BLOODY BELFAST

Sadly in Northern Ireland, the war we were fighting was not recognised, nor the troops, nor the injuries and seldom the deaths; we received our Christmas gifts and letters by default but nevertheless they were appreciated. There was no welcome home, no celebrations; in fact I recall my service medal was thrown at me across a clerk's desk and I was told to sign for it, but that was the way it was.

Lee Sansum, Royal Military Police

This book is dedicated to the following people:

To the memory of the 21 soldiers who died before Robert Curtis, to whom history and our Government have denied the honour of public recognition

To all those soldiers and former soldiers who helped me and became my friends

To every 'Brick' Commander and to every soldier who walked backwards down the streets and roads and country lanes of Ulster

To every CVO; surely the worst job in the world

To Dave Hallam, Tim Marsh, Kevin Stevens, John Moore, Darren Ware, Ken Ambrose, Alan Holborough, Phil Jones and the rest of the Jackets

George Prosser and the 'Kingos'

Tommy Clarke and Kev Wright and the RCT

John Swaine and Mick Pickford and the Royal Artillery

David Dews and the Fusiliers

Arfon Williams and the RRW

Geoff Smith and the 'Arfers' (Light Infantry)

Eddie Atkinson and the Green Howards

To Dave Langston and the 'Slop Jocks'

To Robert Nairac; denied the honour of a known and lasting grave

To Jasmine Curtis whom I have never met; she must be so proud of her Dad

To my late uncle, Tommy Wharton (1935-97)

To all those who wore the badge of the UDR; to every member of NIVA

To the good people of Ulster who never wanted terrorism

Above all, this is dedicated to the memory of the 1,301 identified – so far – who never returned home to their families.

BLOODY BELFAST

AN ORAL HISTORY OF THE BRITISH ARMY'S WAR AGAINST THE IRA

KEN WHARTON

SPELLMOUNT

To my late parents, Mark Clifford Wharton and Irene Wharton.
They brought me into this world and made me what I am today.

This book has been vetted by the Ministry of Defence. They did not ask for much to be changed. The author and publishers are grateful – and to be honest, not a little surprised. They also commented: 'A great read; the book should certainly raise awareness of the British Army's role in Northern Ireland.'

First published 2010

Spellmount Publishers
The History Press
The Mill, Brimscombe Port
Stroud, Gloucestershire, GL5 2QG
www.thehistorypress.co.uk

British Library Cataloguing in Publication Data.
A catalogue record for this book is available from the British Library.

ISBN 978 0 7524 5249 4

Typesetting and origination by The History Press
Printed in Great Britain

Jacket images courtesy Paul Crispin. Front: The dreaded baton gun. Probably seventeen people died during the Troubles from baton rounds. This picture was taken just before the riots that marked the first anniversary of the Anglo-Irish Agreement. Back: the notorious Divis flats. Paul Crispin captured this image having searched a flat and realised that there was no 'resident' backup. He was relieved when the footsteps coming up turned out to be this soldier – who was in turn relieved when Paul exchanged his 9mm for a Nikon F1.

CONTENTS

No matter how well trained you are, as a professional soldier; no matter how hard you think that you are; no matter how impervious to emotion the civvie thinks you are, you never get over the sight of seeing your mate's life blood spill onto the street.

Soldier, Light Infantry, Belfast

To have allowed over a thousand British soldiers' lives to have been lost in our own back yard and to have many, many more injured is criminal.

Pete Whittall, Staffords

So I saw this kid who was about 6 years old, sitting on his doorstep with his little puppy and I thought I would go and sit next to him. I asked him: 'Is that yours mate?' 'Yes,' he replied, but without 'Brit bastard' at the end which was a bonus and a change. 'It's a lovely puppy; can I stroke him please?' I asked. His reply shook me and stays with me to this day and summarises the Troubles for me; 'No, because me ma will beat me if I let you,' he said, looking at me with the saddest eyes.

Craig Laidler, Royal Tank Regiment

The only time I ever felt let down was when our Government started to concede ground to the terrorists, and we became an embarrassment to their political aspirations. While they were busy back-slapping each other for a job well done, they were at the same time slapping us in the face and backsliding against us. They had us over there, trying to do our jobs with one hand tied behind our backs. As you know, there were so many rules enforced on us, that it was almost impossible not to break them and do your job effectively.
Tom Neary, Royal Artillery

But, Ken; it wasn't really a war, was it?

John Humphries, BBC

Opposite: John Swaine (centre) at a bomb blast cordon at the junction of Shankill Road and North Street, 1976. See page 152. *(Via John Swaine)*

THE VOICES OF THE BRITISH ARMY IN NORTHERN IRELAND

Mick Pickford; Ken Ambrose; Andrew Bull; Haydn Davies; Paddy Lenaghan; John Swaine; Andy Thomas; Mick Hill; Ernie Taylor; Eddie Atkinson; Alan Borthwick; Brian Roberts; Jim Seymour; Tim Marsh; Colin Berry; 'Onion'; Craig Laidler; Darren Kynoch; Gordon Vacher; David Harding; Kelvin Brown; James Henderson; David Hardy; Tommy Clarke; Frenchie; Dougie Durrant; 'S'; James Reeves; John Wood; Josef Jurkiewicz; Kevin Stevens; Lawrence Jagger; Marty RGJ; Mick King; Martin Webb; Ken Wharton; Mick Potter; Neil Chant; Steve Wilson; Bill Jones; Big Stevie; Von Slap; Steve Crump; Nigel Barnes; Nigel Glover; Steve Norman; Paul Crooks; Pete Whittall; Phil Hyslop; Richard Drewett; Richard Nettleton; Rob Hughes; Stuart Mallinson; Simon Bromige; Robert Hutton; Simon Richardson; Stephen Durber; Tom Neary; Glen Espie; David Mitchell; Colin 'Jim' Bowie; Roy Davies; Ronnie Gamble; Gavin; Lee Sansum; James Kinchin-White; Jimmy McMaster; Alex, UDR; Micky Lee (71); and the anonymous contributors.

THE TWENTY-ONE SOLDIERS WHO LOST THEIR LIVES BEFORE ROBERT CURTIS

TPR Hugh McCabe	14/08/69	Killed by friendly fire, Divis Street, Belfast
L/CPL Michael Spurway	13/09/69	Shot in controversial circumstances
CFN Christopher Edgar	13/09/69	Violent or unnatural causes
L/CPL Michael Pearce	24/09/69	Violent or unnatural causes
RFN Michael Boswell	25/10/69	RTA involving rioters
RFN John Keeney	25/10/69	Killed in same incident
MJR Philip Cowley	13/01/70	Died on duty
GDSM John Edmunds	16/03/70	Drowned
PTE Peter Docherty	21/05/70	Killed accidentally
SGT James Singleton	23/06/70	Died on duty
PTE Victor Chapman	24/06/70	Drowned
PTE David Pitchford	27/06/70	RTA
S/SGT Peter Sinton	28/07/70	Violent or unnatural causes
PTE Thomas Wilton	22/10/70	Died on duty
PTE John Proctor	24/10/70	RTA
MJR Peter Staunton	26/10/70	Violent or unnatural causes
PTE Brian Sheridan	20/11/70	RTA
TPR James Doyle	24/11/70	Cause of death unknown
SGT Thomas McGahon	19/01/71	RTA involving rioters
CPL James Singleton	19/01/71	Killed in same incident
SGT John Platt	3/02/71	Thought to have been shot in an ambush at Crumlin

FOREWORD BY MAJOR ANDREW MACDONALD, LATE KINGS OWN BORDER

I met Ken in 2007 through a mutual friend – the late Lieutenant Colonel Geoff Moss, Kings Own Border– whose tragic death from a sudden illness in early 2009 left us very shocked. Geoff knew that I'd done several Op Banner tours and that I could help Ken with his new book: *A Long Long War*. Like many, I had countless memories from my seven tours as a Kings Own Border officer but had not taken the trouble to make any sensible records that would exist long after I had forgotten the detail.

I began to understand that Ken's interest was more than that of an author: it was a passion. He possesses a rare ability to galvanise those of us that have stories locked away from experiences gained long before digital technology made it inexcusable not to record what goes on. He has this ability to seek out the latent storytellers who would normally be too modest to relate their experiences, then to draw out their experiences and record them. As an army we needed this catalytic process to help us write down what went on during the long campaign in Northern Ireland so that as we get more forgetful, those that actually did it – the front line soldiers and officers, rather than the official historians, politicians and generals - can record what actually happened. This book is published at a time when the spotlight is on both the Army and defence in general. Whilst the many conflicts in which the Army has been engaged in the era of 'modern' warfare differ greatly, the single common factor has been the soldier. And it is he (or she) that will always bear the greatest burden. Without the courage, doggedness, humour and sheer bloody-minded determination of our fighting men, our Armed Forces would not have the reputation that they so richly deserve. And in this context, we must never forget the other uniformed services in Northern Ireland. Those qualities, so wonderfully revealed in this book, are still displayed today. Indeed, the impediments that our soldiers face in current conflicts – whether for political or economic reasons or through sheer bureaucratic bungling – are, I suggest, very similar to those that we experienced when deployed on Op Banner throughout the campaign.

For me, Ken's books represent one of the best records of what actually went on at ground level since I read George MacDonald Fraser's *Quartered Safe out Here*. Ken's efforts to pull these stories together rightly deserve to put his books in that category. This book is a tribute to all those who served and his painstaking efforts to record the voice of the soldier should be richly rewarded. So even if you come from a non-military background, please read on. You can dip in and out but on every page there's something that you may not find in an official history and you certainly won't be getting military fiction.

I am particularly honoured to have been asked to write the Foreword for *Bloody Belfast*; thank you.

PREFACE BY MICK O'DAY

I first spoke to Ken Wharton on the telephone in 2007 after a mucker in my regimental association pointed him in my direction, as someone who might be able to help put a book together about the Troubles in Northern Ireland. Ken, then a completely unknown, unpublished author, outlined to me in just a few minutes his idea to amass stories written by former British soldiers; stories told from the viewpoint of the ordinary squaddie on the streets of Northern Ireland; often then very young men, who between them faced 30 years of atrocities head on; stories never told before.

Like me, he knew what great evil had been raging throughout that land but these were events I'd long ago consigned to grey memories of a distant past life. Ken was different. From this very first call, it was clear to me that he wanted to do something about it and I knew I was dealing with a straight-up guy who cared deeply about what had passed during the Troubles. From the outset, he made it plain that this book would include no neutral commentary. His intention was to give the ordinary British soldier a voice and let them tell the story, warts and all.

Many would consider this book an impossible task, bearing in mind that these 300,000 former soldiers are now scattered throughout the world. What followed was a roller coaster of activity as former lowly Rifleman Wharton unleashed his passion, his energy, his talent and his total commitment on the world that links former soldiers, civilians now, as they go about their daily lives. No one told him that this would be difficult, if not impossible – had they tried, he wasn't listening anyway. Blind enthusiasm, a belief in his purpose, a book, which as yet had no content, no name and not even a glimmer of an interested publisher, propelled this guy straight through or over all hurdles placed before him, in a way I've rarely witnessed. I had very little doubt that he'd succeed.

My mate Ken, former ordinary British soldier, was now a published author and he could be seen signing books, delivering presentations all over the UK. Popping up on the telly, the radio and in national newspapers, sounding just like the professional author and truly expert voice of the British squaddie that he deserves to be seen as; not by virtue of military rank or social position but by sheer commitment to the task in hand.

If you ask him, he'll tell you that it was I who in some way made it possible; but that's not really what happened. Ken Wharton did it by himself; driven by a deep belief that the telling of these stories, was a necessary footnote to the history of violence in Northern Ireland; a job that just has to be done.

(Mick O'Day is a former IJLB, Scots Guards and 3 Brigade Photographer.)

AUTHOR'S NOTE

When I wrote *A Long Long War; Voices from the British Army in Northern Ireland, 1969-98* I was fortunate enough to be invited onto five different BBC Radio stations to discuss my book and the impact upon those of us who served during the troubles. On one occasion, the esteemed John Humphries on the BBC Radio 4 *Today* programme said to me: 'But, Ken; it wasn't really a war was it?'

I invited him to ask any of the 300,000 who served during Op Banner – the longest single British Army operation in its long and glorious history – if it was a war. I repeat that offer to him and I ask you, the reader, to speak to David Hallam (RGJ), Eddie Atkinson (Green Howards), David Dews (Royal Regiment of Fusiliers), Phil Winstanley (Royal Army Medical Corps) or any one of thousands of former soldiers who witnessed the horrors of Northern Ireland; ask them if it was a war or not.

True, it wasn't the profligate, mass slaughter of the Somme; it wasn't the orchestrated mass battles of El Alamein, or Arnhem, or the Reichswald; it wasn't the major firefights of Goose Green or Mount Longdon or Tumbledown; but it was a war. It was a war fought largely in the shadows, against an increasingly professional and well organised terrorist army. It was a war where a soldier would be shot as he ran to close a gate and where soldiers would be cut down in their beds and their places of rest. Make no mistake; Northern Ireland was a war.

In the early hours of Sunday 8 March 2009, I was awakened by a text; it was a message from Tim Marsh, a Green Jacket friend of mine and it alerted me to the fact that something awful had taken place in Northern Ireland. I put on the television and learned of the killing of two soldiers at an Army base in the land where we had all hoped that the peace was a lasting one.

The following morning, the world heard the names of the two dead soldiers; Sapper Mark Quinsey, 23, from Birmingham, and Sapper Patrick Azimkar, 21, from Wood Green, North London. Barely had we begun to mourn, when dissident Republicans murdered PSNI officer Stephen Carroll (37) at Craigavon. He became the first policeman to be killed since Constable Frank O'Reilly, on 6 October 1998, fatally injured in a blast bomb attack by Loyalists in Corcrain Estate, Portadown. My friend and comrade Tommy Clarke, whilst shooting a TV documentary only a week earlier, had warned that it wasn't all over. Indeed, I had been very cautious in my hopes for peace following my return to the Province in late 2008.

Whether or not this was the work of the so-called Real IRA, responsible for the slaughter of the innocents at Omagh in 1998, or the equally outrageous Continuity IRA or an as yet unnamed Republican group is entirely irrelevant. That some eleven years on, with a hard-won peace still paying dividends, any group, under whatever label, could seek to revive the killings all over again is simply beyond my comprehension. I have never professed to be an intellectual; my writing was described as the 'simple prose of the soldier-scribe'. I am, however bewildered, bemused – not shocked – and appalled that there still exists, within the Republican community, a group of people determined to revisit the Troubles on a country still in the recovery phase following 30 years of insanity.

ACKNOWLEDGEMENTS

In the first two volumes of oral histories of the Northern Ireland troubles, I lavished praise on my many friends in the Royal Green Jackets. I can see no good reason not to do exactly the same again as I acknowledge the many contributors from the finest regiment in the long, glorious history of the British Army.

Ken Ambrose, Dave Hallam, Darren Ware, Tim Marsh, Kevin Stevens, Mickey Lee, 'Vach', Mick Copp, David Harding, James Kinchin-White and all the others; thank you from the bottom of my heart for your help, support and encouragement. 'Always green; forever green.'

To Mick Pickford, John Swaine, Mick Potter and all the other 'Drop Shorts' who helped me. Eddie Atkinson, Pete Townend, Ray Gasgoigne, Phil Brooks and all my other 'Green Custard' mates; lads you did me proud.

Thanks to George Prosser, Paddy Lenaghan, Peter Oakley, Frenchie and the other Kingos. Richard Nettleton and the other 'woodentops'. Tommy Clarke, Kev Wright, Lawrence Jagger and the other 'Rogues, Cutthroats and Thieves'.

Phil Winstanley for all you suffered at MPH; Tiny and June Rose; I can only hope that my eternal gratitude will make up in some small way for the lack of gratitude shown to you by our Government. Thanks to Tim Castle, Geoff Smith and all my new-found 'Arfers' friends in the Light Infantry.

Mike Day, who refused to accept the enormous credit which he so richly deserves.

Andy Thomas, Steve Norman and the other 'angle irons'. You never let me down. Haydn Davies, Arfon Williams and Andrew Bull, Royal Regiment of Wales; you all gave so much and I thank you for your endless support. To Bill 'You can't shoot at me; I'm REME' Jones; a tireless contributor. Dougie Durrant and all the boys at the Army Dog Unit; great canine tails (sic).

To Jimmy Mac, Glen Espie, Jim Henderson and all the others who wore the Harp cap badge of the UDR; you did a magnificent job over there and you continue to do the same for me.

The boys at NIVA have never stopped supporting me and I have to mention Big Stevie, Onion, Andy Bennett, Von Slaps and Dave Langston who keeps threatening to post me a 25-year-old 'egg banjo' via Australia Post; thanks to you all.

This list could never be complete and if you are omitted, please be aware that I will be eternally grateful for all that you have done, for the Army, your country, your family and lastly, for me.

Many thanks to Paul Crispin for the use of his photographs. They are some of the best of images of the Troubles I have seen. Good luck as a photojournalist.

To Helen, my partner; thank you for all your love and patience, and for putting your arms around me when I have sat and sobbed at my computer as yet another tragic story from Northern Ireland has meant that I have had to type through a veil of tears. Too much dust in the computer room!

Finally, to all of you who believed in me and trusted me to tell our stories with honesty and with sincerity; your enthusiasm knows no bounds. With the level of support that you have given me, it's no wonder that we all belonged to the best bloody Army in the world.

INTRODUCTION

On Thursday 14 August 1969, I was a young soldier; only nineteen, with so little experience of this great big world watching a TV in a NAAFI club at a barracks in the deep south of England. When you are a Leeds born and bred Yorkshire boy who, prior to taking a train to Aldershot to join up in early 1967 had only left the confines of God's own county three times, then Hampshire *was* the deep south. It showed scenes – in black and white, of course – of a drama being played out in a country so close you could spit across the Irish Sea and hit it, and yet, it was a country of which I had never heard. That was, until it thrust itself into our newspapers, our televisions, our radios and soon enough, into our collective psyches.

That country was Northern Ireland. A country which was to have a personal effect on my life for several years; an effect on all our lives for almost 30. It will, sadly, for many be a place synonymous with violence, tragedy, intolerance, suffering and sudden death. Did I say that it had a personal effect on my life for a few years? I will be haunted forever by the suffering of my comrades and those wonderful, innocent people of Northern Ireland who neither sought nor supported terrorism.

The net result upon the lives of the people living in both England and Ulster was the loss of over 1,300 military lives, over 300 Police lives, and well over 4,000 lives in total. It also cost billions of pounds in destroyed property; and the emotional and psychological cost that can never be measured. A close friend of mine – and, like me, an ex-soldier – said: 'We were part of the solution, but we were also part of the problem.' I'm not sure that I can agree entirely with what he said, though I do agree that we were certainly part of the solution and the peace that was so hard won. The change that was won over those years of struggle with the IRA and the other paramilitaries was paid for with the blood of British troops and Ulster policemen. That same blood which stained the streets of the Ballymurphy Estate, the Turf lodge, Twinbrook, the Ardoyne, the Creggan, the Bogside and the fields of Ulster, ultimately paved the way for freedom, the removal of fear and the constant threat of terrorist violence that a new generation of Northern Irish no longer have to face.

Let us not forget that the other 3,000 deaths represented an appalling civilian tragedy, as the great majority of the fatalities were not paramilitaries. The innocent bystanders included those caught in the crossfire of the bullets or the indiscriminate terrorist bombs, or those slaughtered because they gave the wrong answer to that most perverted, most evil of all questions: 'Are you a Protestant or a Catholic?'

I recently visited that country for the first time in over 30 years as I had many ghosts to lay to rest. I am pleased to report that although the Black Mountain continues to dominate Belfast and will for millions more years, some things have changed. There are more cars and many of the old blackened terraces of the Lower Falls have been replaced by newer housing. Indeed, the dump that was the 'Murph is changed beyond all recognition; the gardens are tidier, there are no old fridges or cookers in the front gardens and no rusting Vauxhall Vivas or Ford Anglias, propped up on bricks. The outsides of the houses are cleaner and the ubiquitous packs of stray dogs that chased our PIGs around the 'Murph, or Turf Lodge, or Andersonstown, now appear to

The author pictured in Londonderry. *(Ken Wharton)*

have gone to that great doggie heaven in the sky. However, when I walked around the Creggan heights in Londonderry, or Derry, or 'stroke' city, whilst the yellow paint now gleams and covers up the scrawled 'We stand by the IRA' slogans, the underlying menace and threat are still there. Moreover, one does feel that one is in a foreign country and the green painted post boxes, sand stores and the plethora of Irish Tricolour flags give the impression that one is actually in the Irish Republic and not on a British street.

The accents are different in Glasgow and Edinburgh but it is still Britain; the accents are different in Cardiff and Harlech but you are still in Britain. The accents vary in Ulster also, but one-third of the population feel that they are Irish first, second and third. Perhaps when the historical borders – some say arbitrary – of Northern Ireland were drawn up, some of the six counties should have stayed within the Irish 'Free State', and certainly there is a case for Co Armagh to have done so. Whatever the rights and wrongs of this delineation, by 1969, it clearly wasn't working and, whether or not the popularly held views about discrimination were fact or naively held belief, the Army had to go in. On that wonderfully hot August day in 1969, British squaddies in their shiny tin helmets, denim uniforms, SLRs with fixed bayonets at the ready, were deployed onto the streets of the Falls, the Divis, the New Lodge, the Ardoyne, the Gobnascale, the Waterside, the Bogside and the Creggan. Their only knowledge of civil unrest was a brief exposure to an Army training film 'Keeping the Peace, Parts 1 and 2'. Who would have guessed, who could have guessed, that almost 30 years later, those same soldiers or more likely their successors would still be on those same streets, still fighting, by then, a second generation of terrorists?

By the end of that first day's deployment, five people, including nine-year-old Patrick Rooney – killed by a stray (possibly) RUC round and the following evening the first of nearly 1,300 British troops would be killed as he visited his parents' home in Whitehall Row in the Divis Flats area. Trooper Hugh McCabe (20) was on home leave from the Queen's Irish Hussars based in West Germany when he was also killed by a 'stray' round. After that, it never really stopped and even after the 'final' ceasefire, the self-styled Real IRA saw fit to butcher another 29 innocents in the sleepy market town of Omagh in Co Tyrone.

The IRA and INLA took their terror war farther afield and British blood – military and civilian – was spilled in Belgium, Holland and Germany. It stained the streets of London, Deal, Derby, Litchfield, Yorkshire, Eastbourne, Northumberland, Warrington, Guildford, Birmingham and Tadcaster. There was never a let up as the terror gangs sought to sicken the British public into putting pressure on their Government to withdraw from Ulster. I do not class myself as a particularly intelligent person, but I confess my inability to comprehend how the bombers of the 'Mulberry Bush' in Birmingham or the 'Horse and Groom' in Guildford could sit and drink

Republican mural, Bogside, Londonderry. *(Ken Wharton)*

amongst the revellers and then walk out, having planted a bomb, fully cognisant of the death and maiming that would follow amongst those happy, smiling faces. As each atrocity outdid the previous one, as outrage after outrage followed, the terrorists felt that they could push the British over the emotional edge and make them demand their Government pull out of the North. What they forgot and what an invaluable historical lesson they overlooked was the willingness of the British to stoically bear anguish. After all, an Austrian house painter had tried much harder than them in 1939 and had, as posterity records, failed spectacularly. Most people would agree, particularly those who survived the Blitz during those dark days of 1940 and 1941, that the Luftwaffe was a much more terrifying enemy.

This book, in the main, covers the IRA's killing fields of Belfast, where indeed, the bulk of the Army's casualties took place, but I would be foolish to ignore other parts of the Province. There are too many other places where the IRA/INLA and other terrorist groupings practised their evil art and I will step outside the capital in Part Three.

I was asked, during the course of writing this book, what my opinion was of the IRA. I replied that I condemned them – as indeed I condemn all terrorist organisations – for their cowardly attacks and absolute contempt for life. There is, however, one aspect I have never considered and sometimes reproach myself over. Did they grieve for their dead; did they shed tears for their 'volunteers' killed by their own bombs or by our counter-terrorist methods as we did for our fallen comrades? I have often compared the IRA/INLA and the others to psychopathic gangsters who would have been criminals, thugs and murderers even had the Troubles never happened. But did they grieve as we did? Perhaps we will never know.

The original caption to this 1969 picture reads: 'Armed British troops face a crowd after new fighting broke out between Catholics and Protestants. At least eight persons have been shot to death since the rioting erupted here August, 14th. Another 336 persons have been injured, 66 by gun fire.' © *Bettmann/CORBIS*

Over the long and tortuous course of the Troubles which dragged on for almost three decades, the decent people of Ulster – Protestant and Catholic alike – had to contend with almost daily mayhem and death. Those of us fortunate to be on the mainland saw only what the Government of the day allowed us to see. At the announcement of the death of a soldier or a policeman, most of us shrugged and thought 'that's a pity' and then moved on. For the people of the Province and those who had lost a loved one, there was no moving on and Wilson, Callaghan, Heath, Thatcher, Major and Blair continued to send out more soldiers to the 'twilight zone' of Northern Ireland to be quickly forgotten. I swear that through my writing, I will never allow that to happen.

PART ONE

'WHAT ABOUT YE, SOLDIER BOY?'

Northern Ireland was a shit-hole; the IRA and the Prod extremists saw to that, but there were decent people there and we had to go in for their sakes. For every one bastard, there were at least twenty or more decent ones who probably hated the paramilitaries even more than we did, but didn't dare say so.

Private 'W', Royal Regiment of Wales

I do recall on a lighter note one incident that made me smile; a woman came up to me in the street and asked if I'd speak to a very young girl who had never seen a soldier. This young girl was from Canada and just maybe there are not too many soldiers on streets there. I did speak to this very young girl and I think that I made her day but, anyway this made me smile a great deal.

Nigel Glover, Royal Artillery

Too many of this wee Province's citizenry were/are indifferent to the sacrifice made by HM Forces during Op Banner; but there are those who remember and will always be grateful.

Alex, UDR

On 14/15 August 1969, British troops were deployed onto the streets of a part of the United Kingdom for the first time – other than during the exigencies of wartime – since the General Strike of 1926. In Northern Ireland, law and order had finally broken down. The excellent *Lost Lives* states that, prior to that fateful day, eight people had been killed, including several some three years before the 'recorded' start of the Troubles. It is not the brief of this oral history to cover this period and, for the sake of a beginning, it must start the day before, with the first deaths in what the Ulster folk call the 'wee hours' of that August day.

Herbert Roy (26) from the Loyalist Shankill Road area became the first of five people to lose their lives that day. He was involved in rioting in the Divis Street area of Belfast and was shot and died of his wounds around 30 minutes after midnight. Almost simultaneously, little Patrick Rooney (9) was shot and killed in his own bed in the Divis Tower by a stray round. The author, a young and naive soldier, watched with horror and disbelief the TV interviews conducted with his distraught parents; the black and white pictures of a devastated, yet calm looking working man describing how he had to scrape part of his little boy's head off the bedroom wall with a spoon. That interview, those words and the horrific imagination which accompany it will follow this author to his grave. Little did he or any of the watching world realise that many, many more grieving parents would suffer the same way before the Troubles finally claimed their last victims.

Private Hugh McCabe, a British soldier home on leave and merely observing the rioting was shot and killed in Whitehall Row, also in the Divis area. He was buried with full military honours by his comrades from the Queen's Irish Hussars and, by the end of that fateful year, 139 days later, a further five British soldiers would also be dead. Almost seventeen months after the troops had gone in, Gunner Robert Curtis was shot and killed in Lepper Street, Belfast on 6 February 1971, along with his comrade, Gunner John Laurie who died six days later from his wounds. Popular convention has identified Curtis, whose pregnant widow gave birth some months later, as the first soldier to be killed in Northern Ireland during the Troubles. I believe that there is evidence to the contrary and that Gunner Curtis was the 22nd soldier to die.

By the end of the following month, three more soldier's families would have received the dreaded visit by their loved one's CVO (Casualty Visiting Officer), or equivalent, to inform them of the premature ending of a young life. On 13 September Lance Corporal Michael Spurway of the Royal Corps of Signals was killed in a 'friendly fire' incident and the very same day, REME Craftsman Christopher Edgar would also be dead. The circumstances surrounding his death remain highly confused and highly controversial and I am permitted only to say that he died from what the MOD refers to as 'death by violent or unnatural causes'. Eleven days later – and here the author knows definitively the cause of death – Lance Corporal Michael 'Mickey' Pearce of the Royal Green Jackets became the second soldier to die under this 'definition'.

A month later, two young Jackets Riflemen, Michael Boswell and John Keeney were killed in a riot-related road traffic accident (RTA) in the Belfast area. 1970 would continue in the same vein and eleven more regimental CVOs would make that sad journey to a house in Manchester or Leeds or London or any one of those places we all called 'home.' The reality was, of course, that the Army and your new-found comrades were your actual home.

Before that fateful day in the Ardoyne 'interface' area where IRA gunman Billy Reid shot and killed Gunner Curtis and fatally wounded Gunner Laurie, a total of 21 British soldiers had lost their lives through a variety of causes. Whatever the MOD statisticians claim, Robert Curtis was the 22nd soldier to die in Northern Ireland, not the first. Some will argue against this contention, but there were 21 families on the UK mainland who received the tragic news of a loved one's death many months before the Royal Artillery CVO made his fateful visit who would agree with me.

Reid himself would be killed some three months later by a sergeant in a Scottish regiment after an attempted ambush in, ironically enough, Curtis Street, at the junction with Academy Street, north of Belfast's city centre. His short, violent and murderous career would end around 800 yards from where he had bloodily written his name in IRA 'folklore'.

The British soldiers were mostly deployed onto the streets of Belfast and Londonderry, but also in Omagh, Portadown, Newry and countless other places. They were sent in to fill the power vacuum created by the partial retreat of the outnumbered, beleaguered RUC. They were greeted, in the main by cheering Catholic families with cups of tea, biscuits and flowers and quickly – innocently and naturally – assumed the role of liberators. The same greetings were also to be found in the Loyalist or Protestant areas as these communities saw the Army as a buffer between themselves and the Fenians. Were the soldiers confused? Of course they were, as they had to appear to be the saviours, simultaneously, of two differing communities with diametrically opposing religious and political views.

It is certainly true that the Catholics eventually saw them as oppressors as their 'honeymoon' period with the 'Tommies' came to an end, probably about the same time as the other community began calling them 'Taig lovers.' Small wonder, that the ordinary squaddie saw himself as 'piggy in the bloody middle'. These feelings were experienced no less by the young officer classes. For many there, including the author, the streets of Belfast and Londonderry were not a million miles away from their own streets and homes. One Green Jacket remarked, when he first saw the housing of the the Markets area: 'Jesus Christ; I'm bleedin' 'ome!'

As the supply of cups of tea, plates of sandwiches and biscuits began to dry up as the soldiers patrolled the Ballymurphy Estate, the Turf Lodge, the Ardoyne, the New Lodge, Tiger Bay in Belfast, Creggan, Bogside and Gobnascale in Londonderry, so it was soon replaced by other, less savoury and certainly less edible, objects. The soldiers were spat at, had urine and faeces – human and canine varieties – hurled at them; had used sanitary towels thrust into their faces, had women break wind in their faces as they rested on their haunches on street corners. Soldiers had had dead cats and soiled baby's nappies hurled at them as they patrolled. Through all this incredible provocation, they remained, in the main, professional and composed, which reflected the high quality of training a British soldier must undergo before being allowed outside the barracks gates.

One young soldier from the Royal Green Jackets told the author of a moment when he went into a sandwich shop – or 'choggie' as generations of soldiers would know them – and ordered a salad sandwich. The assistant picked one and carefully opened it and asked, 'Ye want anythin' on this, soldier boy?' When the Jacket asked for salad cream, she spat onto the contents and passed it to him with the words, 'On the house, soldier boy.' Soldiers by now, were either declining cups of tea from Catholic households, or pretending to drink them, suspecting that they may have been spiked with all manner of toxic or dangerous substances. The breakdown in the relationship between the 'liberators' and the 'liberated' was starting to gather momentum; it would, inexorably and, perhaps, inevitably, lead to a complete and irrevocable deterioration. Although the following would occur some years afterwards, a Kingsman spoke to me of an incident which involved one of his comrades, Lance Corporal Andy Webster. Both soldiers of the King's Regiment were based in the Andersonstown/Turf Lodge area. Andy Webster had bought his copy of the *Daily Mirror* from 'Andersonstown News' every day since the tour had started some months earlier. One morning he went in, and the newsagent, albeit politely, informed him that he could no longer sell to him or any other British soldier. It does not take a genius to work out that the local IRA commanders had warned the man off. Sadly, not long afterwards, this popular young NCO would be another casualty statistic. Webster was killed in action in Ardmonagh Gardens in the Turf by an IRA bomb on 19 May 1979. Another name for the British media and public alike to gloss over.

From that early 'liberation' period, successive tours of squaddies would be aware that they were *persona non grata* in parts of the United Kingdom. They would know that, in the Catholic/Republican areas, shopkeepers, innkeepers and the like would refuse to serve them and that, unless they were there in uniform, with brick, platoon or Company comrades, these were locations to avoid.

Up until the death of Gunner Robert Curtis the death of a soldier was still a rare occurrence, but afterwards, the floodgates would open. 32 days later, on the evening of 10 March 1971, three young Scottish soldiers, all related, would be lured to their deaths in a sleepy little village just north-west of Belfast. Despite the dangers, unarmed soldiers in civvies, with no personal protection weapons, would still, irresponsibly, be allowed into the city centre and other adjacent 'safe' areas of a night time to indulge in the squaddies' second favourite pastime. Whilst drinking near the Cornmarket in the Markets area of Belfast, two young brothers and their older cousin were picked up by seemingly Loyalist women with the offer of a party.

The three soldiers – according to eyewitnesses, the worse for drink – got into a car with the women, still clutching their glasses half full of beer and set off for an evening's continued revelling. Just north-west of the city, at White's Brae, Squire's Hill, Ligoniel, on a lonely mountain road, the car stopped. Apparently the three young Scots lads got out of the car for a 'pee break' and, whilst they stood, facing away from the road, several members of the IRA who had lain in wait approached them with revolvers. Two of the soldiers were shot in the back of the head and the third was shot in the chest as he turned. The bodies were found the following morning by children; two of them still clutched beer glasses in their lifeless hands. The three were John McCaig (17) his brother Joseph (18) and their cousin Donald McCaughey (23); all were from the Royal Highland Fusiliers and were from Ayr and Glasgow.

The then Home Secretary, Reginald Maudling, a senior member of the Heath Government said, in a statement relating to the perpetrators of these first killings of off-duty soldiers: '... it is a small minority of armed, ruthless men whose strength lies not so much in their numbers as in their wickedness.' These would not be the last soldiers to be killed whilst off duty. The City of Belfast Coroner stated that the murders were 'one of the vilest crimes ever heard of in living memory.' (*Belfast Telegraph*). That Coroner could not have possibly imagined at the time that this was but the first of a whole series of 'vile' crimes which would be perpetrated by both communities' paramilitaries over the course of the next near 30 years.

One of the alleged killers, IRA member Patrick McAdorey, was himself later killed. On 9 August he was shot in Brompton Park in north Belfast during anti-Internment protests, apparently in a fire fight with soldiers, although there is some speculation that, in the chaos, he may have been shot by Loyalists. *Lost Lives* suggests that McAdorey may have also been responsible for the death of another soldier that same day. Private Malcolm Hatton (19) of the Green Howards had been shot and killed earlier during intense gun battles with the IRA in the Ardoyne area. That period of utter insanity, 9-11 August 1971, cost the lives of no less than 23 people; 20 of the deaths were in Belfast. The fatalities included two British soldiers and the first UDR man to be killed by the IRA. Paul Challenor (22) of the Royal Horse Artillery was fatally wounded by an IRA sniper in Londonderry and died shortly afterwards of his wounds. The UDR man was Winston Donnell (22) who was shot and killed by the IRA near Clady, Co Tyrone.

The gloves were off; the IRA had demonstrated, in their own evil fashion, that they were not the IRA of old – amateurs, armed with World War II German Mauser rifles and stolen TA Lee Enfields – but were now practised, professional and cold-blooded killers. They had the deaths of, officially, six soldiers to their 'credit' and unofficially were involved in most of the deaths of all 29. They were now starting to make a mark. Professional and cold-blooded as they already were, they would only get better at doing what they did best, killing members of the Security Forces.

Even the mass, continual rioting followed a set pattern; gangs of younger teenagers would set light to hastily built barricades and then pour a hail of rocks and stones on the soldiers and RUC. Behind them, older men would then run up and hurl petrol bombs and empty glass bottles; the soldiers hated the bursting bottles and the razor edged sharp shards of glass which showered over them. Behind this second rank, would be the shadowy IRA gunmen who would then order the front two ranks to part, like Moses parting the Red Sea, and then either open fire on selected soldiers or simply pour indiscriminate automatic fire at the massed troops.

By 1971, senior Army men knew, before the man on the ground, that the concept of protecting the Catholic communities was dying. The writing was on the wall – in more ways than one. The proliferation of signs demanding that the Brits left was evidence of this. 'Don't ball-lick the Brits; fight 'em' and 'We stand by the IRA' could be seen on every street corner in every Republican enclave in Northern Ireland. The long favoured open riot square formation was out; it had worked in Singapore, Hong Kong and Malaya, but the boyos were distinctly unimpressed. Instead, a formation with riot shields which protected front and flanks, and, like the old Roman 'testudo' shield formations, overhead as well, was developed. This formation was protected by riflemen in flank positions whose job it was to take out the gunman or the bomber. The addition of the famous snatch squads which employed the fastest runners to suddenly break through their shields and literally snatch ringleaders and drag them back behind the lines proved invaluable time and time again.

Later, in 1972, the controversial plastic bullets made it easier to target and temporarily disable people before the snatch squads were deployed. For those who were not caught at the time, where possible, video footage was taken of all the rioters' activities so that they could be identified, traced and picked up at a later date. Another useful innovation were the mobile patrols within Belfast City Centre with the introduction of random VCPs (Vehicle Check Points). Buses were great fun for the soldiers, eager for some payback after all they had endured, where you could spend half an hour 'P' checking all the people on a crowded bus and then move location to start all over again with a line of cars. It is a fact that by constant 24-hour patrolling the Army limited the opposition's ability to plan, to move people and equipment and to set up operations against them.

The need to patrol and dominate all areas constantly was always there. The patrols were up to four hours long and in the worst areas it was hard targeting for all of that time, so if the soldier was not in a fire position he was running and weaving to one. Patrol routes and timings were constantly changed to avoid forming any sort of pattern. A lot of talk went on about building a wall around the 'hard areas' and containing them and although this would have presented less risk to the soldiers it would also have created further no go areas, with a complete breakdown of law and order as a consequence. Another consideration was that maybe 95 per cent of the people in those areas did not deserve to be abandoned to the rule of the gun and terrorism. This had already happened in some parts of Belfast by 1972 and it was only as a result of mounting Operation Motorman that these areas were reclaimed from the terrorists. The pity of it is that the IRA had learnt from the post-Internment gun battles of 1971 and never again came out on to the streets to take on the Army. 'Operation Motorman' was a walkover.

From this point onwards, the pattern throughout the Province would remain largely the same, certainly concerning shootings. Instead of the 'traditional' fire fight, a lone IRA or INLA gunman would stalk the soldier using 'dickers' (a concept which will be explained through the soldiers' own words) or take over a house or a shop, knowing that even irregular patrol patterns would soon bring a soldier into their scopes. The deaths of Blues and Royals' Troopers Thornley and Dykes, shot and killed at the security gates at Andersonstown RUC station in April 1979 typified this approach. IRA gunmen had taken over a barbers' shop opposite the station and waited until the two men were vulnerable at the open gates. The deaths of Kingsmen Shanley and Rumble, which took place in the Ballymurphy Estate in the same month are another example of these hit and run tactics. On this occasion, IRA members took over a house in Glenalina Gardens and a sniper fired shots from an upstairs window and killed both men; Steven Rumble died of his wounds eight days later. Murals on the 'Murph depicting a group of IRA gunmen – and women - in green Parkas, armed with assault rifles raiding as a group are certainly misleading.

The concept of the 'lone gunman' was also a bit of a misnomer, as in addition to the 'dickers' who reported on patrol movements, other supporters would be on hand to try and get weapons out of the area into the myriad IRA safe houses. The gunman would lie on a blanket and shoot at the soldiers from the prone position and, if hit, his supporters would drag the wounded – or dead – terrorist away on the blanket, along with the weapon and important forensic evidence. Another tactic was to get to a pre-arranged 'safe house' after a shooting, where a bath full of water would be ready for the gunman to jump straight into, in order to attempt to wash off the forensics.

Over three decades, generations of soldiers had to be based, safely quartered, fed and watered right in the very areas where they would be needed to make most impact. On the mainland, particularly across the south-east, literally hundreds of Army camps, some as old as time itself, others remnants of an Allied Army in the mid-40s, proliferated. In garrison towns like Tidworth, across Salisbury Plain, in Army towns like Aldershot, Camberley, Winchester, Colchester and the like, a barracks could be found without much searching. In Yeovil in Somerset, the Army had a ready-prepared former US hospital camp, one that, built in the days of segregation, had been for blacks only. That, however, was not the case in Ulster, and the Army had to find bases for the 30,000 troops at the peak of maximum deployment. The Mission Hall in the Markets, Grand Central Hotel, in Royal Avenue, Fort Monagh on the Turf Lodge, Flax street Mill, Ardoyne, North Howard Street Mill, Fort Jericho (also known as 'Fort Whiterock' in West Belfast, Albert Street Mill, Falls area, Henry Taggart Memorial Hall and Vere Foster school on the 'Murph are just a few names that will evoke a host of memories for those who were based there.

The IRA attacked the Security Forces in the Ulster countryside as well as on the streets of the urban areas. However, much of the violence and killings took place in the streets and town centres and suburbs of the two main urban conglomerations of Belfast and Londonderry. The Falls, Divis Street, New Lodge, Ardoyne, Tiger Bay and Short Strand were traditional, terraced workers' housing. The Ballymurphy Estate, Turf Lodge, Andersonstown and Twinbrook were contrasting modern, postwar Council housing estates. I trust that the following analogies will suffice even for the reader outside of my home town of Leeds. I grew up in the terraced slums of Hunslet, a mirror image of the Falls, Ardoyne and New Lodge etc; I was then nurtured in the late-1950s council housing of the sprawling Swarcliffe and Seacroft Estates, which, in turn, were similar to the Turf Lodge and the 'Murph. Can the non-military reader now imagine that sol-

The sleeping headquarters in the mills were not particularly luxurious. *(Richard Lee Nettleton)*

diers and policemen were being shot and blown up in their dozens in Sidey Street, Hunslet or Dennil Road, Swarcliffe? Imagine soldiers being machine-gunned to death on the York Road, Leeds as the three Green Jackets were on Crocus Street in 1982. As I look around Leeds or occasionally around Manchester, York, Liverpool or Newcastle, I find it so difficult to imagine a terrorist organization, armed with largely American-financed weapons, being able to kill both police and soldiers with the same apparent impunity.

If the reader will indulge my analogy further; try and imagine how the following Leeds boys might have felt, viewing the same types of streets and estates in Belfast and Londonderry with which they would be so familiar. Robert Pearson (Coldstream Guards, KIA 20/02/72), George Lee (Duke of Wellingtons, KIA 6/06/72), Paul Jackson (Royal Artillery, KIA 28/11/72), Michael Ryan (Duke of Wellingtons, KIA 17/03/74), Kim Macunn (Royal Artillery, KIA 22/06/74), Dennis Leach (Royal Marines, KIA 13/08/74) and David Wray (Prince of Wales Regiment of Yorkshire, KIA 10/10/75). Imagine the thoughts that went through the minds of Bradford boy John Swaine (Royal Artillery) or Morley boy Richard Smith (Duke of Wellingtons) both of whom, thankfully survived, as they also looked upon streets and estates so like their own? The British Army was fighting a war, albeit on someone else's terms, but in a part of the United Kingdom, on what was, emotionally and physically, familiar yet alien territory. The hard streets and council estates of Belfast and Londonderry represented mirror images of the places most British soldiers had been brought up in.

Large parts of that area of south-west Belfast are very much alike, with the box-style, post-war council housing to be found in Twinbrook and Poleglass and on the Ballymurphy Estate.

Overview of the Divis Flats complex, Lower Falls, July 1972, with soldier superimposed. *(Steve Norman)*

On patrol in the Turf. *(Craig Laidler)*

Belfast Air Army Corps flying over Harland and Wolfe shipyard. *(Dave Harding)*

Regulation gardens, certainly during the Troubles, resembled scrap yards, with old fridges and washing machines or rusting hulks of cars propped up on bricks. Today, they are neater but are still the rabbit warrens of the early seventies where a fleeing gunman could always be sure of a welcome, feigned or otherwise. The Turf Lodge is similar, but with more of the smaller tower block flats or tenements and maisonettes that proliferated at one time in places like Leeds and Manchester. Farther north, above the Springfield Road, is the older, traditional terraced housing of the Ardoyne and New Lodge. Arranged in long, symmetrical rows, with reasonable proximity to Harland and Wolff – once the mainstay of labour provision for the area – they differed only from their Protestant neighbours on the Shankill and Crumlin Roads by virtue of the flags flown.

Make no mistake about it; the war in Northern Ireland was a particularly nasty one; it was, like all wars, a dirty one. It was a war fought largely in the shadows, where undercover soldiers would calmly shoot a known terrorist dead in a darkened Belfast back street. It was a war in which three or four young, heavily armed Catholic men, their heads full of sectarian and political hatred, would burst into the living rooms of off-duty UDR men, or RUC men, or prison

IRA mural, Ballymurphy Estate. *(Ken Wharton)*

warders, and slaughter them in front of their loved ones. It was a war in which men could walk into a crowded bar or restaurant and spray machine-gun fire at the occupants with no more qualm of conscience than if they had just killed a fly. It was a war where men could calmly sit amongst drinkers in a bar, leave a device designed to kill or maim and walk out without a conscience. And it was a war in which men could walk up to an innocent stranger and end his life simply because he was the 'wrong' religion.

Opposite: AFVs and a welcoming party, 1972. © *Leif Skoogfors/CORBIS*

PART TWO

BLOODY BELFAST

I was standing on a street corner in Belfast sometime in '71, when an old dear came up and gave me a bar of chocolate as her way of thanking me for trying to help. I did not want to take it as she was a pensioner, but as she said, she could not afford much but she could afford that. So I took it, and that felt better than any medal or commendation; that is why I was there.

Bill 'Spanner' Jones

Belfast was a place that we travelled through infrequently to get to other places; it held a sombre, hulking relevance. Its very reputation put everyone on their guard; clicked things up a notch. You did the job right there, or you died.

Stevie, UDR

FIRST INTO ULSTER

Roy Davies, Royal Regiment of Wales

We were sent from Lydd in Kent to Ballykinler for what we were told was to be a one month's 'adventure training' period; some adventure! After two days at Ballykinler, we were deployed to Palace Barracks just outside Belfast city centre, 'on standby to assist the civil powers'. On arrival at the barracks we could see that the skyline above the city of Belfast was all smoke and red with flame; flames high into the air just like after a big air raid.

At about 7pm on that hot night, we boarded our open-sided trucks and went in convoy into Belfast. We travelled through streets of burning houses, shops and factories. There was a cinema and no end of cars burning; one could hardly see for the flames and smoke. Our company arrived at the crossroads of Leeson Street and Northumberland Street and I was first out of the leading truck and followed by my mate Adams; I reckon I was the first soldier on the streets of Ulster. We didn't know what to expect, but the locals were immediately friendly, brilliant in fact; they were Catholics and after some hours we had tea and cakes coming out of our ears.

The press arrived and started taking photographs, but we were told not to speak to them or answer their questions. We were in a position immediately in between the Catholics and the Protestants. The 'B' Specials were in the Protestant locations but came out on sorties from time to time. They scoured the area in Land Rovers that had turrets and .30 inch Brownings; they had the muzzles pointing towards us until we told them to 'bugger off'. We wore fighting order, with scrimmed helmets and bayonets fixed, and had ten rounds of ammunition in our magazines and another ten in our pockets. I saw one platoon lead off into Northumberland Street in riot formation, apparently to 'hold back the Prods'. I will, however, never forget the sight of some police helmets and shields lying about the ground as if a big riot had taken place. I picked up one helmet that had the side all bashed in, and the inside was awash with blood.

We slept the first few nights on pavements or anywhere that we could be warm and dry; safety wasn't a problem then; everyone was so friendly and helpful, even to the supply of hot water for washing and shaving.

After a few days, we moved into Springfield Road police station and patrolled from there. We left for home after two or three weeks, but we were quite sorry to leave what was an enjoyable task of being a sort of 'policeman'. In later tours we were always glad to get the hell out of the place and home.

Thus it had begun and though it didn't happen for a while and even then almost imperceptibly, a change from cuppas and cakes to bullets and bombs would occur. This is how it began; cups of tea and cakes; read on and share the experiences of the soldiers who suffered the hatred and violence, caught in the middle of sectarian warfare and ending up as 'piggies in the middle'.

NAVIGATING THE CROSSROADS

Infantry CSM

I hated the crossroads in Belfast. Not the crossroads on the outskirts, but the desolate late night ones in often wet, dark and windy, lethal Belfast city.

They were bloody awful places to have to cross over, because, if you think about it, you stand more than four times the chance of being shot at a crossroads. You were being observed from

Notice how the corner house is painted white so soldiers stood out to the dickers and snipers. *(Craig Laidler)*

Staying low on satellite patrol. *(Craig Laidler)*

eight directions when you consider that a Belfast terraced crossroads has eight rows of houses with all their windows and doors. The derelicts, which were perhaps two houses out of every five, had a dark sinister threat of their own; snipers could get into derelicts and lurk and just bide their time.

The length of time for a patrol to move over the crossroads was another factor; each corner had to be secured in all four directions. This meant that there were often only four of you, and one was moving so he was virtually ineffective while moving sharply over the road, so 25 per cent of observation was lost. The other three in the patrol never seemed to move fast enough doing their individual rush from one corner to the other; not only for your sake but for theirs also. On the move, the others reminded me of the moving targets we used on the ranges; with my one eye on the street and the other on the running soldier, I just waited for that sound of a bullet screaming and echoing its way onwards. I just waited for them to drop, hoping to God they wouldn't. When the crossing was complete I gave a sigh of relief as we all moved off and away from those bloody places.

Some crossroads had their deathly history. One in the Falls had seven soldiers bagged there; others had two or four each. Crossroads gave me the creeps. Death did not seem to feature in my consternation but the loss of mobility of legs or spine did. I didn't want to be blinded either, like an artillery bloke I once had seen in Armagh; all patched up with only half a face and one eye. I always knew that the 'dull thud' was not going to finish me in that place.

But I did hate those bloody awful crossroads. They gave me the creeps definitely!

BELFAST LEGACY

Private Ernie Taylor, Light Infantry

How would anyone describe it? Well no sleep for 30 years; mood swings; wanting to be left alone; aggressive. If I need time to be still; to be in my space; drinking heavy; just to try to sleep and forget for a few moments. Afraid to be awake because your mind is overactive; afraid to sleep because you're always defensive. Where is it the attack coming from? The gentle side of you has gone, you have it but, if you relax, it's like a claw in your heart or a nut in the street that can't understand you are hurting.

So you face them down and chase them off, but this makes you look like a nut yourself, but it keeps YOU together for a bit more until you see the next face. Who is this; who are you; what are you thinking; are you gonna come at me or shall I take you out first? I can't let you get too close because I'm not happy you're near to me. You're boiling over with wanting to be part of the group or party but always knowing you will never be, because you are trained to be with YOUR unit and no one apart from your mates understands. You can't socialise, marry, relax and enjoy seeing your children grow.

A father teaches his children his experience of life. I was on the streets of Belfast shortly after I was eighteen; my experience differs from the norm; I do have mates that I served with, who seem to hold themselves together. Maybe I'm one of the soft buggers.

I want to crawl into a corner that I can defend; wanting to come out of the corner for the need of human companionship. But always afraid that I may relax, and the shot is taken or the blade is in your guts. The shot might be through a pregnant woman's legs or from her shopping bag; maybe it's from a baby's pillow in the pram or pushchair. Hell's bells, I might be out now, 30 years on, but I was in a restaurant and one guy was being passionate with his conversation;

banging on the table. When I asked him to stop, I didn't look at him. But instead at the guy he was growling at. The first guy that was banging challenged me, but I watched the other one. The first guy got rude and I took my ground. The second one told number one to back off, but I had decided to go for number two first.

Well I still can't sleep; I'm wound up over what some would call trivia; I just want peace, quiet and rest. If there is a God, I just want a brain with no memory.

Ernie was involved in a terrible incident in the early 1970s when a fire broke out in a house on the Lower Falls Road. He and other comrades from the Light Infantry were on foot patrol at the time and spotted the blaze at the front of the house. They dashed to the rear, where two small children – left alone by their mother, their father in Long Kesh at the time – were trapped by a door which had been nailed shut. The soldiers desperately fought their way in and Ernie helped carry out a badly burned and dying child; some 30-plus years on, he is still haunted by the memory. The Army showed its usual lack of sympathy and sensitivity and he was eventually discharged and had to fight to receive his GSM. In another incident, he came close to shooting a road worker, mistaking the man's tool for a rifle.

RIOT CONTROL AND TRAGEDY

RSM John Wood, SIB, Northern Ireland

The rubber bullet, or baton round, was introduced in NI during August 1970, and the new ammunition had been publicised on local TV sometime in July. This advance publicity may have led to the death of a young Catholic man in late July during rioting in the New Lodge Road area. Petrol bombers were active and an officer used a loud hailer to warn the crowd that petrol bombers would be shot. A soldier saw a youth throw a petrol bomb and then pick up another which he lit and prepared to throw. The soldier opened fire and the bomber was killed. He had apparently told his companions that the warning was nothing serious, as rubber bullets would be used. Locals denied that there had been any throwing of petrol bombs and that the officer was only part-way through a second warning when the marksman opened fire.

Rubber bullets had a very chequered reputation. A local woman was blinded when she was struck full in the face with one. The instructions were that they be fired at the ground in front of a mob and then bounce up to give a painful but not fatal blow. This random bouncing led to individuals being hit when they had done nothing other than demonstrate, albeit violently. A young boy was killed some time towards the end of 1970 when hit in the head by a bullet fired directly at him.

A total of seventeen people were killed by baton rounds, or rubber bullets, during the course of the troubles in the period 1972–1989; sadly, eight were children.

Another riot control method – CS gas – also came to a premature end. The impression spread that locals were not affected by the gas and vastly inordinate quantities were used. This spread into houses and, inevitably, little old grannies and wee bairns were produced to confirm that they had been harmed by the effects of the CS. I can remember being on the top floor of a bakery in the Shankill Road when rioters were on the ground floor trying to get up to where we were. Me and another soldier were opening boxes of CS grenades with six canisters per box. We merely pulled the rings and then tipped the contents of the box down the staircase. Other variants of irritant gases were trialled but the problem of spread was always there.

Water cannon were also deployed. A couple of ancient vehicles so equipped came from Germany around July 1970. They were used in riots but had no practical use. The force of the discharge was inadequate and would barely knock anyone off their feet. The water tanks were too small and emptied themselves in some five or ten minutes. There was a suitable refill point in Girdwood but this took some 30 minutes to resupply. The idea that locals would be deterred by being made wet was laughable in view of the Belfast weather. There was a move to mix dye with the water and use this as evidence that anyone found stained had been involved in a riotous assembly which was worth a mandatory six months imprisonment. This fell down by virtue of the fact that the spray was not at all accurate. Doctors then raised the spectre of someone drowning when the water jet hit them in the face and that was the end of the water cannon.

The man to whom John Wood refers was Daniel O'Hagan (19) a single man who lived in the 'Long Streets' of the Catholic New Lodge. At a time of heightened tension following several months of being attacked by petrol bombers, the Army was instructed to get tough. A warning was issued that anyone seen carrying petrol bombs or throwing them would be shot. On 31 July 1970, some 319 days after the Army was deployed onto the streets of Northern Ireland, Daniel O'Hagan was observed by a patrol on the corner of Duncairn Parade and New Lodge Road. He was seen to be in the act of throwing a petrol bomb and, after he had ignored a warning, he was shot and killed.

For many, that date, almost twelve months since the Army's deployment, is seen as a turning point, a catalyst for what was to be unleashed by the Republicans on the communities of both sides in general and on the Security Forces in particular.

TO TAKE A LIFE: BELFAST, 1970

'Alex', Royal Tank Regiment

The story you are about to read is true, but names have been omitted, and certain timings have been changed; not just in order to protect myself, but to save the anguish of others. This story would never have been related, without two years of gentle persuasion from Ken Wharton, whom I know, not only as a friend, a former NI vet himself and as a staunch supporter of all servicemen and women who fought in the 'forgotten war'. The story would have gone with me to the grave, because try as I might, I cannot find another ex-British soldier willing to admit the same.

The spring of 1970 saw our regiment based in West Germany, when we were warned for active service in Northern Ireland. Suffice to say that we all cheered, considering it a bit of a lark; words that were to bounce back on many of us over the next 40 years. Following a brief period of training in the UK, which consisted of us throwing bricks at each other, we deployed to Belfast in the summer of 1970.

By the summer of that second year of deployment, CVOs had been compelled to make thirteen trips to the UK. They had visited thirteen grieving families, including the families of three Royal Green Jackets; officially, not a single British soldier had been killed in Ulster.

For those who came much later, the Belfast we all soon learned to hate was a vastly different place from how they would remember it. CS gas shrouded the city for much of the day, and almost all of the nights, making our job of keeping the two communities apart very difficult. Most soldiers wear their respirators during training, and maybe during the odd exercise, but to have to wear the damned things in earnest, for periods of up to twenty hours at a stretch, during a hot summer's night, as well as in daytime, is not funny. The sweat inside slowly built up to our noses, and one would have to take a deep breath, pull the thing up from the bottom, let the river run onto the floor, replace the mask, then breathe out, in order to expel any CS that may have entered. It didn't work. I have seen guys choking in agony when their respirators malfunctioned, and others who just threw the damned things off, and suffered terrible respiratory problems.

We were deployed at a sports arena called Paisley Park. On our second night we took part in a large operation to seal off and search a Republican area of Belfast. Our section's job was to mount a VCP on a main road leading into the city. VCPs (vehicle check points) in those early days could be mounted and kept in position for hours at a time. Woe betide those who tried that trick a few years later! Dusk was settling, and the few street lights that still worked flickered into life. It cast a strange glow through the murk of the floating CS gas, which seemed to combine with the coal smoke and car fumes. I was on 'point', about twenty yards up the road from the VCP, slowing down the traffic, and directing them into the area between the Land Rovers. The first wave of empty glass bottles seemed to come from nowhere, just falling out of the sky, hitting me on the helmet and flak jacket; many smashing in the roadway all around me. More followed, and really I suppose I should have fallen back to the protection of the section, but I stood my ground, even though, as if by magic, all the cars had suddenly disappeared!

From the corner of my eye, I saw three ghostlike figures inching along a tall metal fence to my left, which bordered a school. I watched the repeated sparking of a cigarette lighter. One of the shapes was holding a bottle, and trying to set fire to the top. Petrol bomb! I fell to my right knee, holding my Sterling SMG to my shoulder. I shouted out: 'Drop that now or I will open fire!' Suddenly I felt very calm. The distant bottle flared into life. I cocked the Sterling, and came up into the aim position. 'I said drop that bottle; now!' But far from dropping the bottle, the figure stepped into the roadway, bringing the bottle up behind his shoulder. I slipped the safety catch onto 'repetition'. 'This is your last warning. Stand back and drop that bottle, or I will open fire!' His arm came forwards in what seemed like slow motion, and I fired twice.

Everything seemed to happen at once. The figure went backwards against the fence, and just seemed to crumple out of my vision, as though the very earth had swallowed it up. The petrol bomb sailed into the road, exploding with a great flash some eight yards away from me; harmlessly. I stood up, and dashed forwards. Too late, as my victim's friends were dragging him away, back into the murk outside the feeble glimmer of the single street light. I hesitated; should I follow them? My officer was shouting from the VCP and I doubled back.

Within half an hour I had been arrested by an RMP [Royal Military Police] unit who arrived on the scene and was taken by Land Rover to Palace Barracks. I was banged up in a cell, and then interrogated by two members of the SIB until the early hours. I might still have been locked in that cell now, but for the intervention of my OC, a Major, who came, it seemed, on a white charger to save me! He obtained my release, and we returned to the unit. Within 24 hours, I had been promoted to Lance Corporal, and treated like a national hero! It was three days later when a nineteen-year-old was found in an empty flat off the Falls Road, following a tip off. He had died from two 9mm gunshot wounds to the chest. His blood group matched that from the scene of the shooting.

Four weeks later, I was instructed to attend the Coroner's Court, which in those days was convened in Crumlin Road Courthouse. I stood in the 'dock', facing a sea of angry and threatening faces belonging to the deceased lad's family. Name, rank, number, but then the Coroner asked for my UK address!! No way, and I told him so. He replied that unless I conformed, he would have me arrested for contempt of court!

My wife and six-month-old son were at home, with no protection, so I gave the man my mother's address; what else could I do? It was pretty obvious which side of the street this Coroner lived on! After giving my evidence, I left the court, pursued by a screaming 'banshee' of threats and swearing. They would get me, said the voices, even if it took 50 years!

They didn't, but they did get my mother and stepfather. He's dead now, but my mother is still alive, and I never had the guts to tell either of them where they got her address from. It is enough to say that they both suffered a pretty miserable period afterwards. And so, this strange story crawls to a conclusion. The elation I felt at the time has, over the years, been replaced by firstly doubt, then self condemnation. The kid was just nineteen. I sometimes look at my children, and grandchildren, then think of what I took away from him. OK, so I followed the rules, read right from the yellow card, but does the end justify the means?

Now, 39 years later, and with a conscience, then no, I'm afraid it doesn't.

The author knows 'Alex' and he has been a friend since we met, back on a cold Autumn day as the Northern Ireland Veterans Association gathered at the National Arboretum in Staffordshire in 2007. We marched – at a sedate pace, in view of our advancing years – to the Ulster Ash Grove as wreaths were laid and tributes paid to the memory of our 1,300 comrades and the memories of the RUC and Northern Ireland Prison Officers who fell in the battle against terrorism on our own doorstep. We became friends then – a fact of which I am very proud – and my only regret is that I didn't meet this man years earlier.

THE 'ROCK'

Craig Laidler. 4 Royal Tank Regiment (att: QOH)

I grew up in the eighties watching the news and seeing the bombs going off and hearing about another British soldier being killed (murdered is a better word) by the Provisional Irish Republican Army; how they could call themselves an army is beyond me. As a result, I had a morbid fascination with the Troubles.

I joined the 4th Royal Tank Regiment in the late eighties, although being in this regiment reduced my chances of ever going to Northern Ireland and if we ever did go there it would be as the 'Maze Regiment', basically 'stagging on' in the towers and patrolling the perimeter. So I decided in my youthful exuberance to volunteer, which is something you should never do in the Army; however I really wanted to go there and see what it was like and boy did I find out.

I remember being called into the Sergeant Major's office in Osnabruck in September 1992 and being told my request had been granted and that I would be leaving in seven days for Northern Ireland to be attached to the Queen's Own Highlanders who were starting a six-month tour of West Belfast. Good luck were his last words as I marched out of his office. This is the point when I thought: 'Oh, what have you done?'

I was posted to Fort Whiterock; the SF base there covered Turf Lodge and Andersonstown. The place was to be my home for the next six months, and looked like a prison with huge walls

Getting ready for a night of bricks and bombs. *(Craig Laidler)*

and metal panels all the way around with towers covered with RPG fences around them. Inside was no better, all breeze blocks and double-walled to protect against mortar attacks, inside were beautiful regimental murals painted by previous inmates of the 'Rock'. I shared a room with another eight Jocks which was no bigger than a pub pool room all bunk bedded up, you slept with your 'gat' (SA80) and body armour within grabbing distance. Despite the closeness of the living quarters there was never any trouble or fighting with each other, I think we were all too bloody knackered to anyway and we were fighting for each other against the mindless bastards outside the thick walls and RPG nets.

I remember my first patrol like it was yesterday. In my brick we had Corporal 'X', who carried the first aid kit complete with morphine and saline. We had a purple sifter [electronic counter measure] and then me with the baton gun and white sifter. The first brick belted out of the front entrance of the 'Rock' where there was a road that led down into Springfield Road then into the Turf Lodge. The road seems like it goes on forever until you can reach cover and it is so exposed to the Turf estate and any snipers in the houses that you had to 'bomb burst' out to get to the estate so no sniper could get you in their sights.

Our turn came; there was one patrol covering us out there in the estate scanning the rooftops and windows for any tell tale signs; the lads in the towers were watching the estate and cars with their SUSAT sights trained on any suspect windows. I legged it as fast as I could. I would like to point out to any reader who has not had to do this; it was hard, and you had your helmet, gat, NIBA, [Northern Ireland Body Armour], baton gun and any sifters you had to carry. I ran like I had never run before; my heart was pumping, breathing heavy, swerving from side to side to make it harder for the snipers and looking for the nearest wall to get behind for relative safety.

Above: One of the many murals. *(Craig Laidler)*

Left: View of Fort Whiterock from bottom kennels.

I was thinking 'Not now, God; not now, God.' Eventually I found a wall to get behind and put my weapon up to my shoulder, wiping the sweat off my sight so I could look through it and cover the other patrols out. Then I was looking for my team; where are they? Panic sets in; I'm by myself. 'Oh no, God; don't leave me here by myself, Cpl 'X' came up behind me, tapped me on the shoulder with a smile 'Come on, Geordie, wipe the blood off yer face and let's go.' I had cut my lip running with my gat, or my own teeth or something but in the moment you just didn't know. This was how we always left for foot patrol from the 'Rock', this was the first of many exits; this was Northern Ireland; this was our green and pleasant land.

The Queen's Own Highlanders to whom Craig was attached had lost seven men in tours of the Province between 1972 and 1990; thankfully, after an ND shooting in 1990, when Corporal R.D. Turner was tragically shot, they suffered no further fatalities. The Regiment lost two of their soldiers on 27 August alongside the Parachute Regiment at Warrenpoint when the IRA detonated two devices; a total of nineteen men died that day. The July and August of that 1979 tour saw CVOs make five trips to grieving families within the space of seven weeks. They would lose no more.

ON THE FALLS ROAD

Private Andy Bull, Royal Regiment of Wales

I was just twenty years of age when I was first posted to Northern Ireland with my battalion the Royal Regiment of Wales in November 1983. This tour was to be my first, having just missed out in 1981 where we were stationed in Aldershot at that time, which was during the IRA hunger strikers campaign. At that particular time I was only seventeen years old and the requisite age for serving in Ulster was eighteen. We were to be stationed at McCrory Park police station in West Belfast, just off the Falls Road. The Falls Road, Springfield Road, Andersonstown and the Ballymurphy Estate were predominantly Roman Catholic and one of the hardcore heartlands of the IRA. We were transported from Aldergrove airport to West Belfast in 4-ton Bedford lorries, and it is fair to say that for the youngest there was lots of butterflies and adrenalin pumping. There was also an atmosphere of nervous anticipation for the expected and unexpected.

As you can imagine our quarters were very cramped especially with all our equipment; mostly you were either lying on your bunk bed or sitting on it with a nice brew. When you were not on patrol you took advantage of a nice hot shower or the washrooms to do your laundry, or depending on what time you got back you would get your head down and catch up on some serious sleep. Sometimes sleep would prove very difficult because of the armoured PIGs which would be constantly roaring in and out of the fortified camp as well as the armoured Land Rovers. There was also the noise of the other boys snoring or farting and burping.

I can always remember my very first patrol, and the adrenalin that was coursing through my body at that particular time. When you were in the briefing room and the intelligence officer was showing you photographs and video footage of the IRA players, it suddenly dawned on you that this was the real thing and that there was a great expectancy on you not to let your comrades down. I remember vividly our Corporal as he gave the order for us to load our magazines onto weapons but not to make ready; seeing the high heavy reinforced camp double gates being pulled back and thinking to myself here we go, and the next moment I was sprinting and zig-zagging out into the streets of Belfast. I can remember the strange feeling of nakedness and awkwardness as I saw members of the public walking towards me for the very first time, even though I was armed with an SLR rifle I could still feel my heart racing. I was like a coiled spring, not knowing if at any moment a sniper's rifle would ring out overhead or if a car would suddenly explode. As the patrol settled down into its role I slowly started to relax and to take in my surroundings and to run a critical eye over the painted tricolours and murals depicting IRA weapons on the walls and houses nearby. The civilian population paid us no heed during the day, but at night you were constantly abused verbally by drunks and gangs of youths looking for trouble.

As the days and weeks went by, you patrolled whether it rained, hailed or snowed; you found yourself becoming a part of Belfast, seeing the same people on a regular basis. We knew all the street names, knowing where all the different shops lay; a feeling as if you had been born or lived in Belfast all your life. However you knew this was not true as the hard reality and brutal violence of the IRA would soon bloody the streets of Belfast once again. Sometimes on patrol we would escort the RUC and follow them into the pubs and clubs especially if they were looking for a wanted IRA player. This was a dangerous time and the atmosphere of the pub would quickly change to hostility on seeing our presence. We would take up our designated positions in the pub and take up a firing position to protect the policemen in the event of an incident. If hatred could be a living thing you definitely saw it live and breathe in the eyes of those men in that pub that day; you knew from that moment on should you ever have the misfortune to fall into their hands you would certainly be shown no mercy.

On 23 November 1983 just two months into our tour, whilst escorting two members of the RUC along a busy Falls Road, an IRA bomb exploded, severely injuring myself and wounding my comrades and several civilians in the immediate vicinity. I was very fortunate that the Royal Victoria Hospital was very nearby, and I know that had it not been for their medical and surgical skills that day I would not be writing this account today. That terrorist bomb was to end my Army career, and rob me of something as precious and irreplaceable as my sight. It was to alter my life forever leaving me to begin a new challenge, that of entering civilian life as a blind man.

I owe my life to the Royal Victoria Hospital and to the doctors and nurses there that day. Unfortunately over the years, so many brave men and women have sacrificed their lives on the altar of freedom so that others may live in peace and harmony.

A BEATING

Soldier, Royal Artillery

The year was 1972, and we were embarked to Northern Ireland as part of the Military force to assist the RUC in their duties in keeping the peace. We were sent to Carnmoney first off, and naturally, we took our guns with us. We were located at the Sunnyside Street TA barracks in East Belfast, and from there, we operated in both foot patrols and motor patrols, going pretty much all over the place.

I remember, on one occasion, we were called to do a double cordon of a house in Finaghy. We thought this was just going to be another ring around a house and a search resulting in nothing. The INT on this was that we were looking for a pair of brothers who had gone into a shop and shot the owner and his wife for just a few pounds. It was deemed by the local people as a particularly nasty one as the shopkeepers were well liked and the area was not very hostile. This cordon and search was the result of some weeks of 'homework' by the Int guys and we rolled up to the house in question and threw a cordon around it using stealth. The building was entered and the brothers found on the premises. They were arrested and taken by us to Blacks Road, situated between Andersonstown and Dunmurry in the southern part of the city; Blacks Road was then a rural part of Belfast, in the area of Poleglass. I had been to the INT centre there before and found it very tight on security and a very mysterious place. It was a large Victorian red brick type of house with a conservatory, servants quarters etc. I have to say I never saw inside, but there was a mess room for squaddies and Police who were delivering baddies; it was somewhere for a wash or to get a cuppa or a bit of scran. Sometimes when we were allowed rest, we used to sleep there, but always in our vehicles and in the car park round the back.

This was one such occasion; we delivered the suspects, and we knew they had done it as they were caught on camera. They were taken inside and our Sergeant signed loads of forms to clinch the deal that we had delivered them safely. We were stood down and allowed to use the above facilities. Right opposite was a Land Rover without its canopy and one of the brothers was brought out and manacled to it. A Special Branch officer from the MET, seconded to the RUC, came out and set about the first brother. He hit him several times in the kidneys until the bruises were showing. He was taken away and his brother brought out and the same fate befell him. This happened right in front of us and I personally was appalled by it. I always thought of us military as chivalrous and that we had a sense of fair play. But to be fair, we did only four months in the hole and then went home; these coppers were living it day in, day out.

A while later they were both bought out and were set up for another beating. As they were dragged out, the older one admitted the crime that they were suspected of. The Special Branch officer was joined by another copper who just stood back away from the brothers. He suddenly threw down a 9mm Browning pistol and was goading the brothers to pick it up and shoot him. The brothers were getting very agitated and one of them made a move. The second copper drew a Browning and cocked it and aimed at the brother who had moved. The first copper then told them that if they had touched that weapon they would have been shot dead; right there. One lost control of his bladder and literally pissed himself, the other stood sneering and defiant. They were led away and I never saw them again and did not know what had happened to them. We were all told that this was the sort of interrogation that went on here and we were told to forget what we had seen. After about another two hours we were called to set up a VCP by the Windsor Park football ground and while we were on that job we heard the first sitreps of a shooting in Whiterock parade. I remember it was unclear if anyone was injured and we had to wrap up the VCP and attend as a backup at this incident.

Apparently Blacks Road was a satellite of another two SF bases; Girdwood Park and Holywood. Another place was just emerging; a place called HMS *Maidstone* and I thought: 'Blimey; the Navy's getting involved.' Those of us that saw that incident at Blacks Road thought that it was well deserved and what a bloody shame there wasn't more of it; if there was, those Paddies would soon give it up. I have often thought of military losses in the conflict and measure for measure I think I would have opted for the beating and a cushy time of it in Long Kesh afterwards and then to be released later by the Good Friday agreement, every time.

There are a lot of our dead buddies that would have taken that option, I'm sure, given the chance!

The author has had this story from two different sources and is entirely satisfied that it took place, as described, without embellishment. I seek in no way to justify the treatment of the two suspects, but ask you to put yourself in the place of the policemen and soldiers responsible for bringing two cold-blooded murderers to justice. It was not pretty; what war ever was? What fate befell any member of the Security Forces who fell into the clutches of the IRA? When did an IRA/INLA or other terrorist shoot to wound?

The previous words may well be dismissed as rhetoric, but when the respected former Policeman John Stalker investigated the 'shoot to kill' policy, I inwardly guffawed. That is not to say that I had no regard for the sanctity of life, but I was amused by the assertion that any soldier, in the heat and danger of a life-or-death situation would have the luxury of considering exactly where to aim the round. It is palpable nonsense to even consider that the squaddie on the street had the time to do anything but shoot to kill. In Hollywood, John Wayne could with consummate ease shoot a gun out of the baddie's hands; what happened in Northern Ireland was not Hollywood.

On 2 November 1991, an IRA 'sympathiser' – a hospital porter – placed a bomb outside the Junior Ranks club at the hospital. It exploded whilst the off-duty soldiers were watching television, killing two of them and injuring many. CSM Philip Cross (33) was married with two children and was from the north-east of England. Craig Pantry was 20, single and was from the Gwent area of Wales.

The next piece – from a Medic stationed there – describes the tension and the aftermath of what had to be the most cowardly of all IRA attacks during the Troubles.

WHAT IF?

Stuart Wilson, RAMC

> It had been a couple of weeks since the bombing of the hospital but the Province had been anything but quiet; it was to be one of the most violent few weeks since the early eighties. On the fifth the UFF threw a hand grenade at a mainly Catholic group of supporters of a local football team; luckily no one was injured. The UFF went on to claim that this attack was in response to the IRA bombing of the hospital; funny none of us felt that the score had been settled. The Dublin Corporation voted to stop Sinn Fein from having the use of one of its public buildings for its annual conference, Ard Fheis (Pronounced Ar Desch). To most of us this was a good move but then more bad news. 13 November; the IRA in separate attacks in Belfast killed four civilians; a five-week-old baby girl was wounded twice in one of these. So not only were they bombing hospitals, they were shooting babies also.

The people killed on that night of mayhem were Stephen Lynn (30) and his younger brother Kenneth (28) who were both shot by the IRA as they worked on renovations to a house in the Crumlin Road. The IRA in some sort of sick justification claimed that they were Loyalist paramilitaries; this claim was subsequently disproved. They just happened to be two innocent civilians working on a house formerly owned by a member of the UVF. The other two men killed were Billy Kingsbury (35) a member of the UFF and his stepson Samuel Mchaffey (19) who was not a member of any paramilitary organisation. Both were shot by the IRA in their home in Lecale Street and in the same house Kingsbury's tiny granddaughter was hit six times by the assassin's bullets. She survived after almost eight hours of intense surgery.

> The following day the UFF killed a taxi driver in Belfast and three workmen near Lurgan, Co Armagh. Another fuck up on their part as one of the workmen was a Protestant; in all,

twenty people had been killed in a month. On the desk it had not been quiet but under recent circumstances it was not overly busy. We had to do a run down to the RVH with one of the UDR soldiers, who had been injured in the mortar attack on 5 UDR the week previous, no major problems. We went through the usual arrangements which took a bit of time but it was not long before we were driving up the Grosvenor Road past some shops on the right and then turning left into the RVH. After we had parked up our ambulance we were surrounded by RUC Land Rovers and a lot of policemen who were armed to the teeth. I got the patient out of the back of the ambulance and onto a wheelchair, then we headed for the thick plastic entrance doors. Right behind me were two RUC officers in civilian clothes – my escorts – and we slowly made our way through the busy hospital. The coppers where there for two reasons, one to protect us and two, to stop us getting lost and I was pleased at their presence on this occasion as I had never been to this particular ward before.

We all stood by the lift waiting for the doors to open; a loud ping announced its arrival. The large doors slid back to reveal a man in his late forties, he was about to walk out of the lift but was stopped in his tracks by our presence there. He got quite a surprise to see us all stood there, he made his way past us and we all filed into the lift. We breathed a bit easier when the doors shut, a few smiles and a shit joke out of me about the IRA man who had just left the lift was more for my own benefit as well as an attempt to reassure the patient that we did actually know what we were doing. Once we had got the patient settled in the room, which had a lovely view of the Falls, I turned to one of the RUC officers and told him that I was going to head back. The policeman looked at me and grinned; 'Sorry, but the wagons are not there, something has happened elsewhere and they had to disappear, with your ambulance in tow.'

We had been there for nearly an hour now and I was standing outside the room with one of the other RUC officers, with the other one inside taking to the patient as they knew each other from when the RUC officer had served in the UDR many years before. Still no sign of the consultant. The policeman straightened up as he took in a deep breath and looked past me down the ward. I slowly turned to see what it was that had drawn his attention down the ward; every muscle in my body tightened as a senior leading Sinn Fein politician walked onto the ward. As well as being in Sinn Fein he was also very high up in the ranks of the IRA in Belfast and I had been to briefings which listed what he had done in the past. He had a very violent history and would not be bothered at all if the four of us met our deaths here today. He was promptly stopped by the little nurse who started to bombard him with questions as to why he was here; both of us listened intently.

'No, I don't care; you are not coming onto this ward to see him yet,' she half shouted at him, and I loved it; she was giving him some grief. As I was staring at him I found myself calculating the amount of rounds that I was carrying to the distance he was away from me. Seven to ten feet max. I could get a good group in his head from here easy; a 9mm 'Paracetamol' cures all known headaches. I lowered my head so I was looking at the floor in front of me, where were his bodyguards? The nurse was standing her ground, and he was soon joined by another man whom I did not recognise but I could guess to be a body guard. I did recognise the second man who was 'hanging around' just outside the bottom of the ward.

I took my arms out of my trouser pockets and folded my arms, my right hand reached inside my jacket and felt for the familiar grip of the High Power Browning Pistol which was hung underneath my left armpit. I looked up at the two who were still in front of me, and I was thinking over what I could do and what they might do to react. If I shoot him first, what will he do? Then a little voice in my head made me turn around. The police officer was staring at me, straight in the eyes his facial expression was saying to me: 'No, don't be silly; this is a bad idea!' I unfolded my arms and a small grin appeared over my face, I got the hint. The IRA man would live to see another day, but he was still not getting onto this ward. He had lost his discussion with the little nurse and was at present about to leave the ward. After he and his friend had left the nurse turned around and sighed with relief.

She smiled at us and walked away down the ward, back towards the nursing station. How impressed I was; if she can cook I will marry her. It was about fifteen minutes later when two uniformed RUC officers walked onto the far end of the ward and stopped. A man in plain clothes walked from behind them and up to the officer that was stood with me outside the room. It was time to go. I bid my farewells to the patient and we were gone. The ambulance was still down at the police station so I just got into one of the RUC Land Rovers. It was not until we moved off that we spoke about what had happened.

'I guess that you knew what I was thinking.' I said to him. He answered: 'I am glad that you didn't do it.' He lowered his head again as he sat forward. 'Why?' I asked. He raised his head until it was only a foot away from mine and said: 'As soon as you would have shot him, I would have had to shoot you;' he paused, 'dead, and I would not want to start doing things like that because I don't like the idea of having to shoot a soldier, especially if he had just done this country a service like that!'

AIMING HIGH; BELFAST, 1971

James Kinchin-White, Royal Green Jackets

I was leading my section, just off the Grosvenor Road. There was a crowd on the other side of the road at the junction with Cullingtree Road. I didn't see where the shots came from, but retained enough sense to move my section back about a hundred yards and round a corner; it was then I noticed the flattened imprint of bullets that had hit the riot shields tied to the front of our vehicle; this was parked about three feet to the left of where I'd been standing. The crowd remained at the top of the street and the gunman reappeared and began firing at another patrol further down Grosvenor Road. This was the first time I'd seen a gunman in action.

As I raised my rifle to take aim an elderly lady (actually she was a toothless old witch) came out of the house to my side and stood in front of me saying 'You're shooting no one tonight in my street sonny' – or words to that effect – I couldn't quite understand because she didn't have any teeth, but she was blocking my line of sight! By the time I had shoved her back inside, the gunman had disappeared into the crowd. Amazingly, he reappeared about half an hour later – again, he was shooting down the Grosvenor at another patrol, but this time he was flanked by two other guys who were unarmed but trying to hide the shooter.

As I took aim, unhindered by the toothless witch, I recalled our briefing about avoiding collateral damage and the instructions on the yellow card. I was not confident of missing either of the unarmed people and so I decided to aim above the gunman's head at the street sign – he lived, I lived and I can live with that, but my shot had the desired effect and he buggered off and didn't reappear.

I have often wondered whether he went on to injure others and whether I would have acted differently if I had been through the experience that would emerge over the coming months and years – but that is basically hindsight and it does not exist in reality. I genuinely hope the guy survived; the war is over even if the struggle is not.

The sky above the city was completely black from the smoke of burning Ulster buses and other vehicles. The Lower Falls' ladies 'Bin-Lid Ensemble' entertained us every time we turned up for patrol. During one of the incursions I managed to 're-capture' a truck which still had the keys in the ignition – an exciting event complete with burning barricades and the sound of M1 and Thompson rounds whistling in the wind – only to find that the truck was full of dead chickens! I mean, for God's sake, it could at least have been Players' No 6 or Harp lager; after all, I was now a married man with responsibilities and a wife who smoked and partook of the occasional half.

FOREWARNED

Lee Sansum, Royal Military Police

I had been out on patrol for three days on special Ops, and after only a few hours' sleep during the past 72 hours I was wet, cold and absolutely knackered. The only thing that kept me awake on my top cover position in our Land Rover was my mate's helmet smashing into mine as we occasionally dozed off. Foot patrols, vehicle patrols, route clearances, static Ops constantly over and over; no rest, not enough boots on the ground to give any cover for rest during that Op. This was Northern Ireland 1989, an extra battalion had been sent to the Province to help out with the escalating violence and things were going from bad to worse. There we were, wet, stinking, exhausted and all sixteen of my patrol crammed into a small metal portable container which was doubling up as a briefing room. Bare light bulbs hung from wires tied randomly around the roof and flickered as they swung when the wind blew in through the door. All the lads had dropped their heavy body armour and either sat on in or leant against it; many used to take the protective chest and back plates out to lessen the weight, a practice which became common amongst soldiers the longer they stayed in the Province.

Our team had been through a tough few weeks. We had lost a young guy, the team medic; shot and killed in the most tragic way possible, by friendly fire; blue on blue; mates killing mates. A coffee jar bomb had then taken out four of the team, with the replacement medic taking most of the blast and nearly dying at the scene. We hadn't been able to get a drip into his veins, and he had collapsed with the shock of the blast and the trauma to his body. A local doctor saved his life. He came out from the nearby houses following the explosion and was the only one to help whilst some of the local kids took random kicks aimed at the smouldering bodies which lay around on the ground. There were staggering soldiers, attempting to clear their heads from the ringing and dizziness following the blast. We heard later that this Good Samaritan was punished by the IRA for helping out a Brit.

Our patrol was a simple route across the north of the city; nice and easy, mostly rural with some foot patrols, culvert checks and some vehicle route clearances; nice and easy. That was until the geeky Intelligence Corps corporal gave us the good news. 'Lads,' he said, 'we have a strong indication that you will get shot at in the next few hours. There will be a top cover shoot.' That is when a gunman would take on soldiers providing top cover on mobile patrols. 'Keep your heads down.' The words rang in my ears; no chance of that, I thought; why don't we just stay where we are, or patrol another route, anything for fuck's sake; anything other than do the route clearance, especially as I was one of the assigned top cover guys!

The first few hours were intense, as frightening as I can remember, waiting, watching anything that moved, looking across fields and buildings. I was thinking: 'You are out there, you fuckers, looking for one shot, just to get lucky once and then disappear into the city. I hope it's not me; no, I hope it's not my mate, a younger lad from Manchester; shit I hope they miss.

WELCOME TO BELFAST

Robert Hutton, Royal Highland Fusiliers

On arriving in Belfast, my company was taken by coach in an escorted convoy to Glassmullin camp in the Andersonstown neighbourhood of the city. By midday, 2 Platoon had been issued with flak jackets, ammo, helmet with visor attached and all the other bits and pieces that we might need for the duration of the tour. Once the entire platoon had been issued with their kit, we all had some scoff and even before we could settle in, 2 Platoon was on the move. We were moving to Glenvaugh OP, situated in Lenadoon, a couple of miles along Shaw's Road. Off we went, crammed into PIGs for our first duty of Belfast '74. 1 Platoon was given foot patrols, mostly in the Glassmullan area; 3 Platoon were on mobiles which covered the whole of the Company area, and after three days, the Platoons changed duties on a rotation system.

Glenvaugh OP was a four-storey block of flats, which stood on high ground overlooking the Lenadoon area. The Army had commandeered the top half of the building. The rest of the dwelling was still occupied by its local residents. The front door was armoured and sandbagged, with a sentry on at all times. The top floor had a small OP situated at the corner of the building, which looked out towards the south and east. Also on this floor, there were rooms for sleeping, a TV rest room, toilet and a small kitchen.

Once we settled in, we noticed in one of the rooms used for sleeping that there was a run across the ceiling where all the plaster had been damaged. On enquiring about it, we were told that the Provisional IRA had fired an RPG-7 anti-tank rocket at the OP; luckily it did not detonate on contact but its momentum carried it through the outside wall and across the ceiling and into an inside wall. This was my first forewarning of the reality of Belfast. Certain people there wished you dead, and they fired real bullets.

My first full day in Belfast was spent doing OP duties. Sitting looking out of slits in a wall for two hours at a time could get boring, but you cannot relax in case someone takes a pot shot at your window. The small windows had armoured sliding plates that you close when you were looking out the other; forget to shut the plate and you could be in trouble; consequently you had to stay alert. The small OP faced out to Lenadoon Avenue both ways. A long straight road that approached the flats from the east then curved to the right and continued downhill towards Stewartstown Road. This room was the favourite target of the Provos, as the bullet marks on the outside wall testified. Two men, generally an NCO and a Fusilier, manned the main OP. The observation area of this OP was the downhill stretch of Lenadoon Avenue and westward, looking out over the rest of Lenadoon, including the Blessed Oliver Plunkett (the 'BOP') school. In both rooms we had the 'mug shots' of the local villains on the wall and had small telescopes and binoculars to keep an eye on the locals.

On 28 February 1974, I did my first street patrol in Belfast as part of Geordie Gallagher's section. I acknowledge that I was uneasy, not scared but very nervous. I assumed that every street had a gunman waiting to 'bump' our patrol. I was wondering where all the gunmen and bombs were, and anticipating getting shot at anytime. To make matters worse, I was a 'tail-end Charlie' and had to take turns to walk backwards for 50 per cent of the patrol. On one occasion on that debut patrol, we stopped in a small alley behind some garages for a breather; as last man

I watched the rear; after a couple of minutes I turned around and there was no-one there. They had moved off without telling me. The old 'bottle' went for a few seconds before I calmed down and calculated where they had gone. When I caught up with them, I gave them some heavy verbals. They got the message and it did not occur again.

VCPS

WO2 Haydn Davies, RRW; Att Duke of Edinburgh's Royal Regiment

Often, as I travelled around Armagh in my Mini, I met many a Para road check point and was abused verbally on some occasions. I once handed my work ticket out of the car window as a way of identifying myself. The young eighteen- or ninteen-year-old Para at the checkpoint shouted at me: 'That's no fucking good to me; gerrout the fucking car and give me your fucking ID card!' He helped me from the vehicle and made no remark at all when he saw WO1 on the rank part. But except for his manners he was of course, perfectly right. It was incidents like the above that caused me as an RSM with my own battalion in training for a Belfast tour later, to take them at times on 'Manner lessons' on the square and explained that in no way should they behave like that. I hammered home the fact that the people had been having this treatment of checkpoints and inconvenience for twenty years, and deserved a better attitude than some were inclined to give.

To move through a Grenadier Guards checkpoint was almost a pleasure: 'Won't keep you a moment Sir', and afterwards: 'Sorry to have kept you, Sir.' I think that it was good attitudes like this that kept the shooting down in some particular areas. It is a fact that the local 'boys' weighed up a unit within a day or so of arrival. If a unit needed some extra grief other than that that was on the cards for them, then they would certainly get it.

A NEAR MISS AND A RIVER OF BLOOD

Bill 'Spanner' Jones, REME

It was September 1971, and I was still at the TA camp in Sunnyside. On this particular day, I was going to get cleaned up for dinner when someone called me. 'Spanner; can you do us a favour?' I knew that voice; it was BFJ, the Bombardier who ran the servicing bay. We had first met four years ago, found we shared a surname and both came from Brum, and we had some good times together in Hong Kong. He knew that I would say yes, even before I knew what the 'favour' was.

He asked: 'Can you do the milk run for us tomorrow?' 'Milk run,' I asked, 'doesn't Ringo fetch the milk in the ration truck?' 'We are not actually getting milk,' he replied, 'we have to pick up all the lads going on R&R and take them to the airport and get those coming back and drop them off at each of our locations. Easy job so that's why we call it the milk run.' I asked him why me in particular and he told me that the lads would all be in civvies and unarmed and we would need a PIG. Now the penny dropped; the Humber one ton APC. I took them to pieces, fixed them and put them back together so I was also a designated driver.

So, next morning I met up with BFJ; we were both in DPM combats and carrying SMGs; Ringo had an SLR. He was riding 'shotgun' so the SLR was better suited. About four lads were there in civvies carrying packs, happy to be going on leave. We mounted, with Ringo in the back with the lads; BFJ in the front as commander, and me driving. Leaving Sunnyside, we went to Andersonstown bus depot where another battery was located, picked up more passengers and on to the Belfast docks where 93 Battery looked after a Navy hulk with internees in it. They were all happy and joking and the banter included: 'What's in your bag, two months of laundry for the missus?' 'The second thing I will do when I get home is put my bag down.' The banter flowed, and on we drove to Carmody industrial park on Belfast's north side and collected our last passengers and from there to the airport.

There were barriers and coils of wire everywhere; RUC and military were securing the place and we were directed to an area set aside for military vehicles. I parked up and the lads got out to catch their planes and picked up the incoming soldiers.

We picked up packed lunches and set off on the return journey but it turned out that tragedy was waiting for us. We were going down the Antrim Road, and it was not busy, and was a regular route for military vehicles. However, I couldn't see any ahead of me or in my mirrors. In fact, it could have been a sunny day anywhere in Britain. There was a park and a T-junction to our right, people still in summer office clothes on the corner, waiting to cross; just a seemingly normal day. Then BOOM! The people vanished in a cloud of smoke; the PIG lurched to the left and the back slid away. The door window was an armoured hatch with a grab lever to close it, and I grabbed it and pushed down, briefly feeling something hot brush my forearm as my sleeves were rolled up to the elbow. I could see through the side window a shower of debris coming at us; a whole 'Keep Left ' bollard spinning end over end, glass intact, it would miss us but seemed sinister in that instant. I fought the steering wheel and touched the accelerator to keep the PIG straight, as those lads were depending on me to get them back safely. The vehicle responded, and I heard BFJ shouting in a voice I barely recognised: 'Get us out of here, Spanner!'

I pressed the accelerator a bit harder and he spoke in a more normal tone: 'We can't help those people, Bill. We have no medical kit and these lads would be targets, unarmed and in civvies.' He was right; absolutely right but it was not easy to drive away knowing people were hurt there. A gunner named Ray was sitting behind me, and shouted: 'My sandwich; look at my sandwich.' It had flown across the PIG and stuck to the left inside of the hull. What had hit me was not like a wind or a wave; it was a sudden compression that is very hard to describe and did me physiological harm that did not show up for many years. One of the lads, a sergeant I believe, had fallen from his seat and was curled on the floor; he had only minor bruising and was embarrassed at ending up on the floor.

The explosion is thought to have been the attack by the IRA on the 'Four Steps' pub on the Shankill Road on 29 September 1971. The no-warning bomb went off in the pub which was packed with football fans. Alexander Andrews (60) and Ernest Bates (38) both civilians, were killed and dozens were wounded.

We continued, and I heard sirens as emergency vehicles raced to the area; retracing our route, we dropped lads off at their bases until we were back at Sunnyside and the last few got out. Ringo was looking at the right of the PIG, and said: 'You are going to need your tools Bill; oh, and can you put it on the wash down?' I moved to the wash down and got out, and what I saw was hard to look at; the soft side bins and mud wings were a bit bent, but the hull, the hull was red. It looked as if someone had got buckets of minced meat and thrown them through a giant fan; there was blood and flesh all over the right side of the hull. People do not go 'Argh' and leap through the air when they are that close to a bomb; they shred.

We got a hose and a stiff broom, and we began cleaning; there were no parts big enough to identify as a person, and a river of bloody water flowed to the drain. Ringo climbed on top and brushed as I hosed.

Ringo, BFJ and I spent as much time as we could together afterwards but we could not explain why else we were mates. The flashbacks started a few years on in Germany and went on for 30 years before I got treatment; countless thousands of times I have relived that trip. Some milk run.

Although Bill was badged REME and it was a standing joke at the time that their badge would deter the IRA from shooting at them, their casualties in Northern Ireland were worse than some infantry units. They had nineteen fatalities throughout the course of the Troubles, including one of the first soldiers to be killed in the Province, Craftsman Christopher Edgar who was killed in highly suspicious circumstances on 13 September 1969. The author has one account of his death, but cannot substantiate the claim that it was a 'blue on blue'. Their nineteenth and final casualty was Sergeant Major James Bradwell (43) who died of the wounds he received from an IRA bomb on 7 October 1996 at the Lisburn Garrison. He died four days later and was buried in Sunderland.

A KISS IN WEST BELFAST

Corporal Si Capon, 40 Commando Royal Marines

My second tour of the Province was to West Belfast with 40 Commando in 1993. I had been to South Armagh in 1988, so this was my first city tour. I went out a week early as I was a team commander. We had a week's handover from the outgoing 'Pongo' Battalion.

I remember my first patrol on the first day. I had taken up a kneeling fire position in a doorway whilst a snap VCP was set up. A little girl came over to chat to me; she must have been five, maybe six years old. Chat, chat, chat; 'What are you doing Mister?' All the usual stuff you might expect from kids of that age. 'Can I have a look through your gun?' and so I showed her the SUSAT sight. 'Before I go, can I give you a kiss?' she asked. It was all about winning hearts and minds, so I offered her a cheek to kiss. With that, she spat right in my face and legged it. Welcome to Belfast. I'll never forget that; it just about sums up the place for me.

I seem to remember a shooting on the first day as well. No casualties, just the usual follow up, running round like headless chickens. It's nothing compared to what the lads in Afghanistan etc are facing these days, my hat goes off to them. We were on a foot patrol on the Falls Road, coming up to Christmas, and a passerby came over and whispered 'Merry Christmas' and shoved a small prayer card, I think it was called, into my hand. I can remember thinking how the hell can people live like this? In constant fear from the paramilitaries. At the time, I thought that the whole place was a shit hole and should be bulldozed and turned into a car park. There was something about the smell of West Belfast at night that was gopping. [Gopping: Marine slang for crap, horrible etc.] It could have been the coal fires; it could have been the stash of dead cats and used nappies that were thrown at us. Who knows?

I have looked at the place on Google Earth recently, and a lot has changed; my opinion hasn't.

40 Commando lost four men in Northern Ireland during the Troubles. Marine David Allen (22) from Newcastle-upon-Tyne was shot by an IRA sniper at the Unity Flats in Belfast on 27 July,

40 Commando Royal Marines provide mobile cover while carrying out a search with a foot patrol, Moyard Crescent. *(Dave Harding)*

1972. In mid-September of that year, his comrade Anthony David (27) from Glamorgan was shot whilst driving along the Falls Road. He died of his wounds on 17 October. Exactly a year to the day of David Allen's death, 40 Commando lost Marine John Shaw in an RTA in highly suspicious circumstances; the author is unable to find out further details. That the Royal Marines themselves regard his death as a result of terrorist action is sufficient for the author of this book as firm evidence. On 28 May, 1983, 40 Commando lost Marine Andrew Gibbons who died at Camlough Lake, near Newry.

THE MAN IN THE BATH

Dougie Durrant, Army Dog Handlers Unit

> In 1979/80, the Duke of Wellington's regiment was located in West Belfast. It was my turn to spend two weeks at Macrory Park just off the junction with the Whiterock and Falls Road. It was a typical Belfast summer's day; the birds were singing and the smell of smoke was in the air. Just at that point, a large burst of gunfire was heard from the direction of the Falls/Whiterock Road junction no further than 100 metres from the camp gates. The QRF ran out the gate towards the incident, we knew then there was a man down; I had seen the patrol just leave the base.

I ran to the ops room, kit in hand with my search dog, Bluce, having heard the contact report asking for 'Groundhog' and 'Wagtail.' 'I am ready to go, sir,' I said to the ops officer who at this point was very calm. The tracker dog team was located at Flax Street Mill comprising L/bdr 'Moby' Dick and his black Labrador. A request was sent to 39 Brigade to get the dog on the ground, and, in the meantime I made my way with the QRF to the location on foot. They were just removing the casualty who I believed was fatally wounded. The firing point had been located across the road in a dentist's, and the follow up action was ongoing. However, I knew that no one had been in the house due to the fear of booby traps. I made my way across the road and searched the front entrance of the building but found nothing. I then made my way around the back; Bluce went mad on a bin that was located near the rear of the premises. It was a large explosive device, and by now 'Moby' had turned up and was being briefed by the commander, at the incident control point.

'Moby' got his dog ready and found a point of interest from where to start the track, and tracked from the back door to the main road just a short distance away. It seemed as if the gunman had had a getaway car ready. He then asked the commander if a vehicle had been taken from here during the incident. He replied in the affirmative and said that they had taken the owner's Volvo estate. 'Moby' then informed the commander that if the car was found under no circumstances was he to let anyone near it; the commander alerted the ops room of the request.

A short time later we received information that the car had been found in the Turf Lodge area. We were on our way, and, within ten minutes we had located the vehicle. 'Moby' then got his dog onto the track across the Turf Lodge back across the City Cemetery, across the Whiterock Road and into the Ballymurphy estate. I said to him: 'The fucker has done a 360.' 'I hope so,' said Moby, and we began running at full pelt to find the shooter. The commander asked if we were sure that we had the right man, and 'Moby' replied: 'We will soon find out!'

We stopped at a front door, certain that the track had entered this house, he told the commander and we were ordered in. With this, the door was kicked in and we went straight up the stairs, and there in the bath was a man fully clothed and washing himself and his clothes, desperately trying to get rid of the forensics. Laid on the sink was a loaded AK47; 'Ah, fuck,' was his reaction. He was taken away by the RUC and his house was ripped apart, looking for more evidence. It was an outstanding operation from start to finish with the commander on the ground putting his training into gear that got the result. 'Moby' was awarded Mentioned in Dispatches which he deserved, but I felt very sad for the family for the loss of their son and a good soldier.

The soldier was Corporal Errol Pryce (21) from Sheffield, shot by an IRA sniper at St James Road, near the junction with the Falls Road. The killing, on 26 January 1980 took place after IRA members took a family hostage and opened fire from an upstairs window. Two civilians were also injured as a result of the indiscriminate firing of an M60 machine gun by the terrorists. The IRA used the same M60 in a later shooting in the Twinbrook area of Belfast.

THE SPRINGFIELD ROAD SANGAR

Captain Haydn Davies, RRW

We took over Springfield Road police station from the Royal Green Jackets, and we entered the base and started to meet up with our opposite numbers for a quick brief. 'Relief in the line' is a vulnerable time in any situation and the 'opposition' knew this. Changeovers were kept as secret as possible because the IRA were apt to 'see off' the old and 'welcome the new', the changeover time was an ideal time for it. The sangars and the main gate were taken over immediately, and our first patrols were out on the streets in 15 minutes. We knew the drills well, and security of what the locals called the 'barracks' would be ours quite quickly, so that the 'Jackets' could be on their way home, and we knuckled down to securing the 'Patch'.

Sangars are not the most jovial places to spend time, especially at night. One particular one at the rear of the base was known as a 'dodgy' one where sniping was quite a regular event. Two soldiers from different regiments had met their end due to sniping in this particular sangar. I went my rounds of the sentries and entered the particular one in question. All was well and the sentry stood well back in the 'trapped shadow' of the sangar; he was blacked up and observing through the small slit whilst not making a target of himself. The Green Jacket sentry was still with him and just about leaving.

I noticed an incoming shot hole in the front wall which was facing the street and about lower chest height just below the observation slit. The hole was about 55mm in diameter, and let in lots of daylight. Observing from the slit meant putting your chest to the large shot hole. 'What's that?' I asked the Green Jacket. 'That Sir is the entry hole of the RPG round that got the bloke that was killed here.' I asked why it had not been filled in. The sentry replied: 'Our company commander thought it served to keep sentries "on the ball" and alert.' I said nothing but made a note to have it plugged. The Green Jacket departed and I looked over the sangar. On the breeze block walls and ceiling there was evidence of obvious but small splattered blood spots of the dead soldier.

Within an hour or so I had had the shot hole blocked and had the sangar completely painted on the inside, walls and ceiling with matt black paint. It obscured the blood and the large inlet hole. The matt black paint on the walls also matched the sentry's blacked camouflaged face and helped to prevent silhouette. A little later I went back up to check, and to see the finished work. As I was leaving I nodded to the sentry and asked him if it was O.K. He replied glumly: 'It's a bloody gloomy place now!'

The soldier to whom Haydn Davies refers is thought to be Private Martin Jessop (19) of the Worcestershire and Sherwood Foresters. The single soldier from the Derby area was killed when the IRA fired a Soviet-made RPG7 from nearby Cavendish Street where they were holding a family hostage. He was one of two soldiers to die that day as Lance Bombardier Kevin Waller (20) of the Royal Artillery succumbed to the wounds that he had received several days before following an IRA explosion at Divis Street flats. A young Catholic schoolboy – Stephen Bennett (14) – was killed in the same blast as the IRA showed scant regard for the lives of their 'community'.

The 'barracks' claimed the lives of at least three other soldiers. On 25 May 1971, Sergeant Michael Willetts, GC (27) of the Parachute Regiment was in a foyer at the base. It was packed with civilians thought to be seeking shelter from the violence. An IRA member threw the bomb into the entrance and, realising that there would be a huge loss of life, Sergeant Willetts without any thought for his own safety, threw himself onto the device. It exploded and he was terribly and fatally injured; he died within a few hours. The locals jeered him as he was rushed to hospital. On 30 May 1972, Marcel 'Jimmy' Doglay (28) a married man who had joined the King's Regiment from the Seychelles was killed by an IRA bomb. The device was smuggled into the base by an IRA sympathiser and when it exploded, it left Doglay's four children without a father. Like Michael Willetts almost a year before, the locals jeered his body as it was taken to a waiting ambulance.

The fourth soldier to die was APTC instructor Warrant Officer David Bellamy (31) attached to the Duke of Wellington's Regiment. A married man with two children, from Huntingdon, he was killed at the station when IRA gunmen opened fire from a house at Crocus Street. Several RUC officers were also hit in this attack on 28 October 1979, with one, John Davidson (26) from South Belfast dying of his wounds twenty days later. The author is also aware of a suicide at the station which took place in October 1969.

AFTER THE BOMBING

Kingsman Paddy Lenaghan, King's Regiment

As I write this (on urging from the author) there is a photograph hanging on the wall to my right. It shows my wife, Josephine, in her graduation gown holding her diploma in applied science, in Nursing; Josie graduated in 1987. Our daughter Marika was born at a military hospital, in Malta while I was stationed there with 1 Loyals, and our son was born in Germany, while we were posted to Minden with 1 Kings; our son, Kevin was delivered by a German civvie driver, assisted by Josie.

So my experiences with hospitals up to that time were very positive. The horror of the bomb at Springfield Road police station on 30 May 1972, which resulted in the death of Kingsman Marcel (Jimmy) Doglay and the many injuries sustained in that incident, (including my own shattered finger), the medical staff, both nursing and surgeons, military and civvie, provided first-class care and treatment.

The arrival and reception of the injured at R.V.H. was carried out by medical teams who never appeared to be flustered or found wanting; they were very proficient in the assessment and cataloguing of the victims. After initial treatment I was transferred to Musgrave Park (MPH) and then, after a few days, I was casevaced with about six other patients to Royal Herbert Hospital in Woolwich, London. It was whilst at Woolwich that I found out that I had slightly more than a broken finger when, for the first time, I watched a nurse change the dressing and remove 150 stitches from my left hand; flying glass does tend to shred flesh.

During my stay at the Royal Herbert, I learnt that the layout and design of the hospital was taken from a design by the 'lady with the lamp', Florence Nightingale. I met members of the Regiment, as they were admitted to the hospital; received mail from the Adjutant Major, Mr White, informing me of events and incidents involving the lads still deployed in Belfast. During my stay at the hospital, I received rail warrants to go and visit Josie and the kids, as she had returned back from visiting her family in Malta on being informed of my injury (fallen down drunk I believe the Sergeant had told Josie). She was given a rail warrant to visit me in London; we stayed at the 'Chevron' club, and did a walk of the sites in London which I remembered from my time there on the streets before seeing the light and joining the Army.

I am grateful to the medical personnel who gave to me, and countless others, the treatment and care to recover and to try to get on with our lives.

The author had the pleasure of meeting both Paddy and his wife in Queensland in 2008 and found them a charming and friendly couple. After the Springfield Road police station bombing on 30 May 1972, Paddy eventually left the British Army and went home to his native Australia. Typical of the man they call 'Four Fingers' he promptly enlisted in the Australian Army and served as a weapons instructor for over twenty years.

Kingsman Marcus 'Jimmy' Doglay

On 30 May 1972, the IRA killed 'Jimmy' Doglay at Springfield Road RUC Station in Belfast. Marcus James Doglay (28) known to all of his mates as 'Jimmy' was born and bred in the Seychelles, in the beautiful Indian Ocean, a far cry and half a world away from the blackened stone terraced houses of west Belfast; from a world of palm trees, and the azure blue of the ocean to the filth, violence and sudden death of Belfast during the Troubles.

He was, a fact confirmed by my 'Kingo' friends George Prosser, Paddy Leneghan and Peter Oakley, a very skilful boxer and he had represented his adopted country, England, as well as Ulster and the Army at lightweight level and held the title of Army boxing champion. He had been in uniform for some eleven years, never rising above the rank of Kingsman (Private) in the King's Regiment. He was, unusually for a British soldier at the time, black, and like the Royal Green Jackets (aka: the black mafia) the King's Regiment had several black members. Paddy Lenaghan recalls at least four, all of whom tended to be excellent boxers.

The King's Regiment, like many of the now disbanded county regiments of the time, were a tightly knit bunch of men, recruited from the Manchester and Merseyside area and were known to other soldiers as 'hubcap nickers' no doubt due to the preponderance of 'Scouse' accents; somewhat unfairly, one hastens to add. By the dawn of that fateful day which would rob the Kingos of a popular soldier, they had already suffered some losses in that very month. On the 13th, whilst standing opposite the Whiterock Flats, Corporal Alan Buckley (22) a married man and father of one, was shot and killed by the IRA. A Geordie by birth, he was in the Turf Lodge following a Loyalist bomb attack on a Catholic bar when several gunmen opened fire. A comrade was injured and other soldiers fought desperately to save Buckley's life but his injuries were too severe.

Just ten days later, Kingsman Eustace Hanley (20), like Doglay, black, and known to his comrades as 'Billy', was shot in Springhill Avenue. Springhill Avenue leads south off the Springfield Road and just on the western extremities of the Ballymurphy Estate. Hanley was guarding other soldiers who were dismantling obstacles placed there by rioters; the shot killed him instantly.

In late May, the RUC station on Springfield Road, familiar to the author, was being extended as a permanent base for soldiers and as such, was being decorated by civilian contractors. Despite the fact that security was paramount and armed guards stood watch, the IRA managed to smuggle a 30lb device into the rest area of the station. Soldiers returning from patrol were congregated in that area, unwinding from the day's events when the device exploded. Marcus Doglay was killed and many others were injured in the explosion which blew out almost 20 feet of wall. When the soldier's lifeless body was taken out of the devastated station, crowds of the folk who lived in the area came out to jeer as he was carried by stretcher into an Army ambulance and his body was actually spat upon.

23868738 Kingsman Marcus James Doglay, born in Mahe, Seychelles on 12 August, 1943, is buried in St Patrick's Churchyard; murdered by the IRA, a long, long way from home. He left a widow and four young children.

By the end of that terrible tour, a further four King's Regiment CVOs would be making trips to the UK mainland to inform a grieving family of the loss of their loved one.

'JIMMY'

Paddy Lenaghan, King's Regiment

My enduring memory of Jimmy will be seeing him there at the pool table, near the kitchen serving hatch, in Springfield Road police station, pool cue in hand, lining up for a shot. When we were in Weeton Camp, I often saw him over in the married quarters with his family.

We were not best mates, good friends even, as I mainly knew him from the boxing squad, but he was the sort of person you just had to say 'G'day' to. This was if you passed him in the street, or in this case, the close confines of the cramped living conditions which existed inside Springfield Road RUC station at that time. I don't believe that it ever got any better, even years later.

I came to be in the same room as him on that fateful day. For civvies, the thought that you can be emotional and haunted by the passing of a workmate may be hard to understand. Mourn him and miss him, yes, but to a soldier, our workmates are fellow soldiers who have endured the same hardship, deprivation of liberty and free speech and the same fears as us. Because of the career that we had chosen to follow, we knew that self-discipline was what was required of us and all that went with it. But I digress; there was Jimmy about to take a shot and me getting a light for a cig that I had 'bummed' off a mate; then chaos!

I opened my eyes in a bed in a public ward at the RVH and I was immediately informed by a Corporal when I asked about Jimmy, that he hadn't made it. It was the first time, but sadly not the last, that I shed tears.

On 30 May, every year since 1972, I have managed to find a place, sometimes a physical location, but if not, certainly in my mind, to shed a tear and think of Jimmy.

Peter Oakley, King's Regiment

Trusting my memory serves me right, Private Doglay was originally in my 'B' company. But as we had had a couple of black soldiers shot the OC thought that the opposition were targeting black soldiers so kept him off the street and put him into the ops room on the radio; we really were under a lot of pressure in 1972!

Unfortunately his diction was not good, making him difficult to understand so he went up to Springfield Road. The incident there as I recall (subject to memory) came about as a result of a film show. On that evening the bulb burnt out, so as there was no spare, the film was abandoned and most left. Doglay and a few others stayed behind to play cards. The bomb, I believe, was in a fire extinguisher which was on the wall of the canteen. I may be talking a load of bollocks but that is my memory.

NORTH HOWARD STREET MILL MEMORIES

Rifleman, Royal Green Jackets

I was stationed at the Mill in 1971 and it is a place that I will never forget; the memories of that place are not good and it was where the Bn lost Dave Walker in the summer of that year. It was an old brick cotton mill, about four storeys high with beige-coloured ornamental patterns up the corners and several old spiral staircases made from stone. It was a bugger running up those bastards in full kit, SLR in hand to get to the roof top OP. It was full of old, rusty pipes and always smelled of shit and sweaty socks, and I don't mean the Jocks who had been there before us. There was another mill close by and when trouble started, it started there. I seem to remember that we had a few 'slop jocks' [Army Catering Corps] stationed there and they, bless 'em, did their best to keep us fed and watered and always went out of their way for us. There will be them that take the piss, but as far as I am concerned, I will never hear a bad word about them.

Most of 1RGJ were southern lads, a couple of Taffs, and there was the odd Brummie and a couple of Yorkies whose names now escape me with the passage of time. I live in south Belfast now and occasionally I go back to where the Mill was and it upsets me every time. I keep promising myself that I won't go back, but it has that fatal fascination for me and I see the ghosts of those young, fresh-faced cockney boys who became men on those four-month tours.

I remember the sheets of wriggly tin which surrounded the base and the early stages of the so-called 'peace line' nearby which kept the locals from murdering each other. You know, there were times when I wanted to tear it down and let the bastards have a go at each other; as long as they were killing each other, they were leaving me and my mates alone.

Our TAOR was centred around the Divis, Falls, Springfield Road, Grosvenor Road and the area north of Grosvenor Road, the Rosses, Balkans, Servia etc. The Mill was just off Northumberland Street and was midway between the Catholic Falls Road and the Proddie Shankill and we were right slap-bang in the middle. The area dominated the sectarian line in those days and the street probably still does. We were the Christians, thrown to the lions and the crowd was the local Taigs and Prods. That's how it felt to us; piggy in the sodding middle.

There are too many incidents to recount here and I could fill the book for you, but one I remember took place a month or so before Dave Walker was killed. We were in or around Leeson Street and we stopped a local for questioning. A couple of the lads were sure that they recognised him as a prick who had let loose with half a house brick which had hurt one of the attached personnel we had with us. We pulled him over and he spat at a lance jack who gave him a bit of a slap and we got the usual 'British bastards; fuck off to England, will ye!' A few of his mates had gathered around and they weren't scared of us as they knew that, as much as they hated us that we generally wouldn't lose our tempers. Then a couple of women with greasy hair and miniskirts and no tits (always remember that they were as flat as ironing boards) came out and started banging dustbin lids and blowing whistles. I always felt that had we confiscated all the dustbin lids in Belfast, they would have still found more. We radioed back to base as there was about 50 at this stage and so we let the scumbag go.

I can remember the look on his face as though it was yesterday; he stood his ground and gave us a real mouthful. I called him back but he turned his back on me and farted straight into my face; funny, but it smelled of the boiled cabbage that all the Mick houses reeked of. I thought: 'Sod this for a game of soldiers,' and walked over to him and booted him with my Army-issue size nines right up the backside. I expected him to walk away, but he came straight up to me and stood toe-to-toe and I could smell his foul breath and could see yellowy-brown, rotten teeth. Well, from there it escalated and soon we were in platoon strength and out with the riot shields. These were the days before the long plexi-glass and these were metal things and as soon as a brick hit it, it would fold around your bloody wrist!

We were bottled, with glass shards everywhere and then the bricks started raining down and several of the lads were hit and fell down. Every time a lad went down the mob – must have been over a hundred by now –would cheer. It was like being at a football match when a goal is scored, or at a bull fight when the Spics shout: 'Ole.' It was hairy stuff and I was pissing myself but even throughout all that shit, as each bottle smashed into pieces on my shield or on the walls either side of us, I was thinking: 'There's threepence back on those where I come from!' About a dozen petrol bombs came flying in and exploded nearby but no-one was hurt. After about twenty minutes of this, just as we were forming up for a snatch squad, a couple of PIGs came tearing through us and scattered the mobs. A petrol bomb then hit the roof of one of the vehicles, bursting in bright flame but then quickly died out.

Just after that, a couple of the lads with Federal Riot guns were ordered to fire a couple of baton rounds if the mobs didn't disperse, but they were melting away into their hovels to draw breath and wait for the next moment of Belfast 'magic'. It was peaceful for the rest of the day, but as some big picture star once said; 'Tomorrow is another day.'

Please don't identify me, as I still live locally and I have family here now and I never have told them about my past life as a squaddie; always green!

Rifleman David Walker (30) a single man from Rhyll in North Wales, but living in Staffordshire, was shot in the very early hours of 12 July 1971. He was shot whilst on the rooftop of the Mill following several nights of brief, but regular, gun battles. The IRA lamely claimed that his killing was in direct retaliation for the shooting of two civilians in Londonderry earlier in the week. He is buried in Tidworth Military Cemetery where the Battalion was stationed for a time in the 1970s.

PATROLLING LENADOON

Robert Hutton, Royal Highland Fusiliers

After three days at Glenveagh OP, 2 Platoon moved back to the main camp at Glassmullin, where for the next three days we were tasked to do foot patrols. The area that 'A' Company had been assigned to was the West Belfast Republican stronghold of Andersonstown and Lenadoon. Belfast is made up of a patchwork of areas, some Protestant (Orange), some Roman Catholic (Green), some, though not many, mixed (Yellow), and the City Centre (Grey). West Belfast is the heartland of the Republican movement, Lenadoon, Andersonstown, Whiterock, Ballymurphy, Turf Lodge, New Barnsley and the infamous Falls Road are all included in this catchment area, every one of these areas Catholic and bitter towards the security forces. Lenadoon/Andersonstown had three main roads cutting through it; Stewartstown, Glen and Shaw's. Shaw's Road cuts diagonally across the area and separates Lenadoon from Andersonstown, Glen Road runs across the top of the built up area, to the north lies Black Mountain that rises high above Belfast, giving the city a scenic backdrop.

Glassmullin camp sat in the middle of an old grass square surrounded by houses. It was about the size of a football pitch, into which were crammed portacabins. The portacabins had six rooms, plus a TV room and each platoon had one each. Each soldier had their own bed space, but we had to share lockers due to the lack of space. Unless you were on patrol, this was where you were stuck in camp. You could not go out for a pint down the local unless you wanted your head blown off.

As you walked the streets, you soon become familiar with the Company area; you soon know all the street names and what one led to where, and where the most likely sniper positions were. If you crossed a street, you ran; didn't walk, and if you turned a corner, you peeked round first. Not at head height though, that was too obvious; you didn't poke your rifle around first either, because that would tell them you were coming into sight. If you stopped any time,

Republican propaganda, Andersontown. *(Ken Wharton)*

you stopped adjacent to a door or window, because the Provos don't like shooting at you if there was a prospect of hitting their own; they preferred you out in the open or against a plain wall. If people were nearby, we stood close to them so they acted as a human shield. It may seem callous to use civilians as protection, but it was a battle of wits and using any means possible to outwit the gunman or sniper. If in a garden, get down behind a wall or blend in with a hedge or bush. If in a doorway or near a window etc., you keep moving; move from side to side; kneel down then up again. Move, because even a swaying movement can put a gunman off his aim. It is hard enough to aim at a motionless target, at a couple of hundred metres, never mind a bobbing, swaying one. Derelict buildings, open spaces were kept well clear of, as they were all potential booby trap areas. I think every squaddie who has served in Northern Ireland has had that horrible gut feeling of impending doom in his stomach as he walked or ran by somewhere or something that he thought might be blown up at any second.

All the time you were watching for tell-tale signs; you looked for slightly opened windows, for dickers on street corners, eying cars that drove by, people etc. Your mind had a million things to think about on each patrol, all with one aim, survival; survival for yourself and survival for your mates. One clear sign that something was going to happen is when the streets become devoid of people.

Soldiers dreaded the words: 'Sir, they're taking the kids indoors' as it more often than not heralded the imminent arrival of a gunman in the area. The IRA would nevertheless open fire on soldiers and RUC even if children were in close proximity because they were skilled at the post-incident pious apology. They would, however, send runners into the area to warn parents that a gunman was about to attack a patrol.

While in cover or patrolling along, you would occasionally raise your rifle as if to shoot and point it anywhere you might think a sniper might be; a window, an alleyway, another street, anywhere. If by chance there was a gunman about and he sees a soldier suddenly point a rifle in his direction he will think twice before opening up. Having a rifle pointed at you in Belfast was a heart-stopping experience I can tell you.

We patrolled with a minimum of eight men, sometimes twelve men split into four-man sections; an NCO or a senior Fusilier in charge of each. We patrolled with one group in one street and another group in the next street parallel to you; this way you constantly had back up. Also backing you up were a pair of Land Rovers on mobile patrol which drove around the area and could give you back up within minutes. If you got a 'contact' more back up would arrive from Glassmullan.

For most of the tour I acted as a tail-end Charlie; we patrolled with two either side of the street, each observing the other side as you saw more that way, the NCO and the senior 'Jock' were up front, the 'rookies' at the back, me and someone else. The two men at the rear each took turns to walk backwards, covering the patrols rear arc and it was awkward at first but as the tour went on I became very competent at it.

This was what was demanded of you physically, and with the mental pressure of staying alert all the time, it could become a strain at times. Often, and I did it myself, people would come off patrol, get to their room, boots off, jersey off and collapse on their bed and be out for the count within a few minutes. When you got woken up for your next patrol, you felt as if you had only been asleep for 10-20 minutes; you slowly moved, day-by-day, into the thousand-yard stare.

ON TURF LODGE

Craig Laidler. 4 Royal Tank Regiment (att: QOH)

Our 1992 tour went without any major events, although I would need to qualify 'major'. It doesn't mean nothing happened because it did, and it happened most days; it just means that it didn't make the news back home. This ranged from being pelted with bricks, bottles and paint bombs by kids to which we responded by firing plastic bullets back. We were always told in training not to fire them into the road and bounce them as they lost accuracy and might not hit the intended brick or bottle thrower. However, we were told if you did this, the baton round increased in velocity and took out whoever it hit, a lot harder. Consequently, we enjoyed bouncing them off the road, as it made it more of a lottery as to which brick throwing yob it took out.

Our main role was to support the RUC on their day-to-day duties, which included domestics, serving warrants etc. On 1 February 1993 I was on Red 3s for two nights which meant we followed the Blues (RUC Land Rover) to provide top cover on mobile patrol. We were driving along the Falls Road towards Andytown [Andersonstown] RUC station on a Monday afternoon when there was a massive flash, bang and explosion. I fell inside the wagon along with my buddy on top cover and the next thing I remember, I was outside the back doors with my rifle up to my shoulder scanning kids throwing bottles and bricks at us, my ears were ringing, head was fuzzy. At first I thought we had been hit by a brick or a petrol bomb on the front of our Rover, but when we looked around we saw the RUC wagon on its side with the RUC lads falling out the back. Upon reflection it looked like the keystone cops but at the time it was like a war zone.

Then one of the strangest things happened; other mobiles tipped up and tooled up, and before we knew it the kids had gone and the street seemed normal apart from a RUC wagon on its side in the middle of the road. It was one of the most bizarre sights I have ever seen. I was checked over and we were fine; just a bit dazed and we were sent to check out the firing point. It transpired that PIRA had decided to take out a Rover and fired a PRIG, like a homemade anti-tank shoulder-held weapon. Once the little prick had fired it, this brave 'freedom fighter' used kids to cover his escape by pelting any survivors with bricks and bottles so he could run away and hide.

By this stage of the conflict, the IRA and INLA had abandoned their previous tactic of going face-to-face with the Army and engaging them in fire fights. With that tactic, there could only be one winner: the professional and well-trained and disciplined British soldier. After Operation Motorman, they would shoot from a well concealed firing point, often in a house they had taken over, or from a position where they could easily melt away into the community. Various safe houses – or even Catholic homes where the tenants or owners were too scared to refuse them access – would be open for their escape to other parts of the area, always locked or blocked when the Army came in hot pursuit. A gunman could fire a round at a soldier and then, having ditched his weapon for safe recovery later, could emerge several streets away, looking for all the world like a bystander alerted to the commotion.

The tour was made up of various incidents which you don't hear about; one of the Jocks was shot in the back in the 'Murph but survived because of his NIBA. [Northern Ireland Body Armour] Another Jock got blown across the street as he was walking past a chippy; fish and

Craig Laidler on patrol. *(Via Craig Laidler)*

'Top Cover'. Notice visors half way down so when hit by bricks they dropped. *(Craig Laidler)*

Turf Lodge. *(Craig Laidler)*

chips were off the menu for him for a while. There were various ammo and weapon finds, searches, and even joy riders trying to run you over. There are a couple of things that I remember and I recorded as I have only kept a diary once in my life and it was for the second part of my tour.

The first was a knee capping; the IRA ran the Turf Lodge as a police force of their own and this meant punishment beatings for burglars, joy riders and anyone they didn't like really. We were called out to a victim of a knee capping and our patrol was the first there. I remember turning up to see this guy lying on the side of the road with his trousers rolled up and two bloody holes where his knee caps were meant to be. He was crying in pain; next to him were two plastic bags with the remains of his knee caps in. His crime was that he had burgled a house more than once and he would have to pay his 'compo' from the UK government to the IRA once he had made his claim. We often talked to the younger kids who were joy riders before they nicked the cars and tried to run us over when they were pissed. They hated the IRA as much as us, as most of the kids walked with a limp because of the plastic knee cap they had fitted following their punishment.

On patrol in the 'Turf' you had so many things you had to remember; don't lean on the walls, check for loose bricks as they could have put a small amount of explosive behind it, just enough to blow your leg off. Check before you stop for command wires and bombs; don't pick up anything at all; watch the windows; watch the cars. Why is the street quiet; where have the kids gone, and so on? One of the tricks the kids used to do was to get planks of wood and slap them as hard as they could as you walked past an alley so it sounded like a sniper's shot; it took a while to get used to that and to this day I still jump at loud cracks.

Crazy Wayne, it's finally got to him on mobiles. *(Craig Laidler)*

It wasn't all one-way crap; we had our moments too. One Friday night we were on patrol in Granshas Park in the 'Turf', a particularly nasty street. We stopped again and I took cover in a back garden; I was just doing my 'Belfast Lean' against the back wall (one foot on the wall without your back touching it so not to set of any pressure bombs and it's amazingly relaxing) and the back door opened. This pissed up Paddy came out spitting hate and filth at me, my country, mother, dog, and fish and anything else he could imagine to wind me up. He had clearly been out all night and I couldn't be bothered with it so I asked him nicely to go back indoors and I would be gone in two minutes. I told him not to worry because I wouldn't jump on his prize roses and nick his prize-winning marrow from his garden. I should point out that the garden was a mess with old sofas and dog shit all over.

This didn't seem to work and the finger jabbing started and was accompanied by the usual spitting in the face. At this point Alfie from my team popped his head around the corner to see what all the noise was about. 'Geordie, sort him out mate; everyone will know we're here, pal,' he said. With this, I pulled my head back and head butted the fella right on the nose, and because I was wearing my face shield half way down my face (it dropped the face cover down fully when a brick hit you) it just smashed his nose and he fell back and onto the floor screaming and moaning. 'You were saying about my mother?' I asked.

Alfie looked at the bloke writhing around in the dog shit in the garden, looked at me in shock and said: 'I meant get him back in the house, yer nutter; not smash his nose.' We moved on swiftly with the patrol after that and didn't mention it in the debrief.

GEORDIE AND SWIFTY BLOWN UP AT THE MILL

Steve 'Harry' Crump, Army Dog Handlers Unit

I had just made myself a brew and was settling down to see what the TV had to offer for the evening; I was on location at Fort Whiterock (FWR) or as myself and the other dog handlers called it, 'Fraggle Rock'. FWR was situated right in the heart of Republican West Belfast. I had had a relatively quiet day only being tasked once to carry out a rummage on some waste land in the 'Murph. My dog 'Res' had been fed. I switched on the TV and settled down to wait for something to happen. After about half an hour the phone rang; 'Here we go,' I muttered to myself and answered the phone.

It was the 2 I/C of a light infantry battalion; at the time they were the resident battalion with a company at North Howard Street Mill; one at Girdwood Park and the one at FWR. I was informed that we were on standby to go to North Howard Street Mill (NHSM). I was told to wait, but be ready to move, so went and got 'Res' from his kennel. As I walked to the kennel, I thought it was odd that they wanted me at the Mill because if a big OP was underway they usually tasked the AES team from Girdwood. I hadn't been back in the room long when the phone rang again. I was surprised to hear a dog handler I knew from 8 Brigade on the other end; 8 Brigade worked in the Londonderry area. 'Hello Harry; what's happened at North Howard Street Mill?' he asked. 'No idea at the moment mate; something has happened because we've been put on standby to go there. Why?' 'Haven't you heard?' he responded; 'Geordie and Swifty have been in an incident. Geordie's dead and Swifty is seriously injured!' I couldn't believe it and told him so. 'Seriously, mate!' he replied and I quickly hurried him off the phone and rang the duty room at Palace. It was engaged.

I sat in the room hoping this wasn't true but knowing deep down it was. The call I had just received was really all the evidence I needed. I just sat and waited, occasionally trying to reach Palace but the phone was always engaged. Eventually the phone rang – it was late, maybe eleven at night – and it was the 2 I/C. He was very calm in his voice and asked me to come in and see him. 'No need to bring the dog,' he said. I wandered over, walking down the steps by the cookhouse; as usual there were the umpteen rats that hung about by the bins. One ran past me and I swung my foot and caught it square in the body. 'Twat,' I murmured and went to the OPs room. I went to the 2 I/C's office and went in. He smiled at me and told me to sit down. He then explained that my mate Geordie had died in an explosion at North Howard Street Mill and Swifty had been seriously injured. I felt numb. I already knew but the confirmation was hard to take in. He then picked up the phone and rang Palace. I was passed the phone and at the end of the conversation, I knew the tragic news was true; it wasn't some sick joke. The 2 I/C asked if I was OK. I said yes although I felt sick inside. He said: 'Good man; if you need to talk to anyone tonight I'm on duty till the morning; don't hesitate to come and see me!' He shook my shoulder and I nodded and walked off.

I got back to the room and thought: 'You bastards; you fucking bastards; this fucking country isn't worth the life of another squaddie.' I was filled with rage; these were the first two people I had ever known that had died; these were the guys who I shared my daily life with; ate breakfast with; ogled women with; drank beer with and now some piece of scum had killed them. I sat in the dark all night and just thought. Thought how Geordie had only six months left in the Army after serving almost 22 years. I worried about the extent of Swifty's injuries and a rage engulfed me.

The next morning I was tasked to NHSM. I arrived in the Rover park and was met by Pete, a fellow handler from Palace. I now knew that Geordie had been killed and Swifty injured

Front view of North Howard Street Mill, mid-1995. Home to many a squaddie and location of the death of Corporal Terence O'Neil, 39 Brigade Specialist Dog Section. *(Dave Harding)*

when they were feeding their dogs. I nodded and we wandered off. As I turned the corner the scene took my breath away. The kennels were completely destroyed. I was shocked, because in my naivety I had expected them to be still intact. The ground around them was burnt. We walked away, not speaking; we didn't need to, we both knew what each other was thinking. I was quickly tasked and spent the day doing searches around the outside perimeter of NHSM and around Conway Street Mill which was next door. We found nothing and it hurt; it hurt like hell. We were all desperate to find something that day. Anything; anything at all that would help find the filth that had done this to our mates. I was taken back to the Mill and met Mark, a tracker handler. He told me he was taken to the Mill late last night and had to identify Geordie's body. We sat in silence, each deep in our own thoughts.

I asked him if he knew what had happened. He reckoned a 'Mark 15' coffee jar bomb had been dropped from a balcony on Conway Mill. The two guys were sorting their dogs out and had been chatting in the yard and a terrorist had dropped the device into the yard near them. We looked at each other because, only a couple of weeks ago we had both been in the Mill and had spent a few hours cleaning the kennels and painting them. We both talked of the guilt we felt; had we been watched doing this and had a terrorist worked out a pattern of intelligence on our actions? I silently prayed that my innocent actions weren't somehow responsible for the tragic events of the previous evening.

Geordie was buried back home and we all attended his funeral. A week or so after the incident a few of us visited Swifty in Musgrave Park Hospital; he was waiting to be flown home to continue his treatment. We all nervously walked into his side room, not sure what to expect.

Murals at Fort Whiterock. *(Craig Laidler)*

We were greeted by a smiling Swifty, sitting up in bed. We all laughed and chatted and Swifty offered at one point to give someone his socks; I asked if I could have his boots. Someone commented that it was a shame he never had his nose blown off; Swifty wasn't blessed with a rose bud nose. We weren't being callous; we were coping the best way we could; if we hadn't made crass jokes we would have cried. We eventually left and went back to Palace.

A few weeks later we held a memorial service for Geordie in the Church at Palace. Swifty attended; this incredible man flew from England by himself and walked tall as he entered the church on his brand new artificial legs. He personified courage, sprit and determination. He was and remains to this day my hero. He laughed and he joked and he even climbed a flight of stairs refusing many offers of help. What a guy.

A week or so after the incident at NHSM I was on a search in the Ardoyne. I was knelt down by 'Res' and an elderly couple walked towards me and quietly said: 'We're sorry about your friends.' I nodded and said: 'Thank you!'

I'm glad Northern Ireland is now at peace; people like that elderly couple deserve it!

Corporal Terence O'Neil (44) of the Royal Regiment of Fusiliers was killed on 25 May 1991 when a member of the IRA threw a bomb into the yard at North Howard Street Mill. He was killed almost instantly, but another soldier – 'Swifty' – was dreadfully injured and, heartbreakingly, when he saw the extent of his injuries begged his comrades to shoot him. It was thought that this was the terrorists' first use of the coffee jar bomb, a small device but packed with a deadly amount of the Czech explosive Semtex. O'Neil, originally from Northumberland, is buried in Alnwick in his native north-east.

OVER IN WEEKS: BACK TO BELFAST

Colin 'Jim' Bowie, Royal Artillery

Back in Belfast, but this time we covered the city centre, manning the segment gates and bus gates. The city centre was a complete secure area. And we would spend hours just searching people and bags when they entered the city centre and you ended up with filthy hands from the coats. One of the gates was at the end of an alley at Castle Street, just down from Divis Flats.

We had WRAC searchers for the women, and one was bitten by a rat carried by one of our 'friends' from the markets; nice people. I was on patrol around the city centre one day and watched a lad from one of the other batteries try the door handle of a parked car. I was soon down behind a wall; bloody idiot. I think he got the message that I would shoot him if he tried it again. Several cars were blown up for being unattended in the area.

It was strange, standing on the bus gate outside of Etams, which was a Catholic shop and staff. One girl asked if we would like a cup of tea, but we refused; afterwards, she was told off by her workmates. We had to go onto the buses and check for suspicious packages. I got to know one of the employees for BA, and he was also in the UDR. I was searching him one morning, at a gate and I knocked his .45 personal weapon onto the ground; very embarrassing. Some time later his office was robbed, but he couldn't do a thing.

We were on Segment duty when the Bull Ring in Brum was hit. We all decided NOT to go out, the gates could stay shut. Unfortunately, we were ordered out by those on high, protest over but noted. A very bad day for searching bags etc. Later on returning from a mobile patrol from Hollywood there was an explosion; on reaching the site there was a Ford Escort which had been blown up. Story goes, an officer from Brigade HQ came into the city on a shopping trip and parked his car in the Control Zone. He got back just in time to see Felix do his job.

One of our tasks was to escort the Post Office money transfer around the P.O.s, and we arrived at one twenty minutes after it had been robbed. I tried to remain as diffident as possible during the tours, but alert to do the job, as I didn't believe that we should have been there. We were scapegoats for the politicians. If we had been left to do the job, it would have been over in weeks.

A GUARDIAN ANGEL ON THE 'LONG STREETS'

Mick Pickford, Royal Artillery

New Lodge was nicknamed 'the Long Streets,' because basically that's what they were. Four long, narrow streets, all with terraced housing along both sides. They were separated by Lepper Street which cut all four streets in half; it was also known as part of the 'Killing Triangle'.

As we had to memorise the layout of the New Lodge, we developed the mnemonic 'HUSS'. Hillman, Upper Meadow, Spamount and Stratheden. It worked out that most contacts in the Lodge were on Spamount Street. As this street was in the middle of the Lodge it presented the shooter with the most varied chance of a getaway. At the rear of all the streets were small, long, thin alleyways. These alleys were always knee- to chest-high in shit and rubbish etc. We were very careful of these alleyways for so many reasons.

At the top of the Lodge was a street called Halliday's Road, and before the Troubles began, you could actually walk through to Duncairn Gardens (Protestant) but this had been blocked up a long time ago. What we would do is enter the Lodge from Antrim Road, Halliday's Road, then maybe, depending on order, drop onto one of the 'Long Streets'. The other teams would be using other entry points, such as New Lodge Road and Sheridan Street/Hartwell Place. They wouldn't, however, be too far apart to be exposed, and not too close to bunch up. Therefore, along with RUC and other 'agencies' we had 20–25 men on the ground.

I remember one summer evening, my team and I entered the Lodge to the north of Spamount Street, via Halliday's Road. We moved into the top of Spamount Street and observed children playing out in the warm evening, balls being kicked up the wall, girls hopscotching, and generally having a good time. As the team wheeled into the street, all activity stopped; Mothers were hurrying their children into the houses. In fact, within seconds, the street was empty; even footballs were still bouncing. It reminded me at the time of a spaghetti western, and any minute now someone is going to say, 'You ain't from round here; are ya stranger?' But that thought quickly left me and it was eyes and ears open. My heart was really pumping; I could feel it in my head like a steam train when it pulls away. The hair on the back of my neck was standing up, and my adrenalin was kicking in. I thought: 'This is it; if it happens, it will happen tonight.' We looked at each other, and I swear to this day, we all were thinking exactly the same; you could see it, and you could feel it. Funny thing though, I didn't feel scared; I think I had long since lost that emotion after being there a while.

This was a classic 'combat indicator.' You see 'combat indicators' in films, when, for example, the birds will suddenly all fly from the trees, or from long grass. Sadly, Northern Ireland didn't have dramatic music playing in your ears like Hollywood films do, so we had a disadvantage from the off. Well, this time, it was the kids getting pulled in by their mothers.

The IRA's dickers would have recce'd the area and sent word that soldiers were on the streets and warnings would be sent to their 'community' ordering them from the streets so as to minimise casualties amongst their supporters.

We checked ourselves and moved off; I was the third man in the team, so had to cover the 'tail end Charlie' (Mac); we moved like it was the first day; every movement was done, and done quick; when we'd go firm, we were only there long enough for the 5-metre check. The scope (on our SA80s) was out; we'd check firing points, then hard target [Make yourself a difficult target to hit] to the next point. We then reached Lepper Street, half way down; we were exposed. At Lepper Street, there was a clear shot on, and we were facing either a shot from the northern end of Spamount Street, or from one of the high rise shitholes on the Carlisle Estate; I think it may be Alamein House. Or from where the south end of Stratheden meets Lepper Street.

We had to move, so two of the team hard targeted across Lepper Street, into the alleyway, behind the houses on the south side of Spamount. They did their 'five and twenties' [checks] and then covered our route over. Something was not right, all the alley ways had been cleaned out, and you could actually see the floor. We proceeded on with the patrol. We took our time moving down, around the dog leg, as we had been briefed. PIRA used the alleys for cowboy shoots, and when you were in these alleys, it was not uncommon for someone to pop up at the far end and take a few shots at you then piss off. They also used these alleys for target practice, away from the prying eyes of our OP at Templar House. We could actually see the bullet holes in the wall as we passed the dog leg; shit grouping I may add. But head height nonetheless.

Just then, the two other teams, from Stratheden and Upper Meadow Street reported over the net that their patrol had not seemed any different to any other patrol that we did in the

Thinking of home, Belfast 1986. *(Paul Crispin)*

Lodge. Our Brick commander told them what we had endured at the top and one of the teams reported back that he could observe children playing again. After that, we carried on to North Queen Street RUC station, still wired with adrenalin. When we eventually got back to Girdwood, it was straight into the de-briefing with the Battery Int Officer, Pete Scott. The debrief went as normal; observations, faces, etc. We told Pete about what we had been through, he said that he would get back to me in five minutes; end debrief. Pete did come back to me, and the team, and said that, as far as Intelligence was concerned, a hit was on, and we were the intended; however, the gun had jammed.

Lucky or what? Or did I have an angel on our side; course not, the fucking gun jammed, simple as that!

Spamount Street, where the author parked briefly on a trip to Belfast in November 2008, was the scene of the killing of a member of Mick Pickford's Regiment in 1974. On 22 June of that year, whilst patrolling the 'Long' streets, Gunner Kim Maccunn (18) from the Roundhay area of Leeds, was shot by an IRA sniper and died very quickly from his wounds. With a tragic irony, his parents back in England received a cheerful letter from him on the very day an IRA bullet ended his young life. The author's late father, Mark Wharton who died in 2009, lived in the same area as Kim Maccunn's family. It was always difficult to pass through the area without thinking of the young Gunner or indeed of all the Leeds lads who never returned from across the water.

Spamount Street was the scene of another shooting and mass slaughter was only avoided as the gossamer thread of fate decided to intervene. On 12 January 1974, the IRA shot down an unarmed WRMP, leaving her badly wounded in the face and body; happily, she survived her injuries. A routine foot patrol, consisting of both soldiers and RUC had been patrolling down Spamount at around 15:00 hours. Suddenly, a hail of bullets came out of a window to their left, hitting and seriously wounding the female soldier. The soldiers immediately returned fire and one of them, attached from 2 Para literally went through the window, landed on a settee and 'bounced' after the gunmen. Two were arrested at the rear of the building and an automatic rifle was recovered.

At this point, the story becomes even more interesting. The patrol threw a cordon around the building and was not inside the house when it suddenly exploded. The IRA had relied on the SF staying in or around the house, but for some reason, the drill had changed. Ulster TV's cameras were actually in the street, filming in the aftermath of the shooting of the WRMP, when the booby trap went off, filling the air with dense smoke and the screams of the residents of Spamount Street. The cameras captured clearly shocked children running to their distraught mothers as the IRA again demonstrated their single minded callousness even when it came to killing and maiming their own supporters.

MAZE DRUNK, 1987

Tom Neary, Royal Artillery

On arrival at RAF Aldergrove in 1987, I was immediately struck by the atmosphere in and around the airbase. We were sent to a dark arrivals lounge to wait for our kit to be offloaded from the plane. Whilst there we were greeted by an old lady named Mrs Blackburn, frail and in her 70s I would think. She handed out bits of paper which welcomed us to the Province, along with cards thanking us for our service to Britain. I was only 22 and didn't take too much notice at the time, and it was only later that I realised how brave and generous she had been. She was putting her life on the line just to say thank you to us, and had done so from the beginning of the conflict in 1969. This little kindness is something that has stayed with me ever since!

We were located at the Maze to provide security to the prison, which housed most of the terrorists from both religious persuasions. Strangely our role was not to prevent escape, but to prevent incursions into the prison by outsiders! How mental would you have to be to try and break into a prison? All pretty standard stuff and very boring. However, we were also tasked with carrying out patrols in the surrounding areas and nearby towns. These involved supporting the RUC at Lurgan, Lisburn, Newcastle and Hillsborough. It was here that I first came into contact with the sectarianism that was rife. You didn't really need a map; the streets told you everything you needed to know. The kerbstones painted in their Unionist or Republican colours; the flags wafting everywhere. Most prominent of all, were the murals depicting their heroes or political agendas; and their anti-Army propaganda in the Green areas.

For some reason it always seemed to be raining, even when it was sunny, and the people were always distant. They seemed desperate for a solution but were too afraid to do anything about it. Being semi rural I think they felt that they were more acutely under the scrutiny of the terrorists. There were very few children playing on the estates and generally people didn't seem to leave their homes after dark. I was never happy with that situation when patrolling. At the time coal fires were still very much in use and the smell of burning coal sticks in my mind, especially when it was damp. The clouds of smoke billowing from the stacks were a reminder of normality. There seemed to be something comforting about this for me, because I remember my grandparents had a coal fire and I used to love visits to them as a kid. At the same time, it also brought home to me that I was miles away from my family, in a place which resembled my own hometown of Manchester, but might as well have been on the moon; quite a lonely feeling really!

Whilst we were there, one serious incident stands out in my mind; it involved a prison officer at the Maze PO's club. We were 'stagging' on at the gate and I was manning the barrier when a Ford Cortina came up from the prison, weaving all over the place. I halted the vehicle and was nearly crushed by it, and it only just stopped in time. The driver was obviously bladdered and was gobbing off nonsense and abusing myself and Jonah, the other lad on the gate. We told him to get out of the car as he was liable to kill someone in this drunken state. Taff was on guard commander and rang down to the prison to tell them of this bod's state. In the meantime, this loon gets his 9mm pistol out and starts waving it about. I lost my temper at this point and threatened to shoot him if he didn't put it away. This wasn't working so I cocked my SLR and pointed it at him, and his arse nearly dropped out of his pants.

It annoyed me that we were potentially targets for the IRA/INLA, and there's some fool we were supporting, waving a gun in our faces.

THE DEATH OF BOB BANKIER

Lance Corporal, 23854723, Robert Bankier (25), a married father of two young children was shot and killed in the very early hours of Saturday, 22 May 1971. Bankier, a Corporal in the Royal Green Jackets, came from the Ipswich area, although he was born in Birmingham. He had left his young wife and children in Celle, West Germany and had been in Belfast for less than three weeks. 1RGJ were based in the Markets Area, very close to Belfast city centre and Bankier had led a patrol into the Cromac Street area, shortly after midnight.

Reports had been received that RMP soldiers had been attacked by children and local youths who were blocking the streets and the Jackets were sent in to sort out the problem late on the Friday night. In Cromac Square, their vehicle came under brick attack and the culprits were chased by the patrol into Lagan Street. As Bankier's Land Rover stopped, the crowds of children in the street suddenly parted. Immediately, at least three gunmen opened fire with both single shot and automatic gunfire from the direction of Verner Street, a nineteenth-century row of terraced housing that dominated the area. Corporal Bankier who was operating the RT was hit and fell to the ground, tearing out the radio wires and making it difficult for his comrades to call for assistance. More shots came in from Market Street and then there was the sound of an explosive device being detonated. He had been hit by a single 9mm round – other reports state .45 – and this went clear through both thighs high up, tearing away the femoral artery. Despite the rest of the patrol jumping on him to stop the flow of blood, he died. Several Riflemen had tried to staunch the wounds and save him.

It was quite some time before help finally arrived and he was already too far gone to be revived, dying within minutes, after what was clearly a well prepared ambush. Later on, the Official IRA claimed responsibility for the attack. Speculation at the time was that the Officials were trying to match their murderous rivals in the Provisionals and had set up the attack after having used local youths to lure the Green Jackets into the area. By this stage of the conflict, PIRA had already several British Army 'scalps' under their belts and the officials – known as 'Stickies' – felt that by contributing to the blood-letting, they could be seen as matching, or even surpassing their rivals and seen to be 'defending' the nationalist community. Tragically, Robert Bankier was to be sacrificed in order to aid the Official's internecine struggle with the militant upstarts in the Provisionals.

At the inquest into Robert Bankier's death, the Belfast Coroner stated: 'These gangsters were prepared to use children to lure soldiers into their destruction at Cromac Square. It was a mercy that the whole patrol was not massacred.'

Colour Sergeant Ken Ambrose, Royal Green Jackets

> I can only add that Bob was extremely unlucky because the bullet that killed him – fired from an M1 Carbine – hit the ground first, flattened and came up to enter his thigh and partly severed his femoral artery. The blood loss was enormous and the result was unconsciousness within a minute and death within three minutes. Even if the MO had been standing beside Bob when he was hit, with all his transfusion equipment laid out he would have been hard pushed to save him. As a result of the shooting the whole of the Markets area was searched with all of 'B' Company searching and an additional Company providing the cordon. The whole operation lasted well into the next day and several finds were made as a result.
>
> A little more background; Bob had previously been a dog handler and a bugler and at the time of his death was a full corporal section commander. His wife and small son were both back in Celle when he was killed. In his memory, the Bankier Cane trophy was created, which was given to the top student on battalion NCO Cadres for many years after his death, in fact until the RGJ folded in 2007. His son subsequently joined the regiment and served for a few years.

It was felt, at the time in Intelligence circles that the man who ordered and executed the attack and in all probability fired the fatal shot was IRA leader Joe McCann. Eleven months after the murder of Corporal Bankier, the IRA leader was shot and killed by soldiers from the Parachute

Regiment in Joy Street, Markets area. Shortly after the shooting of Corporal Bankier, he had been briefly in the custody of the Jackets. The 25-year-old IRA gunman was killed on 15 April 1972 just a few streets away from where Bankier had been hit. McCann was a former British paratrooper.

John Wood, Royal Military Police on McCann

He was being followed by a pair of RUC SB and they identified him to a Parachute Regiment patrol as being worth a tug in the event he was armed. He was with his girlfriend and unarmed but took off when challenged. His previous MO had been to get troops to chase him and then have an explosive charge fired as they came after him. Because of this, the patrol did not chase him but shot him. I wrote up that as far as they were concerned, his running was an ongoing part of an attack and this explained the problem of their bending the Yellow Card and shooting someone as he ran away.

Ken Ambrose

In regard to Joe McCann, the man who was reputed to have done the shooting. That fact did not become known until some time later and, during a Markets patrol several weeks after the shooting, my platoon was attacked with a nail bomb. We did a hot pursuit on the perp straight into the local Republican Club and ended up taking the seventeen occupants of the club to Castlereagh police headquarters where they were interrogated at length about the nail bomb incident. No joy there!

Joe McCann was among those lifted and was thoroughly 'beasted' by the RMP who attached themselves to us. Of course we knew who he was in relation to his position within the Official IRA but we did not know at the time that McCann was responsible for Bob's death. The whole lot from the Republican Club was charged with assaulting the SF and were subsequently fined in court the next day. McCann was also released.

BELFAST FROM ABOVE

Lance Corporal 'C', Army Air Corps

I had last seen Belfast in March of 1981 from the back of a Bedford after completing a second tour of South Armagh. After the final handover, 1 Queens Lancashire Regiment had been helicoptered out of Bessbrook to the Maze prison for the road journey to Belfast Docks. I thought the danger was over as the Regiment had once again got away with no deaths in South Armagh. As we got out of the Wessex and Puma helicopters at the Maze, I became bemused by the panic of the other lads as they almost fought and scrambled to be first to get into the backs of the Bedfords for the journey to the LSL [Landing Ships Logistic] moored in Belfast Docks for the voyage over the Irish Sea to Liverpool. Then I realised why they were so concerned to be first on the vehicle as when the tail gate was put up, the lad opposite and I looked out the back to see that we were the first QLR visible for any sniper! Not that a Bedford canopy gave any more protection than the combat jacket I was wearing. My flak jacket had also been handed in back at Bessbrook. I held onto my trusty SLR as a security blanket for all the good it did me to be a company trained sniper as we had no ammo! All ammo had been handed in back at Bessbrook. I felt naked after months of living with my 'gat' and bullets but for the journey though Belfast to the Docks we all had empty mags on!

Four years later I was back in Northern Ireland for my third 'emergency' tour and seeing Belfast from an altogether different view. As an Aircrew Observer in a Gazelle helicopter I had a relatively safer view of Belfast than the lads on the ground. Belfast was at my feet and using a large pair of what appeared to be WWII 'binos' I looked down from 1,000 feet doing 'top cover' for the grunts on the ground. Apparently it was rare for an attack to happen when a helicopter was above.

I had over 850 flying hours in my log book from exercises in Germany, a Med Man in BATUS Canada and had flown in some atrocious weather for a tour in the Falklands (a year after the war). With infantry tours of Northern Ireland behind me I was one of the few members of the Squadron to have urban patrolling experience. I felt as if I was a flying guardian angel to the lads on the ground.

Sadly on 27 March 1985, the day before my first duty over Belfast, a soldier was killed in Divis Flats by a bomb. I can't remember now if there had been a Gazelle in the air on that occasion but one had been in the air above a bombing of a patrol in Divis during that 1985 tour and I have always felt as if the Squadron had let my comrades on the ground down. I repeatedly quizzed the Aircrew man on that occasion to find out what had gone wrong and how I could avoid repeating any mistakes. I was determined to do my best to ensure the safety of the lads I was working for as I knew how difficult urban patrolling could be, having done a bit in Newry and the villages of South Armagh on my previous tours.

The soldier killed was Lance Corporal Anthony Dacre (25) of the Kings Own Border Regiment. A device planted by the IRA in a shed near the Divis Flats was detonated by remote control just as Lance Corporal Dacre was passing by. By some miracle, a small boy who was passing at the time escaped totally unscathed. Dublin newspapers quoted the Irish Foreign Minister Peter Barry: 'In the name of the Irish Government, I want to reaffirm that the IRA have no right whatsoever to bear arms or to take life in the name of Irish unity or in the name of the Irish people.' At the time of day that the murder was committed, children from the nearby St Comgall's school would have been playing outside within the area of the blast. On this day, although the Headmaster claimed that the children were kept inside because of the freezing conditions, it is widely believed that the IRA had pre-warned the school. Even an organisation as cynical as the IRA drew the line at alienating mass sections of the Catholic community by killing scores of schoolchildren.

On a 24-hour duty, the Gazelle would take off from Palace Barracks for sorties lasting from 15 minutes to an hour, flying or hovering over the more dangerous estates. If you did a good job the pilot let you fly it back to Palace. Later in the tour I was doing as much flying as the pilots and got quite good at hovering, even down wind. From Twinbrook in the south, Ballymurphy in the middle and Divis in the north the pilot would come to a hover or slowly circle around the patrol while I used the 'binos' to scan the area around them. The 'binos' had a bolted on gyroscope for stabilisation powered from a socket in the roof. This dampened out the aircraft vibrations but could also make some people violently sick. Later we were issued the Steady Scope, a self contained unit powered by torch batteries. I rarely watched the patrols directly as I knew they would be covering their own arcs. I would scan very closely the area around them watching for signs of trouble or if things did not look right. I would look for firing positions with good lines of sight where an M60 or RPG-7 could get a good field of fire and escape routes. Any quiet areas where I would expect to see kids playing would also get particular attention. In those days sometimes we would fly lower if something caught my eye but not too close as we did not want to be shot out of the sky.

I would report any observations to the ground commanders. For defence, the pilot carried a holstered 9mm with ten rounds, and I had an SLR and a magazine of twenty rounds. Some observers put their SLR in the Gazelle boot behind the rear seat; I stuffed mine along the back of the rear seat. You could still get passengers in the back with it there, but in the event of a crash my theory was I could get to it quicker.

Over Twinbrook one day we heard the dreaded 'Contact; bomb city centre; wait out.' The pilot immediately pulled maximum power and we headed for the centre. We arrived just in time to catch the debris coming up from the explosion on the ground. Not a pleasant experience flying through the after effects of a car bomb in a single-engine helicopter! Nothing major was sucked into the engine and we remained airborne surrounded by loads of flying paper at about 1,000 feet. As the dust settled I was aghast to look down and see a complete block of a street with all the windows smashed. Thinking that was where the bomb had been I told the pilot what I could see. As more of the dust and debris settled I then realised I was looking at the wrong target. Where the van bomb had actually gone off, opposite the one with all the smashed windows, was just not there anymore! No one was killed in that bomb blast; in fact it was a controlled explosion which had been notified on the Battalion net by FELIX.

On the afternoon of 29 June 1985, the City Flight Gazelle was tasked to cover a Green Howard's vehicle and foot patrol close to the Ballymurphy Estate. As usual I was scanning round them, when I noticed a green Ford Cortina drive onto the pavement some streets away from the multiple that I was covering. As the four lads got out and walked north, I noticed the driver didn't look like he had locked the car so I became suspicious. If he had just parked up in the street I would probably have ignored them but I flicked channels and talked another patrol on to the four youths. The Green Howard's Ops Officer sent that day's NIREP to the aircrew City flight with a memo thanking us for catching some car thieves.

My log book records that I passed the thousand hours flying mark, including 200 over the city. Between 3 June 1985 and arriving back in Hildesheim on 13 August 1985, I logged up a total of 1134.7 flying hours. My proudest recollection of that time is in knowing that no one got killed or injured on my watch. Did we deter any attacks? I'll never know.

AN IRA 'COME ON'

Mick Pickford, Royal Artillery

One summer morning we were called out as a back up to one of the other troops that had patrolled down Stratheden Street in the New Lodge nationalist area of Belfast. We were based in the Girdwood Park Barracks which was more or less at the top of New Lodge Road, give or take two streets.

As a suspect Mk15 had been left outside a House on Stratheden Street we were ordered to provide cover and mutual support for the call sign's already on the ground and for ATO [Ammunition Technical Officer – bomb disposal]. ATO was known as the 'NATO Potato', because of the size of the padding the guy wore.

We were soon bomb-busting out of the rear gate toward Antrim Road, then crossing over into the Lodge. I cannot remember what route we took down to the incident area; maybe it

Mick Pickford (right) and Mark Scorer at Girdwood Barracks. *(Via Mick Pickford)*

> was Hillman Street. We dominated the ground and it was soon, in my opinion becoming quite clear this was a come on. The device was very cleverly placed, in a way that would expose each team to certain time in open ground. It would have been better if the two houses on the waste ground opposite had not been blown up some years before. Now, the boss, Mr Brooks, was a great guy; he sees all this going on, so it then turned into a revolving cordon, with us holding teams in reserve down the very narrow alley ways until space could be made. The 'alley way team' could actually keep watch down these points for shoots. The whole experience lasted two hours, in which we had been bricked, spat at, kicked in the shins by the 'scrote to be' and, by the end of it, ATO just picked up the suspect jar, and tossed it into his wagon.
>
> We did encounter quite a few players that day; they moved in between the teams or just made a nuisance of themselves. As the cordon went on longer and longer, we P-checked them more and more and it was getting on their nerves more than it did ours; eventually, they got fed up and pissed off.

A 'come on' could serve two main purposes; it might have been to bring soldiers into the open and expose them to snipers or it might have been to observe response times, deployment and tactics. At Narrow Water, Warrenpoint, on 28 August 1979, the IRA showed that they had learned a valuable and – for the Parachute Regiment – tragic lesson. They had observed that, following an explosion, back up teams would find the nearest cover and observe for secondary devices. On this day, in picturesque Co Down, a three-vehicle Army convoy was en route for Newry and had just reached Narrow Water. An 800lb device had been hidden amongst bales of straw on a trailer at the roadside. It detonated and killed at least six members of the Parachute Regiment troops in one of the vehicles.

Within 30 minutes, several Army back up and rescue vehicles arrived and, true to normal tactics, took up a position behind a wall opposite the initial carnage. The IRA, having painstakingly done their homework, had anticipated this and had planted a further huge device there. It detonated and killed a further ten Paratroopers and two soldiers from the Queen's Own Highlanders, including their CO, who, quite literally, vapourised. It was the worst single disaster for the Army during the entire course of the troubles. Worryingly, it also demonstrated the IRA's transformation into a highly professional and organised killing machine.

'THERE'S A BOMB DOWN THERE MISTER'

Mick Pickford

I remember the metal hooks that were mounted on a length of metal of the snatch Rovers; this was to break any fishing/chicken wire that had been tied between lampposts. Without this, some of us would have been headless by now!

During my time patrolling, I felt sometimes that a few people did not want all the violence; they just wanted to live a normal life. For instance, we had gone firm at the southern end of the 'Long Streets', and there were the usual few people hanging around and I noticed this one boy wander up from nowhere and stand around six or seven feet away from me. He took out a tennis ball and started to kick it, then, he hoofed the ball right at me. So, I took no notice as the first one always came free, and the boy comes over to me; I'm thinking, he wants the ball back, so I leave it near me. As he got closer and closer, he said: 'There's a bomb down there, Mister!' so I played it cool, and said: 'Right; thanks for that,' under my breath. Then as quick as a flash, he was gone. I gave it a few seconds because if it was if true, I didn't want to land this boy in trouble.

I spoke to Jon and then he got on the net, and we were told to about turn and get back up to New Lodge Road via Lepper Street, and back to Girdwood. I still, to this day, wonder if that boy was right; was he having a laugh with his mates, or just generally helping us? Sometimes the best thing to do was just listen, but knowing what and who to listen to was the trickiest part. Sometimes you would enter the Unity flats, where no-one would even talk to you at all; I think that place was stuck so far in the past that even if someone so much as breathed in your direction, they would be kneecapped that night. We saw a well known player come through us whilst we were in the Unity Flats, and we grabbed him and kept him there. It was the only time that we saw this guy and I got the feeling that he disliked being recognised. I knew him, and told him some facts about himself. I generally got the impression that he usually got away with it, and he thought we may have been too intimidated to stop him.

I must admit, the Unity flats were an intimidating place; it was the only place in Belfast that I saw a mural dedicated to the Gibraltar Stiffs. I'm glad that it's no longer there; the people are though.

CORPORAL TURNER'S DEATH

Simon Bromige, 1 Queen's Regiment

Never knew or really wished to have known his name; it was only when I read the author's first book *A Long, Long War* that I recalled the name and events of that day. It was during my third and last tour, and this time I was in West Belfast. I was a platoon sergeant in a rifle company serving in the 1st Battalion the Queens Regiment based at Fort Whiterock strategically positioned between the Turf Lodge and New Barnsley. Our T.A.O.R. (Tactical Area of Responsibility) included the Turf, Andytown, Coolnasillas and the Rossnareens and part of the Falls Road and the AndyTown road.

As our tour was coming to the end and we were having thoughts of home, the Queen's Own Highlanders (QHLDRS) arrived to relieve us; they were last in the Province in the very early 80s and a good bunch of guys they were too. There was always a period of handover between units; the incoming unit would always put their commanders on the ground prior to the main body arriving so that, at least, there was a level of local knowledge regarding the area and local known players. The outgoing units would then send some of their bods back to the UK.

One of the problems we had over this handover was how to conceal the accents (gone were the days of wearing identifiable berets; everyone wore battle bowlers) [Kevlar helmets]. We tried all sorts; one day the Scots lads would speak to the locals and on the radio next day back to Cockneyese/sarf England; in the end every team and patrol did their own thing. To me subterfuge was a good thing but let's get to the basics; know your area, know your enemy and know their tactics.

We took the Scots out on foot and in vehicles introduced them to the esteemed members of the IRA, their acquaintances and mistresses (particularly handy that one, if the wife was within earshot). We did the best for them, and gave as much information and exposure as we could. The last couple of days were a mixture of patrols and QRFs [quick reaction force]. On Tuesday 27 February, I was QRF commander (call sign RED1) and we had two Scots lads attached to us for the day. We did the normal admin runs to MPH (Musgrave Park Hospital) and mobile patrols to support the foot patrols.

Halfway through, the Scots lads changed over so they could spread the exposure of patrolling across the board. We did not have any further imminent patrols so, along with my counterpart from the QHLDRS, I went to the Ops room where we parked our bums in some rather comfy chairs and awaited any further tasking. It was then that a large explosion was heard, and I remember getting under the nearest table (SOP for mortar attacks) watching Capt I. W. 'Blackadder', as he was known because he was a spitting image of Rowan Atkinson. That's where the likeness ended; he was one of the most professional guys I ever served with, a top bloke. He shouted into the radio: 'Hello, O; this is Mike 40; Contact. Wait. Out.' As he did so, the phone rang and he picked it up.

It was bizarre; the conversation went along the lines of 'Really; in the accommodation?' and 'Ok, will send somebody up.' He put the phone down and said to me 'Bromide, apparently someone has shot themselves in the block; have a look will you?' It was then that we found that the noise was, in fact, the blasting of nearby quarries; everybody including myself picked ourselves up muttering about boxing, rugby etc as we sheepishly brushed and smoothed ourselves down. I went out to check on this shooting, envisaging that one of the lads had fucked about with a 9mm pistol and shot themselves through the foot or something similar. As my Scottish counterpart and I started to walk up the accommodation blocks through the maze of blast walls, we came across P.R., a Lance Jack from 9 Platoon running hell for leather towards us. He shouted at me: 'Fucking hell, Brom, he's going to die.' Those words have stayed with me all this time; I started to run to the accommodation block. I kept thinking to myself: please, not one of mine; not one of mine.

I remember getting to the entrance of the accommodation and seeing B.J. the medical sergeant entering at a rapid pace and 9 Platoon's sergeant saying: 'He's in a bad way' I'm now thinking: 'Fuck fuck' and I entered the room. I saw one of the Scots lads we had had with us on patrol earlier lying on the floor; there was a lot of blood under him. I heard B.J. shouting at him to talk to him; to the right was a bed and there was blood on the bed and blood spatters on the wall behind the bed, I could see that he had sustained an injury to the corner of his eye; this was bleeding quite heavily.

Sitting in the opposite corner of the room on a bed was another Scots lad; across his lap sat an SA80 rifle and he was in a complete state of shock, eyes wide, jaw open, totally out of it. I took the weapon from him and made it safe and laid it on the bed, and then took him to an adjoining room. I sat him on a bed and asked him what had happened. He looked up at me, completely vacant, and said 'It was an ND, Sarge; I did it.'

Normally negligent discharges (NDs) are dealt with by a lot of screaming, shouting and occasionally violence culminating in the offender being charged. I felt no anger; there was no point. This poor bastard was in a world of personal turmoil. He'd just accidentally shot his mate. I said to him: 'Do you smoke, mate?' He replied: 'No', but I gave him a couple of fags and a light; 'Well today you do' I replied. I had been joined by one of the lads so I left him to look after the guy, and went back into the room to assist with the casualty.

B.J. was working on the lad like there was no tomorrow, and he had been joined by others, who were stacking up field dressings on his chest and I was treating the wound to his head. We were all beginning to get covered in the blood from this lad, and it was then that I realised that he had been shot in the chest. I later found out that the round had initially hit him by the eye cavity and exited from the chin and re-entered the chest where it hit virtually every major organ.

I heard someone say, repeatedly: 'He's not going to make it.' I looked up and saw it was the MO, and I'm sure that I heard either B.J. or someone else tell him to get the fuck out of the room. The casualty was at this stage semi conscious and kept looking at me, and I was saying things such as 'Stay with me mate; keep looking at me.' I felt totally useless as I was still trying to stem the bleeding from the wound to the head. When we had managed to stem the bleeding, we loaded him on to stretcher and manoeuvred him out of the room around the blast walls and into a medical PIG.

Thus began the move to the Royal Victoria Hospital or RVH as it was known. We headed down the Monagh bypass and came to a roundabout where we were going to go left down the Glen Road onto the Falls Road and in to the RVH. As we came onto the roundabout there was a car being driven in the most obstructive way possible; basically to try to hold us up. We had two APVs (Armoured patrol vehicles and a medical PIG) and the RCT driver did a magnificent piece of driving to get around this clown. Without taking my eyes from the road, I told him that the next twat that tried that, he must ram them off the road.

I could only think of the desperate battle to save that young lad's life as we sped our way along the Falls Road. I recall a crash crew being on standby for us as we arrived and they took him into a side room in the A&E department and started to work on him. We just stood there feeling absolutely helpless as the young man's life left him. We all had blood on our hands and clothing, we all felt totally gutted. The medical staff said we had done a good job but when that

Snap VCP on Monagh bypass. *(Craig Laidler)*

round hit him he was going to die, and nothing could change that. I went outside, sparked up a fag and was joined by the rest of the boys and all the vehicles. The people of Belfast mingled around and I was waiting for someone to make a comment; the mood I was in, I would have filled them in.

We accompanied Corporal Turner to the morgue where the mortician took his personal belongings from him; he attempted to get his wedding ring off but couldn't. He then produced this utensil similar to a coat hanger and began to try to force it off causing damage to his finger and ring. Upon seeing this, C.B. went spare at the guy, threatening to punch him out. He quickly gave up this idea and C.B. and I managed to get the ring off. I later heard that the young lad who had the ND when told that the other had died collapsed to the ground crying; apparently they were the best of mates and one had been the other's best man.

I did three tours in my military service; they totalled some 3½ years, and in all my time in the Province I found this the saddest of all incidents that I got involved in; a total waste of two lives by an accident that should never have occurred. The QOHLDRS Platoon Sergeant said to me 'It will probably happen again.' If that had been one of my own boys I would have been devastated.

Colin Berry, Queen's Regiment

I was Duty Ops officer on that afternoon, when Corporal Warne came running into the room saying that one of the Jocks had been shot. At first I thought he was talking about one of the NCOs who'd been attached to a foot patrol, but he explained that it was in the accommodation.

I ran there, telling the CCTV operator to contact the doctor (Acting Captain Turk and Colour Sergeant Bill Jones. When I got to the room there was a huge pool of blood and the poor lad was on his back blowing bubbles of blood. My mate, Simon Bromige was about 30 seconds behind me; we both looked straight at the guy sitting on the bed opposite, still holding his still-loaded SA80. As I remember it, Brom took it off him, unloaded it and took him out of the room; it turned out he'd been his best man.

By then Bill had arrived and I had turned the wounded lad over to try and find an exit wound. It was the proverbial size of a fist and low down on his right, just under the ribs. I think we stuffed half a dozen field dressings in there and then a pillow case! Fritz Dean turned up with some of our JNCOs and a stretcher and we got him onto it; thereafter it was a bloody nightmare trying to get him round the blast walls without him falling off. He was out of it and barely hanging onto life. We got him into the medical PIG, with one of the RCT NCOs at the wheel. Bill jumped in with one of his medics and so did I, sporting nothing more than desert wellies, denims, sweat shirt and a 9mm hanging from my belt.

We just got to the gate when there was a shout from behind and we stopped; the back doors opened and 'Turk' dragged himself into the vehicle and sat near the back. As we pulled out of the gate I was doing the pulse bit while Bill and his sidekick were trying to find a vein to get a drip into. I told the doctor to get up near to us to try and stem the loss of blood or do something to help out. Anyway he just said to us not to bother as he was no doubt already dead. At that point I felt like kicking him straight out the back of the vehicle and from then on he played no further part in either assisting or talking. Bill opened his ankle with a scalpel and found the remains of a vein and in went a drip; I sort of recall spending the rest of my time holding up his leg and willing him to live.

Our progress was slow on the way to Musgrave, and there were numerous cars that deliberately got in our way, hooted their horns and cursed us as we lumbered passed. On arrival the doors flew open and we helped carry him straight into the emergency room. After that we stood back, I stood next to Bill and the driver (a big bloke) and watched as a team of doctors etc started to work on him, still lying on the blood-stained stretcher we'd bought him in on.

After five minutes and more than his share of whacks from a defibrillator, it all went very quiet. We were all praying that he would live but they pronounced him dead and walked away; the odd look at us said it all. We knew they had tried their hardest and in a way I think that's why we stayed in the room. The field dressings were all on the floor; the pillow case looking out of place and there was blood everywhere. We were just standing there in silence looking at him and then the driver started to cry. Bill had tears in his eyes and started saying he could have done more and I said we'd done all we could or words to that effect and walked over to look at him. By then he was devoid of colour and that white purplish look had set in and his face had turned to wax. The blood-red scar down one side of his young face from the 5.56mm round had stopped bleeding. On its course it had taken off his left eyebrow, sliced open his cheek and entered his body just below the collar bone; exiting as we thought through the open wound in his back.

I did not know what to say, it was over. We were alive but he was dead, the result of a tragic accident. Nonetheless, we were soldiers, brothers in arms. I saw the wedding ring on his finger, and I wondered how or who would explain what had happened. I adjusted his eyelids and at that point I leant forward and kissed his forehead; I whispered that it was from his wife. I then went outside into the late cold afternoon. He was moved still on the stretcher back into the PIG, his chapel. His C.O. arrived with his Adjutant and RSM; they talked in lowered tones to us while the C.O. climbed into the back and shut the doors. After a few minutes he came out; he had been crying, but no one was looking. He said some words of thanks to us and left.

We then took him to the morgue where I got my biggest shock; we were going to leave him with civilians. We took him in like pall bearers and they (the civilian workers) grabbed him by the shoulders and legs and semi dropped him onto a cold slab. I went mad at them shouting what the hell they thought they were doing; I told them to show some respect and worse. By then the RUC had arrived and P.C. Stevie Lyons was with them and he tried to calm things down. At that point, I noticed the 5.56mm round lying in the congealed pool of blood on the stretcher. I bent down and picked it up; it was unmarked except for a small curve to the end. I had assumed that it had exited but somehow it had stayed with him until his back was bowed as he was lifted and it had dropped out. The RUC took it as evidence and the task of removing and recording his belongings began; first his pockets, then dog tags, watch and lastly his wedding ring. I protested that it should be left on until he was back with his family but was told it was procedure. Besides, as one of them said, he did not want us Brit bastards saying they had stolen it! They then used a knitting needle shaped piece of metal and proceeded to stab away at his finger in an attempt to get it off; I think they ended up breaking something. At that point, my pistol was out of the holster and pointing at them both. Stevie jumped in and we went outside. Bill came out and I was asking why the hell we were leaving him there, but no one had the answer except I recall it was a Sunday and therefore there may have been operating hour issues. After a long five minutes we were driving back to Fort Whiterock.

We left there on the understanding that arrangements would be made. Once I'd had a shower and changed my bloodstained clothes I was back on the desk. And he was another statistic for the NIREP. After all we went through during those years, those tours, I still think now how young we were and how much responsibility we had. I do not detract from our professionalism or ability but it all sat heavily on such young shoulders.

Negligent discharges were not, nor have ever been in any army, a rare event. NDs which led to the death of another comrade were few and far between and one is reminded of Tommy Stoker and Owen Pavey. Private Tommy Stoker was shot and fatally wounded near the Flax Street Mill on 27 July 1972 by a Light Infantry comrade in an adjoining room; after a long fight for life, he died on September 19 in the RVH. Private Owen Pavey of the King's Own Border Regiment was accidentally shot by a comrade in a base at Crossmaglen on 11 March 1980. He died after an incident with a GPMG which was, like many NDs, perfectly avoidable.

Perhaps one of the most controversial incidents was the death of Staffords' soldier Sergeant Dean Oliver (30). He was killed on 9 May 1992, after having been hit seven times by a negligent burst of fourteen rounds inside a bombed-out RUC station in Fivemiletown, Co Tyrone. A soldier was later acquitted of his murder.

NEGLIGENT DISCHARGE

Pete Whittall, Staffords

I recall a near-miss incident in Fort George Army Barracks in Londonderry during our tour in 1974. A brick from 'D' Company had just come back to base after being on operations in the Shantallow area. If I recall correctly, we were in a PIG, and the command to debus and make safe weapons was given by the brick commander. Suddenly a round from an SLR went off and ricocheted around the inside of the armoured vehicle. I think one or two of our boys received shrapnel wounds but no one was badly injured or killed, thank God. I am telling you this from third-hand information as I was in Support company and one of my mates told me about it some days later when I was on a three-day rest period after patrolling the Rosemount and Creggan area.

David Mitchell, Gordon Highlanders

It was whilst I was attached to 321 EOD (Bomb Disposal) during 1972 that we were called to an incident at XMG. I was with Corporal 'Yogi' Burnett and another Jock from the Black Watch whose name, sadly, escapes me. We were listening to the RT when news of a contact came in and we could hear an IRA ambush going down and could even hear explosions over the radio. We were ordered to cock our weapons and stick one up the spout, ready for whatever faced us.

321 EOD (Bomb Disposal), Belfast, 1972. Doing a job in Belfast. *(David Mitchell)*

RUC officers guard firefighters from snipers following an IRA bomb, Northern Bank.

We arrived at the RUC station there, in the pitch black and we went inside and then immediately into a small cage to unload; to 'make safe'. As we were doing so, there was an almighty bang right besides my head and I felt the heat of the round which had been negligently discharged. We immediately dived for cover, not realising at first that it was an ND as we feared that we were under attack. Then it dawned on us that the Black Watch lad had forgotten that he had a round up the spout and had brushed the trigger and bang!

He was court martialled for the ND and received 28 days at the tough Gough Barracks where he was seen running around with full sandbags above his head, being 'beasted' by the Gordons' Provost staff. Poor sod; an ND can happen to anyone.

MURDERED BY THE MOB

On 19 May 1988, the world witnessed the horrifying abduction, beating and eventual murder of two corporals from the Royal Corps of Signals. Their murder was not only a seminal moment in the history of the Troubles but probably the most sickening footage ever shown on British television. The two men were abducted outside Milltown Cemetery, savagely beaten, then shot and their bodies dumped at Penny Lane in the Turf Lodge area. (See page 249.)

The two men were Corporal Derek Wood (24) who had been in the country for some time and Corporal David Howes (23) who had only been in the Province for a week; both men belonged to the Royal Corps of Signals. Why or how they stumbled onto an IRA funeral at such a heightened time of tension, following the Michael Stone killings has yet to be officially explained. The men's CO was interviewed on the news, and he stated that the two men had taken the wrong turning off the motorway on their way back to Lisburn. Most squaddies who served there know that the motorway runs all the way back to Lisburn and is signposted, making a wrong turn off highly improbable.

AFTER THE LYNCHING OF THE SIGNALS CORPORALS

Corporal Medic Jim Seymour, RAF

I was a corporal medic in the RAF posted to Aldergrove in September 1987. I had read a lot about the use of helicopters to speedily evacuate casualties to hospitals and improve mortality rates, and I thought that serving in Northern Ireland would give me the kind of experience I was looking for. What I saw on one particular day really made an impression on me and I decided that I could get some valuable medical experience and do a bit of flying into the bargain.

Compared to what the squaddie had to put up with on operations, we in the RAF had a really good life at Aldergrove. We had a resident field squadron of RAF Regiment who went out in makralon Land Rovers on patrol but for the rest of us it was much the same as being back in England, working in support of the flying operations which were pretty much on the go 24/7. The obvious exception was the security restrictions every time we ventured off camp, and I think it's fair to say that even these were regarded in a laid back way. We had all had the security briefings and heard of various incidents but there was a definite 'it will never happen to us' mentality.

This laid-back attitude vanished in March 1988 when the two Signals Corporals were murdered by the mob in West Belfast; of course the whole horrific episode was captured live on the television news and I think this only served to reinforce the tragedy of these guys being lynched and nobody being able to come to their rescue. That night, and for the first time since I had arrived at Aldergrove, there were guys queuing to use the welfare phones to make calls to their families at home and reassure them that they were OK. It's hard to explain, but in a way this one incident seemed to bring home to all of us the hatred and savagery of some of the people we were dealing with, we were all conscious of this hatred being just under the surface.

Various rumours were quick to circulate; the most prominent one was that the experienced guy was showing the new bloke some of the local hotspots and blundered into the funeral procession. At the time we found this hard to understand as so much information had been circulated about what was going on in West Belfast that weekend. Surely these two guys dressed in plain clothes and in an unmarked car would have given the place a wide berth? I know that tensions were running very high at the time; a few days previously the Loyalist gunman Michael Stone had launched his attack against the mourners at the funeral of the Gibraltar bombers killed by Special Forces. The PIRA may have thought that a similar attack was being launched when the silver Volkswagen of the two corporals strayed into the path of the other funeral. Obviously nobody will ever know the real facts of what happened on that day, but I felt physically sick whenever that footage was shown on the news afterwards.

Needless to say we started to take security a lot more seriously after that incident. In the security office where we used to have to book in and out of camp, they had the photos of the two bodies on display, found as they were stripped and beaten on wasteland. Eventually these were removed as I think complaints were received that they were too gruesome, especially for some of the families using the office.

Two incidents in the aftermath of this incident stick in my mind; the first concerns a really nice guy called Pat who was the charge hand over the civilian workers on the camp, cleaners and the like. I went into work in the week after the murders and Pat was in the medical centre to see if our cleaner was ok. Obviously something was the matter and Pat was upset and avoiding eye contact; he looked very uncomfortable. When I asked him what was the matter, Pat replied that he didn't think that any English person would wish to talk to him after what had happened in West Belfast. This kind and very decent man said: 'Jim, I wouldn't blame you or any of your friends if they didn't want to speak to me again after what happened on Saturday, but please don't think we're all like that.' As he spoke to me he was almost in tears.

The other incident was when the two hearses drove onto the camp with the coffins of the two corporals who were being flown back to the mainland. As the two hearses drove slowly down towards the airfield, the coffins covered with union flags, the whole camp fell silent, heads were bowed and service personnel saluted; a very sad and solemn day.

Two weeks after the murders, on 1 April I was on call when we received word that a soldier belonging to 3 Queens had been involved in a road traffic accident and sustained a serious head injury. Consequently he was to be urgently casevaced to the specialist neurological unit at the Royal Victoria Hospital (located on the infamous Falls Road in West Belfast).

I got down to the squadron as quickly as possible, changed into flying kit and got the medical equipment onto the helicopter and joined the crew for a quick brief. The casualty arrived by ambulance and was loaded into the helicopter which then lifted off for Belfast. On the flight the loadmaster came on the intercom and asked me if I would need to go into the hospital with the casualty as they would be doing a 'rotors running' off-load. Due to deterioration in the man's condition, I replied that I would need to go in and give a handover to the medical staff in Accident & Emergency, but this would only take a few minutes.

Anyway, the chopper was met by an ambulance on the sports field at RVH and I helped to transfer that patient and completed my handover to the waiting medical team. Upon leaving the A&E unit I had to walk through the waiting area; I was in flying kit carrying my bone dome helmet and must have stuck out like the proverbial dog's bollocks. As I walked past this little old lady, she hissed something on the lines of 'Brit Bastard' and spat at my back. Not the kind of behaviour normally encountered by RAF medics I can assure you! Worse was to come, however, when I left the A&E department to get my lift back to the sports field and waiting helicopter. I stood anxiously looking up and down for any military vehicles, an ambulance, anything and the realisation quickly dawned that I had been left alone. I've never felt so scared and so conspicuous in all my life, just as I was desperately trying to formulate a plan to get help, a patrol of the Royal Scots ('B' Company I later found out) came round the corner. I was bundled into the back of a PIG and driven to their base at North Howard Street Mill and taken up to the Ops Room.

I then had to explain to a somewhat astounded officer how I had come to be left in the first place. He then told me that in view of recent events I was very lucky not to have been picked up by a black cab instead. To this day the thought of what may have happened gives me a sick feeling in the pit of my stomach, and I owe the Jocks a huge thank you for coming to my rescue. I think the reason for my being left was put down to a breakdown in communication; at the end of the day I was just glad to be back in one piece.

SHANKILL, 1993

Tom Neary, Royal Artillery

I returned to Northern Ireland in 1993, and the same Mrs Blackburn was waiting with her greetings cards and pens. This time I took the opportunity to thank her for her kindness to me back in '87. She simply said it was her duty and pleasure to support the troops. This simple act of decency was the last I would see for a long time and was appreciated!

We were moved to Girdwood by various modes of transport and arrived there in the mid evening. I don't know if it was just me, but there was a far more malicious atmosphere in and around the local area. 46 Battery was tasked to cover the areas of the Ardoyne, Oldpark, Clifftonville, Shankill and Ligoniel. We were also used to patrol the New Lodge when required.

We thought that the outgoing unit would show us the patrol routes etc, but their lads were gone before we had even collected our kit from the wagons. So we had to man the QRF immediately; within fifteen minutes we were out on the streets and providing cover for the ATO on a suspect device at Everton Centre. The following day was spent getting to know the area for real, whilst on patrols. I had studied the maps and was quite confident that I knew my way round the area. This idea was quickly dispelled, due to new blockades having been put up to keep the two communities apart which hadn't been marked on our maps and I found my brick cut off from the rest. There were some young lads in the brick, and one of them had just stepped out of basic a few months before. When they placed him with me late on in the training package, I was unsure how he would cope on the streets. I needn't have worried, he was a good lad and did OK as did all the other settled and confident boys. The lads were Lance Corporal Roki Rokatuni (RAOC), Driver Jock Gilmour (RCT) and Gunner Eddie Edwards from 46 Battery.

On the second night, one of our mobiles was called out to an incident at Yarrow Street off the Crumlin Road. A young girl had been shot dead by the UVF because she wouldn't give them the keys to her car. She was 27, had just passed her test, and two scumbags had seen her parking up and tried to get her car off her; she fought them off and managed to get inside her home. They kicked the door down and shot her in the face, in front of her friend. They panicked and ran away, leaving this girl dying in her hallway. The car cost her more than the £300 she paid, and left a family without a daughter; all for a car they never even took. When I heard this, I was sickened! It made me realise that I had entered Bedlam, where no rules applied! From this point I decided to take no shit from anyone.

Sharon McKenna (27) was murdered by the UVF on 17 January 1993 at Shore Road after she had refused to hand over the keys of her car parked outside. She was shot by a 12 bore shotgun and then shot again as she lay on the ground. The UVF laughably claimed that she was a member of INLA. This was discounted by the Security Forces who stated that the killing was, as the whole world probably knew, purely sectarian. She lived in Newtownabbey and was visiting an elderly friend who had recently been released from hospital.

RHC mural, lower Shankill. *(Thomas Neary)*

Amongst the many tragedies of 1993, several stand out amongst the madness and slaughter. In Warrington on the English mainland, on 20 March, an IRA ASU placed two bombs in the centre of the town, killing tiny Jonathan Ball (three) whilst he shopped for a present for Mother's Day. His father said: 'He is what made me live. He was great. My life is shattered now, absolutely shattered. A child of three years and ten months and they took his life.' (*Lost Lives* p.1314). In the same explosion, Tim Parry (12) was badly injured, succumbing to his injuries five days later.

The young boy, like Jonathan Ball, had also been out shopping, in his case for football gear, when the second device exploded. He never regained consciousness and died on 25 March at a hospital in Liverpool. His father said of him: 'We produced a bloody good kid, one of three, he was a fine lad. He had his moments. He could be a cheeky, impudent little pup, a good kid. The IRA; I have no words for them at all.' (*Lost Lives* p.1317).

Two months earlier, the Troubles had claimed another victim, this time in Belfast when Julie Statham (20) took her own life. The Queen's University student gave up on life some weeks after the UVF murdered her boyfriend Diarmuid Shields in an attack that also claimed the life of his father. She took an overdose and left a note stating: When they killed my darling, they killed me too.' (*Lost Lives* p.1310).

TOWN AND COUNTRY

Phil Hyslop, Royal Artillery

My love-hate relationship with the Province started on my eighteenth birthday, which coincided with day one of the in-barracks training; fitness followed by patrolling techniques, more fitness, boring lectures on weapon velocities and more importantly, first aid.

We deployed to South Armagh and lost a much loved and respected lad within two m to the infamous South Armagh sniper team. Keady will forever be an artillery sore point and from that moment; many lives were changed forever. After returning to Germany I ignored some good advice and volunteered like a muppet to go on an attached tour with another RA Regiment to bloody Belfast. The difference in rural and urban tours was huge even in training but I needed the buzz of being in a real environment and not traipsing around a muddy gun position in Germany or the baking heat of Canada. The early 1995 ceasefire was in full swing as we took command of Girdwood Park patrolling the notorious Ardoyne and New Lodge estates in berets with a low profile; this didn't stop a young Subaltern taking his own life in our brand new accommodation. Two in two tours and I'd not even unpacked properly! [Lance Bombardier Paul Garrett, KIA 12 December 1993 and Second Lieutenant James Fox, death by violent or unnatural causes, 21 January 1995.]

Even in our current climate of the new cease fire I can honestly say the Shankill Road on a Friday night at chucking out time is certainly a good laxative! Although I served in the former Yugoslavia thrice it was the Troubles that made me the person I am today and I'm very proud to have done it. Meeting anyone else who also served in Northern Ireland is very humbling. It is better than a mason's handshake, just an acknowledging nod or respectful grin. Any lad who 'hard targeted' out of an SF base will have known, in the pit of his stomach as he hit the street, that he was 'on offer' and that in itself deserves respect.

PUNISHMENT BEATINGS

Mick Pickford, Royal Artillery

What was not very often reported on the mainland during the Troubles was the amount of punishment shootings and beatings that were dished out by the paramilitaries. Punishment shootings were carried out against the local populace who dared to go against the wishes of the local thugs whether Protestant or Catholic. The offence could be anything from talking to a member of the security forces in the street, or the more serious: dealing drugs without permission. I remember being warned by the Royal Anglians who were putting us through our paces for the deployment training. 'You will see a few young men, walking around with walking sticks; this is not because they have been careless in a PE lesson, it is because, let's say, they have broken the rules.' We all knew what that meant; kneecappings, six packs etc. I'm not sure if the punishment fits the crime, but a 'six pack' was a bullet to both knees, both ankles and both elbows. Kneecapping speaks for itself; a bullet to each kneecap. I guess a beating was 'getting away with it'.

We were aware of the most severe cases, where the defendant would undergo the travesty of a trial and be taken to something called a 'romper room'. All kinds of power tools would be used – sanders, hammer drills, electric carving knives – the list can go on, but you can go to the local B&Q for the ones that I have left out. To give you an idea, a young woman was found in a wheelie bin in the Shankill area during our tour. This poor girl had learning difficulties, and to this day, I do not know what crime she committed, and no amount of searching on the internet can trace her name. This I think, is sad, because when you were in Northern Ireland, death and destruction was all around, so one more 'local' body in the morgue wouldn't be remembered. Unless a) it was a mate b) it was a 'player'.

During my tour, each Brick had to spend a week with the RUC whom we called 'Blacks'. Blacks were a kind of Tactical Support Group; they would go to the major flashpoints and act

This little girl told the brick commander to 'F off'. *(Craig Laidler)*

A quick break and helmets off. What a relief. *(Craig Laidler)*

as the RUC version of QRF. These men had seen it all. We would get up at a ridiculous time in the morning and get in the snatch Rover and drive up to Antrim Road Police Station. I for one didn't mind, because the breakfast they served up there was a lot better than what we got back in Girdwood Park; none of the other guys complained to my knowledge either. The hours were longer for 'Blacks'. We used to 'blue light' from pillar to post, sometimes going to neighbourly disputes, sometimes not. But having the blue light on, charging through the traffic was exciting, I have to admit, but after a while, it became a chore. You would be doing top cover in the following Rover, which was not as fast as the RUC version. And also, being on top cover at 60 mph means that you see fuck all; you get thrown around and things hit you faster.

We would visit the Ardoyne on numerous occasions, up and down the streets we would go, the stench of coal-burning fires, seeing the 'faces' and saying things like: 'Hello, how's the wife, she was good last night, can she still walk?' But they, like us, were used to it. Only when you got a reaction did you know that they had had a bad day poncing off the state. I didn't much care for the Ardoyne; I was aware of the history of the place. After all, it was where Martin Meehan plied his trade years before, and history is the name of the game over there. Seeing the 'Sniper at work sign' on a telegraph pole either unnerved me, or made me angrier; I cannot remember which. I didn't know this area, certainly not as well as I knew the New Lodge. I was kind of in my comfort zone there; I knew the faces, the choke points, possible firing points, but Ardoyne, no, nothing. What I did know, was that the place felt like a tinderbox. The other battery had a few contacts there and I could see why. Hearts and minds were wasted on the Ardoyne – fact!

The other half of the time, we would be going around Belfast Docks, Duncrue Street, Pollock Road etc. This pissed me off no end, due to the early morning temperatures.

One particular time, we had to 'blue light' from the Antrim Road all the way along Derrycoole Way. We had heard that something had happened from the minute we de-bussed. Two of the RUC guys had gone off at a rate of knots and seeing that our orders were to assist them, I went with them; running after – well – I didn't know what to be honest! We turned the corner and found a guy lying on his back, arms behind his head, like you would be sunbathing, with his trousers rolled up, casual as you like. I then saw two unmistakable .22 bullet holes in each kneecap. I said to him: 'You alright?' and he replied: 'Aye, fine; you?' 'No, I'm not fucking fine; you have just made me waste oxygen running across this field just for a scrote like you! I thought I was going to get some action!' This young man could not understand why I had the almighty arse ache. All I can say to him is that a week of getting slung about in a Land Rover, losing vital sleep, getting windburn from the very cold air shifting through the docks, being bottled at speed, abused by the locals from both sides, was just great. But it could have been worse.

*Wheelie bins were used for command-wire IEDs. The UVF used to run a sticker system in the Shankill for wheelie bins that were OK to be picked up; no sticker no pickup. Security Forces were briefed on giving such bins a wide birth due to the danger of getting blown up by a primed bin. My opinion was that the paramilitaries knew this and that is why they were so brazen when dumping a body this way, but I may be wrong.

DEATH AND VIOLENCE ON SPRINGFIELD ROAD

Robert Hutton, Royal Highland Fusiliers

On 24 March 1974, I made my first arrest; a young teenage male, one of the local Fianna. To arrest someone all one had to say is 'As a member of Her Majesty's Forces I arrest you.' That was it. As arresting soldier I had to accompany him to Battalion HQ at Fort Monagh in a PIG. Two days after my first arrest a car bomb went off on Springfield Road, up on Black Mountain, killing one civilian. The Provos were driving the bomb to some location when they spotted one of our mobile patrols heading towards them; they panicked, and left the bomb with timer set, believing that it would go off when our boys were converging on it. It went off before the lads arrived, but this poor bloke was driving past it in his small van when it detonated. It killed him, turning him to toast and blowing his van onto its side. Our boys ran up and cordoned the area off before the police, ambulance and bomb disposal arrived. One of our lads walked past the van, when suddenly the dead man's brain popped like a soufflé; the poor squaddie spewed his guts up and had nightmares for weeks after it. He was so badly shaken by the incident that he was taken off patrol duty for a while to calm down.

The night after the bomb someone threw a nail bomb at the gate of Glenveagh OP. My section was on guard duty at the time. Fusilier Alec Weir was on gate guard when the bomb was thrown at his position. Alec got the shock of his life when it went off and so did most of us upstairs as we raced for our rifles and kit and threw it on ready for action. As I stood there in readiness, I watched the others scramble about in organized confusion; Platoon Sergeant and section commanders grouping their men and diving downstairs, and out onto the streets in 'hot pursuit' of the terrorist. As I stood waiting in full kit with everyone hyped up by the incident and the adrenalin rush, I noticed that the muscles around my knee caps were twitching uncontrollably, as if they were working independently from my brain; my brain was saying 'stop', but my knees said 'No'. I know it wasn't fear, just a weird twitch triggered by the excitement.

As things calmed down a little, I thought to myself: 'What if the bomber had been half an hour later?' Because I would have been there instead of Alec as I was due to relieve him. The bomb had no chance of inflicting injury on anyone; it was just a reminder to us, from the PIRA. A little 'Welcome to Belfast' calling card. The bomber was not caught and life got back on track after a couple of hours, just another almost daily occurrence in Belfast.

The following night two gunmen hit us. The first fired four shots from a Thompson sub-machine gun at the kitchen window, which was shut, and therefore the rounds just pinged off the armour plating. The other gunman fired two high velocity shots at the small OP's window. The gunman fired from the small alley way at the shops, around a hundred yards to the front, and hit the wall causing no damage. Guess who was on duty at the time? Yes, good old Alec Weir! He was sitting in the chair, which was on rollers, looking out through the telescope when the gunman opened up. Alec kicked out with his legs and the chair with Alec still in it catapulted backwards out of the room door into the hallway where it toppled over, spilling Alec onto the floor in a heap of surprise. Fusilier Ian McPhail ran into the room and grabbed Alec's SLR and fired a couple of shots in return, hitting no one. I was on gate sentry at the time and didn't know what was happening upstairs until half the platoon came running down the stairs and dashed out, fully armed to try and catch the perpetrators.

THE LOWER FALLS, 1973

Kevin Stevens, 1RGJ

July 1973 saw the 1st Battalion back in Northern Ireland once more and into an area we had previous experience of the Lower Falls. The Falls have been described in previous books so the reader should be fairly familiar with the layout but in short, like so many urban areas of its era, it was mainly two up, two down houses in long dirty decaying terraces. Its street names were from former battles, Balaclava being one that springs immediately to mind. [The author well remembers Serbia Street, Sevastopol Street and Abyssinia Street, memories of a distant colonial past.] There were also the notorious Leeson Street and Cyprus Street.

I was back in 'A' company and based in Mulhouse, next to the RVH, with two entries, one straight out the front up Mulhouse Street itself and through a high wriggly tin fence onto the Grosvenor Road. The second was a vehicle entrance out the back into the Distillery area which was mainly empty decrepit houses with open areas where houses had been demolished and not rebuilt.

This was the tour immediately following the one which for me had been cut short by ten days by being shot. [This attack left Kevin wounded and in hospital. The incident was described by fellow Green Jacket Ken Ambrose as not actually stopping a bullet, just 'slowing it down'.] I was confident that lightning would not strike twice in the same place, so although I didn't exactly feel fire proof, I was a little more comfortable. Arriving in July we were soon once against in the thick of it, but by 1972 standards it was certainly a lot quieter though that is not to say quiet, far from it. There were the normal bombs and shootings but the tempo was certainly down on 1972.

I was back in my old section 12B commanded by Corporal Bob 'C' but now I didn't have to worry about carrying the lump that was called an A41 radio, as we had been issued Pye pocket phones and therefore the Section Commander carried that. Another innovation was that it was agreed that we should call each other by first names or nick names only on the streets so the players would not be able to identify who was really in charge. This was certainly a cunning plan except our platoon commander Tim 'W.' looked like an officer, spoke like an officer and in the kindest sense acted like an officer and anyway, who, as a Rifleman was going to be brave enough to call our Platoon Sergeant John 'P' by his first name? He didn't even like the abbreviation 'Sarge!'

There were several highlights to the tour and a few spring to mind immediately. The first was a rather boring foot patrol around the Falls. We had been out and about for a couple of hours and were making our way home for lunch, but as we were a couple of minutes early, as we patrolled down from the Grosvenor Road, decided to put in place a snap VCP; just a couple of cars and then a quick walk into Mulhouse itself. The VCP was quickly set up and Bob 'C' indicated that the next car to come along would be stopped. A few seconds later a beige Austin 1100 or 1800 trundled towards us. He was waved into the side and immediately it was clear he was very nervous. As I recall he wasn't known to the security forces as a quick check via HQ showed but something was definitely not right. Bob invited him to step out of his car and assisted by opening the door for him. The door felt unusually heavy for what was a reasonably light car so while he was kept occupied Bob eased off the door panel. Bingo; the door was stuffed full of explosives. The driver was promptly arrested and ATO tasked; well, so much for lunch.

After the car had been thoroughly checked out by ATO and the explosives removed, the car was taken to Mulhouse and impounded. A decent but flukey result; five seconds either way setting up the VCP and chummy would have got through us unscathed. A large amount of explosives were taken out of the equation.

I was in the front sangar early one evening guarding the front entrance when a person appeared around the wriggly tin about 50 yards away and fired a couple of rounds at us. We returned fire, two from me and one from my partner in crime, John R. Very quickly the QRF were deployed. Into the sangar stormed (now) Colour Sergeant John 'P'. Well dones and bol-

Snap checkpoint on the Falls Road, just outside the bookies where the players often went; they didn't like that much. *(Craig Laidler)*

lockings were handed out in equal amounts; the bullet holes in the wriggly tin were found, two at about head height close together and one about nine feet off the ground. The well dones for returning fire; the bollocking for John as he wasn't wearing his tin pot!

We were fortunate enough to have our 3rd Battalion bordering us and the 2nd were also in the Province at the same time. There was a great deal of excitement and, dare I say it, pleasure when we heard that two known IRA men had been taken out by 3 RGJ. James Bryson and Pat Mulvenna Jnr had been setting up an ambush in their area not knowing they were being observed from an OP. Mulvenna died instantly and Bryson a few days later. Bryson was a former British soldier and knew how to shoot. Rumours had circulated about a gunman called 'one shot Willy' meaning one shot, one kill. Bryson was the prime suspect but it could not be proven. However, following his timely demise 'one shot Willy' ceased to operate; coincidence?

James Bryson (26) from the Ballymurphy Estate was shot near the Bull Ring on the 'Murph by soldiers on 31 August 1973, dying of his wounds on 22 September. He was an escapee from the prison ship HMS *Maidstone* and was described by a senior British officer as 'an evil looking man, who joined the IRA to indulge in his homicidal tendencies'. He was, nevertheless regarded as a hero by the locals. Certainly, no member of the Security Forces mourned his passing. Patrick Mulvenna (22) was shot and killed in the same incident on 31 August. Both men were seen driving around the Ballymurphy Estate and were observed to be heavily armed. Soldiers in a covert OP saw the men along with two others and eventually opened fire hitting Mulvenna and Bryson.

Another of the jobs we were tasked to do was to man an OP at the top of the Telex building at the bottom of the Grosvenor Road. This was a terrific little number to get for a couple of days at a time; you were in a secure building and got to eat civilian food. Plus, the staff was friendly and very accommodating, even providing us with a telephone so that we could ring home for nothing. I spent many happy hours either on stag, watching TV in a comfortable chair or learning from the staff how to wire a telephone exchange. The OP was equipped with the biggest telescope in the world; the front lens was about twelve inches across and the detail you could pick up even over great distances was amazing. Windows in the Divis tower block which was almost a half a mile away looked like they were just a few inches away.

I was on stag looking up the Grosvenor Road early one morning about 7am when we had a little bit of excitement. I was looking at the Mayflower pub when a beer lorry pulled up and the dray men started unloading the kegs of beer. I started noting down their descriptions, the lorry, number plate etc as there was something about it that just didn't seem right, whether it was the speed the draymen were moving at or the time of day; whatever it was it worried me. I called through to HQ requesting a vehicle check etc even as the lorry started pulling away; the whole unloading had taken less than a minute. As the lorry disappeared out of view there was a big flash followed shortly by a huge bang which shook the building I was in, even though I was a good 1,000 yards from the pub. As the smoke started to clear I noticed that the Mayflower pub was no more; the beer must have been strong in Northern Ireland! I amended my call from a request for a vehicle check to that of a contact report!

The sadness for me on that tour was the accidental death of Sammy Allen inside Mulhouse. In the last month of the tour I was asked if I would move across to the HQ element of 'A' Company, which I did and in doing so swapped my rifle for an SMG. I will never quite understand the logic behind what happened; I was less then six feet away although there was a screen between us. I know what happened, how it happened but the why it happened is beyond me; certainly I could not have stopped it. Even though I was questioned at length later about it, as it was my SMG and ammunition used, the storage of which etc was in order.

For whatever reason Sammy and the attached RAMC medic decided on a game of 'draw'. Sammy had his rifle and the medic picked up my SMG hanging from its hook beside my bed removing also a full magazine from my pouch. From what the medic said the aim was to see who could cock their weapon, add a magazine and then pull the trigger the fastest. With an SLR as soldiers will know the round is picked up as the working parts move forward but it will not fire until the trigger is depressed, therefore if the magazine is put on after cocking the weapon the working parts will be forward, the breech will still be empty and you can safely pull the trigger. The SMG is different, the working parts remain back until the trigger is depressed and the action of the working parts going forward if a magazine is in place will feed a round into the breech and having a fixed firing pin the round will go off. It would appear that Sammy followed the action for the SLR as I have outlined above and the medic did similar, the difference being that the medic inserted a magazine with the working parts to the rear, then depressed the trigger with the inevitable result.

Apart from the sadness of the accidental shooting there was the stupidity of the ops officer that night refusing to call for the doctor until he got a butt number! Thank goodness for a sensible duty signaller who totally disregarded the officer concerned and got on the radio. It didn't save Sammy but it might have. To be fair he wasn't actually a bad officer; we had always been proud of the quality of our officers, he was having an off day I guess.

In early December the Battalion returned to Celle in Germany. Another tour completed; there were to be many more for them as a whole and two more for me.

A major crime, as stated earlier, in the British Army is that of the negligent discharge or 'ND', which is the accidental or foolish discharge of a weapon. In addition to Nicholas 'Sammy' Allen of the Green Jackets, Tommy Stoker of the Light Infantry was also killed in such a way, dying on 19 September 1972 some seven weeks after an accidental shooting in an OP in Berwick Street, near Flax Street Mill. Private Owen Pavey of the King's Own Royal Border Regiment was killed the same way at Crossmaglen on 11 March 1980. There were several others, although this is not a definitive list; Trooper David Johnson on 18 October 1971 (15/19 Hussars), Lance Corporal D.A. Forman (Parachute Regiment) on 16 April 1973 at Flax Street Mill and Corporal R.D. Turner (Queens Own Highlanders) whose death on 27 February 1990 is dealt with later in this book.

There are many names of soldiers killed in or as a consequence of the troubles and the MOD has chosen to list *c.*731, although the true figure is, as claimed earlier, probably nearer the 1,300 which both NIVA and myself contend. The following is an account of a dead soldier whose name is enshrined on the wall of the Armed Forces Memorial at the National Arboretum in Alrewas, Staffordshire but who is not considered by the MOD to have fallen in Ulster.

TOMMY STOKER (1954-72)

24269674, Private Thomas Albert Stoker (18) was from the same village as the author and, like the author, was a soldier. Tommy came from the then little village of East Ardsley, nestled between Leeds, Morley and Wakefield. In those far off days, it was isolated and involved a bus or train journey to those three larger urban centres; nobody had cars back then.

Tommy was born in Minden, West Germany on 19 June 1954 into an Army family and was living in that little village in West Yorkshire when he joined up, opting for the Light Infantry, known by their regimental rivals, the Royal Green Jackets as 'arfers'. His battalion was already over in Northern Ireland, with various companies being split up in and around the Ardoyne area. When the rest of his comrades went over the water, he was compelled to stay in the UK as he was not yet eighteen. Standing orders expressly banned the posting to an active service area of any soldier who had not yet reached the 'age of maturity'. Following the brutal murders of three off-duty Scottish soldiers at Ligoniel on 9 March 1971, where one of the three was aged only seventeen, the Heath Government had ordered that under-eighteens would not be sent on active service.

He arrived in Belfast on 27 July 1972 and was stationed in Flax Street Mill in the Ardoyne. Two days later, he was placed in a covert OP, in a derelict building overlooking Berwick Road, only a hundred yards or so away from the Mill. Whilst he was keeping watch, a colleague in the next room was fitting an IWS (individual weapons sight) to his SLR, unaware that a round was already chambered. He accidentally squeezed the trigger and Tommy was hit in the back by a 7.62mm round and badly wounded. He was rushed to the RVH at the bottom of the Falls Road within minutes and his parents were rushed to his bedside.

Despite a brave fight for life, Tommy died from his wounds on 19 September, some 52 days after the accidental shooting. He is buried at St Michael's Parish, East Ardsley, in a grave he shares with his mother, Iris, who died not long afterwards; in the next grave is his grandfather. The busy trans-Pennine M62 is a few hundred yards away and, when contemplating the fading headstone, the traffic noise is intrusive and unwelcome. Although fading, the inscription reads: 'Thomas Albert Stoker. Died 19 September 1972.' In another part of the graveyard is the ubiquitous War Memorial on which the names of East Ardsley's fallen from two world wars are proudly etched. There are names such as Broadhead, Binks and Linford, all, by no means coincidentally, names of former school friends of the author. On one side, lonely and clearly added later, are the words: 'T.A. Stoker – Killed in Ireland, 1972.' The last time I stood there, alongside RCT friend and contributor Tom Clarke, we both stood to attention and simultaneously saluted a fallen comrade.

JUST ANOTHER VCP

Stuart Wilson, RAMC

I was sitting in the front seat of my father's car going down the Lisburn road towards Belfast on my way to work. The lights turned to red; I was looking around at the people of Dunmurry. They were walking around and most not even aware that they were under the close scrutiny of my over active mind observing them from my seat in the car. I was looking for faces to match some of the photographs that I had seen from time to time, watching, observing, monitoring.

The clouds covered the sky, and the earlier light rain had now stopped; to our right was a furniture sales showroom which had been firebombed again and was now nothing but a shell of a building. The bright white outer coating was marred with the black flame marks that scorched the surrounding wall where windows had once been. The burnt timber that was dumped over the black floor on the inside was now soaked through with rain; all that timber had once been the roof! 'Looks like he has not been paying his protection money again,' I said with a bit of a chuckle.

Up ahead, we saw a VCP (vehicle checkpoint) and we slowed down, ready to stop. Over the roofs of the other cars we could see the big grey armoured Land Rover of the RUC with its blue flashing light turning behind a metal mesh on top. It was parked directly in the middle of the road with the rear door facing us. The cars moved slowly forward, stopping by the young police officer that was taking his time filling every driver's window, one at a time. His dark green uniform was mostly hidden by his thick, dark green waterproofs, his main torso being covered by a thick black full-plate bulletproof vest. Just below his vest, wrapped around his waist was his black leather belt, on which hung the holster which carried his personal issue .357 Ruger revolver. On the left side was a light green pouch about three inches across and about eight inches deep, I thought that it looked somewhat out of place as it was a standard issue water bottle webbing pouch!

Across his chest was a black Heckler & Koch (H & K) MP5 A2 9mm sub-machine gun; poser! The car in front moved away and we slowly moved forward. The police officer already had his hand out instructing us to stop. Dad had his driving licence on his lap, and the police officer lent in towards the car as he spoke. 'Good evening, Sir; could I see some form of identification please?' Dad and the police officer started to have a brief discussion about our recent movements, all the usual questions, still nothing which we had not heard before. I found myself looking across the road and pin pointing all the rest of the VCP. He covers him, he covers him, and I wondered where the rest were. There were two more police officers standing near a small wall to our right; chatting, but behind them at the other side of the bushes was one officer kneeling down with his H & K 33 Rifle with the stock extended into his shoulder at the ready covering the lot of them. He was in a very good fire position which was unusual for the RUC and I would not have noticed him if I had just been driving through. As we moved off, we gained speed and our conversation remained light; we were now driving down the Lisburn road through Balmoral and we were getting close to our destination. This part of the road was always very busy even in the early hours of the morning. The houses on both sides of the road

Left: Keeping low on a VCP. *(Craig Laidler)*

Below: Neil Scarbro on patrol in the New Lodge. *(Via Neil Scarbro)*

formed a gauntlet for about a hundred metres or so; the trees that stood along the sides seemed to act like putty filling in the gaps between the houses.

On the left side, a bush moved, then stood up and walked forward. The soldier raised his rifle and looked through the scope briefly and continued to walk on. The six-man 'brick' never stopped; all heads turning, moving, watching, looking, praying. 'Real soldiers', I thought to myself and the car travelled on. The trees broke to reveal an old disused petrol station on the left-hand side, with its windows all boarded up and the pumps removed. Only the sign remained to tell the passing world of what it once was; another life down the drain.

A DOG'S LIFE IN BELFAST

David Harding, 1RGJ, Att: ADU, 39 Brigade

The lads, as you will know, came from all regiments; RGJ, Para, Pioneer Corps, UDR, RRW, RRF and Artillery to name a few. They were a good bunch of lads, but as is life, we sometimes fell out. At the end of the day we were members of the least acknowledged unit to serve in Northern Ireland. I left my parent Regiment – 1RGJ – in January 1993 after serving two years in Omagh and then went to the 'Kesh as a guard dog handler for three months.

I was posted back to Belfast just in time for the 'silly season' of marches and on one of my first house searches, I was with Sam, a young golden Labrador. Following a Special Branch tip off, we were in the Moyards, West Belfast [on the edge of the Ballymurphy Estate] and we searched a house where a very good looking single mother lived with her three kids. So in we went with a search team from the Devon & Dorsets; we had a woman searcher, RMP and one RUC officer. We got everyone into the living room and then proceeded to search upstairs; first bedroom was clear, no indications; in the main bedroom Sam's tail perked up and my adrenalin started pumping. He was onto something and I gave him loads of encouragement in the high girly voice you use as a handler and he started to indicate at the side of the bed. I lifted the bed clothes to have a look under the bed and then Sam dived under the bed, then legged it downstairs and I lost all control of him; I was silently shitting myself in case he'd gone with a weapon or device. The whole search team and the RUC man were all trying to stifle their laughs, and the woman's face was pure red; if looks could kill I wouldn't be here now. I looked at Sam who was merrily chewing and licking an, ahem, 10-inch marital aid! There was only one thing I could do; I wrestled to get it from his mouth, wiped it on my combats, offered an apology and passed it back to the lady. I said: 'Sorry, but at least it's ribbed now!'

In October 1993, an IRA bomber by the name of Thomas Begley was killed when his explosive device went off prematurely; he was responsible for the deaths of nine people inside the shop he was trying to bomb. The shop was Frizzell's Fish Shop on the Shankill Road.

After Begley's funeral, we had to search the whole route from the Ardoyne to Andytown. I was tasked with 'H', a fellow Green Jacket, to search the final leg into Milltown cemetery and in and around the graves. We searched with the route no problems, and when we went into the cemetery grounds, he went left and I went right. Where I walked included the Republican plot and Begley's grave. As I neared the grave, the RUC moved the IRA's security people away and just at this moment good old Sam starts to spin; now any handler will tell you what's about to happen! He let rip with a 'chocolate log' but the only problem was, that it was on the soil from

Above: Dave Harding with Sam, North Howard Street Mill, 1993. *(Dave Harding)*

Left: Rear view of North Howard Street Mill. This was the only area where dogs could be exercised. *(Dave Harding)*

the grave and it then proceeded to roll down into the grave! I wasn't going in there to retrieve it, so one of the RUC men kicked a little earth over it and to this day Begley is lying on Sam's excrement.

At the end of the day, we all carried out a very risky and dangerous job but any handler will tell you it was the best time of our lives. The unknown numbers of lives we saved due to the finds and deterrence will never be known.

On 23 October 1993, Thomas Begley and Sean Kelly, two IRA members, entered the Frizzell's fish shop on Shankill Road dressed as deliverymen with a large bomb hidden under a cover on a plastic tray. They intended to leave the time bomb in the shop, where it would detonate once they had made their getaway. The shop was packed with Saturday afternoon shoppers and in the carnage; Begley (23) from the Ardoyne was killed, along with nine civilians, including two schoolgirls. A leading member of the present Administrative Executive – Gerry Adams – attended the funeral, expressing his solidarity with the IRA killer.

AFTER FRIZZELL'S

Mick Pickford, Royal Artillery

The Anglians were still here and gradually stepping back and letting us crack on, and when the time came, they announced their goodbyes and that was that. Our TAOR seemed to have had lost its marbles in a downward spiral of tit-for-tat shooting and attacks. We had Frizzell's Chip Shop blown up by Sean Kelly who lost an eye and use of one arm and Thomas Begley who managed to kill himself in the process. Begley's nickname was 'Bootsy', but Christ knows why, it should have been 'Big-eared wiry-haired murdering filth.' Gerry Adams carried the coffin when the day of his funeral came. I often questioned religion in my youth; the experiences that I had in Northern Ireland repulsed me against the cloth even more so. How could a Catholic priest say all these words at the graveside of a man who had just slaughtered men, women and children?

At the wake, a young soldier from the unit we were to follow, finally cracked and shot Eddie Copeland. Eddie Copeland was a known player and would [allegedly] have known about this attack in advance. Private Clarke fired twenty rounds into the crowd of mourners hitting Eddie Copeland, seriously wounding him. The player had a colostomy bag fitted, was paid out a few grand, but still carried on his job within PIRA, rising up the ranks, whilst the soldier was sent to jail for ten years on the charge of attempted murder. Funny thing, justice.

It is hard to grasp, but when you see death and destruction on the news you are sorry, but you don't 'feel' it. Going past that chip shop, a missing terrace boarded up where it once stood, is quite a choker I can tell you. I found myself just staring at the rubble, bemused, as we rolled past with our heads out of the top of a Rover.

On 8 February 1995, Private Andrew Clarke (27), 9/12 Lancers, was sentenced at Belfast Crown Court to ten years' imprisonment for the attempted murder of Eddie Copeland in Belfast in October 1993. On 19 May 1999, the MOD was found guilty of negligence at Belfast High Court, and Copeland was awarded £27,500 compensation for injuries he received after Private Clarke had opened fire on mourners outside the home of the Frizzell's bomber, Thomas Begley, in October 1993. It was alleged, but never proven, that Copeland was involved in the build-up to the attack on the fish shop.

ON THE SHANKILL: BELFAST 1976

Lance Corporal Pete Whittall, 1 Staffords

By the time I went out for the '76 tour, I was one of the more experienced members of the regiment, but was going to have a much more involved role during this tour. Not only would I be promoted and become a patrol commander but would also be working on attachment to the Intelligence section. Myself and selected other members of the unit had spent many weeks undergoing a very intensive Military Intelligence course specific to operating in the Province and which amongst other things including covert and other surveillance techniques. Also involved were mental profiling skills to enable us to have photographic memory retention of all the 'players' on the patches in which our companies would operate. Support Company was to be posted to the Shankill/Unity Flats area for this tour.

Myself and Jason Mason from the mortar platoon had attended the course together and would be the eyes and ears for the patrols we would support and the undercover operations we would conduct on the patch. I was looking forward to the tour of duty but as soon as we got onto the plane that knot of apprehension returned to my stomach once more. Shankill had a notorious reputation for being a Loyalist stronghold and one that had, and continued to produce, the hardened extremist clusters of terrorist activists that formed the active service units of the UDA, UVF, UFF and others. It was not going to be a picnic keeping the lid on the sectarian divide. The nationalist Unity Flats area on the east/city centre end of the Shankill overlooked the Loyalist Sherbourne flats; this volatile interface was a potential powder keg waiting to blow at anytime and often did. This situation was further supercharged by the Shankill being surrounded on all sides by equally notorious nationalist hot beds.

It certainly was not going to be a walk in the park. Numerous security force organisations had suffered the loss and serious injury of many colleagues trying to protect all communities from the increasing hatred and sectarian war. This was to be 1 Staffords' third tour of duty of NI since the British Army had been deployed in an intended short term emergency peacekeeping mission of its own UK streets on 14 August 1969. What was clear in my mind was that on the previous two tours of duty (Armagh in '72 and Derry '74) we had lost members of our regiment who didn't return home alive, and others who were injured, physically, emotionally and psychologically. For those of us returning to Ulster we knew only too well the risks and the fears that we would experience and feel once again during the tour.

It was early March and as part of the advance party those of us from the unit were to be attached to our areas of responsibility within the battalion operational area. Our job, as was the role of any advance party, was to learn the patch, including the geography, identify the known 'players' including those who were up and coming for the future. We also had to gather sufficient intelligence from our security force colleagues so we could induct our company colleagues sufficiently on taking over from the ASH, [Argyll & Sutherland Highlanders] who were coming to the end of their tour and looking forward to handing responsibility over to 1 Staffords.

I remember my first foot patrol vividly. It was the evening of our arrival, and it was a cold, wet and raining; it brought back memories of most of my time in Derry in '74. We loaded our weapons and I was asked to wear ASH headdress so it would enable me to blend in with the 4-man brick. As the gates opened at Brown's Square Army Base my heart started to race; the patrol commander told us to form up and give 'buddy, buddy' covering fire as we cleared the gates and out of the security area of the base frontage. We turned left onto the Shankill with the

Unity flats, lower Shankill, 1976. *(Pete Whittall)*

Pete Whittall on escort duty at Tennent Street police station, Shankill, 1976. *(Via Pete Whittall)*

Sherbourne flats on our right; as we patrolled towards the west up Shankill Road we came to a large opening on the left that overlooked the Divis Flats and Lower Falls enclave. The patrol commander told us to 'hot pursuit' across the opening giving covering fire for our buddy until the brick was across safely. As we patrolled up through the Shankill it suddenly dawned on me the size of the estate and the width of the Shankill Road itself; it seemed to go on for miles and there were never ending businesses and public houses. Then my Intelligence training started coming in to use them as land marks such as the Bayard and Windsor Bars.

These were frequented by the hardened paramilitaries of the UVF and UFF. There were lots of black taxis going up and down the Shankill, usually associated with the UDA as there was a taxi control room below the UDA HQ. We went on past Tennent Street where the police station was based; I would visit this many times during my tour of duty. We zig-zagged through the back streets and hidden gullies which had become second nature to ASH, who were very good lads, always cracking jokes and loving the fact that they had got a 'new boy' who was English to take the piss out of. But it was all good natured and I gave as good as I got and the guys liked my humour. It seemed we had been patrolling for ages, occasionally stopping for a cigarette break for those that smoked, then the brick commander said to the lads 'Right guys, tea time.' And, into a house we went which erupted into greetings and laughter whilst tea and coffee was made for the four of us. I was introduced to the family but will not mention their names for obvious reasons of security. They were very supportive of the security forces and had no connection with the paramilitaries. Even though we were in a Loyalist area, we would still need to be very cautious in what we said and whom we trusted.

After the tea break we said our goodbyes and proceeded up to Woodvale where we bumped into a couple of known players' meeting haunts and where punishment beatings and more macabre events took place. These were usually in rear rooms that would be guarded by the paramilitaries when someone was being 'interviewed' or tortured. Although there was not the tension and hatred I had experienced in Derry in the Rosemount, Creggan and Shantallow areas, there was a definite feeling of superficial friendliness and you felt as if you were at times walking in on something you were not welcome to. I would experience this many times in some of the social clubs on the patch, whilst in others you felt very much welcome with the odd pint or two being offered you on a genuine basis of friendship. You still had to keep a level head though and not let your guard down. The pubs were the same, usually you knew you were not wanted in those frequented by the paramilitaries and the others were OK. Well we eventually got back to Brown's Square Army Base at some God awful early hour in the morning; wet, cold and the darkness of night still thickened the sky. After an Intelligence debrief with the duty officer it was time to hit the sack; great!

The Staffords' casualties over a 23-year period were relatively light, losing five soldiers between 1972 and 1995. Relatively light that is, unless you were one of the loved ones who answered the door to an Army CVO (Casualty Visiting Officer) and realised with a sick feeling that it was your husband, son, father who was not returning home.

On 15 October 1972, Staff Sergeant John Morrell (29) was badly injured in an explosion in South Armagh. He was a married man with three children and lived in the Macclesfield area. Almost two years later, Second Lieutenant Michael Simpson (21) from Middlesex was shot by an IRA sniper near Racehorse Road in Londonderry. He died of his wounds on 23 October 1974.

Seven years later, on 20 January 1981, Private Christopher Shenton (21) a Stoke-on-Trent boy, was shot and killed by an IRA gunman at Castle Gate, Londonderry as he supervised the closing of the security gates. Controversy still reigns over this shooting, as a 'super grass' later claimed that he warned the SF of an imminent attack that night. On 29 May 1984 Lance Corporal Stephen Anderson (23) from Hednesford was killed by an IRA landmine in the Crossmaglen area.The explosion badly injured several other soldiers.

The Regiment's toll ended on 1 July 1995, when Private Wayne Smith (19), born in Cyprus, was killed in a tragic road traffic accident.

THE COFFEE JAR BOMB IN DONEGAL ROAD; AND TIT-FOR-TAT

David Harding, 1RGJ/ADU

We were on foot patrol on Donegal Road, which is roughly midway between the notorious Falls Road and the equally dangerous city centre, when something went 'boom'. I know that it's an old cliché but when the device exploded, time seemed to slow right down to a snail's pace. I remember looking up and seeing a plume of smoke, some 8–10 metres away from me. I heard a crumpled bang and a then load of cheering from a group of lads sitting on the wall at the point you entered Rodney Parade from Donegal Road.There was also a car that pulled out and was driving towards the barrier and I can vividly remember the pure look of fear from the driver, as no doubt he wouldn't know how we would react.

It's hard to describe, but afterwards I wasn't scared but I had that feeling of being somewhat distant. My mate 'Soapy' then was tasked out with his dog Lucas on the follow up and, despite the shocked feeling following the explosion, seeing Lucas shagging fresh air put a smile back on my face.When I got back to North Howard Street Mill (NHSM), I had a chance to reflect and an Argyle mate called to see if we were OK. It turned out that someone in the IRA had thrown a coffee jar bomb at us, but luckily we were unscathed.

The coffee-jar bomb was a home-made device, filled with shrapnel, Semtex and a detonator, which could kill from over 25 yards away. Often the shrapnel consisted of small coins, collected by activists on tours of Republican bars and pubs.

I stayed in the Mill for one more day as it was my changeover day, and at 05.30 I went out with the Quick Reaction Force to reopen the city centre barriers.The prison guard force from the Maze had sent two teams up to cover for the Marines who were going on R&R, but they were not briefed by them as to what was required to open the barriers, nor on the incident the night before when the coffee jar bomb had blown up.As we reached a safe-ish distance from the barrier I began to carry out a route check and search around them.When I got out of the wagon, my knees were like jelly, but as soon as I harnessed Sam up and sent him on his way with the words 'Seek, seek,' my training and professionalism kicked in. I didn't get an awful lot of sleep the previous night and the constant ringing in the ears was doing my head in. I remember going into the duty room and the boss saying that he wished that he had been in a vehicle when a coffee jar went off, so that he could claim for his hearing. For ages, I couldn't sleep at night and like an idiot, I turned to 'Mr Vodka' as it was my only answer for a good night's sleep.

Later, I sorted the drinking out to a degree, but with the tinnitus and hearing loss even now I find it hard to come to terms with the incident, especially when I can't hear my kids crying at night with a nightmare until they're absolutely screaming; but as the saying goes 'that's life, now get on with it.'

Dave Harding and arms explosive search dog Sam searching the City Hall prior to a VIP visit. *(Via Dave Harding)*

> When Frizzell's Chip Shop was blown up, I was in Palace Barracks, getting my kit together ready to go into NHSM early next morning – Sunday – when we heard the bang over the city. About half an hour later, it was on the telly as a news flash and I saw the devastation, the anguish and anger; I was sort of in limbo trying to understand what I was seeing and not being able to understand. I suppose that's when the biggest word in the English language comes into play, even though it's only three letters; why? Our feet didn't touch the ground during those crazy times with all the tit-for-tat murders and attempted murders etc. But for me, the one thing that stays in my mind was the killing of council refuse workers on the Lower Kennedy Way. I don't know why; maybe it's because we drove past just 30 seconds before the shootings started, to open the barriers. We must have driven past the gunmen and had the top cover been more observant maybe, just maybe, a couple of innocent lives might have may have been saved; God only knows.

On 26 October 1993, in what was described as an 'act of sectarian wickedness' and in direct retaliation for the Frizzell's Chip Shop bombing, the UFF attacked a Council refuse site in south-west Belfast. Protestant paramilitaries, dressed in council work wear, targeted the Refuse Department's depot in Lower Kennedy Way. The site was close to where Andersonstown Road becomes the upper part of the Falls Road in a predominantly Catholic area and would have been targeted for purely sectarian reasons. Early on that fateful morning, as workers opened the security gates, two gunmen got out of a stolen car, burst in and began shouting sectarian slogans, before opening fire with automatic weapons. At least 60 rounds were fired and two men were killed by the assassins.

James Cameron (54) a married man with three children and Mark Rodgers (28), married with two children were gunned down and died at the scene. In an appalling irony, James Cameron's wife was a nurse in the city and only days earlier had actually helped care for wounded survivors of the IRA bomb attack at Frizzell's in the Shankill. In addition to the two murders, several other workers were injured, one very badly, losing an arm. That the workers were deliberately targeted can be in absolutely no doubt and it was clearly yet another escalation in the bloody tit-for-tat games.

THE CARLISLE ESTATE, BELFAST

Mick Pickford, Royal Artillery

Part of my TAOR was the Carlisle Estate, built around the 1960s to house the local overspill of the Catholic population. The estate was made up of four tower blocks, with large open spaces around the base, one of which was an OP (Templar House), which looked over and more or less up towards New Lodge Road and into the 'Long Streets'. One high rise even had a view into the football field at Girdwood Park Barracks, so a screen was erected and only the top two floors could be seen from the pitch.

There were also multiple maisonettes that were linked across alleyways (which nicely blocked out the sun and kept the place in a permanent state of gloom). There was also a religious shrine and it contained the names of IRA 'volunteers'. I always thought just how funny it was that an object of peace could go hand in hand with cold blooded murders. There was the usual graffiti: INLA, Brits Out; so and so was a tout, etc. Then there was the permanent, pungent smell of piss, dog shit, human excrement and the ever-present coal fires from the Lodge.

One time, a child asked me to remove my helmet because she had been taught that all British soldiers were the Devil, and the Devil had horns. So to disprove it, I removed it and proved that her mother was full of shit. John didn't want me to, because he thought it could be a 'come on'. I was so angry that a poor child had to grow up with the bigotry of her mother; it just pissed me off. But sometimes, you had a mean streak, a 'them or us' moment. I'm not proud to say this, but that was the law of this war. Kids on both sides of the sectarian divide used to ask us for sweets or pens or both. With all these kids around you sometimes, you would either feel like you were Jesus feeding the five thousand, or an IRA sniper's worst nightmare.

Often when patrolling through this estate, you would have a lot of combat indicators, for example, people you know avoiding a certain part of an alleyway or going the long way round to their house. This practice could have two meanings; you could be being watched and your drills scrutinised, or there really was going to be a hit. You couldn't tell which until whatever happened, happened.

We had kids around us asking for fucking sweets and bastard pens as soon as we got into the Estate. Our route was to take us through many of the rat runs in the Carlisles, and I could see that John was none too happy about going down this particular alley. I walked up to him and said 'If I throw these 'boilies' (standard issue crap sweets that the top brass thought we liked) down that alley and if the kids go for them, then we go down; right?' 'But,' I continued, 'if they go down there, and it blows up, then we don't; how does that sound?' John, I'm afraid, looked at me as if I really did have horns on my head.

Mick Pickford crouching at the bottom of Spa Street, New Lodge. *(Via Mick Pickford)*

The Provisionals also had an OP. However, they had 360 degrees angle of view and four tower blocks to watch us from. On the first patrol, we were accompanied by the continuation NCO and a member of the RUC who made it known to us which windows to watch, in which tower, and what kind of white goods were on offer this week. 'On offer' meant thrown down from any floor at us.

You really had to get it together to get through the Carlisles; it was the epitome, in my opinion, of 'urban soldiering'. Every part of the estate was a potential shooting and bombing waiting to happen, and before you knew it, you could have been laying in a pool of your own claret, or with your ears ringing. We hard targeted everywhere, covering each other, five- and twenty-metre checks, and also, watching our own Arcs too, all this while trying to keep in mind that you were being observed, not just by our OP, but by all the 'dickers' in the flats also.

The New Lodge, to which the Carlisles belonged, is a working-class Catholic community in north Belfast. The landscape is dominated by several large tower blocks and has a number of murals, mostly sited along the New Lodge Road. The locality is demarcated by Duncairn Gardens, Antrim Road, Clifton Street, and dependent on opinion, York Street or North Queen Street. North Queen Street and Duncairn Gardens have often seen rioting between Republican and Loyalist gangs.

The area was vulnerable to attacks by Loyalist paramilitaries throughout the Troubles, particularly to drive-by shootings and sectarian abductions. During the course of the Troubles, the corner of the New Lodge Road and the Antrim Road was statistically the most dangerous spot to stand in Northern Ireland.

Several other wars took place, occurred, happened, broke out - what is the correct verb? – during the long and tortuous course of the Troubles. The Balkans fighting seemed to last forever; the bloody Falklands War seemed to just come and go, as indeed did Gulf War 1, but Northern Ireland rumbled on. The following account is from a soldier who was given a Christmas package intended for the soldiers fighting against Saddam Hussein in the desert.

WORSE THAN A PAIR OF SOCKS

Lee Sansum, Royal Military Police

The package felt warm in my freezing cold hands and I was glad to be able to put down my SA80 for a brief moment; my body had been heated up the gift from the unknown well wisher and I felt the anticipation of a child opening its first Christmas present. The feeling of cheating a 'proper' soldier out in the Gulf did momentarily cross my mind but was forgotten in a milli-second – 'Fuck you mate!' Here was I freezing cold and wet in Belfast; I carefully unravelled the package. The 'cam' on my face after the OP was now all over my hands and smudged all over the delicate wrapping paper to reveal three small gift wrapped parcels and a Christmas card. The card was very sweet from some elderly lady who knew some grandson's mate who was in the desert. After reading the kind words, I eagerly opened the first gift. We were now mobile again and as I wiped the rain from my visor and peered down to look at what my default gift was, my top cover partner looked on too, as this was more important than any sniper. I stared down and in the darkness eventually realised that it was Factor 30 sun block; I never expected that, but on reflection surely it was to be expected. This was wet cold Belfast, not sunny Iraq.

Ten minutes later the second one was opened, but I was still in denial from the first gift, thinking this must be better. It was a packet of water sterilisation tablets! 'No, no, no; I'm in a fucking rainstorm in the wettest place in the world doing top cover; you stupid civvie; why have you sent me water sterilisation tablets? The last one was quickly opened under the watchful eyes of my oppo; it was a pack of Durex. I looked at my mate and he looked at me, and we both started laughing: 'Fuck; what were we doing in this shit hole?'

MUSGRAVE PARK HOSPITAL, BELFAST

Stuart Wilson, RAMC

I answered the phone and will never forget the words which came loudly through: 'Bessbrook Ops. Casualty. Gunshot wounds, following Contact. Moving to you by chopper.' 'ETA?' I inquired and 'ETA not known,' was shouted back in a voice which was slightly panicked but he had no other details for me that were of any use. He had used a word which I had used many times on exercise in Germany and in England but until now I had never heard for real: 'Contact'.

My oppo spoke out loud the information he was receiving. 'Gunshot wound; lower abdo; lot of blood loss; high velocity; OK, thanks.' The ambulance driver and myself were on our way out the door as choppers do not normally stick to ETAs and the RAF get very upset if you are late for them. This was completely virgin territory for me; nothing could describe what was going through my mind as we went around to the Helicopter Landing Site (HLS). All of the shouts that I had been on during the ambulance strike were nothing compared to this. On the strike which only ended a couple of months beforehand were calls to accidents, but a casualty coming from a terrorist incident was something else. Waiting at the HLS seemed like hours, but it was only minutes, our eyes scanned the sky for the incoming chopper.

I was thinking, over and over about what his wounds were; as medics you are always taught to imagine the worst. The chopper landed about 30 feet in front of us, and the loadmaster raised the thumb on his left hand calling us forward with the wheeled stretcher from out of the back of the ambulance. The noise was deafening, the downdraft from the chopper's engines temporally blocking all your senses, it felt like I was running into a force eight gale as we arrived at the open door of the chopper.

On the right-hand side of the doorway and attached to the main body of the aircraft was a General Purpose Machine Gun. The stretcher was on the floor of the chopper with another uniformed soldier at the far end of the stretcher at the head of the casualty. The casualty lay more than the full length of the stretcher; a clear plastic tube came out from the casualty's arm and up to the intravenous drip where the fluid was being held up in the air by the combat medic. I grabbed both handles on the stretcher and the casualty was lying back and wrapped in a thin blanket. I noticed that he was still in combats and he was still wearing his chest webbing. I pulled on the stretcher after a nod from the other medic and we slowly lifted the fat git out of the chopper and onto our own-wheeled stretcher.

We had to shout over the noise of the engines just to make ourselves heard and once he was on our stretcher I took the head end with the driver at the bottom and we started back towards the white ambulance. The other medic ran along beside us still holding the drip in the air as we made our way towards the ambulance. The back doors of the ambulance were open as it sat in the small car park. One of the soldiers from the echelon camp's Quick Reaction Force (QRF) stood by the doors wanting a quick look at a gunshot wound. The clamps which hold the stretcher in place were not big enough to accommodate both, so the other medic and I had to hold him as steady as we could as the driver drove us back around to the hospital.

The casualty was swearing loudly and was rocking his head from side to side; a large 'M' had been written on his forehead to indicate that he had been given morphine by an inter-muscular injection into his thigh. The main problem with that is that morphine can take up to twenty minutes before it starts to take effect, and it was having no effect whatsoever so far on him. He was lifted up onto the theatre trolley; the IVI was changed and the new one was placed on top of a metal rod that was then attached to the trolley. I then set about removing all of his webbing and body armour. His chest webbing was still full of magazines which, were charged with live rounds for his rifle and I was handling these when the duty nurse lifted out what she thought were some kind of radios. They were similar in size and shape to the Cougar radios which she knew. In fact, they were not radios but were part of the soldier's ECM kit (Electronic Counter Measures; this detected, identified and jammed certain radio and other signals, which the terrorists used in the setting up of certain types of bombs).

As I reached out and took the objects from her I moved to the far side of the white-walled room and started to dismantle the ECM gear and place it in a plastic bag along with the rest of his kit. In the room now was the anesthetist, who was up by his head, the junior surgeon, who was at the far side of the casualty looking at the now uncovered gunshot wounds (as were the nurse and myself). Two theatre techs who had been running back and forth quickly scanned the wounds and went off to prepare the main theatre for the casualty. The round had passed through the left side of the abdomen and had (as we found out later in theatre), damaged his spleen and intestines. The casualty now had a second venflon in his other arm, which the anaesthetist was pumping full of all sorts of goodies. The entire lower half of the casualty was now uncovered, and he had a small red dot which was just over a centimetre in diameter about three inches over from his navel. It was not what I expected an entry wound to look like, and then I looked at the back. Now this was more what I imagined a gunshot wound to look like. The round had hit him at an acute angle as the large exit wound was at the top of his buttocks. The hole measured from three to three and a half inches across and was torn around the edges. I went back over to finish off sorting out whilst the anaesthetist was taking notes of the casualty's military details.

He was asked his name, rank etc but when he told us which unit he was from, it raised a few eyebrows! He told us that he was attached to the Cheshires. 'Attached?' asked the major, 'Why; what is your own cap badge?' 'Royal Army Pay Corps,' he replied. 'Pay Corps! You're a pay clerk?' he asked in a slightly raised voice. When the lad said that he was, he was asked: 'What where you doing out on the ground?' His face was deadpan and he answered: 'I wanted to find out what a patrol was like!'

A smile spread across my face and all heads turned as he went on to explain that he never actually got out of camp. They had been running towards the chopper when the IRA gunmen had opened fire. My smile turned into a giggle, which in turn got me a disgusted look from the Major. He handed me some paperwork as a hint to return to reception to complete his admission. My giggle had now turned into full-on laughter as I reached the desk, the other medic started giggling when I told him what I had just heard; our Medic 'sense of humour' just flowed. 'One way to lose weight, I suppose!' and: 'He is going to save a fortune on tap dancing lessons.' It was all mixed in with other comments, which kept us smiling for a while.

I returned to resus having composed myself, and the casualty was now silent from all the stuff that the Major had pumped into him. A large dressing covered the wounds and he had a tube down his throat to ventilate him. This tube was then attached to the artificial breathing apparatus, which would keep him breathing throughout the operation. When I asked if I could go in, it got a positive response; an extra pair of hands. This was my first time in this theatre, but it was not going to be my last. The operation lasted a few hours and I watched totally engrossed in what I saw. It was late evening when they had finished; another bullet head was found inside him by the X-rays in the entrance wound. Damn good shooting, I thought. Two rounds into the same hole at a moving target from 300 metres! The round head had been spotted earlier by the nurse and she did try and point this out to the junior surgeon, but he did not believe her until he saw the X-rays. This was not something that she was going to let him live down in a hurry; it was a story she would tell many times over.

We had found out that the contact had been a 'Multi-Gun Shoot' on the South Armagh camp, a row of six to seven terrorists at the top of a hill firing down into the camp. This was a type of attack the South Armagh IRA favoured.

The Royal Army Pay Corps was to lose four men in Northern Ireland. Private Michael Prime (18), a young married man from Derbyshire was travelling in a convoy with the Royal Regiment of Fusiliers on 16 February 1972. At Moira roundabout near Lisburn, the IRA attacked with automatic weapons and explosives whilst on top of a motorway bridge. Private Prime was shot and died very shortly afterwards. A second member of his Corps, WO2 George Johnson (37) died on 16 March 1976 and his cause of death is unknown. On 19 March 1980, Lance Corporal Michael Snell died, and later, Lance Corporal Henry McGivern was killed in a road accident. At the time of writing, the author was unable to ascertain any details surrounding the deaths of these latter two soldiers.

MUSGRAVE PARK HOSPITAL ECHELON

David Mitchell, Gordon Highlanders

When the Gordons were in Belfast, I spent some time with the echelon at MPH [Musgrave Park Hospital] and one of our duties was to escort IRA prisoners when they needed operations. For some reason, they had priority over 'Joe Public'. They set aside one small ward just for them and they had 24-hour RUC guards; there were four of us in the Army escort. We would get a photo of each player, plus a list of their various crimes; these included murder, rape and kneecapping etc.

Each player would be cuffed to the side of the trolley and then two of us would push him, often at high speed, down the corridors giving him as many bumps against the walls as we could; accidentally of course. With every bump, the player would give a terrified glance at us, probably wondering if he would ever make it to the operating theatre.

The worst bit was having to stand around in the corridor – no seats – until the operation was finished, then wheel him back the same way. We were always glad to get back to the camp for an egg banjo and a cuppa.

HATRED IN THE ARDOYNE

Tom Neary, Royal Artillery

Patrols in the Ardoyne were very risky, because of the fact that it was a hard 'green' area. It was located in a valley, and the biggest risks occurred when entering and exiting the place, irrespective of route taken. There were 'shooting galleries' everywhere and you were constantly on your toes and had to be aware of 'dickers'. I was always aware when there were no children on the streets because of the fear of an ambush or an IED. That's why the verbal abuse given to us was no problem at all; just an annoyance. Not even those murdering shits would risk killing their own children.

We knew all the main players and they knew us, but we couldn't do a thing about it. That was the RUC's job; we were there to do ours. I had, on a couple of occasions, to prevent one of my lads from battering one of the local players. His frustration could have led to him being placed in the shit and allow that murderer to make a hefty claim against us. I wasn't going to allow either to happen. The RUC was a very suspect organisation in the 80s as far as I was concerned, because they always appeared to appease the terrorists. One incident which sticks in my mind was when the Sinn Fein offices in the New Lodge were attacked. I can't remember the date, but we were on mobiles that day and were called out to an incident in the Lodge. When we arrived there was a huge crowd on the streets opposite Templar House OP. We were told to provide an outer cordon and to control the crowd from there. This we did and all was OK, until a few known players from the Lodge and Ardoyne turned up. They started to try and incite the locals into a riot. They failed because there was genuine fear by the locals that the UVF were possibly coming back to finish the job later. One of the UVF perpetrators was taken out by one of our call signs from Templar house.

What stood out for me weren't the actions of the locals; you expect that, but those of the RUC. While we were being given a hard time, they were appeasing the scumbags at every turn. No wonder Sinn Fein believed they were untouchable! We were there to support the RUC;

they on the other hand didn't reciprocate this mission statement. We were only 'figure 11 targets', there to keep them safe! My opinion of the RUC was not to improve later in the tour.

Back in the 'Doyne our routine patrols were continuing; as the tour went on we were treated with even more contempt by the natives. This could manifest itself in a number of ways. Most common was verbal abuse, which was laughable to us, but I could never understand how people could bring their children up with such hatred. One of our lads saved an old man from a fire in his house on Elmfield Street. He risked his own life to get him out of the fire, but the following day he was patrolling past the same house and was bricked by some of the local scrotes; says it all really!

One of the saddest things I experienced was when I was patrolling up Ladbrook Drive; I was accosted by an old lady who was very distressed. I asked her what was wrong and she told me that the local INLA top brass were trying to force her out of her home. Her husband was an old soldier from World War II and had passed away recently. All her kids had moved away and she was on her own. She was not a supporter of the terrorists and they knew it. They got the local brats to make her life a misery, so that she would leave and they could then move a 'loyal' family into her house. I made the RUC aware of this, but to the best of my knowledge they did nothing practical to help her. So I always made a point of passing her home to ensure she was OK.

We were very fortunate, because we managed to escape any casualties, although there were two incidents that could have ended in disaster. The first was when a patrol from another battery was patrolling in the Lodge when they came under contact. The 'sifter' man was saved only by the grace of God, as his NIBA [Northern Ireland Body Armour] took the round and not him. The other involved my mobile, when on Tuesday 15 June 1993 at about 20.45 hours I was commanding a mobile patrol. We had been out for some two hours patrolling the Ardoyne, New Lodge and all areas in between, in support of various foot patrols. We were tasked with meeting up with the RUC at Old Park RUC Station, and were to escort them on their way to Antrim Road. On completion of this task we were patrolling back to Old Park and following them when they turned into Torrens Crescent. It was here that we came under fire from a house on Old Park Avenue. I sent the initial contact report, whilst we dismounted and started to move into depth. On dismounting I saw a child who was screaming, so I grabbed her and threw her into a doorway out of the line of fire. At this point I looked behind me and saw that the RUC vehicle had just 'done one' and left us isolated. We were watching rounds bouncing up the street near to more kids, and the RUC weren't hanging about to help.

The shooters were also strafing the gable end of the Old Park social club, just trying to hit anything at this point, when, all of a sudden the firing stopped and everything seemed very quiet and still. The only thing I could hear was the cries of the little girl I had thrown into the doorway, but she was OK; just a couple of cuts and bruises probably caused by me. I knew we couldn't catch the shooters but I requested that all available patrols move toward Clifftonville Road to cut off the possible escape route. This they did, but the bleeders got away and disappeared into the New Lodge. It later transpired that they had dumped the car, a red Austin Maestro there on Eia Street and that the actual FP [Firing Point] was a house in Old Park Avenue, which had been taken over that morning. The RUC later reported that the hit men had fired 52 x 7.62 rounds from an AK47. They had also used bedsprings as their platform from which to fire. This, although funny at the time, did I believe, save our skins. They were firing on automatic and their inept choice of platform prevented them from aiming their shots properly.

It has always seemed odd to me, but during the episode, everything seemed to happen in slow motion. I was outraged that those cheeky twats took me on during their ambush and didn't have the courage to fight me in the open! I saw one of the IRA shithouses I believe

'A riot is at bottom the language of the unheard.' Martin Luther King. *(Paul Crispin)*

was involved in the shoot a couple of days later. I stopped him at a snap VCP that I set up on Berwick Road and asked him if he had been a busy boy in the last few days and he said: 'Wouldn't ye like to know.' I told him it would be our turn soon and then started laughing at him. He must have thought I was a loon and that made me smile even more!

Throughout the full year – 1993 – which encompassed Tom's tour of North Belfast, the Royal Artillery lost just one man; still, one hastens to add, one too many. On 2 December, Lance Bombardier Paul Garrett (23) from the South London area was shot by an IRA sniper whilst on patrol in Keady, near Enniskillen. A shocked comrade ran to his side and Paul managed only a few words, and despite the frantic attention of a passing nurse died within a few minutes. The soldier who had served during the First Gulf War in 1991 was described as 'kind hearted, personable and popular' and was a keen sportsman. His distraught father said: 'They shot my boy like a dog, but I just hope that his death serves a purpose. I hope he is the last soldier to die in Northern Ireland.' (*Lost Lives*, pp 1338/9.)

BELFAST ZOMBIES

Richard Nettleton, Grenadier Guards

It didn't matter if it was day or night; Monday, Tuesday, next week or Christmas. We were either on the streets or attempting to rest, which included fatigues, kit cleaning as well as sleeping and eating. We were so physically knackered that we were hardly able to put one weary foot in front of the other; zombiefied we called it. I remember one day when we had finished house-to-house searches, including derelict buildings somewhere in Belfast and were due to be picked up. Whilst waiting for the transport I foolishly squatted on someone's front doorstep (no gardens) and leaned my weary body against their front door.

However, unbeknown to me, the front door wasn't shut properly and as I leaned against it I tumbled backwards into their front room just as the Nationwide news programme theme tune started playing. Looking up I noticed I'd fallen between their settee and armchair and the woman of the house looked over the arm and said: 'Would you be wanting a nice cup of tea?' I had to laugh at my present embarrassing situation but with the amount of kit I was carrying, plus flak jacket and my physical state, I was unable to get myself off the floor and had to call to my mates to give me a hand up.

Whilst on these house searches someone found a suspect army torch and decided to blow it up in situ. But when it went off, it broke all the windows in the surrounding houses. Needless to say, we incurred the wrath and the venom of the local inhabitants. The mostly female locals spilled out into the street screaming choice names at us as well as giving us a demonstration of their spitting prowess.

What galled us, especially when going home on leave, was no-one at home, not even our loved ones it seemed, had an inkling as to what it was like on the mean streets of Ulster. We had gone in with the best of intentions in order to keep the warring sectarian factions apart, but in the main, to prevent the Catholics from being overrun.

Greater minds than mine have tried to put their finger on that exact moment where we were seen as oppressors and aggressive; no one military historian or participant can identify

Above and overleaf: A series of images from riots in Belfast and Londonderry, 1969. *(Richard Lee Nettleton)*

SLRs in the iconic balanced on hip pose.

SLRs stowed, troops man the barricades.

Soldiers respond to a riot in Belfast city centre.

'Another day, another riot!'

Captain Woodrow with Drum Major Trussler. Trussler was responsible for finding one of the first British Army casualties, who is said to have committed suicide.

when precisely that moment came. Gone were the cups of tea and the biscuits and they were replaced by insults, phlegm, bottles, bricks and ultimately bullets and bombs.

I know of no soldier who didn't experience at one time or other hurled urine and excrement, rotting cat or dog carcass missiles, used sanitary ware and a myriad other equally disgusting objects.

Those who watched TV's black and white images, generally night time shots of the rioting, can have little clue of what it was like. My first tour came to an end in January 1970, and up until then it had been tea by the urn and bacon butties by the sack-full and every girl wanting to marry you so they could get out of Ulster. But, when I returned again it was like the Somme without the mud, and no one would speak to you. I think the change may well have been instigated by Bloody Sunday?

THE DEATH OF RES

Steve Crump, Army Dog Handlers Unit

I was tasked with my AES dog Res, on 13 July 1992, to clear cordon positions around the Ormeau Road Railway Bridge. We had been working flat out most of the day, clearing the various routes for the big Protestant marches on the 12th. This year, the marches were being held on the 13th, as the 12th was a Sunday. The UDR team picked us up and off we went to the site to be searched. The team arrived at the area at approximately 17.50hrs. I was given a quick brief by the UDR Colour Sergeant and he told me what he wanted to happen. I was taken to the four-man UDR cover team and the task began. After doing a few rummages on the waste ground around the area, I took Res to the railway line. I planned to do an improvised route clearance along part off the railway track, in order to secure a cordon.

The marches were considered extremely provocative by the Catholics, marking as they did a major sectarian victory by Loyalist forces. The marches were deliberately routed through Republican areas in order to 'rub their noses in it'. An IRA explosion along the route which disrupted the march would be a 'coup'; one which killed or maimed members of the Army or RUC would be, to the terrorists, a 'spectacular'.

We had searched for few minutes, and then, all of a sudden, Res did a double take and went back a few feet on the right hand side off the track. He then began to indicate, his indication being scratching and barking. As he indicated, there was an explosion. The next minute or so was a blur as I was quickly hurried along the railway line to the UDR Land Rover and rushed off to the Musgrave Park Hospital (MPH). As soon as Res indicated I called him off but unfortunately it was all too late! All I can really remember of the incident was the explosion; it seemed deafening and there was a plume of thick black smoke that was acrid. Everything seemed to slow down and before I knew it I was facing the other way, walking off, and then turning around and seeing him, I suppose you would call it, in his death throes. Then I was shouting to him to get up and come to me. The UDR lads that were half supporting me and dragging me along the railway line were telling me: 'Look; he's alright. We'll go and get him in a minute!' I told them: 'I'll get him fucking now!'

The outcome of the incident was that, apart from myself and the four UDR guys being shaken up we were all fine and free from serious injury. Res was killed. He had found an improvised pressure pad and his indicating had set it off. Undoubtedly his actions saved myself and, in my opinion, the four UDR soldiers from serious injury or perhaps even worse.

The full screw UDR lad just put his arm around me and led me away. When we got to the Rover some locals kids and teenagers were yelling and cheering. I had a rush of blood to the head and charged towards them. Eventually, I was bundled into the back off the Rover and one of the UDR guys shouted: 'Don't give the bastards the satisfaction.' By this time I was crying for my mate Res. As I said, I was taken to MPH, where some young doctor came to check on me. He had a quick look at me and said 'You're alright!' and he then wandered off; at this point I threw my search helmet against a wall and shouted: 'Fuck off!' He then told me 'that's not very professional' and I just replied: 'Bollocks.'

The UDR lads quickly bundled me into the Rover and I was whisked off back to Palace Barracks. My mates were there, and one lad, a Lance Sergeant from the Scots Guards called Gordon Battersby came and simply put his arm around me and led me away and gave me a hug in my room and said: 'You'll be alright mate!' Eventually I wandered off and phoned my Mum and Dad and told them what happened and a few tears were shed both ends of the line.

I was upset by the events of that day obviously but although it was never mentioned I knew that I could have quite easily asked for an RTU [Return to Unit]. However the thought never crossed my mind; I maintained the thought that no fucking terrorist was going to stop me doing the job I loved. After I returned from leave I was quickly reteamed with a dog named Zar and was out doing a search in the Ballymurphy before I knew it. That first search back I was nervous for a nanosecond, then the professionalism kicked in and I got on with it.

After I returned from leave I found in my pigeon hole an elegantly addressed envelope with the 39 BDE stamp on it. On opening it I found an immaculate hand-written letter from the Commander 39 Infantry Brigade thanking me for the work that I carried out that day. He went on to add that although Res had died he had undoubtedly saved someone's life with his actions. He then finished by saying how much the work carried out by all dog handlers was appreciated in the Brigade.

Res might have been a yappy little cross bred, German Shepherd/Collie mix but he was my mucker and I still think about him now. No matter where we were, he would climb into the front of the APV and sit on whoever was occupying the passenger seat. It didn't matter if it was a lance corporal or a brigadier who was sitting there; no one ever complained.

The work of the men of the Army Dog Handlers Unit cannot be understated and their courage and devotion is often overlooked by military historians. Equally, the work and sacrifice of the incredibly well trained dogs must never be forgotten. Five ADU soldiers as well as many dogs were killed during the Troubles.

On 22 July 1973, near Clogher, Co Tyrone, RAVC dog handler Corporal Brian Criddle BEM was killed by an IRA bomb; his dog survived the blast. Another dog handler, Sapper Malcolm Orton was killed along with his dog in a terrorist booby-trap bomb at Castleblayney Road, Crossmaglen. He went forward to investigate a box, partly hidden in a ditch and on doing so the bomb detonated.

Corporal Brian Brown of the UDR was killed on 28 May 1986, along with his dog. An IRA bomb planted outside a business in Newry Road, Kilkeel, exploded and both died at the scene. In May 1988 Corporal Derek Hayes from Lincolnshire was killed by a booby trap bomb in Crossmaglen in Armagh. His Labrador dog Ben was also killed; Ben's ashes were buried with him. On 25 May 1991 the fifth ADU soldier to be killed was Corporal Terence O'Neil. He was serving as a dog-handler when a homemade grenade was thrown over the wall of North Howard Street Mill in Belfast.

MAKING FRIENDS ON THE NEW LODGE

Mick Pickford, Royal Artillery

The good thing about being third man in a patrol was if we approached a known player and the first go would ignore him and he'd think that he hadn't been recognised, which more often than not, with John and Paul up front, he was right. By the time he had got to me, I let them know that we going to stop him, and Mac and myself would grab him and do the talking. I'd often ask: 'John, who did he say he was?' The answer would come back and invariably it would be a lie. 'Lying shit; hang on.'

I would go after them, give them their real name and address, and a little bit of personal history and wife's name. That always worked. Sometimes I got the response: 'Well if ye know me, why stop me?' I would reply: 'Well, to be fair, I thought you were a bigger man than what I'm looking at; you ain't much in the flesh. I'm disappointed now.' They must have bloody hated me. Well, they did and we knew it, so that was no great loss. Mac though, used to wind people up when P-checking them, and when they'd answer 'brain surgeon' when asked their occupation, he would respond by saying: 'No you are not, knob-boy; if you are a brain surgeon, why do live in this shithole?' It got to be a bit of a game with the OC of New Lodge (whom I shan't name as he is high up in the Northern Ireland government now). I would respond by sneering at him: 'Brain surgeon my arse; I'm surprised you can see anything in those glasses!' Those were good days; all of which can be counted on one hand.

MY FIRST EXPLOSION: BELFAST 1976

Richard Drewett, Royal Horse Artillery

I was a young Lance Bombardier and on this day, I was with three lads. It was two days into our handover with the outgoing unit and we were in the Funeral Parlour OP at the junction of Antrim road and New Lodge Road. As I walked up the stairs of the OP, there was an almighty explosion. The sound of it made me think we had been blown up because I fell back down the stairs with a tray full of tea. I admit that I pretty much shit myself. There was dust everywhere and as I ran back up the stairs into the OP, the other lads had also been thrown back by the blast. As I got to them I could hear what turned out to be shots being fired at the OP; you could hear them striking the sangar. It was when we had sorted ourselves out that we realised a pub on the corner of the New Lodge Road had been blown up.

There was shit everywhere and the whole street was covered in smoke and debris; there were bodies lying in the road. It was a hell of a mess, and there was a smell of burning and smoke which even today I can still remember and still smell. The whole side of the pub had been blown out. The device which had caused the explosion had been in a duffel bag which had been thrown into the pub. I seem to remember that I couldn't stop my knees shaking for a good while after this happened.

One thing I will never forget was the sight of some of the bodies which I recall were unrecognizable. I remember thinking at the time: 'Thank fuck it's not me that's going to have to deal with them!' I seem to remember it was a Loyalist attack but they didn't know which group. There were quite a few injured/walking wounded etc. Something else I remember is thinking it was like one of those horror movies where they have lots of smoke and people appear then disappear; this was probably because it was confined in the road with all the terraced houses, I am sure you know what I mean.

It was bad enough looking at the scene at probably 50 metres from the explosion; In some ways I was glad we were in the OP as I don't really know whether or not I would have coped with dealing with the injured as it had really shaken me up; I was nineteen years old at the time.

Richard refers to the tragic events of 17 January, 1976, when a Loyalist terrorist group threw a bomb into a bar on the New Lodge Road, Belfast. Sheridan's Bar was a popular drinking haunt for Catholics and was targeted by Loyalists in the ongoing round of bloody tit-for-tats. Sarah O'Dwyer (47) and James Reid (47) were both killed when the device exploded and 26 people were injured. It was alleged that the bomb was thrown into the bar by members of the UVF who later abandoned their stolen car in a Loyalist area.

As you can see there was not a lot of room when disembarking from an APV. *(Paul Crispin)*

Before any area was entered, tentative steps were needed if danger was to be averted. *(Paul Crispin)*

THAT BELFAST SIXTH SENSE

Robert Hutton, Royal Highland Fusiliers

While patrolling on foot in the Lenadoon area on 7 April a bomb went off at Glenveagh OP. We at once did a 'hot pursuit' where we bumped into Martin Peoples, a known terrorist, out with his girlfriend. We arrested them with myself as the arresting soldier. Once more I ended up at Fort Monagh and didn't get back to my bed until 0030 hours.

A few days after that incident my section was out on foot patrol in the Lenadoon area. Walking the streets, we noticed the silence, a dead calm; no one was about. No one out walking; no cars driving by, nothing. Everyone looked at each other and I could tell by their expressions and actions that everyone was thinking what I was feeling. A soldier's sixth sense, something was brewing, was something big going to happen soon? In a situation like that everyone moves into top gear. Check your rifle sights are up and on the right setting, cocking handle out for quick use, check your magazine is secure, thumb on the safety catch, ready to switch off in a millisecond. We carried on patrolling; sure enough, about 20 minutes later we heard 'crack, crack, crack' in the distance in the direction of Glenvaugh OP. Some gunman had taken a pop at the OP once more. By this time we were down the bottom end of Lenadoon Avenue and by the time we ran back up to the top the gunman had made his escape. My main point about this episode was that strange super-sensory feeling that we got when things did not seem quite right.

THE ARREST OF ALEXANDER 'JOKER' ANDREWS: SHANKILL 1976

Lance Corporal Pete Whittall, 1 Staffords

The arrest of 'Joker' Andrews, a notorious, evil Loyalist thug and murderer was a very drawn-out affair. He was wanted on many paramilitary offences but always evaded capture by most cunning means. He was a big, strong violent man, who hated himself as much as he hated his enemies. He was one of the Windsor Bar UVF tyrants who mixed in the circles of Colin Berry, Robert 'Rab' Graham and many others. I can remember that we had received an intelligence briefing from both the OC Major Giles and RUC, and had set an action plan for the next 24 hours as it was known that he would be visiting our patch at some point during the day. He needed to be arrested by the RUC for several crimes including paramilitary sectarian murders.

During the day Jason Mason and I took it in turns to share different patrols as we were the Int support on such operations around the Shankill for the mortar platoon. Our brief was to check in pubs and social clubs likely to have been frequented by him. We knew that covert operations were also taking place by military and RUC surveillance teams to track him down. I remember the day well as it was so hot; in fact 1976 was recorded as one of the longest and hottest summers in the UK. Like we didn't know it; patrolling around in flak jackets and 'hot pursuiting' across wide open spaces during our tour of duty!

The usual riff raff were holding up the doorways of the known 'player' drinking holes. I can remember Colin Berry with his cocky, cheeky grin standing with a group of his mates in the doorway of the Windsor Bar as we patrolled up through the Shankill. He had taken a dislike to me ever since I had rattled one of his new 'recruits', who was an ex-infantry junior leader in the Irish Rangers during the time I was also at Park Hall Camp, Oswestry during the early 1970s. The guy in question didn't know where to put himself when I started asking him about his time at Oswestry. I knew too much of his background and Berry became agitated and told the recruit to get the fuck inside and away from me. I never saw the guy again for the rest of our tour of duty. Anyway, as I walked past the bar Berry held his fingers up in the shape of a pistol and pointed them at me. I smiled, stopped my patrol and said: 'Right lads, let's check the Windsor Bar out.'

Before we entered I radioed the mobile patrol (supporting us) to give extra cover outside, just in case things got nasty. I then instructed my patrol to have two men guarding the main entrance and the mobile patrol covered the rear and outside of the bar, whilst me and my other brick members proceeded to enter. As we did, I gave an instruction to cock weapons and retain the safety catch, and the fear in the faces of Berry and his cronies was an absolute pleasure. I said to them: 'Right guys; are you going to clear the doorway because you never know my safety catch might accidentally be knocked and blow your fucking foot off; by accident of course.' Berry started ranting and swearing but told his boys to move out of the way. As we entered, you could feel the icy atmosphere, and as we moved along the floor area, the commander of the mobile patrol and his cover man came in the other entrance to ensure our safety. I scanned around everyone to see if I could see 'Joker' but no such luck. I then proceeded upstairs to where the 'players' usually hung out and organised their operations. I remember seeing about four or five of them swilling beer and giving me and my army colleagues evil stares. I took a good look around and then said: 'Thanks for your hospitality boys; we are going now, but hey, we will be back.'

As we continued our patrol I received a call on the radio asking me to return to base immediately as the OC wanted me in for a meeting. As the mobile patrol was still out on the patch I asked them to take me and my brick back to Brown's Square. I had to give a quick debrief on my patrol and then was sent straight into the OC's office. In the room was a senior RUC uniformed officer, two long-haired guys in civilians, the CSM and the Intelligence Sergeant. This was very unusual and seemed quite surreal. The OC got straight to the point, telling us that we had a situation developing and that we needed to move fast. He told me to listen carefully to the guys in civvies, told me that I would be working in support of them and that everything was confidential.

Well, these two guys were very thorough and extremely knowledgeable in their briefing on 'Joker' Andrews; they knew him inside out and had been undertaking covert operations on the Shankill for quite some time. They were surveillance specialists from a much respected specialist Army unit. I was to support them in civvies on the patch in their armoured plated, unmarked Maxi. The RUC officer briefed us on the surveillance operation by the RUC Special branch team. Obviously I cannot go into the detail of the briefing or the questions raised for security reasons, but once the briefing was over I signed a 9mm pistol from the armoury and got changed into civvies and took the passenger seat in the undercover car behind the driver. As we left the army base we turned right to go the long way around the Belfast City Centre, past Divis Flats and back in towards the Shankill Road.

We seemed to be out on the streets for hours and my eyes were getting heavy with tiredness. I had logged all the sightings of the 'players' including where, when, who was with who, what were they doing, what were they wearing etc, etc. We were suddenly called to a side street close to the Bayardo Bar where a surveillance officer had seen what he thought was Andrews going into a house; we went to the location but stayed some distance from it, but with a clear view. As we parked up another car passed us and parked further down the street; the passenger in my car informed us that it was RUC SB. God, it was a tense situation; thoughts went through my head of all sorts of things. What if we have been setup? What if it's the wrong man? My nerves were edgy. I kept my composure as best I could. After about fifteen minutes the door of the house we were observing opened and a couple of guys came out and started walking our way; one was tall, with a thick-set body and cropped hair, similar to Andrews, and the other was shorter with a bit of a belly on him; both seemed relaxed. The driver of our vehicle told us to have our weapons at the ready just in case., and I remember getting my 9mm from out of the back of my waist band in my jeans and placing it under my right leg. I then looked across the street and said to the Intelligence guys: 'That's not fucking Andrews, lads; he's a nobody.' They took a closer look, agreed and waited for the two men to pass and drove off in the opposite direction.

As we continued to patrol around the patch I could see my uniformed army mates tabbing it, and passing us in Land Rovers not really noticing we were there but knowing that there was an operation in place to lift Andrews. They would have been told what they needed to know, but no more. Well, as night started to draw in we got called back to Brown's Square to take a rest and change surveillance teams. I thanked the guys for their support and went into the mess area, grabbed a meal and hit the sack; I had been on duty 15 hours nonstop.

I woke up some time later only to find that Jason and a batch of our boys had lifted 'Joker' whilst I was asleep and handed him over to the RUC. I was pissed off but pleased and especially as Jason would have played a major part in recognition as the Int expert; fucking great. Later during the day Major Giles asked to have a meeting with both of us. He said that he was very pleased and proud of the support we had given to the long operation to secure the arrest of 'Joker', who had evaded capture for quite some time. He said that between our support and that of the other surveillance teams, plus the excellent commitment of our own colleagues in Sp Coy we had helped to save many lives and especially those of innocent Catholics. He said that he recognised the potential dangers we had personally put ourselves in to enable the success of the operation and thanked us for our professionalism. Alexander 'Joker' Andrews was believed by some to be a friend of Lenny Murphy, the gang leader of the evil 'Shankill Butchers'.

The Shankill Butchers were a group of Ulster Volunteer Force (UVF) members involved in a large number of Loyalist paramilitary activities in Belfast in the 1970s. Their notoriety came from late-night abduction, torture and killings (generally by throat slashing) of random members of the Roman Catholic community. They killed upwards of 30 people, including a significant number of Protestants, in sectarian attacks, bombing raids, paramilitary feuds, and through personal grudges. Despite extensive police resources being channelled towards the capture of the men responsible, a wall of silence built by a mixture of fear and respect in the Shankill community, provided few leads.

The gang, led by the aforementioned Lenny Murphy, brought a new, frightening level of paramilitary violence to a country already hardened by death and destruction. While the majority of the gang were eventually caught and received the longest combined prison sentences in British legal history, Murphy and his two chief lieutenants escaped prosecution. He was later killed in November 1982 by the IRA. Intelligence circles believe that they (the IRA) acted in cahoots with Loyalist paramilitaries who perceived him as being as much of a threat to themselves as he was to Catholics and Republicans.

I have always maintained that there was an element of pure evil in much of what the IRA, INLA, UVF, UFF et al did during the Troubles. One must however, concede that there were dedicated men and women in the paramilitary outfits on both sides of the sectarian divide who genuinely believed in their cause. They were prepared to commit acts of atrocity because of their desire to win what they perceived to be a just battle. There can, however, be no such rationale behind the activites of the 'Shankill Butchers'; they were pure, unadulterated, evil.

ARDOYNE PROPAGANDA

Darren Kynoch, Coldstream Guards

I was a guardsman at the time the Battalion deployed to Belfast. I was in No1 Company and we got the Ardoyne and luckily the Shankill (any problems meant that we could hot-foot into that area). Being from Birmingham, with its Irish community, I had and still have a lot of mates who are Irish. I am still proud of the fact that one of my mates actually became Lord Mayor of Birmingham. So I went there with this in mind and that also the IRA blew up two pubs in my city.

We only had two incidents of note. One was that my Platoon Sergeant had a run-in, you could say 'argument', with a youth who was about seventeen or eighteen. One day he said to me we were going to arrest him and I was the one who was going to take him into custody. He called me over and I said to him: 'As a member of Her Majesty's Forces, I arrest you.' I put my hand on his shoulder, but this young lad was pretty strong because it took at least four of us to get him into the back of the Land Rover. While we were doing this the barrel of a weapon was rammed into the small of the lad's back. It wasn't me; I had him in a headlock! Inside the Land Rover I said to my mates, 'What bullshit is going to be put into the *An Phoblacht* (*Republican News*). The headline was 'Ardoyne Youth Assaulted.' The story ran that he had been punched to the ground and that he couldn't see his assailants because he had his eyes covered. Also he was hit in the back with a weapon; half of it bullshit. Never underestimate the power of propaganda I say.

The other incident involved my brick; we were round the back of an alleyway while the search team put in a house search. We had put up tape to cordon off the area but some really young kids (eight years old) kept ripping it down. No harm done and we gave it up as a bad joke. In fact we had a laugh with them about it. The search team had been doing their job well, because they had found a weapons hide that actually led from the kitchen through to next door's kitchen, so that place was searched as well. During this time the cordon around the area had been pulled in for some reason, or the roving patrols weren't out. The IRA had, I assume, hastily put together a bomb in a biscuit tin. When it went off, fortunately it only concussed a Guardsman. If it had been properly done, it would have destroyed a Land Rover and possibly killed two Guardsmen. Some of the company gave chase but he was long gone. On hearing the explosion we cocked our weapons and the young kids ran off.

It wasn't till years later I realised, and maybe not at the time, that the Ardoyne was such a dangerous place. Our system of patrolling helped us tremendously so that maybe something could be set up but not initiated against us. I would like to take this opportunity to thank everyone in Number 1 Company, and attached, and the RUC, who helped us get through our tour unscathed. And a footnote I would like to add: to this day I still have to get to know any Irishman, northern, southern, Protestant or Catholic, before I tell them that I served in the Province. I think bitterness still runs deep in some quarters.

ANOTHER NEAR MISS IN BELFAST

Bill 'Spanner' Jones, REME

During the Troubles, the simple task of getting spare parts was no longer a case of a driver and store man going out in a Land Rover. In Belfast we had to take two vehicles with a driver, commander and two men in the back, all armed. Our Land Rovers still had canopies to keep the parts out of sight, but they were rolled halfway forward to allow two of us to stand up with the canopy rails for support. There was a steel plate above the driver and a grill over the windscreen for protection from thrown missiles and an angle iron cheese wire cutter attached to the left door hinge sticking up to protect us from wire tied across the road.

The Regiment was split across four locations so we would go round to each to drop off parts needed by each battery mechanic and usually we were asked to drop off parts for other units on our way, sometimes other units would do this for us. One day, whilst doing a spare parts run, we were on the way to one of the permanent bases, one which had a neat garden with their regimental badge done in flowers out front. They were very close to a Republican area and as we neared, there was a full scale riot going on which we had to dash past. This was the middle of the afternoon; did these people not have work or school to go to?

There were shouts and bangs which we assumed to be the riot guns of those trying for control but as we were about to enter the base, the rear 'landy' in which I was standing, lurched a bit and I thought that I had caught my web pouch containing my spare SMG mag on the rail. Stopping just inside the base we saw that the left rear tyre had gone flat, and, whilst two lads went to deliver the parts, the rest of us began changing the wheel. There was a hole in the tyre wall; strange, we thought, but continued our run.

Back at our base, in my room I was removing my belt with single pouch and field dressing attached and as I laid it down, several rounds rolled out. This was strange, and I checked my magazines. The one I had just removed was fine but the spare was dented, damaging the inner spring which allowed the 9mm rounds to fall out; the spare mag' was always carried top down so as to be ready to slap straight in when lifted out.

I put the loose rounds in a pocket and took the damaged mag' to our armourer, Sergeant Bob Makepeace, and he looked quizzically at it and asked about the rounds. I took them from my pocket and put them on the counter and he picked one up and said: 'Look at this,' holding a round head first against the damaged area. There was a round, neat dent at the centre which exactly fitted the nose of the round. 'You've been hit, he stated, and I tried a round in the dent myself and sure enough, it fitted exactly.

To this day, I smile about that incident and remember the tatty old pouch and second-hand flak jacket that absorbed the impact; for those who have seen how narrow an SMG mag' is, you will know that it was an amazing near thing.

Bill mentions the 'cheese cutter' welded to the top of Army vehicles and the fitting of such an instrument undoubtedly saved the lives of many soldiers. Several contributors have written about how the IRA strung piano wire between lampposts in the hope of decapitating top cover soldiers. The author is aware of several injuries, particularly in the Ardoyne and on the 'Long Streets' of the New Lodge but has been unable to identify any actual deaths.

BLOODY 'DOYNE

Tom Neary, Royal Artillery

Whilst we were based at Girdwood in '93, we were run ragged by the locals playing up and the RUC always wanting to be escorted everywhere. This was despite the fact that they had properly armoured Land Rovers and we had those shit KPIs and Snatch Rovers. They were very secure and we weren't, yet it was us who provided the top covers to protect them. I had a policy where everyone, me included, did their stint as top cover because it could be a pretty vulnerable place to be. As I said before, we were there to deflect any rounds from them and onto us; like fucking bullet magnets! They were earning shed loads of wedge, and we were being paid a pittance plus 60p a day extra. This was insulting enough, but the government added insult to injury by making it taxable. We were over there involuntarily as part of our job, and were pissed on by everyone.

It beggars belief that we continued to perform our jobs professionally, but that's what we did because we had lives and families to go home to. We knew that if we dropped our guard for a second that was when the IRA/INLA would strike! To lose a mate was a constant fear, and just made us more determined to prevent this from happening. Thankfully we achieved our aims and we all came home safe to our families.

2nd Field's time was considered a massive success, because we took the least hits recorded by any unit over a six month period up till that point. We prepped ourselves correctly, and absolutely dominated the ground around us as soon as we got there. Each battery familiarised itself immediately with its primary TAOR. This was achieved by having a heavy concentration of troops on the ground from the word go. They knew that we had just arrived, and wanted to test our state of readiness. This they did regularly for the first month, making hoax calls to get us out on the ground. We, on the other hand, always reacted to these calls by assuming they were a 'come on' and disrupted their plans by making sure we varied every aspect of our routines. Eventually, these calls stopped and we could get on with the job of supporting the RUC and staying alive. This policy paid dividends on a couple of occasions, because we managed to surprise them with our odd patrol times. They could never guarantee that we wouldn't turn up on a patrol, and catch them at their nefarious activities.

One such incident sticks in my mind very vividly. One troop was tasked with carrying out one of those irregular patrols I described earlier. It was an early 'footsie' (05:00), and we had planned our route as usual so as to give us the advantage of maximum surprise. The weather was fairly warm but moist and there was a very eerie mist lying above the estate, which prevented a decent view of the place from a distance. We made our way into the 'Doyne through various entry points so that we would avoid the problem of bunching and making ourselves a bigger target. This also gave us the opportunity to cover a larger area. My team of Private Jock Allen RAOC, and Gunners Dave Close and Dave Welch entered from Crumlin Road and down Flax Street, toward the lower Ardoyne social club and Havanas; always a dodgy route and not one any of us liked. The Troop Commander, Lieutant Phillips and his team made their way down Ardoyne Avenue. Bombardier Keith 'Spoogle' Smith and his lads entered through the Jamaicas. Sergeant 'Dutch' Holland and his team followed Mr Phillips down Ardoyne Avenue. The insertion always took a long time for obvious reasons.

My team had the longest route to enter the Ardoyne, and meant the other teams would have to wait for us to pass through them, and this we did at the RV point of Havana Way. Spoogle's lads in the meantime provided cover for the rest of us from the Jamaicas. Once we got into the old Ardoyne, we took up our normal satellite formations. The patrol reached Etna Drive and was about to carry on as normal, when Spoogle spotted a bod at the far end of the estate acting rather strangely. He was carrying a white plastic bag, which he stuffed into his jacket. Spoogle whistled over to me and pointed this character out; all of a sudden he disappeared sharpish, up Stratford Gardens. We went up Etna Drive in pursuit; this meant he couldn't try and run back and Spoogle took his team down the alleyway between Brompton Park and Highbury Gardens and onto Berwick Road, so that he could question this bod. The other two teams were making their way to the top of Brompton Park to cut him off, this they did. However, we were also aware that this could have been a 'come on' designed to lure us in. This thought was soon dispelled because the twat wasn't hanging about and was running for his life. This indicated that they hadn't been expecting us to be there.

Once we reached the point where this bloke had initially been seen, my team left-hooked it up Stratford Gardens, to join in the hot pursuit. All the other teams were well ahead of my lot, and had just failed to grip this fucker. The screech of wheels could be heard, breaking the silence of the morning. A car was waiting for this lucky bleeder and he got away.

Luckily, Spoogle had spotted this twat launching his suspect package, in the ginnell behind Velsheda Court. At first he couldn't find it, but on closer inspection he realised that it had landed in a shopping trolley. ATO was requested but was busy at another task. So we spent the next few hours in a cordon, trying to prevent the early morning rubberneckers from interfering with the crime scene. Once ATO had cleared the package, the RUC took control of the inner cordon and we formed the outer cordon. It was revealed that our find had produced a tidy little haul, consisting of a butt from an old 303 and an AK47 magazine and last but not least a hand gun with a full clip. The last items were particularly good, because it transpired that this gun had been passed all over the Province and used in quite a few hits. We later found out that the mag had yielded some good prints and prosecutions later took place. Bombardier Smith later received a commendation for his actions and the whole patrol was thanked by the RUC and HQNI apparently, although I can't remember it.

We were relieved on 21 July by the 9/12 Lancers. Unlike our predecessors, we had to spend two extra days showing these 'Cav' lads around the place. It was at this point where I felt most

6 Troop in from Ardoyne patrol. *(Thomas Neary)*

VCP at Holy Cross Church. *(Thomas Neary)*

Berwick Road, close to where Tommy Stoker was shot by an ND. *(Thomas Neary)*

vulnerable. The Lancer with me was very giddy and was hard targeting everywhere. I soon put him straight and told him that it was impossible for him to keep that up and unfair on his lads. But more important to me was the fact that he stood out as new, and might have been seen as an easy target. Also, what did he expect to see if he was running everywhere? When we got back I was relieved because I didn't wish to be hit at this late stage. On leaving Girdwood for the last time and making our way to Aldergrove, I felt happy but empty; lost almost. It was a very strange sensation that I have never been able to explain.

AFTER BALLEYGAWLEY: MEMOIRS OF A MEDIC

Corporal Medic Jim Seymour, RAF

It was in the aftermath of the roadside bomb which blew up the coach carrying members of the Light Infantry who were returning to their base from Aldergrove Airport in August 1988.

Many of the casualties had been taken to various civilian hospitals in Omagh, Londonderry and Tyrone County and where possible these guys had to be recovered back to the military wing at Musgrave Park Hospital, which was a secure location where they could be assessed for aero med flights back to military hospitals on the mainland.

I'm proud of the way we all worked together during this time; we were flying a lot of sorties and trying to get as many casualties retrieved on each flight; this obviously entailed a lot of liaison with the planners on 72 Squadron and the guys on the Puma Detachment. I was fortunate enough to have a really good working relationship with an officer called Reggie Waugent on

72 Squadron (if he reads this I wish him well). A lot of planning went into each flight as landing pads had to be secured, hospitals and the various army and RUC units kept informed and ambulances organised to meet the helicopters. Within a few days we had got all of the casualties who were well enough to be moved back to MPH.

I distinctly remember carrying a young squaddie onto the Wessex at the Altnagelvin Hospital in Londonderry; he had lost his clothes and was dressed in the regulation NHS pyjamas and foam slippers. Due to the explosion he was still deafened and I'll never forget the scared look on his face as we got him into the helicopter. I didn't realise the effect of these flights until a few nights later when I was out with a few of the lads at the NAAFI 'bop' on camp, and, after far too many beers I suddenly found myself crying and very emotional, don't ask me why as I hadn't witnessed anything particularly traumatic. Maybe I was just over-tired and drunk.

On 21 September I had to visit a coach bomb casualty in the Intensive Care Unit at RVH and see how his recovery was progressing; this was part of the process to eventually get him on an aero med flight back to the mainland. I was taken, under armed RUC guard up to the ICU which is how I came to meet David Hardy. He was still in a very bad way and I was told that he hadn't been expected to survive. His injuries were appalling and he was flown back to Lyneham on 23 September and from there taken by helicopter to the army hospital at Woolwich for further treatment and plastic surgery. It felt strange, having to be escorted by armed police to a hospital ward where a British soldier was being nursed, again under armed guard, in a hospital that was technically in Britain.

1988 was certainly a busy year, and another memorable incident took place on 16 November when we were scrambled to casevac a patient from the Altnagelvin Hospital in Londonderry back to the military wing at Musgrave Park Hospital in Belfast. This was a squaddie who was extremely lucky to be alive. Rosemount RUC Station had come under attack by PIRA and this lad (who was off duty) had dashed out into the street wearing a combat jacket and trackie bottoms carrying his weapon, whereupon he was shot by a passing patrol of the Green Howards who understandably thought he was a PIRA gunman. He had sustained five gunshot wounds and was in a very bad way but I think he eventually made a recovery.

Looking back, this was the most rewarding time of my service in the Air Force. It's hard to talk about this time without resorting to the inevitable clichés about teamwork and all pulling together to get the job done etc etc. I don't think you can ever become blasé about dealing, almost on a weekly basis, with young fit guys who had sustained really terrible injuries. Traumatic amputations, disfigurements, burns and blast injuries, blindness; all of what I saw only served to reinforce my belief that what was happening in the Province was a war, plain and simple. I don't think that the various governments ever referred to the Troubles as a war as they had the Falklands War in 1982; even so, these young servicemen's lives were changed beyond recognition forever.

I have never forgotten what I saw in the Province, or the people I met. It was odd to come home on leave and discover that, unless a really big outrage had taken place such as the coach bomb, in the main the Troubles didn't merit much of a place in the news in England and I think eventually the public became sick of hearing about it all.

Eight soldiers from the 1st Battalion, the Light Infantry were killed and 27 injured, including David Hardy, in the landmine attack at Curr near Ballygawley roundabout, County Tyrone, on 20 August while travelling back by coach to base in Omagh from the International Airport at Aldergrove. The men killed in the IRA bomb attack – all privates – were Blair Bishop (19), Jason Burfitt (19), Peter Bullock (21), Richard Greener (21), Alexander Lewis (18), Mark Norsworthy

(18), Stephen Wilkinson (18) and Jason Winter (19). In this tragic instance, the IRA had done their homework and achieved what was, for them, a spectacular. There is some question, however, that they were actually targeting an RUC rugby team's coach, but the deaths and maiming inflicted upon the SF were seen as one of their 'successes' nonetheless.

It is also believed that the IRA were aware that the Army used the Stranraer-Larne ferry line to ship soldiers in and out of the Province and that often, only soft-skinned Bedfords were used for transport. There is evidence in Intelligence circles that the RUC's best ever informant inside the IRA, Martin McGartland, managed to warn the SF of an impending bomb attack and thus, another Ballygawley was averted.

A FOOTBALL CROWD IN BELFAST

John Wood, Royal Military Police, SIB

Linfield FC – 'the Blues' – was a club that received considerable support from the Shankill Road environs, although the club ground was on the other side of Belfast from the Protestant heartland. Fans made their own way there but the main attraction after the mediocre footy was the march home. A large mob would assemble and head back home. Any chance to intrude or pass through a Nationalist area was seized upon. Loyalist hymns were sung and there was always someone with a trumpet for when spirits flagged. The procession – triumphal or otherwise – was attended by RUC who changed as the divisional boundaries were passed. Given the size and mood of the marchers, little control was feasible and most of the police were sympathetic with the mood of the crowd. They were escorts who saw their job as shepherding the fans as best they could.

Their duties ended at Unity Flats. A small choral service was held, and sentiments concerning the Pope were exchanged and the police were told to 'Foxtrot Oscar' as they were no longer needed now the boys were back home. There would always be someone in the Flats who needed to empty a bucket of water (or worse) over the veranda. The mammies had come down to meet their wee lads (mostly in the age range of 19 to 25) and they welcomed, joined in or encouraged the Loyalist concert as they saw fit.

Belfast Commander RUC finally gave in to protests and asked the RMP if they would take over the escort-cum-stewarding task. The OC of 178 Provost Company at that time was a feisty sort of bloke and readily agreed, subject only to the proviso that it would be an exclusively military task with no RUC additions. It was appreciated that things would go pear shaped and every possible Red Cap was warned for duty on the Saturday. All the office wallahs, all the attached elsewhere and all the excused duty – sick – were dragged in. I think we also suited up the tiffy and the cooks. Even I was directed to play, so things were surely being taken seriously.

The tactic was to completely surround the marchers with Land Rovers packed to the gills. We had a mini-bus in the convoy with a prisoner handling team, plus ample supplies of Polaroid film; I put myself in this vehicle. The first mile or so passed with no more than ribald comments, and the first arrest was when a marcher decided to help himself to an apple or two from a street-side display; not too much aggro from that. The rolling armada seemed to be working and the crowd diminished as marchers dropped out in their home areas. We got to Unity Flats with just a hard core of about 60 or so. The usual concert party formed but it was made clear that it would be a very short performance that day. The mammies were not happy with this curtailment and encouraged the wee boys to put a wire barricade across Shankill and the Red Caps were told quite clearly to make themselves scarce as they would not be allowed on the hallowed ground.

This was not appreciated by Mr Hard Nose OC. The radios all blared: 'This is 9er; follow me,' and his Rover charged the barricade. This became entangled with the chassis and formed an instant 'Paddy Pusher'. All hell broke loose and a full scale riot kicked off in a very short time. Arrests were being made left, right, centre, and anywhere else needed. The mini-bus was filled to overcrowding and I decided we should make our way to Glenravel RUC Station and decant some. Before we left I got out of the vehicle to seize upon a big fellow who had just laid out one of our number. I grasped hold of him but the crowd just pulled him away and I was left holding the shoulder pad and one side of a jacket. I was in the parade dress SIB – one of the dodgy suits - but had learned enough from other areas of trouble to have a truncheon taped to each of my forearms which helped when I needed to hand off those who disliked me.

The riot continued about half-way up Shankill and the pressure was taken off us by the timely arrival of the QRF [Quick Reaction Force] from the 'Kingos', whose area it was. We regrouped at Glenravel Barracks and started to process the arrests and hand people over to the RUC. All went well until there was just one man left. He was a small and innocent looking individual. I was unable to find out who had arrested him and asked the Provost RSM if he could assist. Good as gold he said: 'Oh yes. It was me.' 'What offence?' I asked. The reply was that the guy had been shouting FTP at Unity Flats. I told the man to come and stand alongside the RSM to have his prisoner photo taken and then realised why he was small and innocent looking; he was a deaf mute. I pointed this out to his 'arresting officer' and queried the 'shouting FTP' 'Ah no; I remember. He was giving the fingers,' was the amended charge.

The riot that started about 7pm on the Saturday went into the usual three-day scenario. The first day, they bashed us. The second day we bashed them and the third was spent sweeping up the glass and dressing bruises. When it was over there was a demand from locals that some sort of inquiry was needed into the 'Military Police Riot'. It was set up at Tennant Street RUC Station where there was some resentment that Loyalists had been brought under control. We were established in a caravan and complainants directed to two investigators I had brought in from the mainland; all my Lisburn-based guys had been in the team on Saturday. The rules were that if someone said they had been ill-treated by a soldier, a full statement was recorded. If they had merely witnessed a civilian being manhandled, their details were recorded and they would only be used as a witness if the civilian made a personal complaint. Business was brisk.

Local politicians had got press interest and we had a number of TV crews visit the operation. I was asked by the King's PR officer if I would give them an interview and I did a five-minute piece for the BBC's Peter Sissons and a similar bit for local TV. The TV crew remained and the local councillor introduced them to a youth who filed a complaint that soldiers were threatening to arrest him every time he walked past their base. I was still in the yard some fifteen minutes later when this same youth was brought in, in the back of a Land Rover with some very stalwart escorts. I got there before the TV crews found them. The officer said the youth was a known troublemaker and rioter and they had just now managed to secure him. I sent the young officer and his quarry away very quickly; the arrest would have looked good alongside the already filmed complaint!

The saga had a few good results. We had shown the RUC how to conduct the escorts from 'Blues' matches and they did a better job from then on. We had shown the infantry that we could hack it when push came to shove and felt our own stature increase. We got an issue of flak jackets and visored helmets. The wire screening for Rover windscreens was fitted and CS gas and baton rounds provided. Our showing had obviously impressed and General 'Farrer-Para' [Farrar-Hockley] adopted us as his own personal QRF and we got inserted into many interfaces by virtue of being able to deploy quicker than most infantry.

That was not my only TV appearance. A few weeks after the riot I was in an RMP vehicle being driven up the Shankill with the Provost RSM at the wheel when we came across a pub brawl. One of the fighters had been slashed across the throat with a broken glass and was bleeding very heavily. We put him in the back of the vehicle and broke all records en route to RVH. I was in the back applying pressure on the man's throat as he lay on the floor of the Rover. The TV news later showed film of our run to the hospital taken from a car that had followed us. It really did look as if I was throttling the guy.

It wasn't always fun and games for this Corps, which is usually every squaddie's nightmare after a night's drinking in any one of a dozen garrison towns around the world. During the Troubles, they lost fifteen of their men. On 1 March 1971, Lance Corporal William Jolliffe (18) from Chippenham was on a mobile patrol in Westland Street, Londonderry, when it was attacked by a group of petrol bombers. Both he and a wounded comrade were dragged from their burning vehicle by locals who took both injured men to a nearby house and did their best to treat them. William Jolliffe died later from chemical inhalation, as he had been trapped in the back of the vehicle when the extinguishers fired.

On 11 February 1973, to causes as yet unknown, they lost Corpora Alan Holman (23). On 18 May, Sergeant Sheridan Young (26) from Reading was killed along with four other soldiers at the Knock Na Moe Hotel bombing. On 30 May 1973, the RMP lost two of their men in a road traffic accident (RTA) whilst on duty. Corporal Roderick Lane (33) from Gloucester and Corporal Richard Roberts (21), a Wimbledon boy, died. Another tragic RTA on 20 February of the following year claimed the lives of Corporal Stuart Milne (20) from Edinburgh and Lance Corporal Paul Mundy (19) from Wallingford.

On 5 May 1974, Corporal Thomas Lea (32) a married father of two from Merseyside was badly injured by an IRA bomb in the Clonard area of the Falls in Belfast. Despite his terrible injuries, losing a hand and an eye, he recovered and was being trained for another career in the Army when on 21 January 1975, more than eight months after the attack, he collapsed and died from coronary thrombosis. At the inquest, the Coroner said that he was satisfied that Thomas Lea's death was due to the injuries he received in the explosion. Eight days later, Corporal John Booth (22) from Lincolnshire died from, at the time of publication, causes unknown.

On 17 April 1976, to causes unknown, the Regiment lost Corporal Michael Hards (21); the author has no known cause of death for this Oxford boy. On 8 November 1977, Corporal George Middlemas (23) from Co Durham was killed in a RTA whilst on duty. On 25 January 1979, in yet another unexplained death, they lost Sunderland boy, Corporal William Snaith (22).

The penultimate Red Caps' loss occurred on 27 March 1984. Sergeant David Ross (31) from Edinburgh was driving a vehicle near Gransha hospital in outer Londonderry. He was being followed by another soldier and they were due to pick up some Army wives for a day out in the country. The IRA had packed 200lbs of explosives into a stolen car and parked it near the hospital. They detonated it as Sergeant Middlemas drove by, and he was killed instantly. Only five minutes prior to that, a school bus had just dropped off several children at nearby Maydown School. The IRA demonstrated again, that when it came to an opportunity to kill or maim members of the Security Forces, they had absolutely no qualms about whoever was near and caught in the crossfire.

The RMP's final losses occurred on 19 September 1991, when Lance Corporal Duncan Chappell (18) from Sheffield, and then, three weeks later, Corporal Michael Heighton (27) from Southampton, both died in unknown circumstances.

BELFAST CITY CENTRE; LATE SPRING 1975

Gunner Josef Jurkiewicz

> I remember that it was cloudy that day; no sun peeking through the clouds. It must have been lunch time because of the hustle and bustle of the business folk in and out of the security gates. We did a lot of inner city security, so this day wasn't much different. This particular day there were two of us watching over the gate searching the civilians as they went through to go shopping. For the most part they were pleasant, making the usual chit chat and going on their way. After a couple of hours, two young men who appeared to be in their early twenties came through, and I remember having this sense of foreboding. They were quiet, and unlike so many of our prior searches that day, they offered us no pleasantries to pass the time. I was still sizing them up when I decided to give a quick call to headquarters.
>
> With our training it was always best to go on instinct. We gave HQ their names and details, and waited. The seconds ticked by; the silence was palpable. Just then the 'walkie' crackled and headquarters gave the code to hold them; INT was coming over to bring them in! They were IRA leaders of some district in Belfast! However, it turned out that they had no incriminating evidence on them and they were released after only a few days. It would have been great if we could have convicted them but I was relieved as I didn't particularly wish to go to court and testify against these men. Thirty years later, after two tours in Ireland I am still sizing people up with the eye of a soldier; they trained us all too well.

It is worth noting that the centre of Belfast, although safer than the Republican suburbs, could also be a dangerous place. The mass explosions caused by the IRA on 'bloody Friday' on 21 July 1972 proved that. On that day, a whole series of no-warning bombs planted by the Provisional IRA killed nine people, including two soldiers, and injured more than 130. The bombing of the Abercorn Restaurant, near the Cornmarket, on 4 March earlier in the same year, when two people were killed and over 100 injured, is another example of how PIRA terrorised the supposedly 'safe' areas and sought to intimidate civilians and stop money flowing into the Ulster economy. The following are examples of how dangerous the centre of Belfast was; it is by no means an exhaustive list.

Later that same month – after the Abercorn atrocity – the IRA exploded a car bomb packed with explosives (thought to be over 200 lbs) in Donegal Street and killed two policemen, four civilians and an off-duty UDR soldier. On 20 March, Private Samuel Trainor (40) was killed alongside RUC officers Ernest McAllister (38), Bernard O'Neill (36) and the following civilians: Sydney Bell (65), Ernest Dougan (40), James Macklin (27) and Henry Millar (79). Mr Millar died a fortnight later of his injuries. Private Trainor was off duty at the time and was employed as a council refuse collector; he was killed whilst working alongside his work colleagues, the aforementioned Ernest Dougan and James Macklin.

On 13 March 1974, Gunner David Farrington of the Royal Artillery was manning security gates with three comrades at Chapel Lane in Belfast city centre. IRA gunmen, one of whom was using a World War II German submachine gun, opened fire on the four soldiers.

Three were hit and Gunner Farrington (23) from Essex was killed having been hit four times. Eyewitnesses, including civilians, observed that the gunmen had been hiding in the doorway of St Mary's Church across from Chapel Lane. *Lost Lives* quoted a Catholic Bishop, outraged that a Catholic church had been used as cover in the murder: 'Those responsible for coupling murder with sacrilege seem to be emphasising their contempt and defiance of all that Christianity stands for.'

On 3 March 1978, Norma Spence, a civilian searcher employed by the RUC and Trooper James Nowasad of the Royal Tank Regiment were both shot dead by IRA gunmen in Lower Donegall Street. (Civilian searchers were auxiliaries who wore a semi-police uniform and were attached to Army and RUC units to help search civvies at checkpoints. They were particularly useful if it was a woman who was to be searched as there were not always female Red Caps, RMP, or WRACS, Womens Royal Army Corps, available.) Norma Spence (25) and Trooper Nowasad (21) were working in the city centre during a Rag Day event from Queens University. The soldier, a married man from Fifeshire, was shot dead by gunmen in masks, masquerading as students; the same men then chased Miss Spence who was unarmed and shot her down in cowardly fashion. Another civilian searcher, Brian Russell (31) and a father of one, was shot by an IRA sniper in Waterloo Place, Londonderry, whilst working alongside the Military Police. He died of the wound shortly afterwards. The IRA later issued a 'statement of regret' claiming that Russell was not the intended victim. Like so many of their pious – and hollow - statements, it meant little to the families of the 'accidental' victims.

On 24 February 1988, two UDR soldiers, Private James Cummings (22) and Private Frederick Starrett (also 22) were part of a patrol of UDR soldiers closing security gates in Belfast city centre. A massive booby trap had been left by the IRA behind hoardings at Castle Court Shopping Centre. Both soldiers were killed instantly by the bomb, which devastated the Centre.

BELFAST CITY CENTRE: AFTER THE UDR KILLINGS

Stevie, UDR Soldier

My recollection of the attack on the security gate patrol – I had left the 'firm' several years before – was that the Rover had routinely stopped in the same position, at the same time, to carry out this task. Clearly, tragically, this had not gone unnoticed. By 1988 the ratio of the number of attempts to kill related to the number of resulting dead/wounded had decreased enormously – PIRA had learned from the past. What we had learned in the '70s had sometimes to be re-learned ten or fifteen years later. This in no way is a criticism of those who died, but a sad fact of life. This comment is perhaps dispassionate; during my time, it had become habit to analyse every incident to learn whatever could be gleaned, to examine it closely, as what you learnt from the experience of others might help you, or even save your life. By the '80s the opposition did not give too many second chances.

The deaths of Norma Spence and Trooper Nowasad will always bear a particular resonance for me; I arrived back on the ferry from Liverpool from some R&R the day after the killings. I had not heard of the incident, as on the mainland, Ulster and its daily carnage had begun to lose its news-worthiness. Walking from the ferry terminal down to Oxford Street bus station, I saw two stripped-down half-tonner Land Rovers pass by at high speed. The crews had their weapons in the 'ready/aim' position; even for Belfast a very aggressive attitude. I felt immediately that something terrible had occurred, something out of the ordinary even by our standards.

> As the bus passed through the city centre I noticed more Rovers and their crews at every set of traffic lights, in addition to the segment gate teams, and more mobile patrols, bearing an almost tangible aura of menace – 'we're ready to kill, without hesitation.' There was a clear atmosphere of tension that only faded as we left town.
>
> It was only when I returned to the Battalion that I got the full story – of the group of students, dressed in various costumes; of the soldier and the civilian, probably enjoying the spectacle as a break in the monotony; the two gunmen, cynically using the students as cover, shooting the soldier then chasing Ms Spence down the street and shooting her at close range in a doorway. Not assassination, not an act of revolution, not an act of war – just butchery, plain and simple. Sometimes an active, imaginative mind can be a curse; I can see too many pictures.

I would like to add a poignant postscript to this excellent piece of writing by the UDR man, a man I am honoured to call my friend. An eyewitness noted that Trooper Nowasad was looking at the IRA gunman who was in fancy dress and actually smiled at him just seconds before he was shot. It is said that many of the IRA men who killed felt able to assuage their guilt by going to see a Catholic priest and confessing.

Certain Catholic priests encouraged their followers to believe that killing an 'oppressor' could be seen as fighting for a 'free' Ireland. This could mean their Protestant neighbour. A Protestant terrorist was handed no such justification; they, if they told any of their clergy or close family, would usually be encouraged to confess to the authorities. They often became seriously mentally disturbed and either committed suicide, or turned fully to religion and became 'born again' Christians; after a time in prison a Republican terrorist too of course could go the same way, becoming 'born-again'.

If indeed the Catholic priests were duty and spiritually bound never to reveal these confessions, were they also guilty, at least complicit in these crimes, after the event? Further comment from me here would be superfluous.

Whilst the Loyalist killers could be every bit as vicious as the Republican killers they were less likely to gain support within their immediate areas, unlike the Republicans, who could enjoy forced or voluntary support in many areas both urban and rural. This meant little gangs within the various Loyalist areas were continually feuding for superiority; the various groups on the other side of the sectarian divide had this too but it was usually short and sharp. The many Loyalist groups often based their qualifications to be 'top dog' on the number of 'taigs' they had managed kill. PIRA, for example, was more subtle; it knew that it could gain support from killing more selectively. It was also the case that many brave people, Catholic and Protestant, risked their lives and the lives of their families to inform on terrorists within their communities.

OPERA HOUSE BOMB

Gavin, RCT, Attached: Army Bomb Disposal (EOD)

> On Thursday 20 May 1993, I was suddenly awoken from a deep sleep by the tannoy in the room crackling into life. The Young Scots guy who had been on duty all night was shouting: 'Bobcat to Ops; Bobcat to Ops,' and sounding a school bell. That was our signal that there was a ticking bomb somewhere, ticking down to detonation; serious risk to life and property. Without even having the time to wipe the sleep from my eyes, I was dressed and running to the

ops room where the rest of the team had congregated. We collected our weapons and started to sprint to the wagons.

We screamed out of Girdwood Barracks with 'blues and twos' on, and headed towards Belfast down the Crumlin Road past the Jail and down past Carlisle Circus, affectionately known as the '25-metre range' by the troops. Suddenly got an ATO request from Lisburn to go straight to Musgrave Park police station in Belfast and await further information. As we arrived there, we had to do a quick u-turn out of the gates having been tasked to set up an ICP near to the Europa Hotel. For some unknown reason, the blue lights on the front wagon failed and the sirens failed on mine. Don't know if that was a forewarning of bad things to come. We both raced to the scene as quickly as we could, going up and down kerbs and on the footpaths because it was the morning rush hour in Belfast. There was no way we were going to slow down as we knew there was a bomb somewhere.

We quickly set up our ICP and a young policeman came forward to tell us that a 'proxy bomb' had been parked beside the Opera House in Glengall Street. We soon had the wheelbarrow off the back of the truck, had it 'detted' up and sent on its way towards the suspect vehicle. [See page 299.] It was only when the wheelbarrow got to the junction that the boss and his number two saw on the monitors in the back of the truck that it was a skip lorry we were dealing with. A Few expletives followed, but there was no time for a change of plans and the wheelbarrow was about to reach the truck. When it did, a small controlled explosion was carried out to break the window of the cab so the wheelbarrow could place a small amount of explosives inside the cab, which was then detonated. This was to ensure that any wires going to the bomb from a timer unit were severed. The view from the monitors had suggested we had done it right as there was nothing really left of the cab.

The Boss was going to grab his kit and go and search the cab and area for parts of the bomb and to see if it was indeed a bomb as it was known that the IRA would have days called 'D-Days' or disruption days. This was when a lot of false bomb calls were made and a few hijacked cars would be left over Belfast to create as much mayhem as they possible. Monday mornings and Friday afternoon rush hours were typical times for this to happen. As he was eager to see what had been done and was about to leave the ICP, the number two grabbed his arm and told him not to, and that they had to have a 20-minute soak time before the next stage could happen. I have no doubt that this decision saved his life.

About three minutes into the soak time, there was a sudden flash, an ear piercing explosion and the sound of breaking glass. We looked at each other in bewilderment behind the truck. It was suddenly all quiet; no sound of traffic; nothing, just complete quiet. Then we heard a policeman behind us shouting: 'Over here,' and as we turned, we saw a young policewoman lying on the floor; unconscious. We then looked up towards the Dublin Road and saw two policemen lying in the street. There was suddenly the wail of sirens and people shouting and screaming; everything seemed to become 'normal' again apart from the broken glass and shrapnel everywhere.

We had to go and search the rubble of what was the Opera House for the remains of what turned out to be a skip lorry which had an 800-lb bomb in the actual skip; whatever we had done, there was no way we could have stopped it from exploding. As we turned the corner into Glengall Street, what greeted us was a scene more like something from Beirut than Belfast. The damage to the Opera House was such that they didn't know if they were going to pull it down or not. We found a small part of our wheelbarrow and the front of the engine block of the truck; that's all that was left of it.

There had been three RUC casualties and three civilians injured in this bombing. The RUC were still evacuating the area when the bomb exploded.

'RETIRING' A GUNMAN AND OTHER BELFAST MEMORIES

Mick 'Benny' Hill, Royal Anglian Regiment

After 35 long years, I have a kaleidoscope of memories; some funny, some annoying, and some scary ones lurk in the back of my mind waiting for something to shake them loose.

On night in the Lower Falls, a noisy gun-battle was going on, when someone opened up on the blokes on the ground. He was on one of the Divis Flats links, in a good position to fire on troops on the ground between the Divis and the Village area. He must have been an apprentice, because although he was in a good fire position, he was the only firer in probably the whole of Belfast using green tracer. Not a good career move, as we used to say. I think he probably got a 'floral retirement' present that night.

Another day I was searching a derelict building when I overbalanced on the rubble, and put my foot down heavily on an up-turned nail. My size and weight ensured that I had a plank of wood firmly nailed to my foot. The most helpful comment I got from the Toms was: ' Not really a good time to go skiing.' A couple of minutes muffled laughter followed, and then the plank was removed. The ability of the Tom to see the funny side of anything never fails to impress.

On Bloody Friday I had just returned to Hastings Street with my section when I was met by the Adjutant, Capt. G, and given a nominal roll. I was then ordered to go around Recce Platoon and tick off the names of soldiers I had actually seen. It was stressed that I had to see

Above and right: An IRA car blown up with an anti tank weapon. *(David Mitchell)*

and talk to them before I could tick them off. We found out later that the soldiers killed at Oxford Street bus station had not been positively identified, and there was some uncertainty as to how many were there; a nominal roll check was a quick way to find out.

Mick refers here to the events of 21 July 1972, when the IRA brought massive terror and panic to the centre of Belfast as they stepped up their 'economic war' against the British. They detonated a total of 22 bombs which they had planted all over the central part of the city; at the business and commercial heart. Nine people, including two soldiers, were killed and a further 130 civilians injured. The IRA have always claimed that warnings were given via the local media to the security forces before the bombs exploded. Over the course of 70 bloody minutes, the car bombs exploded on an almost regular basis with panicked civilians literally running from blast to blast. IRA leader Sean MacStiofain later claimed that they had given warnings for the bombs but these were deliberately disregarded by the British. The RUC, with inadequate time, were only effectively able to clear a relatively small number of areas before the bombs went off.

The two soldiers killed were Driver Stephen Cooper (19) of the RCT, from Leicester and Sergeant Phillip Price (27) a Glamorgan man from the Welsh Guards. The two men were killed instantly as they were standing by one of the car bombs.

BLOODY FRIDAY

Steve Norman, 3 Royal Anglians

The day started off with a lot of tension in the air, as only a few days earlier we had lost two men from our battalion to snipers and the Provisional IRA had called off their ceasefire after talks had broken down.

We were stationed in Albert Street Mill and this state of high alert meant that when my platoon were on our stand-by day, we had to be in full combat kit, including flak jackets and have our SLRs with us at all times, in case of being turned out. We were dozing on our beds, completely knackered, having nearly come to the end of our punishing four-month tour. Suddenly, an almighty bang shook the Mill and the windows shook and rattled and our room was covered in dust. No-one said a word except one bloke who shouted: 'Shit; that was close!'

We didn't need orders and we ran down the stairs like rabbits to get to the PIGs and, just as we reached them, another bang boomed across the city followed by the wailing of sirens from all directions. We just piled in and headed out the main gate, to God knows where! Eventually we de-bussed at the bus station, not far from the Mill, among scenes of absolute chaos and devastation. A bomb had gone off and people were panicking and running in all directions; thick black smoke and debris were everywhere. Somewhere in the distance, a woman was screaming at the top of her voice: 'Oh my God! Oh my God; I'm hurt; someone help me.'

Just then, another bomb went off and birds were flying around just as panic-stricken as the humans, not knowing what to do. By this time I was crouching down in a gateway waiting for orders and still the sound of bombs continued to echo across Belfast; it seemed like Armageddon had arrived! Just then, I came across a young mum with her little boy; they were both terrified and crying. She looked at me and asked in a terrified voice: 'Soldier, soldier, where shall I go?' I felt absolutely bloody useless as I had no more idea then her where the next bomb would go off. I just said: 'Stay with me,' as it was all I could think of. I shoved them behind me in the gateway and just waited.

As I began to get my bearings I looked across the road and in the distance I saw what had only a few moments ago been a human being, now completely unrecognisable, male or female, young or old? Only God could tell. I'm not afraid to say it, but the tears came into my eyes; a mixture of boiling anger and pity. I just thought what kind of sub human could do this to another human being just to further their own political ends? The bombs continued to go off all over Belfast; this was terrorism on a scale that no one could have expected.

The next few hours went in a blur for me, but I could not get the sight of that poor person out of my head and to this day I still do not know who it was. Eventually we returned to Albert Street Mill, just in time to see the late news on TV, which informed us of the extent of the bombings and who was responsible for it. In that news report was footage of a fireman shovelling up body parts into a plastic bag. That image and the victim I had seen earlier remain with me to this day and will never go away; suppose it's a piece of mental shrapnel that most squaddies have of some sort and it's something we learn to live with.

God may forgive those bombers but I never will.

SUICIDE AT THE GRAND CENTRAL AND THE UNLUCKY BRICK

Brian Roberts, Royal Army Medical Corps

In 1977 I was working in the Medical Centre at the Grand Central Hotel in Belfast, covering the ATO teams and the Royal Engineers. Some time during the day of 8 August, we heard the bang of a weapon being fired very close by, but none of the sentries had seen where it came from or fired any rounds off. We were left wondering where it had come from and then there was a shout from the third floor that someone had been shot inside the building. All of a sudden, the loudspeakers blared out a call for a medical team to report immediately to the fifth floor.

I was the first on the scene as I had already been heading up the stairs and I was directed towards the toilets. As I entered, I found a young lad with a gunshot wound to the face and head. For reasons of his own, he had taken his SLR into the toilets and put the barrel in his mouth and pulled the trigger; the round was never found as it had gone up and out of the roof. We found out later that he had been punished for a minor misdemeanour and wrongly informed that he would lose his chance of a commission after we got back to Germany as a result. He had a degree in engineering science and was being fast-tracked for promotion. Tragically, this had preyed on his mind as we found out from the goodbye letter he had written to his parents.

On that day, a young 21-year-old from Edinburgh took his own life; in the ROH his death will be recorded as being by 'violent or unnatural causes'. The author has identified this young soldier but his name will not be revealed here so as to not re-open the wounds suffered by his loved ones. During the course of research, the author has identified the names of at least 43 soldiers who chose suicide as the balance of their minds was disturbed by the trauma of life as a member of the security forces in Northern Ireland. I strongly suspect that there are more.

Not long after this, I was called to a road traffic accident (RTA) at the gates as one of the Royal Engineers' Land Rovers had skidded on the wet cobbles and crashed into a wall. I got there to find that the brick commander – who lived in the same block of flats as me back in Germany – had suffered 23 fractures to his, foot, ankle and lower leg and was in a bad way. He was taken to Musgrave Park Hospital. The next day, after an explosion at the Post Office sorting department, I was called out with both medical teams. One of the lads we treated – a neighbour and a boxing champion - had lost four fingers in the explosion and I realised that it was the 2IC of the same brick as the previous day. Just two days later, I was called out to a shooting on the east gates where a young lad had been shot whilst on a foot patrol. You guessed it; he was the third member of the same brick to be injured! The fourth and so far, uninjured, member was sent out of Northern Ireland that very night; he was worried – for good reason – that he might be next.

That tour was a very busy one from a medical point of view as we had a lot of IED incidents and it was also the marching season with all the trouble that brings. I am pleased to report that we had no further serious injuries after that.

SANGARS AND STREETS

Colin 'Jim' Bowie, Royal Artillery

I started my first tour as the Troop Commander's driver, and we were based in the grand Central Hotel in Belfast City Centre. Interestingly, it turned out that my uncle was there as a chef before the war. The market was at the rear of the Hotel behind the Post Office. It wasn't a nice place to be, mind you, the rest wasn't very pleasant either.

We used to go out to visit the sections on the ground; in the fixed OPs or the sangars on the street corners. For some reason I was often left guarding the Rover outside whilst the OC went in to the telephone exchange to visit the lads at the top. For those of you who don't know it, the Republican Markets area was just over the square. I used to hate being in the sangars, as you never knew what was going to happen, and you could be there for up to four hours, usually on a street corner. Tin and sandbags, quite often smelly, day and night, and usually in a sectarian interface. You were never sure as to what would come first, your relief, a local with a cup of tea, or a bullet or bomb.

It depended where you went on foot patrol as to how alert you were. We went from the Catholic Markets to the affluent Ormeau Road and University areas. Usually the University area was by mobile. In general the Protestants were friendly and the Catholics were not, surprising as they asked for us to be there in the first place. I know I shouldn't say this, but you just knew when you had changed areas. The Protestant areas were clean and tidy, but the Catholics ones never were. Lavinia Street, off the Ormeau Road, opposite the Donegal Pass area apparently was once a very nice street but not when I was there. I remember going past one evening, and a car backfired. For some reason I knew what it was, but I was the only one standing, the rest had disappeared! We would patrol the Markets, not a very nice place, not nice people, and be followed by youths on horseback. You would find dead greyhounds in bags on dustbins, outside the vets.

The base we used there was the old Mission Hall. We lived there for a week, and then eventually had a patrol base in the old gas works and this enabled patrols to cover the others. One patrol was shot at from the 'Mothers Pride' bakery, but we weren't allowed to search the place properly: politics. We were held back on the first tour, just to play nursemaid for the Orangemen to parade through Belfast, annoying the Republicans.

Continuing on that tragic thread of suicide, or apparent suicide, the following contributor gives an insight into the largely unseen world of the Army's dedicated team of medics and nurses and surgeons, part of whose job was to deal with this terrible phenomenon.

THE PRICE OF A LIFE

Stuart Wilson, RAMC

It had been quiet through the week until Friday 31 May, 1991, when a UDR soldier had put his own gun under his chin after he had filled his mouth full of water. The bullet passing through the water caused an explosion inside his head and spread his head all over the room he was sat in. Death was instantaneous. Saturday night another UDR soldier had shot himself in his head while sat in his car with two other soldiers in Ballykinler, highlighting the incredible pressures these soldiers were under.

It is understood that the 'other' UDR soldier who shall only be described as 'Richard' was shot under highly debatable and controversial circumstances whilst sitting in a parked car. To spare further pain to the soldier's family and because nothing can be substantiated, I can say no more than that there is much controversy about this incident.

Then, as they say, these things come in threes, and we were informed that a young Gunner had also tried to kill himself in the Bessbrook area. The difference this time was that the bullet entered the front right hand lobe of his brain and did not kill him. He was being brought from Ballykinler to us by emergency helicopter.

Both the driver and I sprinted out the door to the large white ambulance parked outside, and then we heard the sound of the chopper. I was out of the ambulance before it had completely stopped; the noise of the engine of the chopper blocked out nearly everything, and the down draft from the blades hit me as I rounded the rear of the ambulance. Right in front of me was a figure with his back to me: he was wearing black army issue boots, combat trousers complete with a Royal Army Medical Corps stable belt and a green issue shirt with a crown on each shoulder. I recognised the Major as the RMO from Bessbrook as he had been up a couple of times since arriving in Province. He turned towards me and he threw this body at me, he was shouting something, which over the noise of the chopper I could not hear. I caught this body under the arms, he was face down and his head fell against the right side of my chest and his arms flopped beside my legs. The top of his head was only inches from my face, the back top left of his head started to open like a bud opening to reveal a flower. I pulled the stretcher out and I was moving back when, out of the darkness behind the driver stepped a soldier in combats with his rifle held up over his chest webbing. The visor on his helmet had been raised; he was one of the HLS guard. He took a step forward and stared, and muttered: 'Oh, God.'

The casualty was lying face down; his arms were hanging over the side of the stretcher like a rag doll and the blood poured over the black leather. It took about another two or three seconds before the stretcher was inside the ambulance. The back doors slammed shut and the wheels of the ambulance were spinning in the mud; the wheels caught the tarmac and the ambulance shot forward and both myself and the medical officer were thrown rearwards, the stretcher had not been attached inside the back of the ambulance yet and swung across and hit us. The medical officer was kneeling beside the casualty's upper torso, and he was very panicked; he was shouting at the body lying beside us. There was nothing from him, and it was then I noticed his young face, his mouth was open showing his teeth, his eyes were closed and his hair was soaked with blood which was sticking to his face as if he was sweating profusely. His head was lying on his right side, the hole was right at the top of his head and it was nearly four inches across. Strands of his brain tissue lay over the ragged edges of the skull, which stuck up in the air; a large field dressing which at one stage had mostly covered the hole had fallen onto the floor of the vehicle. The Medical Officer picked this up and replaced it over the hole. The dressing was thick and heavy with the blood that it contained, the MO was still constantly shouting at him and getting little or no response. Looking at his young face I could not imagine him to be more than twenty years old. It took about thirty seconds to get back to the hospital building but it seemed to take a lot longer.

Once there, we got a theatre trolley and the casualty was lifted up onto it; he was still lying face down with his head pointing towards the wall and blood pouring all over the place. The duty theatre sister was stood at the far side of him and she had already started to cut his clothes off so after liberating a pair of large scissors off one of the techs I helped her with this. I could not really say how I felt; it was strange, as I had been in similar situations before. I felt nothing; this wasn't the time or the place to worry about how we felt; top priority was to save his life.

The Orderly Medical Officer (OMO) was standing beside me and was working around the casualty's head with the rest of the crash team running around like blue arsed flies. The OMO had managed to get the lad's eyes open; he was still alive, his mouth was moving, opening and closing but nothing came out. We could see that the entrance wound was just below his right eye on his cheekbone. It was about an inch across and most of his right cheek resembled a deflated balloon, as his eyes moved so did the top ridge of the entrance wound. He turned his head slightly and stared at me; I had eye to eye contact with him. 'Help me, help me; please help me.' It was no more than a whisper, but this was a whisper which I will never forget. The voice was English, but the whisper didn't hide the pain and the look on his face didn't hide the fear. Here was a boy who knew that he was going to die and he was scared; he was very scared. For a second my mind blanked out all other sights and sounds except the sound of his voice and the look on his begging face, tunnel vision.

The anesthetist also heard him and started talking to him and he started answering to those who were trying to save his life. I turned and lifted the plastic bag into which we had just finished placing all his clothes and the contents of his pockets. I walked out the doors and remembered what an instructor had once advised me: 'Don't get emotionally attached to casualties.'

I went straight into the male changing room and undressed. I could feel the sickness of the drying blood on my skin; it felt like I had honey or syrup poured over me. Afterwards I went back to where the surgeon was and he was on the phone; presumably to the ICU at the RVH [Royal Victoria Hospital]. 'Yes, as I was saying; I have a nineteen-year-old soldier with a high velocity gunshot wound to his head.' He went on to describe which parts of his brain the round had passed through. He paused, as he did so he slightly lowered his head and from underneath his glasses I thought that I could see a small red line appearing around his eyelids. 'Yes, I agree bu-…' He was not being allowed a word in edgeways. A minute passed, he bit his bottom lip, thanked whoever he was talking to and said his farewells. The surgeon was still sitting, pondering what he had just heard for a few seconds, and then he spoke: 'They said: let him die!'

We both looked at each other; our faces shocked at what we had just heard. 'They do not want to put a soldier into their ICU who will be dead by morning when they can put a civilian patient in instead.' I finished my mug of tea in one mouthful and followed him back into resus [resuscitation]. 'We will take him into theatre here,' he announced loud enough for everyone to hear. Nobody said anything; everyone paused slightly, looked at each other and then fully returned to the jobs which they were at. It was only a short time later that we could hear the wheels of the trolley trundling off towards the new theatre complex at the far end of what used to be ward one but was now the admin corridor and theatres.

The admin officer had come in early, and after a visit to his office he approached reception. 'Right; his mother and father have arrived in the Province and will be here shortly; direct them to my office, the Red Cross Lady is with them.' I walked towards the admin officer's office but I was stopped by what I heard from up the corridor. The junior surgeon and a nurse were talking. 'Time of death, put down as 07:30hrs; I will tell the AO.' The nurse nodded and turned and pushed past the closed doors into resus.

Another life lost. A boy, a fucking boy, typical of the army; sends a boy to do a man's job. Shortly afterwards, the front door opened. The Red Cross lady walked in followed by a man and a woman; both looked to be in their late fifties. I motioned with my head towards the corridor where the admin officer was waiting. I watched as they passed, I felt my heart sinking, my eyes closed briefly, I felt a cold chill pass over me.

Afterwards, I walked up to the accommodation with my head slightly bowed; I didn't speak to anyone. One of the gate guards wished me a good morning and it passed over me like the wind. I trotted up the stairs and lay down on the bed; I knew that I would be awake for some time to come.

During the course of 1991, 25 members of the Army or former members were killed in, or as a result of, the Troubles. The author is aware of the identity of the young soldier who died in this incident. Whatever the cause of his death, he was one of 25 men who died in the ongoing quest for peace in the troubled Province during the 22nd year of deployment.

I have mentioned several times the sanitised term 'death by violent or unnatural causes' when dealing with the painful subject of suicide. During the course of writing, I have felt compelled to use this 'sanitised' expression, partly because of my desire to protect the feelings of the loved ones of such a soldier and partly because I have been instructed to do so by the MOD. I will always accept the MOD's ruling because they can slap a 'D' notice on me whenever they wish and because I signed the Official Secrets Act and will comply with its conditions.

The following account relates to the death of a well respected soldier in a well established traditional county regiment and I use it in the full knowledge of who the soldier was and what regiment he belonged to. Please God that, through my words, his family do not recognise him and nor will I ever reveal his name. However, I will add my profound thanks to the following contributor for what he did to preserve the memory and integrity of a man who had reached the end of his tether.

RSM John Wood, SIB, Northern Ireland

I may be able to add a bit of detail; I think he was just as much a victim of NI as was any soldier shot or blown up there. I was the RSM of the SIB NI. I was called to Henry Taggart Memorial Hall, a base on the Ballymurphy Estate. He was in a locked lavatory cubicle and had a gunshot wound to the head. A Browning 9mm was on the floor between his feet as he was seated on the lavatory bowl but with his trousers not lowered. He had been in a staff post and his posting to the 'Murph was his first on return to regimental duties. He had spent the previous ten days or so taking over the area from a RA unit. They had kept the whole area of operations under a very tight hold using very rigorous policies not necessarily recommended in any manual.

The Battery Commander of the RA unit had commented that the officer was worried about how he would fare. His regiment was due to go live, in charge of the area on 26 October. He had drawn his weapon about 10:00 but was still in the building at 12:20 when he was seen by his driver going into the lavatory area. A shot was heard soon after. Troops going into the room saw blood coming from under a door. One climbed up and saw that the officer was – he assumed – dead. I called a pathologist to the scene and he confirmed that death would have been instantaneous. A post mortem established that the muzzle of the pistol was in contact with the officer's head when it was fired; a typical finding in suicides.

His CO confirmed to me that the officer was fresh back in the Regiment and had been showing nerves at his responsibilities. He had a family; a wife and couple of young kids. There would be no insurance provision in the event of suicide. After I had been informed of that, I spoke with the Coroner. He arranged that his clerk select a jury of RUC pensioners, including three or four former 'B' Specials. The pathologist gave his evidence, and he did not mention significance of skin contact wound and was not questioned on this. I arranged to take three or four 9mm Brownings into Court when I gave my evidence and we let the jury 'play' with these. I was asked if there were many instances of accidental discharge and was able to confirm that there were, generally from not checking that the weapon was properly safe. I showed the jury how this could happen.

They came back with an 'Open Verdict' and the insurance was paid out. No dishonour to the name of the officer concerned and his family were spared financial problems which would have only added to their emotional grief. I realise this account might not be deemed suitable for publication but you might find some way to attribute his death to the emergency rather than just 'violent or unnatural causes'.

'DAYS, NOT YEARS': ARDOYNE 1976

Colin 'Jim' Bowie, Royal Artillery

Int told us that there were no rifles in the Ardoyne, but one was found in a derelict house by the main road. I think Gerry Adams was on a building site next to Flax Street Mill, which was our base, and he was warned that if a shot was fired, the second round fired was his.

We were returning from foot patrol in the Old Ardoyne when there was the sound of a bomb going off. We ran towards the sound, and I was out in front, and stood in the road just up from the Mill gate and saw a VW had stopped. I shouted: 'We've got one,' and found myself surrounded by locals and no patrol in sight! A pipe bomb was under the driver's seat and had gone off when the car went over speed bumps.

We used to have to search the waterway under the Mill, as they had tried to float a bomb down the stream once. Happily, it only got as far as the grille, under their own drinking den! That was not a very nice tour at all, and one of the more onerous tasks was the 'school patrol'. We had to stand on a corner making sure the two different lots of school kids stayed apart. We were told from the start that no mobile patrols were to enter the Ardoyne; foot patrols only.

I was on guard duty, we were upstairs in the rest room when we heard a lot of shots; I got everyone downstairs before the Provost had reacted, I was sent with the ambulance to the hospital, not knowing what had happened. I found out that contrary to orders, two Land Rovers had been sent to pick up a foot patrol, not sure where from. For some unknown reason an idiot tasked them (sixteen men) into the Ardoyne to investigate an incident. It was up a cul-de-sac, and as they reversed to turn around they were ambushed by gunmen using an M40 machine gun. They didn't stand a chance and it is still unbelievable that there were only two casualties and an SLR stolen but later recovered.

So we lost two men for nothing but a show of total stupidity from those on high. This reinforced my belief, that if we had done it properly at the start it would have lasted days and not years.

The two soldiers to whom John refers were Gunner Anthony Abbot (19) from Manchester, who was killed in the IRA ambush In Oakfield Street in the Ardoyne on 24 October 1976. The young, single soldier died very shortly afterwards in hospital. Gunner Maurice Murphy (26), another Lancashire lad, hailing from Bolton, was badly wounded. Despite the amputation of his leg in order to save him from infection, he died in hospital on 22 November.

It was a bad year for the Gunners, losing a total of five soldiers. On 17 January, Gunner Mark Ashford (19) from Willesden, London was shot whilst manning a checkpoint in Great James

Street in Londonderry. On 13 March, Gunner James Reynolds from Eastbourne was killed in an RTA the day after his 22nd birthday. On 3 July, Gunner William Miller (19) was shot and badly wounded by an IRA sniper at Butcher's Gate in Londonderry. He was rushed to the RVH and his father was flown to his bedside from their home in Lanarkshire; William died of his wounds.

SOME LUCKY ESCAPES

Alex, UDR

It was 21 December 1971 and I was on the fourth floor of Progressive House, the NI Housing Executive HQ in College Square East (see page 56 of the John Chartres/Bert Henshaw/Mike Dewar *Northern Ireland Scrapbook* for a look at it) when, just after lunchtime, the internal PA system advised all staff to move to the rear of the building as there was a bomb scare in King Street. As always, that was the cue for everyone to move to the front windows for a grandstand view. Yes, I know; incredibly stupid, but the Provos' so-called 'commercial campaign' was only just getting up to speed and these events were still a 'novelty', thus the reaction. Gass's Cycle Shop was without doubt the best-stocked bicycle retailer in Ireland, with all the latest kit, multi-speed gear sets, lightweight racing frames, rims, etc, for enthusiasts, but it became the 'freedom fighters' target when they carried in a hold-all, shouted a warning and legged it towards Smithfield. Within minutes the EOD Saracens came growling down College Square North from Durham Street and parked up directly below us.

We watched the ATO (a captain, from memory, but 39 years on, I can't be sure) suit up and, with his No 2, make the long walk 100 yards or so to the shop entrance, deploying a line with which to haul out the device. Both disappeared and wouldn't have been inside for twenty seconds when, without deference to rank, the No 2 charged out the door and and back towards his colleagues. On his heels, and not much slower, came the encumbered ATO. He'd barely reached next door and relative safety when an enormous blast of smoke, flame, glass, aluminium shop front and shattered bicycles roared across the street. I've often wished them continued good luck; hoped both survived to retirement, wondered who they were and what prompted the get-out-of-here-now decision that saved their lives.

It was 9 November 1972, and I had my first lucky escape of far too many. It was mid-morning and the PA announcement wasn't directing us to the rear of the building this time, but ordering: 'Clear the building. This is not a practice drill. Leave immediately via the rear fire escapes.' The gated ramp to the underground car park was only unlocked for arriving and departing NIHE employees. A Provo 'volunteer' had waited until the gate was opened, raced across from Durham Street, stuck a revolver in the unarmed security man's face and ordered him to allow a stolen car to be driven in. The guard raised the alarm when the two heroes ran off, thus the 'leave now' tannoy message. 300-odd staff ended up 200 yards away at the junction of Great Victoria Street and the Grosvenor Road – where the ABC and Odeon cinemas used to be – watching and waiting. Felix arrived on cue, waited half an hour or so and decided to disrupt the thing with an RPG practice round, a generally used method at that pre-wheelbarrow time. Loud Bang! Whoosh! Then a small bang and the flickering glow of flames reflected on the side walls of the ramp. We watched and waited some more as the vehicle continued to burn. 50-50 chance I suppose as to where the detonator was located in relation to the fire that was safely consuming the HME, but the ATO's bomb-disposal luck wasn't in that day. No recrimination though as no-one was hurt, and the damage was 100 per cent the responsibility of the scrotes who made and planted the bomb. The resulting (enormous) bang took every window out of our offices, the Skandia restaurant next door, the Progressive Building Society above it and the Belfast College of Technology across the street. The cascade of glass looked like a waterfall, and I began to think that spectating at these events mightn't really be the cleverest idea. If, hopefully, he's still around enjoying his pension, the ATO will definitely remember it.

The sight that met us next day when we were allowed back into the building was awesome. A steel frame/reinforced concrete construction built in 1967 or '68, it was still structurally intact. On leaving we'd lowered the venetian blinds, but the glass had shredded them, blasting foot-long shards through internal partitions, into desks and drawing boards, protruding like daggers from solid internal walls. Large site layout negatives on the drawing boards were sliced to ribbons and a further sobering thought was that our section had been evacuated via the wrong route, down the fire escape at the rear; directly over the ramp and the car bomb. The metal staircase was buckled and had been torn away from the external wall. Had the bomb detonated either as an 'own goal' when the planters armed it or during the evacuation, there'd have been a massacre. Our personnel department, with about fifteen staff, was on the first floor, directly above the ramp, and its floor slab was driven vertically up into the ceiling, with the room's contents ending up as the 'filling' in a concrete sandwich. Definitely no survivors there and the glass would have done for the rest of us. Today, the horizontal alignment of the front elevation of the building is out by about an inch between the former NIHE section (now the Belfast Weather Office) and the building society, solely due to that explosion.

The third incident occurred on duty, so, as I didn't keep a diary (that still annoys me) the only date reference I have is that it was between April 1974 and March 1976. It was a blast incendiary that our platoon 'discovered' on the window sill of a terraced house in the small hours of the morning. Late the previous evening while we were manning a VCP on the Kings Bridge, along the Stranmillis Embankment, something detonated. Minding the Rover as usual, I'd seen the flash and counted: 'Thousand and one, thousand and tw-....' 'Boooom.' Hmmm, not too close, but not so far away either. Anyway, we continued the mobile; two vehicles as usual with a six-strong foot patrol deployed occasionally. About 03.00 I'd half-registered Liz, our Greenfinch signaller, acknowledging a call, but driving on autopilot with thoughts of packing it in for the night, it was a thump from the vehicle commander, our beloved sergeant, that brought me back to reality along with his 'Alex; for fuck's sake; waken up! (Whatever) Street! Now! Didn't you hear our call sign reporting they'd found a bomb?' Nursing my broken shoulder (felt like it!) I raced the Rover to the scene to find ourselves in charge of getting the family out of their house as well as waking and evacuating the neighbours.

That was sorted by the time the ATO arrived and, as we'd found it, he invited us to stay within the cordon and watch the 1-gallon oil can and attached explosives being dealt with. I'd thought it was one of the 'Holy Land' streets off Stranmillis Embankment/Ormeau Road, but a Belfast newspaper account of an 11 July 1974 incident records: 'A 1½ lb bomb with a five gallon can of petrol attached was discovered on the sill of a house in Sandymount Street, Stranmillis Road. An Army bomb-disposal officer defused the device.' The same article also reports a blast-incendiary demolishing an unoccupied house in Agra Street (just outside our TAOR) on the Annandale Embankment the same night and that would tally with the earlier explosion we'd seen. I definitely recall the house owner telling the ATO that, as a Catholic family in a Protestant area, they'd move out if it was a real device and that under no circumstances were the soldiers to risk their own lives trying to defuse the bomb. The ATO thanked him for his concern and got on with it, rigging up the wheelbarrow, sending it forward with lights and camera and letting us have a look at the B&W TV screen in their vehicle.

My memory is of one of the EOD team taking a scope-fitted .303 Lee-Enfield out of a hardwood case and having a chat with his boss at the TV; the ATO indicating on the close-up picture which wires he wanted cut on the package taped to the can. Everyone had moved further back by the time the marksman took cover across the street and, with the tin illuminated by the wheelbarrow floodlights, fired the first round at it. Bang. Silence; and a neat hole through the front window. ATO and sniper returned to the screen, had another few seconds' discussion, then went back for a second shot. From memory that sorted it, though there may have been a third. At any rate, it was successfully neutralised, with the only damage to the property being the broken glass and two or three rounds embedded in furniture or walls in the house. We never knew what became of the family, but were told it had been a viable blast incendiary with a timer, so we'd probably saved their lives. That one night made my two years in worthwhile.

CONTACT IN GARTREE PLACE

Robert Holland, Royal Highland Fusiliers

On the 9th, Belfast suffered a day of non-stop bombings and shootings. I was on patrol at 1500 hours on Shaw's Road, when someone fired at Glassmullan camp. With weapons cocked we went looking for the gunman, but did not catch sight of him. Later that night while out on foot patrol in Lance Corporal Bobby Jones' brick, Corporal Geordie Gallagher's brick got a 'contact'. We were stopped and hiding in someone's front gardens when Geordie's brick in the next street – Gartree Place – opened fire. As one of the passengers got out of a parked car, Jimmy Morrison saw a weapon (an SMG) under his coat. Jimmy shouted at the guy to stop and put his hands up but the guy took off over some waste ground. The lads fired some shots after him but missed due to the darkness. Meanwhile the car had revved off and was zig-zagging down the street. One of the passengers pointed a pistol out a window and fired a few shots at Geordie's men. This was the sign for our lads to fire back and around twelve shots were pumped into the retreating car. The car kept going and disappeared out of sight. While all this was going on myself and the rest of Bobbie's lot were haring it up to the top of the road to try and cut off the car's retreat, but we didn't make it in time.

The car was found in the early hours of the morning, a couple of streets away in Ramoan Drive. When it was examined, there was blood all over the dashboard and seats. A trail of blood went up to a house then disappeared inside. Although no bodies were found, we at least know that someone was killed and the others wounded because varied blood groups were found and pieces of a human heart were found embedded to the dash. There was also a considerable amount of ammunition and explosives material found. My one regret on that 'contact' was that I would like to have been in Geordie's brick so that I could have got a shot at them. At that time I was the best shot in 'A' Company, and one of the best in the Battalion with an SLR, and I consider that I would have hit the car with more accuracy as it sped away, consequently causing more definite damage and casualties on the Provos.

That day, Belfast was a real battle zone, and we calculated that at least a hundred-plus shots were fired at 1 RHF that day alone. The Recce Section had a 'contact' and fired back. One of the Recce's rounds missed its target and carried on for a distance where it penetrated a pub wall, ricocheted off a mirror and killed a civilian, standing at the bar having a pint. Tough luck on him but we soldiers felt indifferent to it. Some of us had a laugh about it; some of us said:

'Who cares?' Some of us didn't even bother. Ireland can kill your senses of emotion; survive the tour and look out for your mates while doing so, that is the main aim of Northern Ireland; survive and go home!

RPG ATTACK

Robert Hutton, Royal Highland Fusiliers

As I have said, things were quiet until 24 April, three days before my nineteenth birthday. We were back at Glenveagh OP. At 2130 hours a Provo stepped out onto the top end of Lenadoon Avenue and fired an RPG-7 anti-tank projectile at the building. Sitting in the TV room of Glenveagh OP, appreciating the rest and peace of not being on patrol, I enjoyed the relative liberty of not being on duty. Slouched on the couch, which was against the outside wall, I watched TV with some of my comrades – would you believe we were watching 'The World at War' – some sat around stuffing their faces with the ubiquitous 'egg banjos', some were sleeping and the rest stared blankly at the television. As the American plane *Enola Gay* closes in on Hiroshima, the whole building shakes and shudders to the accompaniment of a loud explosion. I immediately hit the deck. 'Shit,' I thought, 'someone is trying to blow us up.' For a split second I froze at the shock of it all, then my brain triggered into instant reaction mode. I scrambled/crawled to my rifle, belt order and flak jacket and threw them on with unsteady fingers. I returned to the TV room ready for action, awaiting orders.

I was not needed for the 'hot pursuit' follow up and was kept indoors. As I waited as back up, my thoughts attempted to recall the incident. When it happened I thought that someone had thrown a bomb at the base of the building. Now I was told it was an RPG warhead. All the thoughts go through your head after a major 'contact' like this: 'Where did he fire from? Why did the OP not see him and fire first? Where did it hit the building? How close to injury or death had I been?' Many, many thoughts fly through your brain, but at the end of the day I'm alive and unhurt, and the rest of the platoon are unscathed.

We were lucky that night, because the Royal Engineers had been putting up mesh fencing all around the block to prevent such things and they had just finished the last portion that day. The point of the mesh was, apart from stopping bricks and nail bombs being thrown against the building, it also in the case of an RPG caused the warhead to detonate on the wire many feet away from the walls. This lessened the damage as only the remains of the warhead carried on through to hit the outside wall, leaving a small hole on impact instead of taking the wall out completely.

When I looked at the building whilst out on patrol the next morning, I calculated that if the fencing hadn't caused the warhead to explode before it hit the brick wall and had been four or six feet higher, it would have hit squarely where I had been sitting. It had in fact hit the junction of the TV room floor and the ceiling of the room below. It would have probably taken out all personnel in the TV room, me included. I would have been a dead man along with three or four of my mates. It was lucky for us the protective fence had been completed. This was the first of a few incidents during my three tours of N. Ireland that I was lucky to survive. Boy, did that explosion ring in my ears.

The rest of the tour went by with only a few more incidents. There were only a couple of small escapades, like a civilian setting off a booby trap intended for us. He wasn't hurt. A car bomb was also detonated; once again no one was hurt. We continued to patrol day and night, keeping the IRA guessing. On foot patrols at night we would search out the street lampposts that still worked in our area, open up the small plate at the base and cut the wiring to extinguish the light. This was done so that they did not illuminate the patrolling soldiers in their beams of light, which made us easier targets as we attempted to blend in with the shadows and background.

On 26 June the Battalion left Belfast. We sailed through the night to arrive in Glasgow the next morning. We then boarded buses and returned to Redford Barracks in Edinburgh. After getting paid I went for a drink with Davy Hind – himself to become a murder victim of the IRA in Crossmaglen in 1977 – then home.

David Hind, who was 23 and came from the Kilmarnock area, was shot and killed by the IRA at Crossmaglen on Sunday 2 January 1977. His four-man brick came under sustained automatic fire and he was killed instantly. A comrade bravely held off the attack by an apparently large number of gunmen; he was later awarded the MM.

AN ELDERLY PROD DOES THE SPOTTING

Lance Corporal Pete Whittall, 1 Staffords

I recall a number of incidents during our month on advance party in the Shankill area. One night I was out on a two-vehicle patrol made up of two four-man bricks. We had been supporting the foot patrols when a call came over the radio to set up an instant VCP on the Shankill Road as there had been a shooting in Woodvale and the suspect vehicle was last seen heading towards Shankill Road. Within no more than five or ten minutes a car swerved into a side road on seeing the VCP and headed north towards the Crumlin Road area. We quickly got into the Land Rovers and went in hot pursuit of them whilst our brick commander radioed into control to tell them what was happening. Luckily we managed to get the registration plate number and do a vehicle check; surprise, surprise it had been stolen in the Ardoyne the day

The notorious flashpoint between Sherbourne and Unity flats. *(Pete Whittall)*

before and guess where we were heading towards? Yes, the notorious nationalist stronghold of the IRA in the Ardoyne. Unfortunately the Crumlin Road was our most northerly demarcation line and so we had to pass on the info to the unit responsible for the Ardoyne; the Royal Marines I think.

On another occasion whilst on foot patrol along the interface between Sherbourne and Unity Flats there was this all too familiar rat-a-tat, tat of an Armalite being fired from Unity flats. We hit the deck as there was very little cover and the brick commander ordered us to scan the upper level of the flats for any evidence of the sniper. Suddenly there was another burst of fire as another ASH foot patrol came to support us. Soon the rapid response section in two PIGs arrived, followed by the RUC and other support troops.

There was a yell from a window above us from Sherbourne Flats: 'The bastard is in the top flat; six from the right. Get the friggin' bastard taig.' We all looked up and there was a middle-aged man directing us to where the gunfire had come from. By now soldiers were saturating Unity Flats and starting to cordon off the rabbit warren of escape routes. After a lengthy stand-off, ASH found the flat and spent ammunition cartridges but no gunman. It was a close call, which luckily resulted in no injuries. Some days later, as part of a joint RUC/Army covert operation, both the weapon and the IRA gunman were apprehended; nice one guys, another weapon off the street.

SHANKILL: BOMBS? WHAT BOMBS?

Lance Bombardier John Swaine, Royal Artillery

3 June 1976 and on the Shankill Road and North Street Belfast; just like our '74 tour; Belfast city centre was just like Beirut when it came to car-bombs and other devices. The sound of blasts was just about the order of the day on any given day.

It was just a toss-up as to which location was to be next and the impact of what a 200lb car or van bomb can do to an enclosed area is unreal; it's just total carnage. On this tour we had five or six in one day, which left most of the city centre blitzed; the whole area was up to the roof tops in the foam that ATO used. Luckily no deaths. Things were not so lucky in Castle Street though. It leads up towards Divis Street, where a car bomb went off without warning which almost killed two RUC officers. However, not long afterwards a small radio device was left in Castle Street on a bookie's window ledge for an intended Army foot-patrol but was picked up by an old tramp. He just turned it on and 'boom'. Not much was found of him.

My brick – call sign '22 Echo' – was on foot-patrol round the Smithfield Markets when a bomb warning came over the Pye-Set at a location in North Street with the junction of Shankill Road. We had about two minutes legging it; 'Fuck me,' I said to the lads; 'this is going to be tricky.' The whole of North Street, right up to the Shankill Road junction was as busy as fuck with shoppers! We located the target shop which turned out to be a massive paint store, some four to five storeys high. The owners were outside telling us quickly that hooded men with large hold-alls had planted them and run. No time before detonation had been given; that's when the terror hits you!

By this time, other patrols on the ground had moved in to assist including our Battery Commander who was in a mobile. No time was wasted as we began to clear the whole area, which turned out to be a fucking nightmare, because although many moved away quickly, lots refused, saying it was just another hoax. Time and time again, we all ran from building to

Shankill Road, looking towards Woodvale on an unusually quiet day, 1976. *(Pete Whittall)*

building, shop to shop, screaming get out. It's a day which lives with me forever now as we passed time and time again near the target shop, not knowing if it was to go boom at that very moment! After what seemed like hours but was over in about fifteen minutes we had cleared the whole area and by this time ATO had been tasked. No sooner had ATO arrived, than the biggest of fucking booms sent my ears rumbling with the high pitched sound of the explosion as the bombs went off. We watched from the location as you see us in the picture [see page 7] as the whole shop blew out from about two storeys up, sending most of the building over the other side of the road and smashing into the adjacent shops. An intense fire started straight away with the mass of paint inside and it was totally destroyed within 30 minutes.

Our job was done well that day and luckily no one was killed but the calm of the locals always stuck in my mind as if they had not a care in the world. The picture just tells it all; look at the small kid of about four years, leaning on the lamp-post with his sister and Dad. They were only 75 yards away from the blast; God knows what his father was thinking! If the kid who's about 36 years old now, could see this pic, he would bollock his Dad for getting them all so near to death. But this was Belfast in '76; what you saw was what you got!

The author is pleased to report how easy it was, over the course of interviewing this former 'Drop Short', to become friends with John Swaine, a fellow 'Yorkie'. He was asked by a documentary maker: 'Were you ever scared?' John looked at the questioner and replied, 'You show me someone who wasn't scared on service in Northern Ireland. Yes, I was scared, especially on patrols with all the bombs and shots being fired. Whether you were in Belfast or Londonderry or in the border country, you were always scared.' May I absolutely identify myself with John's eloquent words.

24 NOVEMBER 1983, WEST BELFAST

Private Andrew Bull, Royal Regiment of Wales

We were the primary brick (call sign Lima); the patrol consisted of me, Lieutenant Brayshaw and Sergeant Rummage, who was attached from Int Section; also on with us were Private Pember and two RUC officers. As we made our way down to the junction from the Whiterock estate we turned left onto the Falls Road.

I was the second man in relation to the formation of the patrol, and on the immediate left as we turned into the Falls Road. It was really busy, being late evening and rush hour traffic, everyone having finished and wanting to get home. As I made my way along the road, I passed a pub on my left known as the Rock Bar; up ahead of me and on the opposite side of the road I could see Lt Brayshaw and just in front of him the two RUC officers. I was carrying a special piece of equipment, which to the everyday person looked like a normal military Klansman radio. It gave this impression because I was wearing a headset that had a mouthpiece very similar to the ones you saw in Thunderbirds. This particular piece of equipment would over-ride and cut out the signal being emitted from a remote control device used by the IRA in the detonation of their bombs.

Unfortunately for me and everyone else injured that day, the IRA chose instead a command wire to detonate their bomb. Had the bomb been remote controlled I would have heard a series of intermittent high pitched tones in my head set. I often wonder, now and then, had the bomb been detonated by remote control, would the equipment have done its job that day? As the patrol continued, the traffic was a constant stream of noise and hustle and bustle as it flowed into the city centre of Belfast. Walking towards me was a young woman and as we passed one another I wished her a good evening.

I can't remember if she answered me or not because no sooner had we passed one another there was a tremendous explosion. I never heard the bang or if I did my brain couldn't comprehend what had happened; my only recollection of that day was the terrible high-pitched, screaming, buzzing sounds in my ears. It was like a giant switch had been thrown, because all the sounds from the immediate traffic and the normal everyday sounds of a busy city environment had disappeared. I can only describe it as a sea of silence apart from the high pitched buzzing in my ear drums. To my left was a wall that ran for at least a thousand yards or more into the city and it was made of the old dressed stone that was quite thick. It was behind this very wall that the bomb had been placed; it was a large welder's acetylene bottle which had been packed inside with nails, nuts and bolts, and about six pounds of Semtex plastic explosive. As I was saying, all I could remember was this horrendous high pitched buzzing that was in my ear drums and it was pissing me off big time. It also felt like there was a great weight on my chest and I couldn't fill my lungs with air. It was a feeling that I can only describe as drowning. In the meantime, I was subconsciously trying to lift my hand towards the headset, to remove it in the hope of releasing the noise in my ears. I was as weak as a new born baby, and try as I might I just couldn't work out why I could not perform this simple action.

All around me was mayhem and destruction; there were people screaming, some bleeding, some crying and many just stunned into silence with shock. The Falls Road had been turned into a giant scrap yard at the flick of a switch. In the distance could be heard the mournful cry of the sirens as the emergency services raced towards the scene. As the carnage unfolded around me I was totally oblivious of it all, I didn't know half my face had been crushed in, or that my throat had been sliced open by shrapnel and that my jugular had been nicked. Most of my upper body had been peppered in shrapnel; the reason for the drowning feeling was not only the blood pouring down my throat, but one lung had collapsed. As my comrades from the other patrols hurried to secure the area and give assistance to the wounded, they described to me many months later how they couldn't see for five minutes or so because of black billowing smoke and debris still falling to earth. They told me of how their training paid off that day, especially following the four Bs rules of first aid; Breathing, Bleeding, Breaks, and Burns. They told me of Brayshaw's injuries, whose femur had been snapped and that he was screaming like a banshee, but they realised immediately who was the priority casualty and that was me. I was on my back, not moving and as I found out later a good rugby friend and colleague of mine, Private Wayne Bragger, was working over me trying to save my life.

He couldn't work out where the blood was escaping from, that was until he opened my combat jacket and unzipped the bulletproof plate that was covering my heart. My flak jacket had pushed up against my neck and the bulletproof plate had wedged under my throat. He told me that he had never seen so much blood in his life and was only too grateful when the paramedics arrived and took over. I was quickly put in the back of the ambulance and Wayne came as well, not only for emotional support but as protection. It would not be the first or the last time that IRA terrorists had murdered members of the security forces in hospital.

I will always remember in years to come as the ambulance 'blue lighted' away and I lay on the stretcher and the paramedics fought to save my life. Wayne said that I spoke out and said 'Do you fancy pie and chips from the chippy then?' All I know on that day was that one moment I was in the land of the living, and the next moment I had been beamed up to a different planet.

I left behind me a road full of crushed and smashed cars, as well as wounded people. Where the bomb had exploded, the thick dressed stones of the wall had been flung brutally broadside into the busy traffic. The youngest casualty that day was a six-month old baby, who was lying in a baby seat in a car when the rear windscreen exploded, covering the baby in glass and debris. From the moment the ambulance arrived at the Royal Victoria hospital a trauma team was waiting to receive me. My clothes and equipment were cut off, and I was rushed into the theatre immediately. I don't remember how many hours I was in there, but I was told was that when I came out, I was hooked up to a life support machine and two RUC offers stood guard over me whilst I lay in intensive care. The next 48 hours would be the crucial time as to which way I would go; either I would make it, or I would become yet another British soldier to be murdered by the IRA in Northern Ireland. I made it, but I never saw again.

Andrew continues his story later on in this book. It was a feature of the IRA's war of terror against the Security Forces that they also hit many innocent victims in their quest for 'State blood'. It was in addition a feature of these 'own goals' and crossfire victims that before the dust had settled on an incident, Sinn Fein would have wheeled out an apologist in order to assuage their guilt. That the innocent child, caught in the blast asleep in the back of the car did not die is, of course, a cause to celebrate. That the child didn't become yet another innocent victim of the IRA's bloodlust is not in any way due to them.

FROM THE GRAND CENTRAL HOTEL TO ANDERSONSTOWN

Gunner Nigel Glover, Royal Artillery

The Grand Central Hotel (GCH). This sounds a grand place to live, maybe in the 1940s this was a very grand hotel. However, time had taken its toll on this building and no more was it grand. I was introduced to the Guard Sergeant at the reception desk, where I was signed in and told that my accommodation was on the sixth floor. There were twelve flights of stairs to negotiate, and I looked up the stairwell to see the top floor some way in the distance. At this point I was told that we could not use the lifts and had to use the stairs. On reaching the top floor I was knackered from the climb, which was to be a regular four times-plus a day treat for me; I was then shown my accommodation.

The room which was to be my home for the next four months was no more than 10 x 10 feet. This room had four beds and two lockers and one wash basin; 'what luxury' I said to myself. There was one plus side to this accommodation, there was a great view over the city and to the mountains.

We were then moved out to West Belfast and there I was, looking at this corrugated-iron-fenced encampment; it was something that was a shock to me. Behind the screen of corrugated iron were some low rise buildings; the next thing up from a derelict building site. What a hell-hole; it made the GCH look like a great place, I thought to myself 'this lot have a shit deal being here.' After an introduction to the unit and my patrol I was briefed on what we were about to be doing and how we exited this encampment. It was time for me and my new brick to start our patrol. My heart was pounding and I was feeling very nervous. The gates opened and we ran out across the street and down the road for at least 100 yards before stopping and taking up the patrolling position of two soldiers on the left, two soldiers on the right of the road.

The patrolling formation was that each soldier was staggered from his counterpart on the opposite side of the road, the reason being that if one of the patrol was shot, the bullet would not go straight through him and potentially into another soldier. The rearmost soldier spent most of his time walking backwards guarding the rear of the patrol; this job came to me on this occasion. We were in Andersonstown. I had never seen such a place in my life and I can only describe it as being a very rundown, dirty place with crap everywhere. There was old car tyres, paper and rubbish in the street, in fact, a real shit hole; I was thinking how on earth can people live in these conditions? I soon learnt the reason: there was inequality between the Catholic population and the Protestant population, with the Catholics living in shit holes. I believe this is the main contributing factor for the political and religious unrest in the Province of Ulster. This was for me, very unfamiliar territory, coming from a very rural part of England to a city, unlike anything I had ever seen before.

Walking backwards through a council estate has its drawbacks, in that you had to be constantly turning and looking where you were treading as well as where you'd been. Some of the children thought it was great fun to try and trip you up by placing obstacles in your way, such things as skipping ropes tied across the path, or their bikes to trip you up and all the other crap too. I can remember one poignant part of this patrol when the brick became stationary. Myself and the soldiers at the rear turned and knelt down alongside a low garden fence trying to make ourselves as small a target as possible. Both of us at the rear were facing backwards. After a short while a young voice said to me: 'The other soldiers have gone!' At this point we were in great danger; two soldiers left in the street only looking one way; we are fucked here!

Debrief at Andytown RUC centre. *(Craig Laidler)*

Often the OC of a company would take to the streets to control big operations or incidents. This usually meant that most if not all of his company were deployed out on the streets and would therefore require careful and precise co-ordination. *(Paul Crispin)*

One recalls the tragic and terrible killing of nineteen-year-old Private Gary Barlow of the Queen's Lancashire Regiment (QLR). Gary was on foot patrol in the Lower Falls area of Belfast when he was separated from the rest of his comrades and was immediately surrounded by a gang of women from the area who forcibly removed his SLR. He was then held there and – according to some accounts from women who tried to rescue him – became distraught and called out for his mother. An IRA gunman was sent for – apparently the same age as Gary – who then cold-bloodedly shot him in the head from point-blank range after he had been pushed into a garage.

Remember that dream you have when you fall over the cliff; how that feels and how your heart pounds? That was how I felt right then. At that point we both looked at each other and got up and ran in the opposite direction hoping that the others in the patrol were close by. As luck would have it the rest of the patrol were just around the corner. There was some choice words exchanged but you cannot imagine the feeling that went through me being left there. Had I been on my own I do not know how it would have turned out or what I would have done finding myself in an unfamiliar district; the consequences could have been grave.

1972: 'I DIDN'T THINK IT WAS THAT BAD!'

Gunner Mick Potter, Royal Artillery

I went home to quarters and told my wife that we were going to have to go to NI and that it would involve time away for training. And later, when training was over, it would result in a potentially life threatening posting.

This was met with that awful feeling of flatness and worry. We visited Lydd and polished up on riot drills etc and it was like going to school again. Do you feel compassion for a kid that is throwing rocks at you? Oh Christ, will I ever remember what is written on that yellow card? I have no live rounds, empty cartridge cases, blanks or pyrotechnics in my possession, sir!! Some of the millions of things you are faced with. Training completed, we went back to Catterick to find the Battery was being posted to East Belfast. Other batteries of the regiment were posted elsewhere (Andersonstown, Finaghy, and Markets), so generally we felt as if we had got off lightly. Our gun park at Bourlon was not workable at the time for whatever reason, so we took our 105 pack howitzers with us. We joined a car ferry at Liverpool and were told that were the only occupants of the whole ferry and would be sailing past the Isle of Man in the night. It was a rough crossing and in the morning we went on deck to see church spires, and tall buildings in Belfast. Funny how you smell land after being at sea; none of us slept. I have since read somewhere that the crossing from England to Ireland is one of the worst in the world; I can say that in my case it was. I have never felt so bad, indeed in later years, I sailed on the old HMS *Fearless* to Puerto Rico for seventeen days and it never even started to compare with that night to Belfast.

Belfast was cold and damp and a mist hung just over the rooftops; I felt as if every second that we were unloading our stuff someone somewhere had the crosshairs of a rifle on me. I felt the next second would be my last. I was not alone; we all looked scared, never having been to 'hot' postings before. I remember the distinct smell of 'Holland House' pipe tobacco. I wished I was somewhere else! We disembarked at Harland and Wolff's shipyard under that big yellow crane and were driving in order of march from said yard. When we got to the entrance, there were MOD police holding back traffic for us to exit as a convoy. A 'Modplod' [civilian MOD

Police] nearly flaked out when he saw the guns on the back of the Landys and said 'Be Jaysus; I know'd it was bad, but I didn't think it was that bad!' Poor bloke thought that it had escalated so badly that we were now using artillery. Squaddie humour what it is, we told this man that were going to call in air strikes too if they didn't behave themselves. At that time we had no idea who was the baddie or the goodie; anybody from NI was the enemy. It was only later that we learned the subtle difference.

We trundled off into Belfast and noticed all the shop fronts that had been boarded up and houses that had been on fire. I had absolutely no idea where we were going; everywhere smelt of soot. You know the smell of a chimney fire? I remember being relieved that we didn't have to stop at traffic lights and we eventually arrived in Sunnyside Street T.A. Barracks, in the south of the city and about three miles east of Andersonstown. We placed the guns in heavy preservative grease and went about our tour.

I remember one foot patrol, or 'footsie', in particular. We were about halfway up Rosetta Road. 'Point' observed wires from a house to a parked car. Felix was called and the car was blown; doors, boot, bonnet; the whole thing was decimated. The poor owner was only charging a flat battery. We all walked back to Sunnyside Street, smirking and giggling at this poor unfortunate's loss. We had struck a small blow and to us it was blessed relief for a couple of hours. We all got back in one piece and settled down to letter writing and a nice cuppa tea, but inside my head I longed to be out of the place. Oh well; another day crossed off my homemade calendar.

It wasn't all fun of course, and we lost a comrade in Gunner Paul Jackson to a bomb blast. I distinctly remember the first radio sitreps coming in. We all thought: 'No, not one of ours; can't be.' It was eventually confirmed that, sadly, it was true. You are so torn by this news. I remember thinking 'Christ, I know that bloke!' You are torn by conflicting emotions; thinking 'Oh Jesus; poor bugger!' then 'Thank Christ it wasn't me.' A raft of thoughts goes through your head in a nanosecond. I saw my comrades change; it was as if we had to get the bastards at all costs. It wasn't the fact that Paul was gone. It was the fact that these swine had had a go at us and won. Every patrol, every search, every roadblock was done with aggression and revenge. As I write this 30 years on, I am shaking with temper! The culprits had to be brought to book. I am unaware if they ever were. All who served with us then remember Paul; what a tragic loss. It is especially difficult around 'Poppy time'.

That time in my life is so profound; I have some funny memories and some not so funny. I think of NI with humour, remember some brave people and still enjoy a drink with my muckers, who were with me 30 years ago. However, I still shake my head at the frustration of it all!

Gunner Paul Jackson from Glasgow but whose family had settled in Leeds, was aged 21 and a father to two very young children. He was in an armoured vehicle and was taking photographs outside a supermarket on the Strand Road in Londonderry where it was believed that an explosive device had been planted. It exploded and he was hit in the head by shrapnel which penetrated the viewing slit and he was killed instantly. The author understands that there is a differing, although highly unofficial version of Gunner Jackson's death. A source close to his unit alleges that the soldier was ordered to put his head outside the Saracen in order to take a better photograph. It was understood at the time that a warning had been telephoned through to say that the device – at Long's Supermarket – was on a timer device. It was, in fact an RCIED and the bomb was detonated remotely when the firers saw Gunner Jackson's head emerge from the vehicle. He was the 22nd soldier from the Royal Artillery to die and the 11th from the Regiment to lose his life during that terrible year of 1972.

RECRUITS OF A DIFFERENT MOULD

CSM Haydn Davies, RRW

Woolworths was bombed and the Anti Tank platoon dispatched to help the city centre battalion to stake out and stop any looting. They returned with half a dozen female mannequins dressed in flimsy underwear. They placed these in their billets in compromising positions. The section NCO placed his in his bed for something 'to come home to'. Eventually a military use was found for them, and with blackened faces and combat jackets they manned the empty sangars.

TANGOING WITH OSCAR

Neil 'Arfur' Chant, Army Dog Unit, Northern Ireland

It never ceased to amaze me how many units operating in Northern Ireland were ignorant of our dogs' capabilities and limitations; also how they could be so tactically unaware.

On one particular occasion I was deployed with my AES dog Oscar to clear the barriers at the bottom of Kennedy Way in Belfast. These were periodically locked to restrict movement around West Belfast, and in the past, terrorists had placed devices painted the same colour on the barrier. The morning my dog and I were deployed the conditions couldn't have been better, and there was a light breeze blowing up Kennedy Way from the direction of the barrier. The control point was set up a good distance from the barrier and I got Oscar out of the vehicle to let him settle and relieve himself.

While I was harnessing my dog and preparing him for work, the control point commander then ordered two soldiers to run down Kennedy Way and take up position on the roundabout on the other side of the barrier. I watched in disbelief as the two soldiers did exactly that, climbing over the barrier I was to clear for any explosive devices, effectively doing me out of one job, then taking up position upwind of my dog carrying weapons, presumably freshly cleaned and oiled! No matter how I tried to explain how the dog had now been made redundant, it just wasn't registering. So I watched Oscar do a textbook route clearance down Kennedy way, and make a distinct indication on two British Army SA80s!

A very similar incident involved Oscar and me in Belfast. Every morning at the time 7/10 UDR would open the gates to the city centre, and, before this could be done the AES dog would be sent to search for any devices before it could be approached. Oscar, myself and a full complement of soldiers packed in a Makralon Land Rover drove past the gate and took up position a few yards from it! As we had just driven within five metres of the gate, any device that was on it would have been detonated and killed us all for sure. So sending in a dog afterwards was a bit late. When asked why I wasn't deploying my dog, I explained. It took a while for the penny to drop, but the realisation on all the faces concerned was worth the wait!

I was involved on a big rural search operation and it was lunchtime. We were all sitting around eating our 'haverbag' rations, and Oscar was milling about scrounging as usual. Two soldiers were sitting on top of a Land Rover and throwing bits of chicken skin to him. As one of them finished his chicken he threw the bone over his shoulder, Oscar tracked it through the air and was poised, mouth open ready to catch it. Chicken bones are very dangerous for dogs, with a shout from me of 'Leave!' he immediately sat down and looked straight at me. One side of his top lip had caught on his lower canine; a comical expression at the best of times, as the chicken bone bounced off the top of his head. He just glanced at the bone and back at me and forty other soldiers, on our backs with laughter.

In RUC Woodbourne, Oscar and I were in the canteen awaiting deployment. Some RUC were playing pool and Oscar was at my feet looking for a spare pie or sandwich. One of the pool players stood on his tail and Oscar turned on me. He was a stroppy bastard at times and periodically would have a go at me. Today he was on a mission, he was snapping at me as I was trying get to my feet to fend him off. A full-scale scrap ensued where tables and chairs were knocked over, drinks and meals spilled. I managed to avoid his pearly whites and eventually get the better of him, pinning him by the neck to the floor. As peace resumed I turned to see a sea of faces, all staring in abject horror of the terrible cruelty I had inflicted on that poor dog!

Then there were the times when after giving Oscar ample time to relieve himself before an occupied house search, he defecated in bedrooms. And of course, the occasional snacking from children's potties!

PERSONAL SADNESS IN THE 'TURF'

Craig Laidler. 4 Royal Tank Regiment (att: QOH)

Another memory and saddest time of my life didn't involve the usual abuse, spit, bricks and bombs. I was on patrol in the 'Turf' and we stopped as an RUC officer was doing a 'P' check on a vehicle. As per usual, we took cover, checked the wall, checked the hedge, and moved away from the car. We watched the windows etc., as one of the tricks we learnt was when you

Fixing the kid's brakes, Turf Lodge. *(Craig Laidler)*

in areas unannounced and tooled up with non-issue weapons probably looking to create mischief. Using weapons that were non-issue would not draw the immediate attention of any of the security forces if an incident took place and where forensics may have checked out any wounds. Their activities could be used to stir up some internecine rivalry, an ambition that was to be realised in grand fashion in 1975, the origins of which can only be guessed at, but which did not involve them.

This unit were disbanded, as far as I know, having been used as an experiment, and evolved into another unit with a more acceptable face, some time in 1972. But only a few people would really know how this unit was formed and when; I am not one of them. How I came across the first one was by helping stop one of their cars near the Martin Forsyth Republican drinking club in Turf Lodge one late night, near to the time when many of the incumbents were going to be leaving. My patrol was in loose support of the company 'squirrel patrol', which operated in a different role from standard patrolling. The occupants of the car seemed also to be very interested as they parked nearby. They were approached by our squirrel patrol commander and asked to produce ID and the car was searched as per the standard procedure. 'C' Company KOSB used a squirrel patrol to dig out more information in their area of responsibility and as such operated as an entity on the fringe of standard Company activity. It consisted of one officer and about eight other ranks working in uniform. They worked in and around the general military activity in the area often using it as cover for longer surveillance and quite often would be out on the ground when everyone else was in. They would often be used for a specific 'lift' of a suspect and hence would need quick support cover to be on standby to support them if a rumpus ensued.

Lo and behold, they were in possession of weapons that were not standard issue and we only narrowly averted a serious incident when the man in charge of the car produced an ID card and quickly explained who they were. A code word was verified from HQ and we had to let them go. They were told by the 'squirrel patrol' commander, to clear off out of the area as they were disrupting our operations. There was a bigger session than usual at the Martin Forsythe club that night and it was hoped to pick out a sought-after face or two and make an arrest. With the subsequent events occurring, the opportunity was missed. We can only guess what they were planning when the club disgorged its occupants. And so began my awareness of a war within a war that was unfolding under my feet.

On occasions whilst deployed on normal patrol duties I would be informed to keep out of the area I was to be patrolling as another operation was underway. This would last only for a few hours and rarely would I know what was taking place. I don't think murder was on the agenda though, perhaps a meeting with a tout or an arrest that would need to be done without drawing a lot of attention to the event. We would pick up the flak later! As time went by speculation was minimal about that aspect of the situation we faced. I think that the ranks were of the opinion these undercover operations involved the specialist units and they could do as they liked in given situations and that was all right by us. It was much further into tours of duty that I became aware that a lot of the 'spook' activities did not involve the specialist units but a plethora of operations in civilian garb that gave cover when convenient for a variety of reasons. Some local commanders wanted easier access through Belfast, wanting to visit someone, wanting to meet someone. Local commanders may choose to carry out a low-key operation out of uniform such as a recce or just to visit a cash-and-carry! Other operations were controlled from higher up and the only time I would know anything about their activities would be when I was told to keep out of an area for a while. This was all only the beginning for me. Certain other tasks requiring covert activity needed other personali-

Bad luck; your turn to check. *(Craig Laidler)*

Down the hole looking for arms. *(Craig Laidler)*

ties to be recruited on an ad hoc basis. People already deployed and very familiar with the poisons of Ulster would be selected and asked to get involved in tasks – some short term, others much longer term – depending on the role envisaged. Mostly covert intelligence gathering. No extra training. If the person did not fit then he or she could be pulled out and replaced as necessary. I entered this nether world, one which I had never thought of but was invited into at short notice. In hours my world was transformed. Ulster now looked a different place.

The adrenalin began to pump differently in this world, with virtual carte blanche as to movement. It was a heady mix to travel around the Ulster countryside, meeting contacts in pubs and hotels, rubbing shoulders with those who could be players, watching who was going where and meeting whom, picking up a lot of secondary information not generally available in an orthodox setting. I had contact with everyday work locations and this was valuable. Someone, somewhere, will know the extent of this type of information gathering and what use it may have been in the bigger picture but in those days of constant evolvement of terrorist cells the more information that could be collated the clearer the picture. Finding out about newer personnel being recruited into the insurgent network and their movements could cast light upon this evolving situation. This would require a lot of surveillance of people and their contacts to build a picture of who could be involved by association. Loose talk and other verbal information could supply more clarity. I was one of those who found himself in a number of advantageous situations for these purposes. I was fed quite a lot of sensitive stuff. The boldness of some of the paramilitary 'rent collectors' (racketeers) was pointed out to me clandestinely by the occasional member of staff I had befriended socially and through work. Go into a certain establishment at an appointed time and a couple of faces would be indicated. A cloth money bag would sometimes be handed over and at other times a wedge of folded notes. This helped my portfolio and if I did not know them from already gathered information I would remember their faces and rake through 'mugshots' to find a match. A photo opportunity could maybe be arranged but great care had to be taken with that. Not impossible though and at times some beauties were achieved. Get a fix on one then those with him, if not already known, could be involved. Even better was to casually open conversation with staff once they felt confident about your presence. If they felt you were not a threat then a name of one person seen 'collecting' might be forthcoming. Cross verification could be tried then and if nothing so far known, no form, then we have discovered another possible activist who would need watching. I would then go orthodox and inform the unit looking after the area where I was told he was from, to add him to the list.

CLOSE TO DEATH ON THE ARDOYNE

Guardsman Peter Miller, 1st Battalion, Coldstream Guards

I was nineteen years old when I first served in Belfast. Joining the infantry in the 1980s meant a certain posting to Northern Ireland, something I welcomed at the time. I'd grown up with images of the Troubles on television; the huge funeral parades, city centre explosions and covered bodies lying in the road. These were not pictures of horror or death to me but naïvely, images of excitement. My preparation for Belfast included the usual round of military training but I also found myself becoming increasingly fascinated by the conflict and its history. Our tour began shortly after the murder of two Royal Signals corporals during a funeral parade in

March 1988, a reaction to the actions of Loyalist paramilitary Michael Stone at Milltown cemetery days earlier [see page 249]; it was a violent yet fascinating time.

I arrived in Belfast on a typical autumn day. Drizzle hung in the air as we drove from Aldergrove airfield towards the city in an old Bedford three-tonner, protected only by a sheet of loose canvas. I quickly volunteered to sit at the back of the truck acting as a sort of sentry, eager to get my first glimpse of this turbulent land. We entered Belfast from the north-west, passing through Ligoniel, a drab, grey estate on the fringes of the city and on to the Crumlin Road. I was immediately struck by the murals painted on the sides of houses. In this area of the city they were predominantly Loyalist. Vast walls of bright, patriotic colour seemed to light our way. One stands out indelibly in my mind, an artistically intricate image of Michael Stone, pistol in hand, loosing off rounds and grenades in Milltown cemetery at the funeral of three IRA members killed in Gibraltar; underneath were the words 'Michael Stone V.C.'.

The work routine quickly became second nature. Patrol briefings outlined the planned movements of our teams, indicated the routes to be used and any potential 'players' (known or suspected terrorists) who might be around. I had developed a reputation for spotting players on the street from the mug shots pasted over the ops-room wall. Soon, I was face-to-face with known members of the IRA, trying to engage them in conversation whilst searching them in the futile hope of them carrying something incriminating. Some spoke, some stayed silent. There were jokes, insults, intimidation and threats from both sides. I was nose to nose with people who wanted to kill me and I had never been happier. There was a constant and palpable tension in the air; you knew that at any moment, this seemingly ordinary city with its plain houses and its grey streets might explode in a flash of violence. This became the paradox of the place. I patrolled streets populated with elderly ladies carrying shopping bags and I chatted with kids who got excited if you gave them a pen. Daily life simply carried on as normal and we had to fight not to become complacent.

The Shankill area of Belfast is surrounded by hostility. To the north the fiercely Republican Ardoyne offers an ideological contrast to end all others. My young eyes had never witnessed such hatred and to this day, twenty years later, I have yet to encounter anything stronger. Such public displays of tribalism spilled onto the street in the form of painted kerbstones and flags hanging from telegraph poles. You always knew where you were. At that time, the Loyalist community was very supportive of the army. At Christmas time, patrols were offered tea at almost every house. Once, when our vehicle was parked at the roadside deep within the estate, the rear doors were opened and crates of beer were pushed in until there was little room for the crew. I had my first taste of potcheen in the Shankill; a sweet, strong and oddly pleasant spirit, illegally distilled from potatoes and given out by an elderly woman with blackened teeth and an accent so impenetrable I could hardly understand a word. It seemed strange that the handshakes and the gifts might have come from men who had killed other men.

A tour of duty was six months and for most of this time, routine was king. Briefings, patrols, de-briefs, food, washing and sleep became the pattern of my life. And for weeks this cycle remained unbroken. Then the routine search of a house in Etna Drive, Ardoyne broke that routine and nearly resulted in death. The RUC told us they had sound intelligence of a 'serious weapon' in the Ardoyne that was being prepared for use. Searches were planned and two specialist teams deployed to addresses within the area. As part of a search team I found myself wading through the everyday detritus of people's lives. I searched drawers and cupboards, attics and kitchens. We found nothing. After about six hours in the area, we moved to try one final address. No one was home so the door was smashed down and we began our search. I was in the kitchen, rummaging through rusty oven trays and greasy plates when the owner of the

One of the many Belfast murals, Turf Lodge. *(Craig Laidler)*

house came home and the usual shouting started. But then something odd happened. The householder became quiet and nervy. He wanted a glass of water. He wanted to call his wife, his daughter, his mother. And then he told us; two days previously two men had knocked at his back door and pointed a gun at his head. They told him to go out for a few hours. When he returned they were in his kitchen drinking tea. They told him his house had been chosen to hide 'equipment' crucial to the cause. If he told anyone of this, he would be killed; then he pointed to the kitchen floor and wept.

The house was part of a terrace, and, under the kitchen floor the foundations ran the length of the houses. A small crawl space led to a shallow pit that lay under the next door's kitchen. The prize was a GPMG, 1500 rounds of armour-piercing ammunition in link, a series of detonators and a small quantity of Semtex explosive. We had to dig through the next door's kitchen floor to get at it. We'd been in the houses for over five hours and our protective cordon outside even longer. Once the weapon had been cleared for booby-traps, I carried it out to the waiting Land Rover. As I climbed into the back to gaze at the find, there was a dull thud from the roof before a colossal noise filled my ears and the metal armour of the Land Rover echoed to the explosion. I was thrown against the bulkhead and must have been knocked unconscious as the next thing I recall is stumbling from the back of the vehicle and waving my weapon around like an idiot.

I was grabbed and led to a waiting ambulance, my eardrum perforated by the explosion. Apparently our vehicle had spent so long in one place that it had given the local IRA time to get a hand grenade, step out from an alleyway and lob it just as I was climbing in. No one was seriously hurt and the attackers made good their escape, but it was close.

I returned home and could not settle. I struggled to rationalise the intensity of feelings that I had sat in between for six months. The grey city of Belfast had got under my skin. The grubby kids who threw stones at me were no enemy. Neither were the elderly men who struggled to carry their shopping home or the housewives struggling to raise their families without a husband. The boyish excitement of conflict remained but the context seemed to affect too many innocents. I learned that in any conflict, it is the humblest of society that suffer most; working families, private soldiers, the old, and the lonely. I wanted to go back, now that I felt I understood.

'C' COMPANY IN BELFAST, 1972

Rifleman Tim Marsh 2, RGJ

Our company was sent to Belfast to reinforce the Belfast Brigade troops on the ground. I remember the company moving about a lot in the bombed-out city. Our sleeping arrangements could be anything from a disused cotton mill to an abandoned slaughter house in Lenadoon. We also had one night sleeping onboard the prison ship *Maidstone*, which had been anchored in Belfast Lough.

'C' Company had patrols to carry out in the Markets area of Belfast, and we also were tasked to go to the Ormeau Road and patrol around Belfast University campus plus the Botanical gardens. Our company thought we were being used by the Belfast Brigade when really we should be in Londonderry supporting our fellow Riflemen in 2 RGJ as it was getting close to 12 July. [12 July, as every squaddie or NI observer knows, is the date on which the Loyalist marching season commences.]

Anyway, one of our tasks in Belfast was giving cover to the RUC and salvage teams cleaning up after bomb damage in the city. As our section was giving cover, we looked into the wrecked Burtons the Tailors to see RUC constables trying on all the coats, so our lads decided to do the same. But unfortunately some of them went a bit over the top, trying to put coats on under their uniforms; it was extremely funny to watch, with them all looking like Michelin men. On returning to Londonderry, the SIB [Special Investigation Branch of the Army] swooped into the company lines to retrieve said Burtons 'purchases'! That night we stayed on the Maidstone, which was eventful. One guy from our company dropped his SLR into Belfast Lough while he was crossing the gangway. It was only a rumour, but we heard on our mess deck that 'C' Company had asked if a naval diver could retrieve the rifle from the bottom of the Lough.

We also got tasked to a suspect device in a huge grain lorry on Oxford Street, down by the river Lagan. We cleared the area as much as we could and just waited, and few minutes later there was the biggest explosion I had heard to date; grain and pigeon shit everywhere!

Now looking back on this quick tour of Belfast, it was rush here, rush there and everywhere; sleeping, eating and surviving on the streets; sleeping in disused mills with only the rats to keep us company.

SPRINGFIELD ROAD

Soldier, Welsh Infantry Regiment

I had first entered Springfield Road police station in 1970, and at that time I was a platoon sergeant. 1970 was the era of the 'Disco tours' when little came at you except abuse and the odd hand-thrown missile. In 1984 I was a captain and commanded the location. In the interim period the situation had escalated somewhat and over that time I had served about seven and a half years in total in Northern Ireland, collated in short tours and residential tours.

In 1984 there was a change in me. In the early tours I had taken it all in my stride; riots, shootings, death and the injuries. It did not bother me much. I personally escaped serious injury, although I did have some very narrow escapes. Being infantry we always got the hard areas, and my seven and a half years were not without strife. I was hardened to it. I felt that the 'dull thud' would never get me. I also had little compassion. I remember turning a soldier over with my boot to see if I could bring him to life, I wanted to keep both hands on my rifle; a selfish act. I was different in 1984. I saw life as precious. I began to dread the soldiers leaving the base. The sound of explosions and shootings within our 'patch' made me think 'What poor soul is it this time?' I would wait for the contact report to come over the radio. The wait was quite unbearable.

One night I was working in my office within the base, when suddenly there was a very loud explosion; it was quite near and just outside my office wall. Plaster fell from my ceiling and crashed onto my desk, my ears rang. There was shouting of orders and running feet. A patrol leaving the base had been bombed by a remote control device. A young soldier was down. I knew him well and liked him even more; he was a cheerful and energetic little character. I did all that I could, I left it to the experts and came back into my office and sat down and just looked at the wall. In the silence of my office, tears flowed hot down my face. I knew it was time to leave and that this was best left to younger men.

This contributor is a man for whom I have the greatest respect and admiration. I feel no shame whatsoever in admitting that I have wept openly at the death of a comrade. There is no such thing as a tough soldier; only a human being who is trained to act tough. In the end, it is just a façade.

RUMOURS

Brian Roberts, Royal Army Medical Corps

After reading some of the comments in your first book about life over the water, one thing that was brought back to me was how our wives and parents must have suffered. Whilst on my second or third tour, my late wife – who was PA to the Brigade Commander in our part of West Germany – was walking to work one day and noticed a group of Army wives just standing about talking. One of them noticed her and asked if she knew that a Medic Sergeant had been killed in Northern Ireland. The only Medic Sergeant she knew over in Ulster was me and she just keeled over in shock. The next thing that she remembers is coming around in the BMH [British Medical Hospital] in Munster; she had been diagnosed with stress-related asthma which, sadly, she had for the rest of her life.

This rumour about me had apparently been started by a soldier, who, as far as I know, had never been outside the gates of the base over in Ulster. He had, allegedly, phoned his wife and passed on – third hand – false information, which caused so much distress. Needless to say, I heard none of this until I got home and she had no desire to upset me and make me lose concentration when I needed it most.

DIVIDE AND RULE

Soldier 'A', King's Own Scottish Border Regiment

> Sensitive areas such as prisons would see such people acting as couriers for the detained, ferrying information in and out via the prison visiting system. Remand prisoners claiming special category could have a variety of visitors not restricted to family and therefore their visitors would be worth watching. I had some experience trying to get the best out of this situation but it was fraught with obstacles. Some days, if properly co-ordinated, could prove very fruitful. Every little bit of intelligence coming in from wherever it could be had would give us a bigger picture. There was of course a lot of rubbish coming in too but that would filter out. Some information could be used to stir up suspicion and internecine rivalries by those better placed than me, especially when splinter groups were already forming in the Province. The old theory of divide and rule could be tried again. Someone hit the jackpot in 1975 triggering a serious feud in the Republican body or so the story goes. As I recall it some 35 members of proscribed Republican organisations were assassinated or badly wounded during a few weeks of mayhem, many in Belfast, in the summer of 1975.

During the course of this year, a total of 58 paramilitaries on both sides were killed by the Army or by the other side, or during the internecine feuds which took place. A violent split during the course of year between the two wings of the IRA led to many deaths as the tentative *entente cordiale* broke down. There had never been any love lost between the Officials and Provisionals and a total of 31 IRA/INLA were killed in 1975. As a soldier from the Royal Green Jackets told the author: 'There was evidence that the UVF/UFF were more successful at that time in 'offing' the IRA and lots of rumours about Special Forces. There was also talk that they were killing each other. That sat well with me, because it saved us a job!'

> I was bemused by events. Who was doing it? Several contacts spoke to me with a little concern. Was it an Army unit on the rampage? Had the Loyalist paramilitaries achieved lethal sophistication without us noticing? Weighing up the evidence to date those contacts of mine who had in-depth knowledge of Loyalist capabilities just said 'they wish!' Discussing things in the military community, the initial feedback to me was that no-one knew, but that it was bloody great! The targets picked needed to be taken off the streets; all influential within the Republican cause, but not removed according to the rule of law so it would not have been us. No, it was definitely them. As each hit was reported more intelligence came in supporting the view that this was a full blown internecine feud. Exactly what it was about I never was privy to.
>
> Top men like Billy McKee were being 'whacked' and it did not make sense even if it made good reading. I was just 'around the corner' when McKee was hit in North Queen Street. Out on an errand, I heard some shots. Thinking things were closer than they were, I got a shift on and changed my route away from the direction of New Lodge Road and veered away towards the York Street area. I initially thought it was a sniper attack on Unity Flats. I learned later of McKee's demise. I was on foot and had taken a short cut so it was a sweaty ten minutes or so until I got clear of Republican streets.
>
> It could well have been about the control of funds and who may have been dipping in illicitly. New groups were forming out of existing cells, groups such as Saor Eire and the IRSP with its militant wing the INLA, groups that may have had possession of funds previously earmarked for PIRA but were now flexing their own muscles. They may have stolen some of the

newly arrived weapons from Libya to back up their ambitions. I was picking up intelligence, I intercepted messages found on a courier in one instance that indicated that an AK47 had been newly acquired and needed to be secreted. This was in Short Strand and the urgency in the message suggested that they were not supposed to have it there and to get it, or them, moved quickly. The Quartermaster of the Short Strand Provos had just been locked up on remand and messages via couriers were flying about to sort this out. Who they wanted to keep the AK47 from is part of the puzzle preceding the next event. Someone observing from close to the heart of events, with more information than anyone, saw an opportunity to set one against the other. My information was that a well placed and trusted 'player' was also working for the security forces. His handler advised him on a course of action and the ball was set rolling. Inevitably, after much damage was done, the suspicions pointed towards this person. He would have had to be spirited out of Ulster or face death but he had sown the seeds of suspicion amongst insurgent groups and that had longer term consequences. Paranoia was setting in. The terror cells became tighter and more enclosed with only the immediate members knowing each other. This would make for a difficult programme of control at PIRA council level, heightening their fears of being got at; but they had to tighten security or lose face. I think they never had tight control of things anyway but now it was going to be tested.

The response as viewed from the eyes of troops on the ground was to carry on as we had been doing. I recall that we only had the information on PIRA restructuring and that it may be more difficult to gain wider information as regards any 'grand plans' they may be making. PIRA had gone retrogressive at this time. The interest was centred more on the IRSP [Irish Republican Socialist Party; the political wing of the INLA] which as an emergent body was rapidly gaining converts to its ranks. I remember the whole of Divis Flats being referred to as 'Planet of the IRPS' because so many were involved. How big a threat were they going to be?

Skirting past the Divis Flats one day on my way from a meeting in Ardoyne and heading for Lisburn I was intending to nip down the Falls Road as a short cut. I noticed that the general area was buzzing a bit more than usual so I turned left into Grosvenor Road to head back into town when I was stopped at a road block. Not just any road block; this was a plain clothes operation by locals. [Commonly known as IVCPs; illegal vehicle checkpoints often put on as either a show of strength by the paramilitaries or because they had intelligence that undercover soldiers or their other 'enemies' might be in the area.] I was waved into a short queue while the cars in front were being searched in broad daylight. They had one man posted twenty metres to the front of their search and two to the rear by a wall next to waste ground. They were watching both the activity and access to Leeson Street. One of them wore a long trench coat, hands in pockets and moving with a stiff leg. This was a warm summer's day! Yes, I suspected a rifle held down the inside of the coat.

I began to sweat a little and rapidly thought of an escape plan. Suddenly there was a nod from the front man, a wave from the pair at the rear and they made off in the direction of Leeson Street just as my vehicle was to be searched. Panic over. These were players, but were they IRPS or Provos? Who and what were they looking for? This was just around the time that the internecine mayhem was about to erupt. I think they may have been looking for someone or something being moved out of the Falls area. A show of muscle in an area where dominance could be about to change hands. It was so brazen. They even carried on while a vehicle patrol from the Scots Guards passed by on the other side of the road.

The IRSP began with a flurry in Belfast but ultimately failed to become the main protagonist in the conflict, losing out to PIRA which, with hindsight, held the main Catholic support in the Province. The name Seamus Costello comes to mind as a wanted leading light in the

IRSP; more wanted by PIRA it seems. Seamus' luck ran out and he fled the scene. With him out of the way the IRSP's thrust was not the same; I think he was assassinated some time in the late '70s.

Seamus Costello (38) was a leading INLA player and was shot dead by the Official IRA in Dublin on 5 October 1977. His death sparked off a series of killings in a Republican feud which clearly had its roots in the period that Soldier 'A' speaks of.

On 10 March 1971, off-duty members of the Royal Highland Fusiliers were picked up in the Markets area of Belfast and driven to their deaths on the promise of a party. They were taken to Ligoniel, on the outskirts of the city, and when the car stopped and the three got out to relieve themselves at the roadside, waiting IRA gunmen cold-bloodedly murdered them. Two of the three were brothers, Fusilier John Boreland McCaig (17), Fusilier Joseph McCaig (18) and their cousin, Fusilier Dougald Purdon McCaughey who was 23.

'ALLIES' ON SANDY ROW

Steve Norman, 3 Royal Anglian Regiment

The PIG rumbled to a halt and the back doors were swung open and, adjusting my eyes from the dark interior, I saw for the first time Albert Street Mill. It was as its title suggests, an old Victorian building, dilapidated and now used as an emergency Army billet. It was situated in the very heart of the Falls Road. Overlooking the Mill was the infamous Divis Tower surrounded by the Divis Flats complex. These flats were to play a major role in my life over the next few months. They were the epitome of 1960s bad design and had quickly become modern-day slums. They were a fertile ground for discontent and social deprivation and an absolute godsend to the IRA.

All three of us new recruits got out the PIG and followed Corporal Jim, known to all as 'the Col' up some old, dark, dank, twisting stairs to our allotted platoon's room. We were now members of 2 platoon 'A' Company though it would be a while until the 'old sweats' accepted us as such. 'Right,' he said, 'get your civvies off; get your combats on and go to the QMs to draw your flak jacket and SLR.' The SLR was affectionately known as the 'Paddy Whacker'. He then introduced us to the rest of the platoon. Nobody said a word except from the back came a muttered 'Bloody hell! Just what we need. More fucking Nigs.' (Nigs being an Army term for raw recruits.)

Over the next few hours we found out why the lads were so pissed off; only a few days earlier, the Platoon Commander, Second Lieutenant Nicholas Hull, had been shot dead in the back of a PIG. He had been mapping the area around the Divis Flats and a burst of gunfire aimed at the PIG had entered the observation slit. One round hit him under his arm and traversed through his chest. He never regained consciousness and was pronounced dead at the Royal Victoria Hospital. Nick was a great loss to the platoon. He was a very popular officer and was very much admired and respected by all ranks. He was also our first fatality and sadly not our last.

Nicholas Hull was 22 and was born in Bow, East London, but lived in Bedfordshire. He had been directing the removal of makeshift barricades in Durham Street when an Official IRA sniper fired into the PIG from where he was directing. He died shortly afterwards from his wounds.

My first patrol was not what I had expected, because, for some strange reason also incorporated in our predominantly Catholic area was the staunchly Protestant area of Sandy Row and it was here that I first learnt to be tail-end Charlie. This involved, as you might imagine, being at the tail end of the patrol and learning to walk backwards so as to cover the patrol from attack from behind. I soon mastered the art and still to this day find it easy to walk backwards. Sandy Row at that time was bedecked with Union Jack bunting and the curbstones were painted in red white and blue and the welcome from the residents was both warm and genuine. These people felt that we were 'their boys' and here to sort out those 'Fenian Bastards'. Cups of tea and biscuits and warm soda bread were on offer at every turn and all the local teenage girls flirted with us outrageously.

I remember our patrol sitting in one house in the Sandy Row having tea and cakes with the lady of the house and her young son. Whilst chatting away the little boy suddenly said to me: 'Can I have a look at your gun, mister?' I looked over at Jim who nodded and said: 'Take the mag off and check it's unloaded and let him have a look.' I handed it to him and he then proceeded to strip the working parts out and told me how they worked! I asked him how he knew so much about the SLR and had another soldier showed him? He replied: 'No; me daddy's got one but he won't let me play with it.' There followed a stunned silence quickly broken by the mother who had turned bright red. She said: 'The little bugger is always joking; take no notice, it's only make believe.' We did not search that house which I suppose we should have done, so I shall never know if the 'little bugger' nearly gave the game away.

Well my first patrol had been a doddle and I thought this is not so bad I can now drink tea while walking backwards; boy, was I in for a surprise.

There has been much talk about alleged collusion between the Army and the Loyalist paramilitaries such as the UVF, UFF, UDA etc and the Ulster Defence Regiment have their critics amongst the Republicans. But, in the words of Lord Profumo's lady friend, 'Well they would say that, wouldn't they?' This author has no views on this subject, but if the Army, or individuals within the Army, saw the 'Prods' as their natural allies against the Catholics who had developed into their 'natural enemies', who could be surprised? If the allegation is correct and there was an SLR within that house on the Sandy Row, it is entirely possible that it came from an institutionalised military source: the Security Forces.

There was a tight and vicious and well organised 'policing' system within both the Republican and Loyalist movements. Stepping out of line was dangerous; even talking to soldiers in the Catholic areas was likely to merit vicious punishment and it was also, of course, dangerous not to appear in certain areas to support the Loyalist movement too; but they were less cohesive and more randomly vicious and their areas of control smaller and more easily penetrated or disrupted by Security Forces. They had of course no bolt-hole across the Irish border.

MURDERS AT LIGONIEL: THE RECKONING

RSM John Wood, SIB, Northern Ireland

The murder of the three members of RHF had some interesting tags. Immediately after the bodies were identified, SIB set about interviewing all soldiers who had been out on the town that night. They found one who had seen the trio leave a pub in the company of a bearded civilian. The witness was old enough to describe this beard as identical to one worn by Philip

Searching waste ground in west Belfast.

Harben, a celebrity TV chef of the times. The RUC artist worked with our soldier and produced what was reckoned to be a good likeness. The civil police provisionally identified the man as Patrick McAdorey, a known member of the IRA.

In discussion with the RUC it was clear that they did not intend to pursue the investigation into the murder of the three Jocks. This situation was put to GOC NI and he spoke with the Commissioner of the Met Police. A team of Met detectives – murder squad, intelligence and SB – was already in Belfast and were investigating the death of a civilian where the RUC inquiry was deemed to have been biased. The services of this group were made available immediately. They soon discovered that there had been three players in the abduction and murder. One had gone to earth in the South and the other was thought to be somewhere on the mainland; his brother ran a pub in Birmingham. This last was thought to have a British Army connection with the Parachute Regiment; story was that the IRA had ordered him to join to learn tactics and other useful terrorist skills. News of this leaked out to Palace Barracks and we had to dash off to Aldergrove when the cook sergeant drew a Browning and two magazines with the stated intention of expunging the dishonour brought upon the Regiment. We stopped him just as he was about to board his flight so a Birmingham publican had a near miss he never knew about.

However, there is a God! McAdorey came onto the streets on the day of internment and did the 'High Noon' scene of standing in the middle of the road whilst firing off a revolver. He was put down. Almost all of the Met team were photographed shaking hands with him as he lay on his cold slab at the Lagan Bank mortuary, along with myself. The ex-soldier deemed the UK too hot and went off to assist in raising funds in New York. He died after a drunken escapade ended in a shooting. I cannot remember what happened to the man who went to the South.

Patrick McAdorey (24) was shot dead by soldiers on 9 August 1971 in Brompton Park, Belfast; he was one of thirteen people killed on that day of insanity throughout the Province. All but one of the dead was killed in the city of Belfast and they included two soldiers.

AFTER THE BOMB

Private Andrew Bull, Royal Regiment of Wales

That same night as I lay in intensive care linked to a life support machine, my parents were being called upon by the local police. They broke the sad news to my mother and father informing them that I had been severely injured by an IRA bomb whilst on a routine patrol in Belfast. My parents had never flown in their lives and to this day my elderly parents have no recollection of the flight or landing at Aldergrove airport. They were taken to the Royal Victoria Hospital where they sat vigilantly at my bedside, my mother holding my hand. The next 48 hours passed and the doctors made a decision for me to have further surgery, as my head apparently had swollen to the size of a pumpkin. I went down to theatre once more and was then taken back up to intensive care, and when my parents next saw me, my mother burst into tears because she thought that the doctors had amputated my ears. There were big red plastic bags covering my ears and protruding from them were long drainage tubes; we sometimes laugh at this when looking back.

I think it was about a week to ten days later before I regained full consciousness. I had no idea where I was or of what had happened. I thought that it was so quiet that I had died and gone to heaven and this is what it was like on the other side. Finally a voice spoke to me from the darkness, and told me that I was in hospital having been seriously injured. I thought I had bandages over my eyes because of not being able to see; I couldn't touch my face as both the backs of my hands had tubes going in and I was still connected up to the respirator. I knew I had stitches in my face because I had asked the nurse who had spoken to me first; she told me that the consultant would be along very shortly to speak to me. When I finally spoke to the consultant he gently told me in the best way that he could, the severity of my injuries and that considering how close I was to the explosion it was a miracle that I had lived. I just lay there absorbing the reality of his words; that I had lost my right eye completely and that they had tried to save my left eye but unfortunately it was beyond their medical skills.

I had thought my lack of sight was due to the fact that I had bandages over my eyes, but the truth of the matter was that I no longer had my eyes. I found out later that the doctors had asked my parents if they wanted to break this devastating news, but my Mother and my Father could not bring themselves to do this, and I respect them both for what emotional turmoil they were going through at that time. I was still trying to absorb and register the news of what the consultant had said to me, but for whatever reason there was a sense of denial and that he must be mistaken. My Company Commander and CSM came to visit me as did many of my comrades on numerous occasions. Most of the bones were broken in my face including my upper jaw, stopping me from being able to talk. Apart from my jaws being wired together, I also had what can only be described as a mini scaffold screwed into my face known in the medical profession as a 'Mount Vernon' halo frame. When I had visitors my only means of communication was by pen and paper; I would use a medical chart board for support whilst I wrote what I wanted to say. This caused great consternation because my writing was perfectly legible and straight. Everyone couldn't get their head round as to how I could still write when I was totally blind, but the doctors explained that this is a purely normal reflex because of how long I had already been writing, but in time this would deteriorate. I can still write today, however I am told it is very childlike and this is purely down to having not written for so long; when you have sight you reach for a pen automatically, when you are blind you reach for a Dictaphone or typewriter. Eventually the visits from my mates were stopped. The reasons given were that my mates were getting upset and that I was still in a much weakened state and I wouldn't argue with that because I would get tired very quickly.

As the weeks went by I formed a very strong and loving bond with the nursing staff, and we would have some great laughs on occasions. I was six feet two and about sixteen stone when I was rushed into hospital, and I lost about five stone as a result of my injuries. As the saying goes I was like a stripped down racing pigeon. Every day one of the nursing staff therapists would lower me down flat and then push down on my chest and get me to try and use my lungs independently. I used to fucking dread it when she came in because it felt like she was pushing all the air out of my lungs and I felt like I was going to have a heart attack at any moment. Although I used to give her a hard time she knew what she was doing, and in my own ignorance at that time I didn't appreciate that she was doing her best for me.

The only way I could have food was through a straw so my food was always liquidised, and all of my medication was given through the drips in the backs of my hands. Sometimes the nurses would describe my dinner by saying 'it's a good job you can't see your dinner Andy because it looks like baby shit' and we would laugh together. Then came the time when I needed to have a shit and I asked one of the nurses to give me a hand, this was the first time that I had been out of bed and on my feet since being admitted. I could not believe how weak I was and the only way to describe it was like the Walt Disney film *Bambi* when he was on the ice with Thumper the rabbit. When we finally got to the toilet and the nurse left me I couldn't understand why nothing was happening, I wanted to go but I couldn't. I shouted for the nurse and explained to her as best I could my predicament, she laughed and told me that I was constipated and she would be back in a moment. She came back and dutifully shoved up my arse what felt to me like two L2 hand grenades; the next day after several attempts I finally managed to get my bowels moving. I can now sympathise with pregnant women and can relate to what pains they go through, because I certainly thought I was giving birth that day; never again would I want to be constipated.

One evening as I lay on my bed listening to an Elvis Presley song, whether it was the relaxed melancholy atmosphere or not I don't know, suddenly the words of the doctor came flooding back into my thoughts. 'You're blind; you're blind; you're blind.' The enormity of his words had finally breeched any barriers of denial that I had built, and the full impact of this hit me with the force of a hurricane. The dam finally burst and I could no longer hold back my tears, I don't remember which one of the nurses held me that evening, but she held me tight as I threw my arms around her and buried my face into her neck as I shook uncontrollably and cried my heart out. Eventually the river of tears receded and finally stopped, and the nurse and I talked into the early hours of the morning until I finally surrendered to sleep.

I thought I was the only blind man in the world, or the only blind person in the world; at no time did it cross my mind that there were millions of people that were blind or partially sighted. I never thought of children being born blind, people losing their sight as a result of cancer or some other disease. I thought of how I had asked the nurse who would want to marry a blind man, and putting to her would you marry a blind man, and remembering her answer. 'It would make no difference whether he was blind or not; it's the person's personality that is the most important. If I loved that person his blindness wouldn't matter one bit.' From that very next day

> I went from strength to strength; it was as if by opening the flood gates the despair and vulnerability and reservations that I had held had all been washed away in one great tidal wave.
>
> Soon came the time where I was well enough to leave the RVH and be transferred to Musgrave Park Military Hospital. This was a sad time for both the staff and myself because we had all come a long way; however, as time has passed we have unfortunately lost touch with one another. I didn't enjoy my short stay at Musgrave, because I found the nursing care very poor and nothing in comparison to the high standards I received at the RVH. I found any requests that I made to the nursing staff either fell on deaf ears or were responded to very slowly. I couldn't wait to be transferred to London and get away from the miserable place and my parents were of the same opinion because they could see this in my change of mood. Finally I was to be flown back in a Hercules aircraft and taken to the Woolwich Military Hospital in London. I remember being stretchered from the back of the ambulance, and as they carried me up the ramp of the Hercules and strapped me in I was the main focus of attention for a number of squaddies who were also in the back of the Hercules but they were going on leave. As the two nurses attended to me I can only imagine what the other squaddies were thinking at that time.

I have come to know Andrew as a happy-go-lucky, funny guy who doesn't offend easily. Given his awful injuries, whether I could be as sanguine or as cheerful under the same circumstances is doubtful. That he is alive is down not only to the incredible skills and devotion of the entire medical staff at the RVH but also to his inner strength. Over a quarter of British soldiers wounded in explosions during the troubles succumbed to their wounds. I attach below a copy of the Hostile Action Casualty System report into soldiers' deaths, written in 1989.

> Death and injury due to terrorist bombings continue to exercise civilian and military surgeons alike. In this paper 828 servicemen killed and injured by explosions in Northern Ireland have been studied, using data stored in the Hostile Action Casualty System (HACS). Because of the nature of the conflict in Northern Ireland, the magnitude of each explosion and the distance of the victims from it are quite accurately known. The overpressure (blast loading) to which the victim was exposed can be estimated from the information on the HACS forms and standard tables, giving overpressures for a given charge at a known distance. Using the HACS data, the numbers of injuries due to overpressure (primary blast injury), missiles energized by the blast (secondary injury), displacement of the victim by the blast wind (tertiary injury) and flash burn can be determined. Of the 828 servicemen involved in explosions, 216 were killed, most of them before any treatment could be instituted. Of the servicemen in the survey, 90 per cent were wearing body armour. Although body armour affords considerable protection from secondary missiles, it is unlikely to reduce the number of deaths due to primary blast injury. [www3.interscience.wiley.com/journal/112185256/abstract]

A BAG OF ALMONDS

Gunner Nigel Glover, Royal Artillery

> I was in the guard room one day, and my troop WO2 brought in a suspect whom we had to entertain in our holding room. In this room, the suspects had to stand up against the walls for a long time. You may think this is not too hard standing there, but, with their legs and arms

outstretched at an angle touching the wall, it wasn't the most comfortable position to be in. Anyway the WO2 said that they were being held for having handled or having had explosives on them. Innocently, I asked: 'How do you know this?' He handed me an old bread bag and told me to have a smell of the inside. This I did, taking in a nice strong smell of the bag. I called out: 'Bloody hell!' as I got an instant headache and my eyes were watering. After the initial shock, I could smell almonds which, I was told, are the smell of explosives.

HM Prison Maze was also known as the 'H' Blocks. 'Long Kesh', or the 'Kesh was a prison used to house paramilitary prisoners during the Troubles from 1971 to 2000. It was located in a former RAF station at Long Kesh near Lisburn, nine miles outside Belfast, in County Antrim. The prison and its inmates played a prominent role in recent Irish history, notably in the 1981 hunger strike.

IAN METCALFE

Eddie Atkinson, Green Howards

I don't want anyone to think Ian Metcalfe is any more deserving than anyone else who lost their lives or was seriously injured in the Northern Ireland conflict. I would like to think this could be a tribute to all who lost their lives or suffered because of their service. Ian Metcalfe was my mate; we met in 1972 when we volunteered for a mortar platoon course. We became close friends because we supported the same team Leeds United and came from the same area; Ian was from Wyke in Bradford.

What kind of man was Ian? He was the type of bloke you would always know wouldn't let you down; he would stand with you 100,per cent but he had a wicked sense of humour, and on occasions it did get him into trouble with his mates as well as authority. It wasn't unknown for him to let everyone's tents down, and then as an afterthought he realised if he left his own up everyone would know who had done it, so let his own tent down. On the streets you knew he was with you and that he would always watch your back. As a soldier, isn't that all you need to know? That you had a mucker; a buddy who would never let you down was all that you needed to know. We all knew we could cop it any time because that goes with the job; we were doing a job but we have to think that all those deaths and injuries were in an attempt to bring peace to Northern Ireland. We had to try and take the centre ground until the politicians could be coaxed round the peace table.

But the way Ian was killed seems such a waste; he was killed with five others on a mini bus in Lisburn 1988 after completing a fun run to raise money to send two Irish babies to the USA for eye surgery. I still can't think that was a legitimate target. I've been reliably informed by Ian's widow, Rita that women and children were supposed to be on the bus. Would that have been a legitimate target? I think not. I will never forget him as thousands of others will not forget their friends and that is why Ian was no different or more deserving than anyone else. God bless him; God bless them all.

This atrocity took place in Lisburn on 15 June 1988. Six soldiers who had been on a 'fun run' in the garrison town in order to raise funds for the local YMCA – an organisation that cared for both Catholic and Protestants – were killed when an IRA bomb planted underneath their vehicle exploded. In what many view as an alarming lapse of security, the six men were allowed to climb on board the vehicle which had been left unattended and was therefore an opportunistic target for the IRA bombers. Many have felt that since Lisburn was such a major garrison town, full of military personnel, attacks were highly unlikely. The IRA later claimed that the device – at 7lbs, bigger than that normally used in UVBT attacks – had been designed to explode upwards so as to minimise civilian casualties. The remark attracted derision in Army and Government circles as it was shown that, had the area been packed with civilians, scores of others might have been killed or injured. But then, when did the terrorists worry about 'collateral damage'?

Had there been other deaths, there is no doubt that a statement from the IRA would have been hurriedly issued to the media, expressing regret. There were far too many of these sickening attacks on 'soft targets' to recount here, but one has only to look at Omagh, Ballykelly, Shankill Road Fisheries to name but a few of their many outrages.

Ian Metcalfe was 37 and married with two children. He was a professional soldier and had been in the Army for almost eighteen years.

On that terrible day, the following soldiers were killed alongside Ian Metcalfe: Sergeant Michael Winkler (31); Lance Corporal William Patterson (22); Mark Clavey (24) and Lance Corporal Graham Lambie (22) all from the Royal Corps of Signals and Lance Corporal Derek Green (24), RAOC. Whether the Army and RUC had become complacent in the area or the six men were tired and distracted after their exertions will never be known.

WORK TO RULE

CSM Haydn Davies, RRW

We had been searching outlying farms just south of Belfast for some weeks; nothing of worth was found, but it appears we were being watched and the IRA found us. Many of the farms in the area, although they were farmed, were unoccupied and the farmhouses empty, often derelict. Two patrols were working some way from the Company firm base. They had an unusual experience. On entering a farmyard there was a loud explosion near the empty farmhouse and a mature pig sailed through the air on its way skyward.

ATO was summoned and the farmyard staked out for eventual further search. ATO worked at his unenviable task and before he left he came over to brief us on what he had found. The explosive charge laid was a large one containing a huge amount of 'commercial explosive'. It had only partially exploded. The pig had tripped it in his wanderings and the poor thing had paid the ultimate sacrifice that had been destined for the patrols. Had the whole charge been activated we would have lost some soldiers.

Dog handlers with explosives search dogs arrived and they started to scour the area. They had been working for about two hours when our CO arrived. The CO heard one of the dog handlers say. 'That's it for me; my time's up.' He then descended on the handler, and leaning his six foot frame into his face, towering over the little dog handler, he bellowed aggressively: 'What do you mean? Time up! Where the bloody hell do you think you are? What bloody trade union rules are you operating under!' 'No, no, Sir; not my time, but the dog can only work for two hours before he becomes ineffective.' It is search dog rules Sir.'

Exit embarrassed CO stage left and a company of tired soldiers were left to chuckle on the way back to Palace Barracks. End of another routine day.

THE BATTLE OF THE DIVIS

Steve Norman, 3 Royal Anglian Regiment

A two-week-old ceasefire involving the IRA had ended abruptly on the night of 9 July 1972 in the Lenadoon Estate. This also ended for us, what had become a surreal existence in our own bit of the Lower Falls/Divis Flats area. We had for the past few days been patrolling without flak jackets and magazines on our SLRs. This was a visible effort on our behalf to show the locals we could adopt a non-aggressive stance and indeed, we even did a litter clearing up operation around the area during the ceasefire.

The tension in the air was broken on the night 12/13 July as we lay on our beds fully dressed, SLRs by our sides on standby. The first few shots had been aimed at the sangars in the Mill from the links within the Divis complex; fire was returned and a steady crescendo of gun fire could be heard all around the flats complex. We were under attack from all sides. 'Right,' said Sergeant Major 'B' (known to us all as 'Snuff'), 'you lot get into the attics and knock the roof tiles out and get into position. The lights in the area are going to be turned off any second now; it should help to see where the fire is coming from.' Sure enough, within a short time the whole area was blacked out and we could see the muzzle flashes from the gunmen coming from various positions in the flats. 'OK,' said 'Snuff', 'engage but make sure you have a target.' Within a split second my whole platoon began firing into the flats; the noise was deafening and we began shouting to each other where we could see the fire coming from.

This went on for what seemed an age but was probably no more than half an hour. Then came the order 'Right lads, get your faces cammed up; we're going in.' In the meantime, we had just heard the news that Lance Corporal Martin Rooney had been shot and killed in Clonard Street a while earlier. This fired us up and we could not wait to get out and have a go at them. We stormed out of the Mill and ran, zig-zagging towards the flats, as one or two dropped down and gave covering fire into the links. Sergeant 'K' told me to stick with him and I didn't need telling twice, this man was a brave soldier and very experienced. As I followed him into the flats, we could hear firing from above us at the top of the stairs, and he did not hesitate; he went up those stairs so fast I was left standing.

By the time I got to the top, he was firing at two figures that were by now running for their lives. One dropped down and I heard a long moan. We had been joined by dozens of other lads and firing was going on all around. It was complete mayhem. Sergeant 'K' turned to me and said: 'Stay here and guard this link; I'm going to push forward. If anyone comes, challenge them with a word that only we would know and if they don't know it let them have it.' Bloody hell, I thought; he meant it! And he did. Whilst in the prone position at the top of this stairwell I had crawled forward and could see through the railings a 'Knights of Malta' ambulance pull into the centre of the complex. I could see that several men were waving white sheets and dragging two figures wrapped in blankets. They proceeded to bundle them in to the ambulance whilst calling out: 'For God's sake don't shoot.' Luckily for them, no one did. I lay there for over two hours until the dawn began to break, and as the light grew stronger I noticed what I had thought was a puddle of water but which now was quite obviously a large pool of congealed blood. It was complete with drag marks leading along the walkway and down to the next set of stairs. This had in all probability come from the man I had seen the Sergeant drop earlier.

At last I heard footsteps coming up the stairs and my bum was squeaking like a mouse but I did as I had been told and shouted: 'Halt! Who are you?' A voice came back: 'It's me!' 'Well what's the name of our Choggie shop man?' I said rather stupidly. 'Gunga fucking Din,' came

Falls Road, July 1972. Divis Tower can be seen on the left and Hastings Street on the right. This photograph was taken during the rioting following the breakdown of the ceasefire in the Lenadoon Estate. *(Steve Norman)*

the reply, 'now get you skinny arse over here; we are going back.' Later on that day, we found out that we had lost another of our lads. Corporal Kenny Mogg had been killed at the junction of the Falls and Grosvenor Road during gun battles in the area.

This night would become folklore legend among the 3rd battalion as we all had a tale to tell and was ever after known as the Battle of the Divis.

On the night of 9 July 1972 ten people would be shot dead in the fierce fire fights which echoed through several parts of Belfast. Four Catholics were killed in the crossfire between soldiers and the IRA and this tragically included a thirteen-year-old school girl, Margaret Gargan from the Ballymurphy Estate. Four Protestants were killed by the IRA in more ruthless sectarian slaughter as tragedy showed it recognised no sectarian boundaries. Additionally, two IRA members were shot and killed during gun battles with soldiers.

July 1972 was amongst the worst months of the Troubles, as a total of 96 people, including eighteen soldiers and two police officers were killed. This period of savagery included the Claudy bombing (six civilian dead as a result of an IRA car bomb) and 'Bloody Friday' when the IRA killed nine people in a score or more explosions that devastated Belfast city centre. 30 years after the killings the IRA issued a statement of 'apology'.

TRAGEDY FOR THE ANGLE IRONS

Steve Norman, 3 Royal Anglian Regiment

> I first joined the Army on 4 January 1972, and did a basic fourteen weeks before being detailed to join my battalion who had just started a four-month emergency tour of Northern Ireland. 'A' Company was situated at Albert Street Mill in the Lower Falls area of Belfast which included the notorious Divis Flats complex. This was a very strong Republican area with overwhelming support for the Provisional IRA. Myself and three other new recruits were picked up from the Belfast ferry terminal having arrived that morning and were taken straight to Albert Street Mill and allotted our respective platoons. I was placed in 2 platoon 'A' company and I knew something was terribly wrong as soon as I met the platoon lads, because they completely ignored me and hardly spoke to each other and seemed very down and tired looking; I soon discovered why. Only a few days earlier on 16 April, the platoon commander Second Lieutenant Nick Hull had been shot dead on the Falls Road. He was in the back of an armoured PIG when a burst of gunfire came through the observation slit and hit him in the chest; he never regained consciousness and was pronounced dead at the hospital.
>
> 1972 turned out to be the most bloodiest and violent in all the subsequent years of the Troubles and a year I shall never forget.

He is not wrong. During 1972, in incidents related to the Troubles, an appalling 158 soldiers, including UDR personnel, lost their lives. To put this into some kind of perspective, approximately the same number of British personnel killed in Afghanistan over the years 2001 to May 2009.

> I was soon patrolling the streets and remember thinking that only fifteen weeks earlier I had been a young kid, daft as a brush with not a care in the world and now I was walking around with a powerful weapon being shot at and shooting back. This was a different world and I grew up fast. Those first four months changed my life forever, and I would never look at life the same way again. In all we lost four dead in Belfast; Nick Hull, John Ballard, Kenny Mogg, and Martin Rooney, together with numerous injured, some seriously.

There were a total of eight 'Angle Irons' killed in action that year. Second Lieutenant Nicholas Hull (22) from Bedford, shot by an Official IRA gunman at Divis Street on 16 April; Private John Ballard (18) from Grimsby, shot by an IRA sniper, Sultan Street, Belfast on 11 May; Lance Corporal Martin Rooney (22) from the Irish Republic, killed by the IRA at Clonard Street, Belfast on 12 July; Corporal Kenneth Mogg (29) from Melton Mowbray killed by the IRA during a fire fight at Dunville Park, Belfast the following day; Lance Corporal John Boddy (24) from Peterborough was shot and killed by an IRA sniper in Grosvenor Road, Belfast on 17 August. Corporal John Barry (22) from Kirton, Lincs, was shot in Cyprus Street in the Lower Falls area of Belfast on September 23; he died of his wounds two days later with his young wife at his bedside. Four days later, Private Ian Burt (18) from Essex was shot and killed in a fierce fire fight with members of both wings of the IRA. Finally, a year of tragedy for the Regiment ended on 24 October, when Private Robert Mason (19) from Wisbech was shot by an IRA sniper in the Grosvenor Road area of Belfast.

Steve Norman, aged nineteen at Bligh's Lane Camp, Londonderry. *(Via Steve Norman)*

The next year saw us posted yet again to Northern Ireland; this time to the notorious Creggan Estate, Londonderry, another hardline Republican IRA area. This time we knew what to expect and we knew it was a numbers game and some of us would not return. My company was billeted at the Bligh's Lane camp just up from the Bogside in Derry. It was a very vulnerable camp as the whole of the Creggan looked down on it, and as proved by later events, so did the IRA. 27 April is a date burned in my memory; this was the day my platoon mate Tony Goodfellow was shot dead by a sniper at the permanent VCP in the Creggan. He had just stepped out to take a driving licence from a car when two shots rang out and he fell to the ground hit in the chest. One of the lads (Andy) tried to give him mouth-to-mouth but he was dead within seconds, never knowing what hit him. The sickening thing was how the locals came out and laughed and jeered as he lay dying; that was the level these people had sunk to and frankly I felt sorry for them, because they had lost much more than Tony; they had lost their souls. Little did I know within a few weeks, I too would fall victim to that hatred.

Anthony Goodfellow (26) from Rushton, Northamptonshire was killed by an Official IRA sniper in Creggan Road, Londonderry. He had earlier rescued a Catholic girl who had been 'tarred and feathered' by a barbaric Creggan mob and had moved her to England where they had intended to get married.

It was the Fourth of July and we suspected the local Provos would try something as it was American Independence Day – the Americans being the people that they got most of their

Steve Norman (front centre), 3rd Royal Anglian, at the police station being built opposite the Unity Flats, July 1972. *(Via Steve Norman)*

funding from. We were on patrol and it all seemed too quiet; as we returned to Bligh's Lane, we got as far as the unloading bay when an almighty bang occurred and then something lifted us up and threw us down like rag dolls. The Provos had watched us and had fired an RPG 7 Russian anti-tank rocket at us. It hit the wall just above our heads and at the same time an IRA ASU began firing down at us. My section commander Bill immediately realised if we stayed where we were we would be sitting ducks so all his ambush training kicked in and he shouted to us to get up and attack the gunmen.

As I stood up, my left leg buckled under me and I felt a hot searing pain just above the back of my knee. I knew in an instant that I had been shot. Bill could see that I could not move so he shouted for me to stay down while he and the rest of the lads charged up the hill and engaged the IRA. The gunmen immediately legged it, but not before Bill shot one through the neck. For his actions that day Bill was awarded the Military Medal and if ever a man deserved it he did. Meanwhile, the medics had got to me and cut away my combat trousers to see what damage had been done. I had a hole roughly the size of a golf ball in the back of my leg right through to the bone. Amazingly there was very little blood as the red hot shrapnel had cauterised the arteries. They gave me a quick shot of morphine and got me to the Altnagelvin

Hospital in Derry, and there on a stretcher next to me in the emergency room was the IRA man who had been shot by Bill.

This cheered me up no end! I had an operation and stayed for a week before I was flown by helicopter down to Musgrave Park military hospital where another operation took place, this time to remove the shrapnel for forensics. It took me a full year to get back to fitness in order to return to platoon lines and when I reported for duty I was told they had gone back to the Creggan! So off I went back to the now dreaded place for one last tour.

Luckily, no one was killed on that last one and Bligh's Lane had been closed as being too vulnerable; a bit too late for some of us but I think we all lost something of ourselves in Northern Ireland. Part of us will always remain there.

BATTLE OF LONG KESH: SUMMER, 1974

CSM Haydn Davies, RRW

The battle of Long Kesh was the night that the prison was burned to the ground. Our Company was on 'stand down' at Palace Barracks, Belfast, and during the early evening we were changed from '24 hour standby' to 'Move in one hour' to 'Move now!' All three orders were issued within a period of about five minutes. Off we went as a company, at speed, in our armoured vehicles towards Long Kesh, thinking it was just another exercise. We had completed lots of those in the past, only to be stood down on arrival at the Kesh and sent back to barracks, after testing our ability to get there properly equipped.

As we approached the prison area, the skyline above Long Kesh in the distance told us that this one was different. Flames were flying in some places well above the prison to about fifty feet into the air and over a very large area. The whole night sky was well illuminated with a massive glow. We arrived outside the main prison gates, two very large tin gates about 30 feet wide and about 20 feet high. The gates were opened slowly by some RMPs that were standing outside them. In we went, a platoon at a time, line abreast and close behind each other, three platoons in all. Inside the gates all hell was let loose. The noise was deafening.

We went in at about 8pm, and we came out quite exhausted 24 hours later. The prison warders – about a hundred of them – passed back between our ranks as we moved forward through the gates to relieve them. They had been very badly beaten up, and there was hardly one of them that was not injured somewhere on his body; mostly head and facial wounds; some with front teeth missing, lots of blood on faces and heads. They had held their ground very well but were quite glad to get out of it. A few refused to leave and stayed with us.

As we moved towards them, the prisoners stopped and stared; there was a short lull, they just gazed at us for a moment, an eerie silence, and then recommenced the rioting. We set about subduing them with baton guns, tear gas and the riot club. Our Welshmen were in their element, but we were hard pushed because of the numbers involved and the number of missiles flying about. I cannot remember the numbers of prisoners but I think we were up against about 5,000 of them. We were only one company strong until two companies of the Royal Hampshire arrived a few hours later.

During the time before the Hampshires arrived, about eight or ten weapons that we had not seen before or since were issued to us by an ordinance officer. They were like baton guns with a cocoa tin fixed to the muzzle. One popped into the tin a close-fitting large rubber grenade with a metal base. When fired it gave an airburst above the crowd, exuding a storm of a jellified

CS gas downwards. It was very effective and went into their eyes and on their skin and clothing; there was no escape from it. It brought forth screams of: 'You British bastards,' followed by their departure from the field of battle and some very short quiet periods.

Then they returned with their ultimate weapon: full LPG gas containers with lighted cotton waste tied to the outlet valves. The gas containers were being rolled towards us on mess hall food trolleys. They ran them on their wheels at speed and released them to run into us. They exploded with a terrific 'thump' and sent a burning circular cloud of flame up into the air about thirty feet, then it drifted down and burnt out after some minutes. The cloud came down so slowly that it was easy to run away from its burning effect. We had no real answer to the LPG except to move back some yards and give volley fire with the jellied gas. On the whole it was a great night to be a soldier, all the excitement and none of the killing.

Some war dogs arrived with handlers. The dogs were, huge vicious, snarling bloody things; they frightened our soldiers more than they frightened the rioters. Two RAF Pumas arrived and started dropping large canisters of CS gas from the air on top of friend and foe alike; bloody dangerous! This was the first time that I realised that one can become immune to CS gas once all one's tears and bodily sweat is expended. Also that dogs do not have tear ducts, and are unaffected by CS gas! It was well after midnight when we had a quiet period for about two hours. In the meantime we could hear the prisoners singing in their burning compounds. Their morale was quite high. I can remember thinking what great people the Irish are to have on one's own side.

During the lull we had our briefings for the following morning's plan of attack. Other units had arrived to strengthen the cordon on the outside perimeter. The RRW and the Hampshires and also the DERR were given various compounds to capture at first light. Our Company target was to be Compound 13; this was the compound that contained the convicted IRA murderers.

At about 5am we went in hard and fast on a blind side to the compound occupants, but met resistance at the prisoners' aid store, which was attached to Compound 13. It was a little like the hospital scene from the film *Zulu*. We were battling to get through the breezeblock walls within the building in order to get into the compound, only to get bricked from within the compound. I seem to remember some soldiers behind me busy filling their pockets and ammo pouches with tins of polish, toothpaste, soap and so on. Finally, in we went and battled for about ten minutes; then suddenly the baddies all stopped and threw down their bed ends etc. They fell in facing us in three ranks of their own accord. One prisoner acted as spokesman, he marched forward and halted like a guardsman, and asked for food and water and medical aid, and, as we had a medic set him to work. Food and water we didn't have. We lined them up against a fence, body searched them and called the roll, but they refused to give names. We took their cigarettes from them and placed them into a big pile a metre high to one side.

Food arrived; cheese rolls and a pint of milk per prisoner; nothing for us. The qualification for the prisoners to have breakfast and a smoke was to answer the roll call, which they did. One gave the wrong name, but he was recognised by a warder who told us of this. His milk, rolls and fag went over the fence. He answered up correctly shortly afterwards.

We spent the rest of the day collecting various prisoners from other compounds and placing them back into their own compounds. They didn't want to do this and many had to be dragged screaming from compound to compound. During all this mayhem a new prisoner was admitted and arrived with his escort from the courts; he had a guitar on his back, a hold-all in his hands and a look of utter confusion on his face.

We started to pack up and leave during the late afternoon. As we did so our 'B' Company arrived, and they were tasked to protect two squadrons of Royal Engineers who were to rebuild the prison. They don't give up, the British!

At about first light, whilst on our way to Compound 13 in an alley way we came upon four brutish looking prisoners. We moved towards them, prepared for close quarter stuff, but good naturedly they held their hands in the air and sat down on the ground saying, 'Hold on fellers, we're going to sit this one out.' I enquired, 'Had enough have you?' 'We have that,' was the reply. His black head of hair was a mass of blood, and a passing soldier threw him a field dressing. Of all the fighting in Long Kesh that night, there was a certain amount of chivalry between the prisoners and the Army; there were no unnecessary beatings or vicious wounding from either side. The only real visible animosity was between the prisoners and the warders.

THE MAZE RIOTS

Stephen, Staffordshire Regiment

I was about three months into my first tour of Londonderry and we had spent endless weeks patrolling the streets of Shantallow and Carn Hill. During the evening of 15 October 1974 our Platoon was put on standby with rumours rife that the Maze Prison just outside Belfast was ablaze, and that the PIRA Prisoners interned there were planning a mass breakout. It seemed that the monotony was going to be broken and we were soon receiving our orders to jump in the three-tonners and head towards Belfast. I recall our Platoon Sergeant at the time – Paul Mullingani – flying up to the Maze complex by helicopter from our Fort George base in order that he could attend a briefing.

It was early evening when we reached the Maze and we were held in a secure area along with hundreds of other troops. I recall smoke coming from the area of the prison and it was, in fact, burning. It would appear that inside the camp all the prison officers had withdrawn and the PIRA Members had started to empty the contents of their Nissan huts. All of their personal possessions had been stacked outside the main door and the huts systematically set on fire. They then moved into the middle of the complex where the football fields were situated. A decision was made that no troops would enter the Maze that evening; we would wait until first light and then we would enter armed only with baton rounds and long wooden batons.

The next day – 16 October – along with 2,000 other troops, we entered the prison complex to be greeted by some 1,500 convicted or remanded IRA terrorists. It's interesting to note at this stage that the Loyalist prisoners wanted no part in the proceedings and 'Gusty' Spence, the leading figure from the Loyalist internees, indicated to commanders that his men would provide first aid assistance! I can still remember entering the compound and seeing the Loyalist prisoners standing on the roofs of their huts, watching the action unfold.

I think that we were one of the first to enter and, as we ran towards the football pitch, I remember looking to my right and seeing members of another regiment charging towards the fencing that surrounded the field. I ran straight towards the fence, and all kinds of missiles were being thrown; because I was so close, the majority of objects were missing me. As I stood there and caught my breath, standing right in front of me was a prisoner who was wearing sections of bedding mattress which he had cut up and tied around his body to protect himself. In a surreal moment, we made eye contact and he gave me that look as if to say: 'I know that I look a complete wanker,' and we both smiled.

In front of me were hundreds of prisoners, some even dressed in Army issue flak jackets and tin helmets. Some had improvised and had made respirators from the foam from mattresses. Prisoners then ran up to the wire fence with containers and threw kerosene over us, after

Member of 14 Platoon D Company 1 Staffords. Maze Prison riots, October 15–16 1974. *(Stephen Durber)*

Damaged caused by internees at the Maze riots. *(Stephen Durber)*

Surveying the damage. Four guard dogs were burned to death. *(Stephen Durber)*

which, someone would throw lighted matches at us to try and set us on fire. I soon became soaked and made my mind up not to have a ciggie until I changed out of those clothes. As you can imagine all kinds of chaos erupted, and to my right I saw that a soldier from another regiment had somehow got through a small wicker gate and had entered the main football field, where he was immediately set on by prisoners. What he was thinking about or what his intentions were I don't know, but I watched him fight for his life and, fortunately for him, he managed to get back through the gate with the help of his colleagues. Behind me screaming and shouting continued as an Army Saracen armoured vehicle came racing through the ranks. As soldiers scattered, it rammed the fence and on the second attempt the fence collapsed. From above an Army helicopter arrived and swooped in very low. I don't remember at what stage I put on my respirator but I do recall a guy leaning out and firing masses of tear gas out of the open door.

By this time the fence had been destroyed not only by the Saracen but the several hundred soldiers that were moving through. Baton round after baton round was fired at the prisoners who were determined to stand their ground and fight. My section alone fired 400 baton rounds that day, to put the whole thing into perspective. It was baton charge after baton charge as we tried to force the hundreds of prisoners over to the far end of the football field. CS gas still continued to be fired from above and due to the amount of it, my respirator was worse than useless and I had to withdraw and cough my guts up. I went back in and came out a further three times due to the amount of gas I was inhaling.

Members of 14 Platoon D Company 1 Staffords feel the effect of CS gas. *(Stephen Durber)*

Members of 14 Platoon reorganise. *(Stephen Durber)*

Situation contained. The Maze closed in September 2000. *(Stephen Durber)*

14 Platoon D Company 1 Staffords, team photo. *(Stephen Durber)*

On entering for the last time, I recall running across the football field where the majority of the prisoners had now been lined up against the wire fence. I ran past some prisoners who were stacked some five or six high in a pile not moving. I thought: 'My God; what's happened to them?' They looked dead.

I have no idea how long this operation took, but I know at the end I followed a medical officer around the fence who examined the now spread-eagled prisoners. Each prisoner was then photographed and then it was me who ran them out into the centre of the football field, where some cakes and milk had been left in bread baskets. They were then to collect this and take their place back against the fence. Not many made it back with full rations, as the chasing Alsatian war dog made sure that much of it spilled on the journey back.

One other memory was that of a PIRA prisoner, a giant of a man, refusing medical treatment. His top lip was hanging on by a small piece of skin and he looked in a bad way from other injuries. He refused all treatment. I asked the medic why this was and he replied: 'He was scared of the needle.'

We returned back to Fort George in Londonderry and we were debriefed. It was then off to the stores to be re-issued with kit that did not smell of kerosene!

Three prison staff were kept in hospital after rioting prisoners set fire to the prison, and more than 130 prisoners were injured; nine needed hospital treatment. One officer was treated after suffering a fractured skull.

UNDERCOVER IN BELFAST

James Kinchin-White, Royal Green Jackets

On returning to Belfast, I had a different role, albeit back in the Lower Falls. Amongst the various responsibilities of the Intelligence Section NCO are skills in nuclear, biological and chemical defence, photography and the collation and dissemination of information. I kind of guessed that we weren't going to nuke Ballymurphy or gas the Whiterock.

To say we didn't have much in the way of information is a little misleading; in fact, there was probably lots of it. Every time a patrol stopped someone in the street it was the usual spiel: Name? Address? What colour are your curtains? I mean, for fuck's sake, we must have been the best qualified interior designers in the whole of Ireland. The real problem was that people didn't share information. Now I can see reasonable cause for PIRA to keep their secrets, they weren't on the same side after all; but we had MI5, Special Branch, HQ Northern Ireland, the RUC and Battalion Intelligence.

Add to this the operations of a number of different specialist Army units and you have a right mixture of vested interests. Information, as I found out during '72, had its own hierarchy – the lower down the pecking order, the more likely you were to specialise in interior design; higher up you got to dabble in the Republican Who's Who; and if you were really important, well, you got the MBE complete with a 30-year order prohibiting anyone finding out what you did to get it.

In any event, my life in the world of sneaky beaky came to an abrupt end when it emerged that the political sympathies of my new family were somewhat Republican. I suppose it might have been different had my other half not decided to move back to Belfast while I was there on duty – or perhaps it was the family home's proximity to TAC HQ – I must have been the only squaddie that didn't need a phone to talk to his spouse while on duty in Belfast. All I had to do was go to one of the roof-top sangers and we could almost hold hands when she appeared in the attic window. Neither chief sneaky nor beaky were impressed however. I was effectively judged to be a security risk and banned from the Ops Room until arrangements could be made for my transfer back to the UK. But not yet!

Having arrived with the advanced party in '72 and being responsible for the collation and dissemination of mug-shots of known players and other 'persons of interest', I was assigned to another location to introduce some of our new arrivals to people and places of interest. (I wonder if I could get a job with Black Taxi Tours – perhaps as a homer from my day job in interior design – Join the Army, get a trade eh?) During one such period of induction I had pointed out, in passing so to speak, a person of interest who was engaged in that highly suspicious act of standing outside a pub having a fag. I did it in passing because we were belting up the Falls Road in Land Rovers when I spotted him. The general noise level in an open-topped Land Rover belting up the Falls Road is, believe it or not, incompatible with normal conversation and thus I disseminated this piece of 'intelligence' by pointing to the appropriate mug shot and pointing towards the said public house, whereupon the head honcho decided to u-turn the vehicles and effect an arrest. In the resulting melee the poor lad was unceremoniously 'lifted' together with another pub patron whose consumption of the house beverage was sufficient to lead him to believe that he could get away with calling us a bunch of 'effing Nazi bastards' whilst taking a swipe at a junior born leader. Frankly, in his situation and in the prevailing setting he might have had a point, and if I hadn't been on duty I might have helped him stiff the junior born leader since he was a pain in the arse anyway; but life is rarely simple.

After depositing our captives at TAC HQ we were heading up the road to return to base when the unmistakable sound of an Armalite broke the night air. An immediate anti-ambush drill was executed as the occupants of both vehicles de-bussed and took up defensive firing positions. For my part, I was last out of the rear vehicle and took up a kneeling position next to the front offside of the Land Rover. I had fired two rounds to take down the street lighting (and to make the opposition think they were being fired upon) when a blue flash struck the vehicle antennae just a few inches from my head.

On reflection, my training took over; I moved, rolled and took up a new position of cover behind another stationary vehicle and the event passed without further ado, until the next morning when I inspected the damage to the Land Rover antennae box. The round which had struck it was embedded in the casing; it had been fired not from in front of me, but from behind, and it was an SLR round from an Army rifle! The only 'friendly forces' behind us were the soldiers in TAC HQ, about one hundred metres away. I have always believed that, in the dark and perhaps turning at the sound of gunfire and seeing my muzzle flashes, one of them mistook my fire for enemy fire. I never did get to follow up the question as I was sent packing the next day, back to base in England.

WHAT CEASEFIRE?

Andy Thomas, 2 Royal Anglians

It was 29 January 1997 and we were based at Springfield Road RUC station [known to the locals as 'the barracks']. We had been in the Province about two months now, and there was talk of a renewed ceasefire again! However, what they (the IRA), said and did were two different things.

In the incident which lives with me, my platoon was out on the ground and I was part of QRF [Quick Reaction Force]. Our brick consisted of Lance Corporal Hedge, Privates Squibb, Killingsworth and me. We were to deploy for a fourteen-hour shift on the streets at 1700 hours, and we were just chilling out. A few minutes later, we heard an almighty bang. It was not too far away either! Suddenly, we heard a big explosion and we were immediately 'crashed out'. We star burst – nervously, I might add – out of the RUC station and into Springfield Road. My head seemed fuzzy and my nerves were on edge and my heart was racing as I sprinted along the road. I was shaking with fear and adrenalin and did not know what to expect, but I do remember a scene of chaos. An APC was parked close to what I later learned was the impact area of the Prig missile where it had hit a training centre. I was crippled with fear, but also felt a sense of aggression – ready I thought to take out one of them. I was ordered by Lance Corporal Hedge to go static in hard cover, in a good firing position. By this time, there were RUC vehicles (APCs and Land Rovers) on the scene and there were even a couple of Gazelle helicopters above us.

After some minutes, and with the area cordoned off by the RUC, all seemed calmer, I started to breathe easier and my guts seemed less tense! There were crowds gathering outside the cordon, and the local kids were taking the piss as usual. A mortar had been fired at a joint Army/Police patrol and I just remember a burning smell where the missile had hit the Springvale training centre. Two armoured Land Rovers were on patrol under the command of a lance Jack called Oldenburg and two Privates – Perry and Gill – were on top cover. The lead vehicle was blocked by a vehicle, probably driven by members of PIRA in what was clearly a 'come on'. The mortar, a homemade device, was fired from an alley way at the second vehicle – commanded by Corporal Riley – and it just whizzed past the two top covers (Privates Sell and Fennell) missing them by inches. In all the noise and confusion, the IRA suspects just melted away and, by the time we got there and took up firing positions, they were either in a safe house or supping a pint in a local pub. The searching carried on long into the night and on balance, we were lucky. The mortar hit an empty building.

Our call sign N35 commanded by Lance Corporal Hedge carried on for a longer shift. It made for a very tiring night, after the nerves and adrenalin had gone.

On another occasion, we were on duty inside Fort Whiterock and we heard what we took to be an explosion coming from the New Barnsley/Ballymurphy area. A patrol from our 'A' company had come under an IRA command wire IED attack in Glenalina Park. Thankfully, no-one had been hurt in the attack. Although they had all been shaken they had managed to lift a major PIRA player, Christopher 'N'. This took place on Thursday 6 March 1997, and we remained on high alert inside Fort Whiterock.

I have to admit that I felt the butterflies and my guts were getting tighter and tighter; I knew that I had to fight my fears but it got no better. We occasionally had bricks and other debris come flying over the perimeter walls and our lannies [Land Rovers] and sangars took a real hammering. All the time, Sinn Fein was supposedly pressing for peace: or was I being naïve?

Some time later, I was on patrol in Glenalina Park and I saw the huge hole in the wall where the IED had gone off; from that day on, I have never walked close to walls. At the time I really wanted was to be at home in England and not in imminent danger in bloody Belfast.

A glance at the date of the second incident that Andy describes speaks volumes about Sinn Fein/IRA; it was on 2 March almost a month after the 'final ceasefire' which was heralded by the murder of Lance Bombardier Stephen Restorick at Bessbrook Mill on 12 February 1997.

Royal Anglians at New Barnsley RUC station. *(Andy Thomas)*

Fortified OP at the top of New Lodge Road. *(Neil Scarbro)*

The fact that soldiers continued to die either directly or indirectly connected to the Troubles/IRA shows what a sham it was at the time. The fact that a lot of the later deaths such as Private Andrew Richardson (12 March 1997) and Corporal Gary Fenton (22 June 1998) went largely unannounced by the government of the day again reveals a lot. The newly elected Blair government was wooing the terrorists and incidents like this, if made openly public, could well have jeopardised the 'peace process'.

PARTING GIFTS FROM BELFAST

Lee Sansum, Royal Military Police

It was nearly the end of my 104 weeks in the Province and strangely I was going to be sad to leave; one gets addicted to the adrenalin, the boredom, the constant threat, the bullshit and the rain. You could tell when it was summer in Belfast, the rain was warm. Two years was officially your limit in Ulster, any more and it could seriously damage your health. I did meet soldiers who had stayed too long, a Para who had done the best part of four years in the city; he got posted quickly after a patrol discovered him out for a run with his dog down the Falls Road at three in the morning.

A close friend had served three years constantly out on the ground in West Belfast, and I last saw him in the city leading his team back into North Howard Street Mill having survived a coffee jar bomb attack. The wounded were being taken off the ground by armoured vehicles, but he insisted that the rest of his team who were able to walk would do so. 'No Fenians are going to see me run away; we will walk back to camp,' he said. I first heard the commotion inside the Mill by the loading bay, and then looked on at the Gate guard in his full body armour taking up his position as the massive armour-plated gate automatically opened. This was the shittiest job in Belfast, some poor Tom would get dressed up in the most ridiculous looking full body armour you could imagine, in fact you could be mistaken for thinking you were looking at some huge green robot shuffling in a strange way because of the sheer weight of armour. Mind you, he needed it, as he was the poor unfortunate soldier that always exited the base every time the gate opened and was the softest target in the Battalion.

I saw Corporal 'B' walking towards me, still some 100 yards away; his clothing was still smoking from the dockyard confetti thrown from the bomb that had embedded in his body armour. His face was blackened and he was strolling without a care in the world. The rest of his patrol were hard targeting like crazy but he had lost the plot and looked like he was on a summer's day stroll. He was soon posted.

MORE TRAGEDY FOR YORKSHIRE

Mick Potter, Royal Artillery

I have been reading *A Long Long War* and I noticed that one of ours (25 RA) had submitted an article on page 100. I also noticed your comment that it was 'thought that it was Gunner Clifford Loring'.

It pains me to confirm to you that it was Cliff; unfortunately. The buzz went round that he had been 'tapped' on a VCP on Stockmans lane and we were gutted; this was our first. Not for the RA, but for 25. I remember the lad was sent to us as we were under strength as per nominal roll. He had just turned eighteen and was terrified that he was going to get it. We – as older vets, if you like – took him under our wings and looked out for him. All was going well and he was catching on. He was deployed to the VCP; his last deployment. Whilst the VCP was being set up, the Sergeant told him to stay close and 'watch and learn' how it was done. Consequently he was trailing the Sergeant closely, making mental notes for the future so that it all became like clockwork.

He was standing next to the NCO, when a gunman opened fire, presumably at the senior man. The round entered the collar of the Sergeant's flak jacket and exited through the collar and caught poor Cliff in the temple, causing him serious head injuries. He subsequently died of wounds received. The Sergeant concerned was shaken, naturally, bearing in mind that he was the original target. He later rallied and was soon back on the job. I have no contact with him these days as he is a bit of a recluse. The poor man always felt guilty about that incident. Peculiar that, when something like it happens, you see past rank and you see a hurting, terrified human being and cannot help but to try to make it all go away for them.

Cliff was flown home to his family and was given a full military funeral. He is gone, but for all who knew him, he will never be forgotten. This is just one story of several that dominate the uselessness of all that went on. The cost to us all was just too high both in terms of loss of friends and things we have to bear until we reach 'Rounds complete'.

Looking back at this incident and another in '72 when we lost Gunner Paul Jackson to an IED, it still hurts to think of people we knew and shared our lives with suddenly taken from us. I hear the words of the infamous Rev Ian Paisley in my mind, though a little faded now: 'No surrender.' I wish it was possible to find these people who committed these murders. How long would they last in a fair fight? Who knows?

The young man of whom Mick Potter writes so fondly and who had been with his comrades a very short time, died of his wounds two days later. He came from the Barnsley area. Gunner Paul Jackson (21) a married man with two young children was killed in the Londonderry area whilst filming an incident outside a supermarket in Strand Road. He was another son of Yorkshire and his family lived in Leeds.

Bill 'Spanner' Jones, REME

When Gunner Clifford Loring came out from the School of Artillery to the 25th RA, he was still seventeen and was unable to join us in Belfast in the summer of '71. However, when his eighteenth birthday came around, he was sent out to meet up with his unit.

He got on the ferry in Liverpool on Friday evening, arriving in Belfast Saturday morning, and, as he was officially eighteen, he went straight to the Andersonstown bus depot to join his Battery. Two days later, on the Sunday, he went on his first duty, manning a VCP, where he received the fatal wound. The news filtered through to us at Sunnyside; a group of us, REME and RA sat in the NAAFI discussing the loss of the new lad. It was Ringo who put it best when he said: 'I am not sure if I am more shocked by his death or ashamed that I never got to know him.'

That summed it up pretty well; just eighteen; just arrived and murdered so cruelly. Clifford Loring; gone but never forgotten.

So many people have used the same words to me over the years; I went to Ireland a boy, and came back as a man. Tragically, Clifford Loring, like Tommy Stoker (18), John McCaig (17), his brother Joseph (18), William Jolliffe (18) and Miles Amos (18) all died as boys over the water; and this list is by no means exhaustive.

Gunner Clifford Loring (18) from the village of Grimethorpe was shot and fatally wounded by the IRA on 29 August 1971. Clifford Loring left England on a Friday, was shot on the following Sunday and died on a Tuesday.

SPOTTERS

Steve Norman, 3 Royal Anglian Regiment

I was now ready for my baptism of fire and we left the Mill in the small, claustrophobic, confines of the Humber PIG. A section of us all crammed in; it not only rolled around like a fat pig but smelt like one too; a mixture of sweaty socks, cheap choggie burgers and fag smoke. As we neared the Divis Flats we pulled onto the waste ground opposite and de-bussed. I had barely got three paces, when I heard a 'clack, clack, clack' from the flats and a shout of: 'Fucking hell, they got me ear' from inside the PIG. I dived to the ground and cocked my weapon. Looking into the vehicle I saw little Jock clutching his ear with blood oozing out between his fingers.

Just at that moment the OC of 'A' company turned up in another vehicle and you had to admire the man because he stood out in full view of the Divis and shouted at the top of his voice: 'The next time anyone fires at you, let the buggers have it!' This was clearly done to let the gunman know if he fired again up to twenty SLRs would respond and we would not be too choosy where we fired. The ball was in his court and no more shots came from him. The OC shouted: 'Anyone hurt?' Little Jock replied: 'Sir, sir they shot my fucking ear hole!' and they had indeed taken a nick out of it but he was one lucky guy that day. Of course from then on at any company booze ups back in Germany, when Jock turned up he got the inevitable: 'Sir, sir, they shot me fucking ear' shout from the lads.

The night of 13 May 1972 was one I shall never forget as long as I live. We were on patrol when there was the sound of a bomb going off in the distance. We later found out that Kelly's Bar in West Belfast had been the target. Within a short while all hell broke loose with gunfire coming from all directions. Loyalist gunmen were engaging IRA gunmen and we as usual were stuck in the middle. It lasted what seemed to be hours. We had taken cover behind a heap of broken rubble and bricks and were trying to see where the fire was coming from with not much success, as none of us had fired at any targets. Suddenly from behind us came a young voice: 'Hey mister; they are over there by the church; there's two of 'em.' We could hardly believe our eyes, because, not more than two foot behind us lay two young lads no more than twelve or thirteen. 'What the fuck are you doing here?' asked our Corp incredulously, 'are you mad?' 'We've come to spot for you, mister; that's the Fenian fuckers' area over there. We know this place better than ye do.' And so for the next thirty-odd minutes that's exactly what they did, pointing out possible targets and showing no fear whatsoever. Eventually one said: 'Sorry, mister; got to go now. Me mam will be mad at us if we stop out too late' and with that they just upped and ran back down the road. We never even got to know their names but somewhere in Belfast today, there are two Protestant men – possibly in their early 50s – who will recall what they did as kids that night.

NORTH STREET PAINT STORE BOMB

Gunner Nigel Glover, Royal Artillery

One of the most unforgettable events that I had in Ireland was when we were coming back in from patrolling the city outside the segments. We turned the corner onto North Street leading to Smithfield market. Normally this was a very busy street where a number of black taxis were parked waiting for their fare but on this occasion there were not any taxis to be seen, the place was deserted and there was a deadly silence all around; it didn't look good. We then contacted the operation room over the radio and informed them of the situation.

We had only walked a short distant along the road when we heard a sound coming from a derelict, burned-out building on the opposite side of the road. Now I was even more on edge and I could hear my heart pounding at a rate of knots; we could be in the shit here. We crossed the street to carry out a visual check into the old burned-out building; we could smell burnt wood, just like a bonfire smell. We did not see anything at this point nor did we venture inside. The Lance Corporal radioed in that we could not see anything or anyone. We moved off and made our way toward Smithfield and turned the right-hand corner and walked a short distance to enter the rear of the segments gates back into the GCH. On entering GCH, we had to unload and make safe our weapons in the unloading point. I had just cleared the unloading bay when there was an almighty explosion that shook the whole building. Like a rocket I was running up those bloody stairs. I couldn't see much from our window, so I ran down the corridor to another room with a better view. By now there were a number of others looking at what had happened. At the time I had a small 110 Kodak instamatic camera that was always in my flak jacket breast pocket and I started taking pictures of the billowing acrid smoke coming out of what was the paint store.

Then the fire-fighters were on the scene and up went a fire-fighter on the extendable ladder. At times he was covered by the smoke and disappeared from sight, but by now the building was an inferno. We were all laughing at the fire-fighter on the ladder in his efforts to put out the fire, seeing this poor sod going back and forth. Then came another explosion and a fireball of flames engulfed the remains of the building that shot up skywards in the air. The ladder operator must have had sharp reflexes to get that fire-fighter out of the flames, because in a split second the ladder shot back like a catapult; how he stayed on the ladder I do not know. Had it not been for the quick reactions of the ladder operator there would have been another casualty. Though there was laughter at the time at the efforts of the fire-fighters it brought it home to me that not only were we soldiers and police in the front line of the terrorist attacks but also those brave fire-fighters.

This day's event could have been a very close call for us on that patrol, had we taken just that little bit longer investigating the derelict building or taken another route back to the GCH. Had we gone past the paint store and around Smithfield market maybe all of us would not be here today to tell this story. I have always thought that the bombers had waited until we were out of range before setting off their bomb; it could have been so very different.

UP AGAINST THE IRA 'TOP BRASS'

Mick King 1st Battalion Royal Regiment of Fusiliers

When 1RRF was posted in Ballykelly in the early 1980s, I was a 'full screw' Search Team Commander. One day all the search teams in the Battalion did a joint operation in Londonderry; we were given early morning briefings and I was given the address that my team would be searching. I remember at the time that we were nervous but dead keen, having completed our search cadres not long before that. We were told to look for IRA 'uniforms', weapons, ammunition, or anything that might have been used in recent post office robberies.

We were all given an RUC man to join us and we arrived at the houses at 6am screeching up in Land Rovers. I also had a search dog and handler with me; a lovely black Labrador as I remember. Our RUC officer banged on the door and we heard people come downstairs all half asleep like. I remember the police showed the people the paperwork and we all barged in. There were six people in my team; myself the Search Commander, a door man, two lads upstairs and two lads downstairs. The search began with much vigour and enthusiasm.

Before the search began, the dog did a cursory search around the house which was dirty and quite smelly. It was the home of a PIRA member who was OTR [on the run]. His father was upstairs in bed and he was an old IRA volunteer with only one leg. The story was that it had been blown off during the Troubles. To our astonishment and amusement, the search dog decided to pick up his artificial plastic limb and carry it around the house! This didn't go down well with the already angry household.

I positioned my door man and gave him the orders: 'Don't answer the door and no one gets past you! Understand?' Anyway, after about 30 minutes into the search, I heard a commotion at the front door. My doorman who was a sprog (new lad) opened the door to be confronted by a very angry Martin McGuinness and his henchman Mitchell McGlaughlin. I ran downstairs because they had barged passed my door man using force and I was stood face to face with McGuinness. His face was that close to mine, that I could feel his agitated breath on mine. Neither of us was willing to back down. I told him that he was not getting past as we were doing a house search. I told both of them that if they didn't leave the house, they would be moved forcibly. I asked for back-up from the cordon patrol outside; Corporal Joe Brown, a fellow Geordie, who was only about five foot two inches. He came around the corner, saw the situation, and dragged McGuinness forcefully out of the house! Little Joe 'Broon' and McGuinness were basically scrapping in the street, and I was left fighting McGlaughlin in the corridor, who was a big man, by the way!

In the end, our policeman, who was an old part-time reservist, told us all to stop; very much like a boxing referee would stop a bout! We all stopped, fighting for breath, and he got on his radio to police headquarters. Much to our annoyance and to stop the situation from escalating, McGuinness and McClauglin were allowed to come into the house and supervise our search to make sure we were not harassing the one-legged IRA member. I remember McGuinness walking past me in that corridor, looking me straight in the eyes and smirking as if he'd won the battle. Alarm bells started going off in my head. Out of all the house searches that were going on in Londonderry, why would Martin McGuinness come to the house that I was searching? I sternly warned McGuinness and McGlaughlin to put their hands in their pockets and not to take them out. Every time they took their hands out of their pockets, I would physically search them. Not a nice experience if you have ever been searched by a soldier, especially around the groin area!

Our search intensified and much to our satisfaction, we found IRA 'uniforms', ski masks, and £35,000 in cash, which we assumed had been stolen from a local post office to raise funds for the IRA to buy weapons and munitions.

For my actions and for not backing down and for my performance as a Section Commander in Northern Ireland between 1984 and 1985, I was awarded a commendation in the Operational Gallantry Awards list for service in Northern Ireland. I'll never forget that black Labrador running around the house with a plastic leg in its mouth! Every time I see Martin McGuinness or Mitch McGlaughlin who are now high ranking members of the Northern Ireland parliament, I always think to myself: 'I had a fight with them!'

THE SEVEN DWARVES: 1 RRW BELFAST 1974

Company Sergeant Major George Harris had an expansive sense of humour, abnormal in fact, and so much so that it sometimes got him into trouble, but not on this particular occasion. The whole battalion called him 'George' but not to his face of course. George's sense of military etiquette would never have taken that, not even from the CO.

George was on a day task with his company at a Protestant area of North Belfast on some sort of standby. Riots were expected, it was the time of the Ulster general strike. Nothing happened all day and George had time to think; this was bad for him as a rule. However, back to the story! The whole Company were sheltering up behind the Company PIGs whilst sentries had the area staked out; all was quiet and relaxed in a comparatively safe area.

Towards evening a crowd of over a hundred or so people were seen to be gathering in the road and forming up for an advance on the Company position. George casually walked out into the road and stood and faced them. There was about a hundred yards between George and the small Protestant crowd. Suddenly, as in Disney's *Snow White and the Seven Dwarves*, George put his two hands to his mouth and bellowed out two very loud and slow 'Hi – Hos'! There was silence for a few seconds, and then from his obviously well briefed company came the return call, 'Hi Ho!' from a hundred men, and all done in the fine Welsh choral style. Another 'Hi Ho' from George, then around from behind the vehicles came his whole company in two marching groups singing loudly the dwarf's marching song. 'Hi ho, Hi ho, it's off to work we go!'

There were no riots that night!

TEETH AND TAIL

Mick 'Benny' Hill, Royal Anglians

There has always been a lot of friction between the 'teeth' and the 'tail' troops in the Army; any Army in fact. This is probably caused by each being somewhat unaware of what the other half actually does; the 'tail' resent the 'teeth' for being scruffy, abrasive, and often extremely profane. The 'teeth' resent the fact that the 'tail' has pressed uniforms, regular hours, constant hot water and showers, and enough sleep. They seldom meet on neutral turf, and rarely get to see what the other half actually does. Our own attached personnel were marvellous; the battalion couldn't have functioned without them.

Farther back down the line it did not always appear to be the case. Our RCT drivers were always there when needed; most of them would gladly go out with us on foot patrols if they were having a less busy day. The medics were fantastic, as were the REME, both armourers and mechanics. There always seemed to be someone in their workshop getting oily and mending things that some Tom had managed to break. Any request for something to be repaired was usually greeted by the traditional REME reply of: 'You fucking wanker; go and get a cup of tea, and I'll see what I can do.' Invariably it was fixed. The cooks performed marvels. At Albert Street Mill, it was possible to get tea and a 'banjo' 24 hours a day; even for visitors. The three cooks at Hastings Street had a kitchen the size of a normal living room, two domestic cookers and one sink, and they still turned out quality scoff for over 100 all ranks. What hours they worked or how they managed to produce the goods so consistently is completely beyond me. I just did what squaddies have done for years; turn up, moan about the choice, slag off the cooks, then go away and enjoy the meal; what would we have done without them!

The 'tail' at Lisburn was a different matter. Very early one morning in '72, I had to go to Lisburn to collect a dog and its handler to deliver to Mulhouse to take part in a search; in those days, there was no NI Dog Unit, and not many dogs and handlers. All were RAVC, and mostly based in Lisburn, and sent to Units on an 'as and when' basis. I rendezvoused with the handler, and enquiring about his lack of flak jacket was informed that it was up to my unit to provide one. I told him in no uncertain terms that I wasn't taking him to Mulhouse without one, and that we would both go and see the store man. The store man, somewhat smugly I thought, informed me that flak jackets were only to be issued as short term loans.

I explained my position to him. When a pissed off 6 foot 3 inch Infantry Sergeant is squeezing your Adam's apple in a very unfriendly way, you can sometimes realise that perhaps the rules are a little inflexible, and open to re-interpretation!

Amen to that; you will not hear one derogatory comment from the author in regards to the 'tail' troops, whether or not they were RCT, ACC, REME or whatever support unit was there in Northern Ireland. They were as equally vulnerable to attack as the front-line infantry units when out on foot or mobile patrols and they were also equally vulnerable when off-duty also. The IRA/INLA was not too much concerned about the colour of a soldier's beret or the shape of his cap badge when it came to killing troops.

The single highest number of fatalities among the mainland units was suffered by the Royal Artillery, the unit most infantrymen would refer to as 'drop shorts' and 'long range snipers'. Basically used as a front line soldier, the Gunners suffered 70 deaths in or as a result of the Troubles. Other 'tail' unit fatalities were as follows: Royal Engineers 40, RCT/RLC 35, Royal Corps of Signals 29, REME 19, Army Catering Corps 9, Women's Royal Army Corps 8, RAMC/QARANC 7, Royal Army Pay Corps 4, Royal Army Veterinary Corps 2, Royal Army Education Corps and Royal Army Dental Corps 1 each. This totals 155 'tail' troops –excluding RA – or almost 12 per cent of all identified fatalities in Northern Ireland. I have deliberately excluded the 'blanket stackers' of the RAOC from the 'tail' echelon of the Army as they were in the forefront of bomb disposal and can, therefore, in this context, be seen as 'teeth' troops.

HOME ON LEAVE FROM BELFAST

Lee Sansum, Royal Military Police

Eventually I would intentionally bring Northern Irish currency back to my Lancashire home as I could find myself in West Belfast in the morning, and drinking in a local pub in the afternoon. After a few beers the Irish notes would come out and so would my rage. I would always drink a third of the beer then give the note over the bar. 'We can't take this; it's foreign!' That would be the trigger; the pint would then be sunk and I would go into my rehearsed patter. 'You're telling me that I am fighting in Northern Ireland to keep the Province part of the UK and you won't even take the currency? Don't you know what going on over there; what's wrong with you?' This was usually said in a loud enough voice for the other people in the bar to overhear.

That's what I wanted; confrontation, violence, a vent for my anger; shit, what had I to be frightened of? Admittedly I was seen as a tough guy on my massive housing estate but this, Northern Ireland, the War, the Troubles was something different; that was tough. I wish the public had witnessed, as I did, the nineteen-year-old Para with the back of his head blown off; the entry wound on his young face barely visible. Or the young soldier and colleague on 'cut off' who died at a VCP, shot in the shoulder, with the round slowed down by his body armour, before spinning around the body cavity and exiting through his groin hitting most major organs on the way through. Or the wreckage caused by countless bombs and the effect the war had on our troops and civilians alike.

DEATH AT LISBURN

Lance Corporal 'S', Royal Corps of Transport

I was born in Belfast at the beginning of the Troubles, and it was normal, when growing up, for us to see soldiers and be stopped by them all over the city. It was also, sadly, normal to hear bombs exploding and shootings also. I joined the Royal Corps of Transport in 1989 hoping to get away from the Provence and the Troubles and to see a bit of the world. Unbeknownst to me at the time, I would spend five years out of nine serving here.

It was early on Monday 7 October 1996 that I was tasked with taking vehicle equipment to Kinnegar for an annual inspection. I got back to Lisburn just after 13:00, and spent the afternoon helping out on the troop lines. Everything seemed just like a normal Monday afternoon, until, around 16.20, I was asked to hand a set of keys into the Op's room. As I left the Op's room I noticed two female soldiers who had been down the town shopping that morning. I shouted at them to stop so I could chat to them. Suddenly, there was a sound of what I first thought was a shot. Instantly as I was spun around, I saw in slow motion a fireball rising up from around the nearest car in the car park.

It's true what they say about a second seeming like a minute, and I was thrown to the floor and everything went very quiet. I tried to sit up but noticed that my femur was poking out the back of my left leg. I also saw blood spurting a few feet out of my right hip. I looked to my left side and saw one of the girls lying on her front. She had what appeared to me to be a lump of metal in the back of her head. The other girl was standing at my head, and she had a quizzical look on her face. It was like she didn't know whether to laugh or cry. I put my right hand over my face and wondered what it was that had just happened.

I thought it might have been an under-car booby trap that had exploded, and I found out later that it was an 800-lb car bomb. I knew that I was injured in a bad way and that I wanted to make my peace with my maker and just closed my eyes. I began to take control again and said to myself that they weren't going to kill me this way and I shouted for help as loudly as I could. After a short while I was being asked the usual; name, rank, number, unit by someone who was at my side. I was put onto a makeshift stretcher (a mattress) and was taken away from the blast site. I was being carried to the medical centre when a sharp pain in my right foot (I had a big bit of shrapnel stuck half way into it) caused me to scream with pain. I screamed at the people who were carrying me to put me down, and then one of them lost his grip on the mattress and they decided to put me down to get a better control of it.

Just as they put me down there was a second explosion. Then they picked me up and regained control of the mattress. It was then seen that the medical centre had been demolished by what turned out to be a second 800-lb car bomb. They took the injured from the first bomb to a side gate where a padre was trying to comfort the wounded. I was unceremoniously dumped into a waiting ambulance and rushed to the Lagan Valley Hospital. I finally lost consciousness in the back of the ambulance.

I awoke four days later in the RVH intensive care unit. When I awoke, a soldier (WO1 J. Bradwell) in the next bed to me, passed away from his injuries. It was only in the following days and weeks that I found out that many people had been injured in this double car bombing. Five of us were put into intensive care and many others were wounded. I also found out that as I left the Op's room, I had actually held the door open for Mr Bradwell to enter. He left just as the first bomb exploded and, sadly, he took the full force of the blast. He was taken to the medical centre, where the doctors and medical staff were working on him when the second bomb exploded, burying him in the rubble.

I was discharged from the Army in 1998 due to the numerous injuries I had received from this incident.

The longest period of the Troubles without loss to strictly terrorist activity of military personnel came to an abrupt end with an apparent major lapse in Army security on the Lisburn garrison. On 7 October 1996, two IRA bombs were smuggled into Thiepval barracks and in one of the explosions, Sergeant Major James Bradwell of REME, who was 43, was critically injured. A married man with four children, he was from the Gateshead area; he died four days later in the RVH having fought bravely for life. He was buried in a cemetery in Sunderland and his loss was a kick in the pants for the Army whom it was felt had 'taken their eye off the ball' with most of the violence at the time being directed on the British mainland. It was a message that the IRA had not gone away and there were still more CVO visits to come; more heartbreaking news to impart.

PART THREE

THE OTHER KILLING GROUNDS

From a soldier's perspective, the name Londonderry was synonymous with fierce Republicanism and rebellion, and to be told that you were going to Londonderry was enough to cause you some concern, particularly the young soldiers. In short, the name Londonderry to me means defiance, confrontation and trouble with a capital 'T'.

Jimmy McMaster, UDR

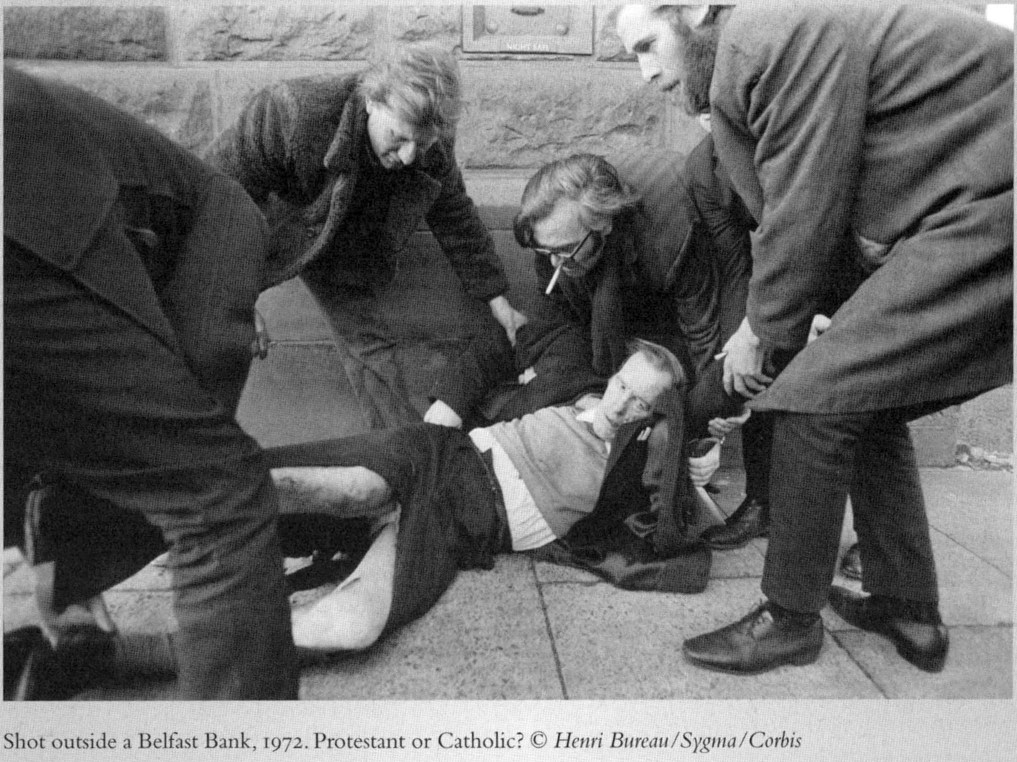

Shot outside a Belfast Bank, 1972. Protestant or Catholic? © *Henri Bureau/Sygma/Corbis*

THE 'B' SPECIALS

James Henderson, UDR

I read Ken Wharton's earlier books and, whilst I enjoyed them, I am afraid I cannot support his judgement of the Ulster Special Constabulary when he uses the term: 'the brutality of the infamous 'B' Specials'. I firmly believe that this is a harsh and unfair judgement of the thousands who for many years held the terrorists at bay before the advent of Operation Banner.

I have some memories of the elections of the early 1970s when the British Government of the time – the Prime Minister then was Harold Wilson – was attempting to manipulate the local government voting system to enable the minority nationalist population to obtain a greater number of elected positions. They introduced a singularly unsuccessful early version of proportional representation.

I have memories of two such elections while commanding a UDR platoon – more than half of whom were ex-B Specials – which was tasked to provide security in an ultra-Republican area of County Londonderry. The IRA had threatened to take ballot boxes from polling stations by force because, in their opinion, any election should be 'all Ireland'. We took over the area around the local primary school late on the previous evening and set up a discreet cordon after clearing for devices. There was half a platoon on stag. We stayed there through the day of the election and accompanied the RUC to the counting hall that night with the ballot boxes. The irony was that up to 75 per cent of those who voted there were Republican by inclination, whilst only a few of my platoon managed to get to their own polling stations. When this was later pointed out, arrangements were made to get postal votes for the next election for those on duty. However, postal votes then were difficult to arrange (strong justification was needed in the application), and telling someone you were serving in the Security Forces was a security risk as more and more Republican sympathisers were being employed in this aspect of Government.

Also in the early 1970s, my Company lost three soldiers (two of whom were Ex-B Specials) to terrorist action. These two were Captain James Hood (a personal friend) and Private George Ellis Hamiltion. The third was Staff Sergeant David Deacon, ex-RN, who was taken alive and tortured. All were off duty when murdered. Losing three very popular soldiers in such a short time from what was then an under strength company was a heavy blow. However, it did not deter the rest and while later assassination attempts resulted in serious injury there were no further deaths within the company.

The majority – almost 53 per cent – of the UDR who were killed between 1969 and 1998 were actually off duty at the time. The IRA/INLA deliberately targeted these courageous men and women at a time when they would be most vulnerable. They were targeted when they were alone, as they arrived home from work, were en route for work, or in their very places of work. 312 serving UDR men and women were killed during the Troubles. This included a very high number (68) killed in road traffic accidents (RTAs) and it has been ascertained that an incredibly high proportion were on duty at the time. It would be disrespectful to the memory of those killed in such a way to even attempt to break this down into those who lost their lives in RTAs whilst on duty and those who were not. Additionally, 65 former members of the UDR were killed by terrorists despite the fact that they had resigned and were no longer connected to the Regiment. Guilty by association was clearly the watchword for the IRA/INLA, as they made no distinction between serving and no longer serving.

Thus, 377 or 29 per cent of all military or ex-military personnel identified to date who died in or as a result of the Troubles were members or former members of the UDR. Of the 312 serving members killed, at least 164 were killed by terrorists whilst off duty. The vagueness in that last sentence is a result of the fact that I have identified 37 UDR personnel for whom I have no cause of death. Additionally, there are about another 80 UDR names that require further research.

James is both a contributor and a friend, and, whilst he does not agree with me in terms of my assertion that the 'B' Specials used brutality and intimidating tactics on those who crossed them, I respect his comments. This book is not merely a forum for my own personal opinions, but also for all those who served, irrespective of whether I agree with them or not. I do not for a second dispute that most Specials acted correctly and in a disciplined and professional manner, especially in view of the quite savage provocation. (Editor's note: for an arguably balanced account of the early, terrible events of the 'Irish question' from 1920 and an indirect foreshadowing of the 'B' Specials, see Richard Bennett's *The Black and Tans*.)

On 4 January 1973, Captain James Hood (48) a married UDR soldier with three children, was shot and killed by the IRA as he approached his home. His killers had hidden behind a low wall and shot him as he entered his front door, with his son close by. Private George E. Hamilton (28) a married father with one child was shot by an IRA sniper on 20 December 1972, whilst working as an electrician at a reservoir near Londonderry. He was badly injured and died within hours despite being rushed to hospital.

On the same day, apparently in a Loyalist tit-for-tat reprisal, four innocent Catholics and a Protestant were gunned down by the UVF in a bar in the city. The 'Top of the Hill' bar was in a sectarian interface area and was considered unsafe for Protestants and, as such, the murder gang would not have expected a Protestant to be present. The dead included a male nurse, a barman and a father of seven children. The final soldier to whom James Henderson refers was UDR soldier David Deacon (39) from Londonderry. The part-time soldier and father of four children was abducted near the border and later found bound, hooded and shot in the back of the head near Molenan on 3 March 1973.

'B' SPECIALS: ANOTHER VIEWPOINT

Stevie, Ulster Defence Regiment

Your comments are fine; they are just the facts, as you see then, in relation to which you have stated your own position. You would get a similar, if not more forthright response from opponents of the 'Bs', and, while in some instances your assertion with regard to the behaviour of some 'B'-men is correct, any criticism is a very sore point and simply not tolerated. It is as if the behaviour of some is to be accepted and 'only to be expected', in the face of their losses to, and the activities of, the IRA/PIRA over the period of the life of the Specials from the 1920s to their disbandment in 1970.

With a basis in truth, they feel that they saved the Province from both the terrorists and successive British governments, who might have caved in to pressure and offered up the North as a means of dealing with the 'Irish problem'. I don't know if you have read Max Arthur's book *NI Soldiers Talking* but in its UDR section it carries a comment from a UDR company commander, who says, 'One night my platoon of Specials handed in their kit and disbanded. The next night they paraded en masse as the new UDR platoon.'

This sort of service passed from father to son and onward; it was seen as a duty that could not be shirked or avoided, and nor would it be. They were part of the community and knew their area best, and who lived in it. In 1970 when the Specials were disbanded, local level intelligence was lost that took valuable years, years where many died, to re-kindle and amass.

Operation Demetrius – internment – could have been a disaster as it was based on old records from the border war (1958–62) and even the internment lists from the 1940s, instead of up-to-date info and local knowledge. Fathers were lifted instead of sons, uncles instead of nephews, and grandads instead of grandsons. That is why so many were released shortly after arrest, when the RUC got them sorted out. And the ringleaders, for the most part, still avoided being lifted.

Tradition, discredited by some, is still defended strongly; and for very good reason.

RTAS

Ronnie Gamble, UDR (Author of Echo Company)

The RTAs were caused mostly by exhaustion. They were usually part-time soldiers holding down two jobs at the same time. Most of the men and women were doing a normal day's work in civilian employment and at least two nights out on patrol as well as their four-hour training night and training/operational weekends. Their civilian bosses stopped making allowances for part-time soldiers when the war went on for so long. At the start many employers let the men sleep on and come into their civilian jobs by 10am. Working all hours was a normal week for a good soldier who wanted to meet all their training and operational commitments and qualify for their military pay grades and annual bounty. There were also extended duties or sudden operational requirements that cost some men and women their civilian jobs. I put it across in my book that the soldiers did get tired and often fell out of the back of Land Rovers while out on patrol.

Before I joined up in '74 I could see the part time soldiers in their civilian jobs falling asleep during their lunch breaks or whilst travelling by coach to work. So, if they were driving themselves, hell's bells!

Some members of UDR patrols were travelling around the country totally exhausted from doing a full-time job and then volunteering for night patrols. Every third night was an operational night but in between you were expected to meet your training commitments. Sometimes other platoons were short of men and volunteers were always being called upon to ensure that the patrols were up to strength. It's not surprising that some people made mistakes.

On one occasion I was driving the rear vehicle when I saw the front vehicle start to swerve a little bit. We approached a bend on the road and the front vehicle went through the hedge. It did not stop until it crossed the bend and reached the road again. It stopped there until the rear vehicle caught up. When the patrol commander spoke to the driver and the crew none of them could recall going through the hedge. None of the crew believed what had happened until the patrol commander took them back to the scene of the 'short cut'. Sheer tiredness caused this accident but luckily no one was injured.

One night we were on a country mobile and finished off the night with a VCP at Ringsend. I was doing cover man in the hedge and when it was time to go the patrol packed up and headed for Coleraine. It was only when they reached Coleraine that someone noticed I was missing. The patrol headed back to Ringsend to find me fast asleep in the hedge! This incident highlights the extent to which we pushed ourselves physically. One night there were three of us in the rear Land Rover. Usually there were four soldiers in the vehicle. This included the driver and the vehicle commander in the front and two riflemen in the back. I was sitting in the back half dozing on my own and I heard someone say VCP. That was my cue to leap out and act as stopper (the traffic stopper) so that the VCP could be set up.

I thought the vehicle was preparing to stop so I leapt out. The vehicle was travelling too fast and I rolled up the road. I finished up sitting on the ground with the Bardic lamp between my legs and my rifle was still slung on my back. I did not have a clue where I was or what had happened. Luckily I still had my 10p piece, which everybody carried for an emergency. But I was unsure of the area I was in and could not risk knocking on any doors to use their phone.

I elected to hide behind a large tree at the roadside until I got my act together. Luckily the Bardic lamp was still working and I was able to retrieve my ammunition, magazine and beret. I settled down behind the tree and recharged my magazine. There was a stop sign at the end of the road I had landed on so I waited there. Very soon the Land Rovers came back; I waited until the second vehicle drew up beside me. I jumped on board and scared the life out of the two rear passengers. What had happened was the vehicles had changed around so that the rear vehicle had the lead and was able to retrace the ground where I most likely fell.

After that incident it was always said that you weren't a UDR soldier until you fell out of the back of a Land Rover. In the following years more people admitted that this was a common occurrence. Many people became hypnotized by looking out of the back of a Land Rover at the road. Sometimes you were unable to tell if the vehicle had stopped moving. The constant supply of petrol and diesel exhaust fumes that billowed into the back of the vehicle also contributed to this condition.

The following account, written by a remarkable UDR soldier, encapsulates what it was like to be a member of that Regiment, the one that suffered by far the most fatalities among the Security Forces. And this isn't the only dramatic account of survival from him.

AMBUSHED BY THE IRA

Glen Espie, Ulster Defence Regiment

Just before my eighteenth birthday, I applied to join the UDR as a part-time soldier, following in my father's footsteps and other family members who were already serving in the regiment. This would be the best of both worlds where I could complete my apprenticeship and service as a soldier, doing my bit in the Province. I was duly accepted into the regiment in January 1975 and served with 'G' Company based in Cookstown. I was a young soldier, serving with tough soldiers who had experienced landmine and gun attacks on their patrols since its formation in April 1970.

These old soldiers kept you switched on and you quickly learned from them the dos and don'ts in an internal security situation. Being a soldier in the area in which you lived and worked was a bonus because you were well aware of who the terrorists were, their family connections, where they lived and the vehicles they used. Unfortunately this worked both ways and you were stopping players who in reality were your neighbours who lived in the next village or farm. We didn't ask these players for identification when stopped at our VCP; they were addressed by their Christian names and in many cases they answered you back calling you by your surname. To hide one's identity from the players working within the same area of operations was next to impossible. Many of our part time soldiers lived in isolated farms or homes within what were deemed Republican areas.

Being a part time soldier was in reality a 24/7 total commitment; we patrolled on average twenty duties a month at night and weekend. You were never off-duty as far as the terrorist was concerned and you were an easy target for them to ambush at home. Whether at work or travelling between these, you had to be aware that they would know of your route and timings; they would know when you started and when you finished.

These were the main factors required to set up any ambush; target, time and place. Therefore, on a daily basis you were consistently alert for anything out of the ordinary in your routine. When driving you didn't get boxed in coming up to junctions; you slowed to ensure when you arrived at the junction you didn't have to stop and could drive through without stopping at what could be a possible ambush site.

The first time I was ambushed was on 22 March 1978. My Platoon Commander Lieutenant Robin Smyrl, MID, was a natural leader of men and one who led by example. This did not escape the notice of East Tyrone PIRA. Thus, the most inspiring leader I have ever had the privilege to serve with and the one who gave me the confidence to believe in myself, was ambushed and murdered by heavily armed gunmen. Armed with assault rifles, they shot and killed him as he slowed to negotiate a bridge on a small country road outside Plumbridge on his way to work.

Lieutenant Robin Smyrl (25), part-time soldier in the UDR and manager of a clothing factory was killed by the IRA on the road between Omagh and Newtownstewart on 13 September 1977. He was from Cookstown and in the company of a colleague who was wounded in the attack. It is estimated that the two gunmen fired at least two dozen rounds and forced the car to lose control and smash into a telegraph pole.

The morning of 22 March 1978 was a normal March morning; not too cold with a cloudy overcast sky. I left for work about ten past eight, but before leaving my house I would look through the window to see that there were no suspicious vehicles parked near my home that could conceal an ambush team in waiting. Then I would check for under car booby traps before driving off. I was unable to vary my routes to and from work to any degree because of the locations of my home and work place. On arrival I would park in different places in the car park trying not to set a pattern. After clocking into work I would check my works van for under vehicle booby trap bombs, under the watchful eyes of some of my work colleagues who were players or suspected PIRA members.

My first job that day was in Parkview Pomeroy, a Republican estate to the north of the village. At lunchtime, the foreman called me over and said that he had just received a call that the copper cylinder had burst at 3 Killygonlan beside the Diamond in Ardboe. This was on the shores of Lough Neagh about eleven miles from Cookstown and a Republican area. This could be a 'come on' situation as there had been a lot of PIRA activity in this area. Undercover soldiers had shot and killed a terrorist loading a bomb into a car at a derelict house close to the village three weeks earlier. [Paul Duffy (23) an IRA member was shot and killed by soldiers in Washing Bay, Co Tyrone on 26 February. He was a member of the Tyrone brigade of the IRA.] Two weeks earlier, a UDR soldier was travelling through the Ardboe area on his way home when PIRA fired 23 rounds, striking his car but fortunately not hitting him.

I worked in these areas daily, and my civilian job was as a plumber with the Northern Ireland Housing Executive (NIHE). I was always wary when called out to emergency jobs as the house could have been taken over by PIRA and used to mount an assassination attack. On my way to 3 Killygonlan I called at home and put on my concealed body armour. I didn't always wear it at work because of the physical activity involved and you sweated like a pig wearing it.

The day had cleared up with some hazy spring sunshine as I drove a roundabout route to get to Killygonlan. The properties are pre-war two-storeyed, three bedrooms with a downstairs bathroom at the bottom of the stairs. The properties are set in a square bounded by the main road; six terraced houses facing the main road with two semi-detached houses at either side of the terraced block. On arrival I drove up to the house and reversed my van up to the door and kept the wing mirror in line with the front door. I never took my eyes off the door watching for signs of suspicious activity. I got out of the van and walked towards the door; my heart was pounding, expecting the door to be flung open, or a burst of gunfire from the house or entry on my left as I walked the short distant from my van.

I stood to the side of the door and knocked so that if someone fired through the door they would be unable to hit me. The door was opened slightly by a male. I advised him that I was there to repair the burst cylinder from the Housing Executive. He said: 'OK son, go ahead; it's at the top of the stairs.' I pushed the door open as the male in the house went through a door on my right into the living room and closed the door behind him. I assumed he was the tenant. I relaxed, as it appeared to be just another burst cylinder; all in a day's work. On entering the hall of the house, I turned left and walked to the bottom of the stairs. I became aware that the curtains were pulled on the circular window at the bottom of the stairs and the hall, even though it was about 2.15pm – it was very dark.

The door into the downstairs bathroom was open; it was to the right of the hall at the bottom of the stairs. As I was taking all this in, a male of stocky build emerged from the downstairs bathroom, in front of me. I saw that he was wearing a black balaclava mask and I could see his eyes and mouth perfectly; he had a pistol in a two-handed grip pointed at my chest literally inches away.

The initial shock to the system stopped me in my tracks as I stared at this frightening figure. My first thoughts were: 'Fuck; this is it!' He fired and hit me on the left side of the chest, just below the nipple, in the heart area, and the force of the shot was like being kicked by a horse. It lifted me off my feet and propelled me backwards and I fell to the ground lying against the open front door. As I looked up at the gunman, he had stepped forward and levelled the pistol at my head. In those milliseconds, my life really did pass in front of me, like a cinema screen in fast forward; my wife, children, Mum and Dad; all the people who really mattered in my life flashed across my brain in a fraction of a second.

As the gunman levelled the pistol at my head, I ducked and rolled out of the open front door, and getting to my feet, I ran past my parked van to get away from the gunman who fired again. I could feel rounds going past my head and had covered about 10 to 15 yards when I was hit again in the left shoulder; the impact of the bullet spun me round and down with the impact of a horse's kick. As I was running, I was trying to get the zip down on my boiler suit as I had a .22 Walther Pistol tucked into a holster on my left side. I was now lying on my back on the ground looking over my head back towards the door. Two PIRA terrorists ran from the door of the house towards me to finish me off. They looked to be running in slow motion and it was only later I discovered that, because of the adrenalin pumping in my system, my brain was thinking so fast that everything in real time looked to be in slow motion.

As I lay on the ground, I was able to pull my pistol from its holster, but because of the gunshot wound to my shoulder I couldn't pull back the slide to cock it in the normal manner. I pushed the pistol into my left hand, held the slide and pushed the pistol forward with the right hand, chambering a round, and as I did this, I brought the pistol up and over my head and fired at the two men. I can still see them to this day, and by this time, they were about half way between me and the house. When I fired, both gunmen hit the deck, and I rolled over onto my belly and went to fire again, but nothing happened; the pistol had jammed. I couldn't clear it as they were too close, so I jumped to my feet and ran around the side of the last two semi-detached houses at the end of the square. There was a five-foot-high chain link fence at the rear of the garden and I jumped clean over the fence; adrenalin does work! I ran behind a filling station, over a wooden fence and across an open field for about 150 yards.

As I ran, my breath was coming in large gasps; my heart was pounding and my lungs were on fire, and the hedge at the far side of this open field seemed so far away. I was expecting to be shot again, but I jumped up into this large thorn hedge and tore through it. I was able to clear the jammed pistol and take stock of my situation. I looked back towards the rear of the filling station and could see men moving about and pointing towards the hedge where I was. I was aware that the front of my boiler suit was all bloody; it was coming from my mouth because the round hit my concealed body armour and impacted against my left lung. I had never been shot before and was alone and wounded in this Republican area with the nearest haven of safety the Unionist village of Coagh five miles away. To get there I was going to have to commandeer a car and either drive it or force the driver at gunpoint to drive me there.

I was very much aware that this being a Republican area, no one would have reported the shooting to the Police. Therefore the gunmen involved could still be looking for me in the area. I used the cover of hedgerows to make my way across country to a bungalow. To get to the bungalow I had to cross a secondary road about 350 metres from the house in which I was attacked, so I waited until there was no traffic and scrambled over the hedge and ran up the drive and to the rear of the bungalow to be out of view from the road. No vehicle was visible but I tried the rear door which was unlocked; on entering I found the bungalow unoccupied. I remember checking out each room in turn and finding a very large map of the Ardboe Area fastened to the wall in a bedroom; I wondered had I stumbled into a PIRA ops room? This was long before mobile phones, and luckily for me, the bungalow had a telephone. I dialled 999 and asked for the police; on speaking to them, they thought it was a 'come on' situation to get Security Forces into the area to ambush them. I told the police operator my name and that I was a part time lance corporal with 'G 'Company 8 UDR based in Cookstown. I also told them that my civilian job was a plumber for the Housing Executive and I had been shot and wounded twice and needed help and medical attention.

The telephone was on a hall table just behind the front door, which was entirely of clear glass. All my senses were working in over-drive, so I set the phone down and looked out of a bedroom window and saw a car coming down the road with three men, driving very slowly, looking out across the fields to both sides of the road. On looking into the hall I could see that the floor was covered in blood. I remember thinking if they look into the hall and see the blood they would know I was there. I took the Yellow Pages and opened it, setting it across the pool of blood and took up a fire position in a bedroom. It was so quiet except the noise of my laboured breathing because of my injuries and my heart seemed to be pounding out of my chest. I tried to take deep breaths and slow down my heart rate. I watched as the car came up the road and ducked down as it drew level with the bungalow, praying that the car would drive past and not stop. It seemed like a long time until it drove past; I really felt like a cornered rat in that bungalow and a .22 pistol doesn't really inspire confidence when the enemy is armed with heavier weapons than you.

I made across country trying to put distance between me and the ambush point, using the hedgerow as cover and keeping the main road to my left about 200 metres away. I was going across the front of what I believed to be a derelict farm house, but on looking up at a second floor window, I spotted movement and pointed my pistol but an old man who must have been bedridden with his bed pulled up to the window, raised himself up on one arm. On seeing me pointing a pistol in his direction and taking into account my boiler suit covered in blood his face turned ashen; his eyes seemed to get larger as he stared at me and he was frozen to the spot. As I left his field of vision I could see him falling away out of view. I had covered about half a mile and was becoming weak and weary; the adrenalin was wearing off and the pain was starting to set in. The weather was spring sunshine and I could see my shadow in the grass to my front and right.

To get to another bungalow, I had to cross the main road about three-quarters of a mile down the road from Killygonlan. I used the cover afforded by the hedgerows that are common in Tyrone, and was able to cross the road undetected and made my way to the rear of a bungalow. No-one was at home and the property was locked. I lifted a milk crate and smashed a bathroom window and climbed in and again used the telephone to contact the police. The operator listened to what I had to say but gave no hint of how they would respond. I was repeatedly asked the same questions; who was I; what had happened etc. I was becoming tired and weary and slammed down the telephone and went into a bedroom and lay down on the bed. I was drifting off to sleep and just wanted to rest, however the will to survive kicked in as I believed if I fell asleep I could die there. I had been wounded twice and my breathing was becoming laboured now. I was in pain, and didn't know the extent of my injuries and I was still in enemy territory. My fear was that I would fall asleep and die there or be discovered and captured by the PIRA; after all I was in in their 'back yard'.

I left and went to the farmhouse beside the bungalow; as I walked into the farmyard from the rear, I saw a Mini parked in an open shed with the keys in the ignition. I got into the car and thankfully it fired up first time and reversed out of the shed. As I drove round the side of the house to gain access to the main road, I saw a closed gate. I got out, opened the gate and lay across the passenger's seat as I drove away, half expecting the farmer to give me both barrels of a shotgun for stealing his car. I was thinking after all I had been through, just to get shot for stealing a car. I made good my escape to the safety of Coagh village about five miles away, driving into the village, lying over the steering wheel. I stopped on the main road outside a house where people I knew lived. I rolled out of the car onto the side of the road in great pain and, as it was on a slight hill the car rolled on and crashed into a fence were my granny used to live.

I saw a young chap about fourteen who I knew across the road and shouted at him to get help, but he stood there, frozen to the spot unable to recognise me; all he saw was a man lying at the side of the road with a pistol in his hand, covered in blood. As I lay on my back looking up at the clouds, the earlier sunshine had been replaced by swirling grey with puffs of white cloud which matched how I felt at that moment in time. The youngster went and got help and I was taken into the house and the he was sent down the street to summon the local doctor who promptly arrived.

As I was lying on a couch being examined by the doctor, I heard the most welcome sound of Saracens driving through the village on their way to the ambush location at Killygonlon Ardboe. I now felt safe again for the first time since the ambush about 45 minutes earlier. I was taken to Magherafelt hospital and there, police and Army personnel visited and wanted to hear how the concealed body armour saved my life. I was told this was the first time that this type had saved someone's life in the Province.

On leaving hospital I made repeated visits for skin grafting to my shoulder wound. After six months I returned to my civilian job as a plumber and reported to the Army doctor at the

Military Wing of Musgrave Park Hospital. The Doctor told me that he could give me a medical discharge with a pension. I advised him I didn't want one and wanted to return to my duties with the UDR as soon as possible. I just wanted to be back on duty with my comrades, not wanting to let the side down; such a prick!

In November, 2008, the author returned to Northern Ireland after an absence of many years (see *Return to Ulster* in Part Four) and met Glen Espie. It was a great pleasure to meet this remarkable – and incredibly lucky, though clearly resourceful – man at Palace Barracks in Belfast. The sandbagged sangars there, the razor wire, the miles of fencing and armed soldiers, were a sure sign that peace has still not returned to Northern Ireland. ('Bomb bigger than device at Omagh "would have blown up houses and killed civilians"' – headline in *The Times*, September 2009. The 600lb bomb was discovered near Forkhill in South Armagh, the command wire running from it for a mile to a firing point across the border.)

Glen showed me his bloodstained body armour, a grisly souvenir of his brush with the IRA and death. Despite being a former soldier, I was fascinated by his other mementos from that day in Killygonlan. The first round hit him in the region of his heart and drilled holes neatly through his pack of cigarettes, warrant card holder and his wallet. Inside that wallet are two five pound notes, both containing a bullet hole; he could never have been a Yorkshireman because they would have been long ago spent, holes and all.

THE DEATH OF CAPTAIN YOUNG

David Mitchell, Gordon Highlanders

In 1972, I was sent out on my first tour of Northern Ireland and was based in Lurgan in the northern part of Co Armagh. I was part of 'B' company and, along with a Corporal Burnett and a couple of Black Watch lads, we were attached to 321 EOD [Explosives Ordinance Disposal]. We were to be escort and close protection for ATO for the four months of the tour.

On 17 July 1972, we were called out to go to a place called Silverbridge near Forkhill. A milk churn had been discovered in a ditch with wires leading from it, and crossing the road to disappear in an adjacent field. On that day, the ATO was a Captain John H. Young and we arrived in South Armagh at Bessbrook Mill where the Duke of Wellingtons (DWR) was based. We never unloaded our weapons as we were usually escorted straight up to the incident. For some reason never explained to me, Captain Young was taking a long time to come out of the company office. So, myself and my driver went into the choggies to get something to eat and a cup of tea, but when we came out a Sergeant Major of the DWR was holding our SLRs and barked at us: 'You're both charged for not unloading your weapons.' However, just at that moment, Captain Young came out and informed the Sergeant Major that he would deal with it later; file 13!

When we reached the suspect milk churn, we tried to manhandle it out of the ditch, but it was far too heavy, so we had to pull it out with a rope attached to a Land Rover. We couldn't, however, get the lid off, so Captain Young asked his driver for a hammer and ordered us to get back about 50 yards, which we did. I watched him as he struck the lid about seven times, but on the seventh time, the churn erupted in intense fire and smoke, killing him instantly. The force and heat of the explosion was such that it incinerated every single trace of his 9mm Browning.

321 EOD (Bomb Disposal), Lurgan, 1972. *(David Mitchell)*

321 EOD (Bomb Disposal), with Humber PIG in the background. *(David Mitchell)*

Captain John Young (27), of the RAOC was killed when the suspect milk churn exploded. He was born in Berkeley and his funeral was held at Aldershot Crematorium in Hampshire, the spiritual home of the British Army.

> We were given the following day off to recover and then we were back on ops the very next day. On the same tour, my Battalion's search team lost three men in a booby-trapped house in Lurgan. But, at the end of the tour, we got out unscathed and were awarded our coveted 'Felix' ties, which you only got if you had faced live bombs. Myself and Corporal Burnett were the only Gordons to get these ties; I wear mine with pride.

On 18 June 1972, three members of the Gordons were killed together in Lurgan. The three soldiers were Sergeant Major Arthur McMillan (37) a married father of one, from Hull in East Yorkshire; Lance Corporal Colin Leslie (26) from the Orkney Islands and Sergeant Ian Mutch (31), married, from Nairn, near the Moray Firth. At the time of the explosion, seven soldiers from the Gordon's search team were inside the house at Bleary, near Lurgan, searching for arms after a tip off which, with the benefit of hindsight, was clearly an IRA 'come on'. The other four soldiers were injured, one very severely.

The house belonged to a recently released internee, who was subsequently cleared of any complicity in the attack; even in Ulster, even during the Troubles, coincidences did happen. All three men received military funerals in their home towns.

TRIBUTE TO A GREEN JACKET OFFICER

Marty, Royal Green Jackets

> Major Robin Alers-Hankey died on 30 January 1972 after being shot in the stomach as he deployed his troops to protect firemen who had been attacked by rioters in the Bogside area of Londonderry. He was just one of the 158 military personnel who died in this year as a result of the Troubles; this was the highest number of military deaths during the Troubles, indeed a total of 496 deaths occurred in this bloody year. To many people these are just statistics – but what of the individuals?
>
> He was my OC; as a 'Nig' with less than two years service, I found him to be an inspiration; a leader of men in troubled times and a gentleman. I recall him always being out and about visiting all the locations of his men and directing them on the ground regardless of what, or how serious, riots were going on as if things were normal. I had on occasion to give him cover from rioters as the stones were raining down upon us; he seemed to be able to ignore the dangers as he directed his troops. As a radio operator, for a short time, I listened to him directing troops and reacting to events with great speed, I was impressed with his ability to constantly keep up-to-date, as situations changed so quickly.
>
> As a gentleman, who wore a pin striped suit and bowler hat, he couldn't have been more far removed from many of us from the inner cities. I knew very little about the man but often thought of him throughout my Army service and feel he never, like others, got the recognition he deserved, he became just a statistic as other brave men did.

Major Alers-Hankey (35) was shot during the late summer of 1971 at the junction of Abbey Street and Frederick Street in Londonderry. An officer in 2RGJ, he was a married man and father of two, living in the Winchester area. He spent a long time in hospital before being med-evaced to the UK. Shortly after New Year 1972, he was readmitted to hospital and died, ironically, on Bloody Sunday; 30 January 1972. With the world's attention focussed on the events of that day in the Rossville Flats area of the Bogside, his passing was largely overlooked. He was buried at the Magdalen Cemetery in the Green Jackets' spiritual home of Winchester, where he was born.

CLOSE CALLS IN LONDONDERRY

Lance Corporal James Schwarz, 1 Royal Regiment of Fusiliers

The posting to Londonderry was not an emergency tour and was for a full eighteen months, and I thought that this would mean we would have an easy ride of it, with those troops on an emergency tour taking the brunt of it. No such luck, as I was to find out. My first patrol out was in the Waterside. The Fusiliers I was with had already carried out previous patrols, and as we toured the area, two large explosions went off, one after another. I quickly took cover against a nearby wall, until I saw the others were totally unfazed. It turned out the bombs had gone off across the river, some distance away and were no threat to us; what an introduction to my start in Ireland.

As I said, I thought it would be easy, until I saw orders. We were tasked in three-week stints. Our first stint was to cover Ebrington Barracks side of the river, taking in the waterside. For the next three weeks, we had to carry out on a rotation basis six-hour foot patrols, followed by six-hour mobile patrols and then six-hour standby. In the standby, you got fed and watered, washed and shaved, and got whatever sleep you could. If you were unlucky, as I subsequently was, to be 'turned out' during your standby, you missed your sleep and started again: six-hour foot patrols, six-hour mobile. This resulted in some sections not getting any rest for 36 hours or more. During this first three-week stint, probably late September 1973, a bonded warehouse was bombed and set on fire. My section had just started a six-hour standby and we were turned out to guard the warehouse for the entire time. It was a full 30 hours on the streets before we got any rest.

As you can see the hours were very long and tiring. Just before one mobile patrol commenced, two new recruits joined us. As we patrolled the Waterside in a PIG with just a viewing slot open at the back, we were all knackered. The driver pulled over and we all decided to have 40 winks. The two recruits were told to keep their eyes peeled and the rest of us dropped off. Some time later I opened my eyes to see everyone asleep, including the two recruits. I thought 'Fuck it' and dropped off again. It was only after that I thought how easy it would have been for one of the 'Boyos' to drop a pipe bomb through the viewing slot, but we got away with it, so all's well as they say.

The city of Londonderry has a large wall surrounding the centre. Whilst on top of that wall I was told by a Fusilier that a week before my arrival, the Army had a sniper shooting from a position up there. It was only reading your book, [*A Long Long War*] that I saw a photo of that sniper: Sergeant Major Haydn Davies. There was an incident of note about that wall. I was in charge of a mobile patrol coming out of the city gates. As you turn right, the road leads down to the Bogside Inn, a well known trouble spot and I didn't know my way around at this time; neither did the driver. To avoid any trouble at the Bogside Inn, we turned immediately right down the side of the city wall. Unknown to us, the road petered out. There was insufficient room to turn around so the driver tried reversing the PIG back up the hill. Unfortunately, the vehicle had been armoured to such an extent, that it was way overweight and broke the drive-shaft. Engineers with a heavy recovery truck had to haul us out, and take us out past the Inn. The turning circle of the heavy recovery truck towing our PIG made it very difficult to get around the end of the road, and, alerted, the patrons of the Inn came out, stoning us and leading to a full-scale riot. Extra troops were drafted in to keep us safe until we eventually manoeuvred around the corner. This was only the first of a number of riots I was involved in.

An easier three-week stint guarding the married quarters took place before going across the river to what my Battalion called 'the Saracen factory'. This was located just up from the Creggan and the Bogside, and was the hardest soldiering I had done. This side of the river was so dangerous that we were not allowed to walk our patrols. Everywhere we went was at the double. Before we went out on these patrols, we were given 'Bingo books' with photographs of wanted IRA players. On one of the first patrols I saw a wanted player by the name of McCartney. He was lurking down an alley way. I indicated to an officer who took some troops around one way and we caught him in a pincer movement. The officer told me to arrest him; I looked blankly at him. Again he said 'Go on; arrest him.' But I hadn't got a clue what he was on about and another Fusilier stepped in and said 'As a member of her Majesty's forces, I arrest you.' It turned out this was important and featured in the Induction course that I missed out on.

One of the fixed positions to be covered whilst in the Bogside was a static observation point on top of the Rossville flats. This gave a bird's-eye view of the surrounding area to look for bombers, snipers or mobs congregating. As I recall this was a three-day stint and involved six of us. The sleeping arrangements were located in the switchgear room in the top of the lift shaft. Whilst three of us rested, one was in the rooftop OP keeping watch. The other two were posted on armed guard outside the top floor lift doors. Two things stick in mind about my time in the Rossville flats OP. One was that the toilet arrangements were a dustbin with a toilet seat; this was located in one corner of the rooftop, adjacent to a two-foot parapet. When I went to use it for a number two, I found I had just as good a view overlooking the Bogside as did the soldier in the OP. I then realised that if I had a view onto the Bogside, then a sniper could easily have a view of me. I had horrid thoughts of the headlines in the papers if I had been shot whilst on the throne. It was at this point that I leaned over out of sight, making it difficult to do my business. It is only as I write this that it occurred to me, it would have been so much easier to move the bin away from the edge. The second reason I remember the Rossville Flats, unfortunately, had far more fatal consequences. A short time after leaving Northern Ireland, I saw on the news that two soldiers had been shot dead whilst guarding the lift doors on the top floor. I felt extremely saddened by this; having carried out the same duty only a few months earlier I had a real feeling for those guys.

Whilst I was in Gibraltar, I had been with a Fusilier called Mick Shipley; he was an unfortunate casualty of the war, getting shot in the neck by a sniper. I was told he survived, but lost an arm.

After three months on the streets I was seconded to 321 EOD [Explosive Ordinance Disposal] as NCO in charge of the Escorts for ATO, (ammunition technical officer) the bomb disposal experts. The set up was three teams; one for the city, one for the surrounding country and one team on standby. These teams rotated daily. In essence it meant I had a day off every third day; an absolute luxury compared to the previous three months.

On two occasions during my spell with 321 EOD, I nearly copped it. The first time was my own stupid fault. A bomber had gone into a butchers' shop and planted a bomb on the counter

Bloody Sunday mural, Londonderry. *(Ken Wharton)*

telling everyone to get out. As the city crew, we turned out to this, and as the armed escort, I just had to keep an eye on the ATO. The rest of the team prepared the 'wheelbarrow' and sent it trundling past the front of the shop window to the doorway on the other side of the shop. As the wheelbarrow turned into the doorway, the batteries gave out and it just stopped in the door. Me and another member of the team volunteered to retrieve it and ran forward, past the shop window and grabbed the wheelbarrow handle. We dragged it backwards and a got it a few yards back from the shop when the bomb exploded and blasted the shop window in a wave of shards across the road. If it had gone off some ten seconds earlier we would have been shredded.

The second occasion involved a suspect car bomb in Cookstown. This was in the middle of the night. The car was situated on a hill and our officer had a quick look at the car from a distance. He then stood under a lamp column and called us together to tell us how he intended to deal with it. The local troops had the hill surrounded and the area was believed to be sterile. However, this was not entirely the case and the IRA had a machine gun set up on adjacent hill, which overlooked our position. As we stood under the lamp, they opened up at us; or more precisely at ATO, the prime target. The rounds were striking high up on a house wall a few yards from us. No surprises in that we all took cover. We left at that point for the bomb to soak, and came back the following day; the car turned out to be just a 'come on'.

Those two incidents were the closest that I came to death or serious injury and after seven months in Ireland I was discharged upon completion of the three years I signed up for. I know that my Battalion served a number of tours in Ireland, and didn't get much mention in your first book, so this can give some recognition to the 1st Battalion Royal Regiment of Fusiliers.

Five members of James' and the previous writer Mick King's battalion never made the journey home back to their loved ones alive. Fusilier Anthony Simmons (19) from Manchester was shot by an IRA gunman hiding in a derelict house in Fountain Street in Strabane. The gunman shot the soldier whilst he was illuminated in the lights of a passing car; there is still speculation that the illumination was deliberate and was the work of a 'dicker' working with the gunman. On 24 January 1981, Corporal Philip Barker (25), a father of two from Oldham, was manning a VCP at the security gates in Belfast city centre. The VCP was approached by two men who shot Corporal Barker at close range. He died of his wounds in the RVH the following day.

The Battalion's final losses took place in Enniskillen with the deaths of two off-duty soldiers and the later death of another wounded comrade. On 18 May 1984, three members of the Battalion were taking part in a fishing contest at Enniskillen and on returning to their parked car triggered off a UVBT, which killed two and wounded a third. Corporal Thomas Agar (35) from Jarrow, Tyne and Wear and Lance Corporal Robert Huggins (29), a father of three from Manchester were killed instantly by the IRA device. Their comrade, Lance Corporal Peter Gallimore (27) from Bolton was badly injured in the attack and eventually succumbed to a heart attack in Woolwich Hospital on 18 October the same year.

STRABANE: A 'BEAUTIFUL HELL'

Frenchie, 1 Kings

Travel roughly south-west out of Londonderry following the course of the Foyle and in around half an hour, you will come to a quaint Northern Ireland town called Strabane. I could describe the area as a 'challenge' for any security force to operate successfully. The strange mix of rural lanes surrounding city-like terraced streets in the centre of town contrives to make it a difficult TAOR; usually I just describe the place as a hellhole!

The army manned several 'temporary' bases in the area, including the RUC station in the town centre. In another area just a couple of miles outside of town, a tin-covered scaffolding fence surrounded and protected a strange mix of Nissan huts and portacabins, which stood out starkly against the surrounding public housing estate. This was the Sion Mills base camp; it could just about support a platoon-strength unit and all the kit they needed to carry out their daily duties.

Just outside the town centre towards the Foyle, a narrow road led to the South and crossed the border at the 'Hump Back VCP'. Soldiers usually dropped the 'Back' from the title and referedr to this as the 'Hump VCP'. On the southern facing line of the rough billets at the Hump was a tall sangar, if I recall correctly it reached around thirty feet in height. Climbing the steep steps into the cramped sangar, all who did their share of stags in it got a stark visual reminder of the dangers presented here; this was in the form of rows of small holes in the scaffolding tubing and some of the surrounding tin sheets. Once, an ambitious IRA gunner had sprayed the position with a powerful machine-gun from the direction of an isolated hotel just over the border in the south. This had to be one of the loneliest stags in the Province, though all the better for it as the IRA seemed to have given up on the Sustained Fire Role exercises against the position.

Back in the town centre, the RUC station, the main façade and gate of which formed one side of a small, open square in the centre of town, was a different duty altogether. Foot patrols left the station every day to gather Intel and show strength. On the side of the square facing the station was an old church, which was built on ground a good bit higher than the rest of the square. A five to six foot sandstone retaining wall topped with shrubs and with small trees growing on the higher ground on the other side of the wall gave excellent cover to any attacker who was determined enough to have a go at the station or the front entrance sangar there.

The missile/rocket defence screens were not as sophisticated as they later became and whilst doing sentry duty in that sangar, my attention often strayed to the sooty starburst stain between the first and second floor of the station behind me. An RPG round had hit the front of the station earlier, flying not far over the sentry's head before exploding on the front wall. The attacker had fired the RPG from the high ground behind the wall opposite; it made for itchy trigger fingers on dark winter nights, watching threatening shadows in the bushes topping and hanging over the church wall.

From the RUC station we would engage in extended patrols up to and around the Townsend. Needless to say, this was a 100 per cent dyed-in-the-wool Republican area, even the dogs had been trained to attack 'the Green' (a term drawn from the soldiers' uniform while in the Province). The Townsend was a small housing estate which covered the floor of a three sided valley just outside the main town of Strabane. There was one road in, which travelled around the estate in an elongated horseshoe. The inner roads, tracks and alleys traversed the valley floor connecting the two sides of the perimeter horseshoe road. It made for great cover for any gunmen down on the estate.

Far worse for the hapless patrols though, was the dirt track that followed the perimeter road from start to finish on the high ground on all three sides of the estate. My first patrol through this estate was made even more nerve wracking when I noticed the painted lines across the road at regular intervals and the short vertical upturns which the lines made as they reached the fences or gateways on each side. In the centre of the road, alongside each line was a number; 300, 200, 100 and so on. On the way out of the valley the road markings reversed; 100, 200, 300. We patrolled this 'firing range' many times, even carrying out 'baiting patrols' at the same time every day for a week at a time. Along the dirt track running around the top of the valley the IRA placed two black marble plaques.

I remember the day I had a young woman's life in my hands. I still think about her sometimes. I let her live. I wonder if she knows this.

Proudly displayed in the ground floor window of a house was the ubiquitous symbol of the early IRA weaponry – a 'Tommy gun'. It sat on a wooden rack in full view of anyone passing by. We knew it had been there a while although we never had the opportunity to inspect it close up. I assume an earlier unit had already done that.

This day as I was leading my stick out, a young woman, 19 to 23 years of age, took the Thompson from the rack and pointed it at me. She wasn't smiling. I lifted my SLR and sighted through the bulbous active sight. I centred on the bottom centre of what I chose to be the target, just as the book says. She didn't panic; she just slowly placed the wooden gun back into its cradle. She stayed staring out through the window as I lowered my weapon and turned to lead out.

I let her live; I didn't have to, but I let her live.

Seven members of the British Army were killed in Strabane, this 'beautiful hell', between 1972 and 1990. On 3 August 1972, Sergeant Major William Clark (34) of the RAOC was killed whilst defusing an IRA bomb outside Strabane. He was the father of four children, and was buried in Middlesbrough. On 1 February 1973, Colour Sergeant William Boardley (30) of the Kings Own

Scottish Borderers was shot and killed in the centre of Strabane by an IRA gunman. The married soldier was the father of two and came from Cumbria.

The following summer, Corporal David Smith (31) from the Cardiff area was killed by an IRA booby trap in a derelict house on the Ballycolman estate in Strabane; he was a member of the Royal Welch Fusiliers. On 15 November 1974, Fusilier Anthony Simmons (19), a Manchester boy was shot dead by the IRA in the centre of the town. He was in the Royal Regiment of Fusiliers. The final three to be killed were a serving member and two former members of the UDR.

On 19 November 1981, Lance Corporal Johnny McKeegan (49) a married father of three, was lured to a house in Strabane which IRA gunmen had taken over. He was shot and killed whilst the family who lived there were held hostage. six months later, Thomas Cunningham (23) a builder was targeted by the IRA as a former member of the UDR. He was working on a building site in Strabane when a gunman approached him and shot him several times. His wife was heavily pregnant at the time of his death. The IRA's 'Department for Pious and Meaningless Apologies' issued a statement after the murder claiming that they had only killed him because they were unaware that he had retired from the UDR.

On 20 October 1990 David Pollock (30) was driving through the town. As he passed a Catholic church in full view of the departing congregation, his car was rammed by another car, carrying IRA gunmen. The masked men jumped out and shot Mr Pollock; despite the best efforts of two passing nurses, he died at the scene. He had left the UDR as far back as 1983.

Readers of the author's first book might recall the poignant story of the RRW soldier assigned as a sniper on the city walls in Londonderry. The soldier, Haydn Davies, had an IRA gunwoman in his sights but deliberately missed. The follow piece concludes that incident.

THE LONDONDERRY SNIPER: AFTERWORD

RSM Haydn Davies, Royal Regiment of Wales

The young girl was arrested some minutes after the incident, about two hundred yards to the rear of the Bogside Inn. She had done very well to have got rid of the rifle in less than about two minutes, when she was arrested by a foot patrol of the Royal Fusiliers. They were talked on to her position behind a low wall where she was hiding; the directions were done by radio from the city wall position, and I watched it being done.

As with other incidents, I thought I would hear no more of it; however the following afternoon, after my disciplinary 'interview' with the CO, I was called in by the Adjutant. He told me to get into some civilian clothes and to be at the court house in Derry at about two pm that afternoon to speak as a witness to the shooting incident. I had no civilian clothes, so I borrowed a female shirt from a WRAC girl, and a pair of over-size trousers from a civilian kitchen worker. An officer loaned me his gardening jacket and I wore my army boots. I looked and felt like a sack of spuds. The court house as I remember was in the area of Woolworths, and I was dropped at a place called the Irish Kitchen and with an escort I did not know or trust, I made my way to where I was told to go.

The escort moved into a doorway and though I did not see it I heard him cock a 9mm pistol. I faced him in the doorway and asked could I carry it. He looked me in the face with what I remember to be extraordinary piercing blue eyes and replied: 'You do your bloody job and I'll do mine!' I thought, 'Cheeky sod!' Then he nodded his head in the direction of the city centre and said 'Let's go!' Sometimes he was behind me, then over the other side of the road, then behind me again. He certainly did not relax as I made my way to where I had to go.

I entered the court and was directed to sit by two men in civilian clothes; they beckoned me as I entered. I sat with them and waited. The thin, small, young girl was ushered into the court with two female policewomen and perhaps it was her mother with her. I cannot remember the exact details but Ivy Terrace was given as her address. She either lived there or she stayed there with an aunt. I identified her when asked to do so by a single magistrate whom nobody could hear properly. I was shown the coat and indentified that also. I examined the coat and saw that the right pocket had been cut out of the coat to facilitate carriage of a weapon. There were circular rings where the black fouling of a recently fired Armalite rifle muzzle had fouled the light silk lining up under the shoulder. There were fouling muzzle rings from another larger muzzle weapon, perhaps a Thompson.

The girl was only briefly questioned and then left the court. There was a lot of whispering between the sole magistrate and men in civilian clothes. The case against the girl was dismissed. I was told that I could go. I remember thinking: 'What a waste of time.' The two men in civilian clothes called to me and took me to a small space at the back of the court house. They introduced themselves as 'Intelligence HQNI. One was a major, the other a captain. They explained that they realized that the girl was implicated and that indeed forensic had told them that. They then explained that they did not want her arrested because she was more use to them on the loose. They felt the need to tell me that, on the grounds that the bullet from the previous day had missed me by only inches.

Whoever the girl was, she will surely, for all of her days, remember the awful sound of rounds landing each side of her. I remember hoping at the time that it would deter her from further such activities. I looked out for her over my remaining six weeks or so in Derry, but I did not see her again.

'CONTACT ALL AREAS': LONDONDERRY 1974

Private Pete Whittall Mortar Platoon, 1 Staffords

This was my first tour of duty in the Province; I had only recently turned eighteen years of age and was inwardly fearful of the reality of what this was going to be like. I had seen the news flashes, the odd documentary and the whole violent image of what was happening in Ulster. My family were worried sick but understood that the very reason I had got to where I was now, was because from the young age of nine or ten I had dreamed of being a soldier and serving and protecting my country, my people, my family. Little was I to know that within months of joining the Staffordshire Regiment I would be facing the reality and horror of NI for the first, but not the last time.

On 26 July 1974 I flew out with the main body of my Company to the military section of Aldergrove Airport. It was an uneasy flight with loads of apprehension, but the experienced guys who had done the Lurgan, South Armagh tour in 1972 were very supportive of us young sprogs and I was very grateful for that. On the Staffords' first tour of duty in the Province Colour Sergeant John Morrell had been killed in Drumagh as a result of an IRA booby trap explosion. No sooner had we taken off than we were landing, going through the security procedures and dumped on a series of blue/white Ulster buses to go to Fort George Army Base in Derry.

Colour Sergeant Morrell – on attachment from the Prince of Wales Own – was dreadfully wounded on 15 October 1972, following an IRA bomb explosion at Drumagh and he was eventually casevaced to hospital in England; he died of his wounds on 25 October. He was aged 32, a married man with three children and came from Macclesfield.

> Our armed escort and minders were two Grenadier Guards we were replacing. They seemed good guys, very switched on and were very good at their job I have to say. They told us not to stand up at any time during the journey to the base and to keep a constant lookout for the unusual or the potential for trouble. They did not mince their words and rightly so. One only needs to remember that Derry was a very volatile area to patrol and it was only two years after the Bloody Sunday events that took place in the Bogside around Rossville flats on 30 January 1972. The British Army was not best liked and tensions were still understandably high. We arrived at Fort George safe and sound and then after a bite to eat and sorting our bunks and rooms and NI gear etc we were given a briefing on the areas that 1 Staffords would patrol during their tour. If memory serves me right it was 'A' and 'C' companies based within the Creggan; 'B' and 'D' in Shantallow. Support Company was given Rosemount, Cloughglass and Buncrana; on PVCPs we would give extra support to the Creggan and Shantallow areas as required. We ended up doing about four days patrolling in Rosemount, four days Buncrana, four days as response team and so many days off and rotated again. We did do patrols in the Creggan and Shantallow at odd times throughout the tour and especially to support the need for more troops during searches, riots and hot pursuits.
>
> The first incident was the night that my section was on a rest period and suddenly, all hell broke loose. There was the noise of sporadic high velocity gunfire from all around us and then the tannoy said: 'Stand to, stand to, contact all areas.' What this meant was that the IRA ASUs had set up an all-round ambush of the Rosemount police Station/Army base and was giving us a good going over. I remember quickly putting my flak jacket on and being called by my section commander to load weapons outside and follow him. Alan Wassall, me and, I think 'Kipper' congregated outside, loaded our weapons and made for the gate out of the base. Jim Swain, our patrol commander, radioed in to do a radio check and was told to go hard and hot pursue towards the top of Creggan Road and out towards the Westway where the RRF sentry guards had seen gunfire flashes. Now, Rosemount police station was in a much built-up residential area; easy target for any coordinated ambush group. It was, and needed to be, heavily fortified and guarded; even though at best there were two or three police officers on duty, not counting the regular mobile patrols that visited the base to check on things and get a cuppa; the rest was made up of army contingents.
>
> I remember that my adrenalin was flowing and as soon as the gates were opened, I ran with Alan to take up a defensive position at the front of the zig-zagged, high rocket defence walls that covered the front side of the base. My heart was pumping with fear and my mind was everywhere: 'Will I be shot tonight? Where's Jim and Kipper? Are they OK?' Just then, I heard another splat of gunfire and a PIG armoured vehicle came out of the base and the vehicle commander told Jim to get his section behind and use it as a shield until they got into a clearer area. Jim shouted us on, and we followed behind and as we got through the fortified chicane, another heavy set of gunfire started coming our way. I remember cocking my weapon and looking through my IWS to see if I could see any gunmen; I saw a figure run to ground by some derelict houses, and I shouted to Jim and Alan: 'Target ahead.' Jim said right: 'Go, go, go.' and radioed in for backup. The PIG went up the Westway to check out something they had seen and Alan and I hot pursued towards the derelict houses. Alan shouted to Jim and Kipper:

Pete Whittall, 1st Staffords, patrolling the Rosemount area, Derry, 1974. *(Via Pete Whittall)*

'You take the outside; we'll go through the buildings.' I remember taking up a defensive position so that Alan was covered whilst he checked the entrance way into these old houses and then I followed him in. In no time backup had arrived and they were surrounding all sides of the buildings with Jim and Kipper. Other than streetlight silhouettes and our torches, there was not much light in the disused buildings.

As we came to the last couple of interconnecting areas, I saw a shadow and raised my weapon and shouted: 'Get the fuck up slowly or I'll fire,' upon which, the shadow assumed the same shape as my own. I could see now that the shadow was mine and boy was I relieved – Alan called me a bastard for putting the craps up him. Worse was to come because as we came to the end of the row of houses, Alan and I heard the rush of someone running away into the dark. We legged it out into the open and as we got outside a group of our colleagues raised their weapons and cocked; shit me, we both hit the deck and as flat as we could and shouted: 'Mortar platoon; don't shoot.' The lads dropped their weapons immediately and a 'blue on blue' was averted, thank God. Christ, it was frightening; if the guys had opened fire, there would not have been much of me and Alan left.

Whilst we were dealing with this side of the base, other colleagues including the RRF were hot pursuing down towards the Brook Park and Marlborough Road area from where another IRA ASU had fired several shots. No one was found but plenty of spent cases from rounds were retrieved and taken into the base; we counted over 50 rounds from both sides of the ambush attempt and we found more during the next few days as we patrolled around the area. Looking back now the outcome could have been so tragic; what if Alan and I had gone into a booby trap whilst hot pursuing into the derelict houses? We came so close to being shot by our own friendly forces; what would have happened if the PIG commander hadn't seen sense to give us a shield with his vehicle as we were coming out of the entrance of the base?

MY FIRST FOOT PATROL

Frenchie, 1 Kings

It was just after 6pm and it was already dark. Second platoon, 'A' Company had just settled in to its billet at the RUC station in Strabane, but there was no time to relax; unpacking personal kit would be done later, after our very first foot patrol. We had been out 'on the streets' before of course, but only as passengers in military buses or Makralon armoured Land Rovers, while moving from base to base around our TAOR in the Londonderry area.

Now it was time to get out for real. We were to carry out a two-hour recon and familiarisation patrol of the Strabane town centre and surrounding district. The four weeks intensive urban warfare training was supposed to prepare us for this moment, and of course we were well hyped and raring to get on with the job. But the stories that every one of us had heard time and time again about the ambushes and the dustbin bombs, the pram bombs (nowadays known by that popular acronym, thanks to Iraq and Afghanistan – IEDs), were the only thoughts running through everybody's mind.

The dim red lighting in the Ops room was supposed to preserve our night vision so that we would be alert and vigilant as we exited the station into the small square in front of the building – nice idea. The briefing finished, and we were led out into the dark night. No more than three steps away from the gate sangar a car came roaring into the square, caught full in the headlights; my carefully preserved night vision was torn away in a crazy dance of dazzling sparkles behind my eyelids. I remembered only too well the stories about the sniper's accomplice [A common practice known as 'dicking']. lighting up the victim in a blaze of vehicle main lamps. I hit the deck. The car roared past, the dodgy exhaust pipe clattering between the rear wheels. I felt a lot better when I looked around to see the rest of the patrol had also taken cover. My heart was beating like an express train; I stood and continued with the patrol into a narrow street leading off the square.

We were in a built-up area of narrow terraced streets which curved up and around the rear of the police station before eventually widening out into slightly more modern tarmac roadways, which led out away from the town centre. There were surprisingly few people about as we patrolled the town but there did seem to be a few cars lighting our way. I thought I saw the same car that had been outside the station as we started our patrol on two more occasions. I learned later that this was an old tactic, and used to full effect on new units, just to let us know that they had our number. Every incident that the crafty instructors played out in training came and went on that first patrol. Every high window hid a sniper, every doorway and dustbin concealed a bomb which was going to blow my legs right off from under me. Those people we did see spat on our backs or breathed out: 'Bastards' softly as we passed.

I had to grip my SLR tightly so that nobody would see how badly my hands were shaking. Every possible enemy position screamed out to my heightened senses; it wasn't supposed to be like this at all. Gradually, after about 90 minutes my heart slowed to something like normal and I was even able to look around for the more mundane, but equally important little things which may have been important on the debrief when we got back in. Then we were on our

Two soldiers just in from patrol catch their breath from the long run in. *(Craig Laidler)*

way back to our base at the police station. Once again the nerves took control; eyesight became so much more intense and aware of the slightest changes around. We were back into the square, less than fifty yards to go to the safety of the fortified fence surrounding the building. More car headlights, soldiers silhouetted against the silver tin sheets of the security fencing. More stories, more warnings jumping into mind. Never relax at the end of a patrol; that's when you are at your most vulnerable; that's when the shot will come!

It didn't, and we went in and made safe at the butts. Made it! They were playing with us. They knew it was our first patrol. They knew so much about us. They were just playing with us. They would pay for that later. Just as soon as we learned the rules of the game.

BOGSIDE: 20 MARCH 1972

Marty, Royal Green Jackets

I remember this day quite well; we had been in Londonderry just a year (2 RGJ). The riots continued on a daily basis, but we had our routine and we could always contain the riots to within the local area. We had become quite expert at moving into certain positions and remaining there, letting the rioters vent whatever anger they had and doing little damage other than to the areas that they lived in.

We moved into position in the area of the swimming baths at the top of William Street where rioting had been going on for some time; the smell of CS gas was a constant reminder of a city in turmoil. We moved into a vacant house facing the baths and took up fire positions.

I remember the sounds of blast bombs, small arms fire all being directed at the house and it was a constant and sustained attack. We realised after a short time that we couldn't get out of the house as the rioters had moved in around us. Others in my section were returning fire and these actions seem to go on for some time. I recall being in a fire position looking down William Street and being a bit envious of others who had targets to fire at.

We did eventually get relieved by another section and returned to the police station for a break. It was while we were on our break that we were told the sad news that Rifleman John Taylor had been shot and killed; I believe he was part of the section that had relieved us that day. A tall, quiet man aged just nineteen; a sniper had fired one shot and John was hit in the stomach and was declared dead on arrival at hospital.

Rifleman John William Taylor (19) from the Wanstead area in London was shot and fatally wounded by the IRA in Lower Street, Londonderry. He was rushed to the Altnagelvin Hospital but had succumbed to his wounds before the ambulance got there. John's tragic death was largely overshadowed as news came through of an appalling attack by the IRA in Donegall Street in Belfast. Seven people were killed by the 200lb device left in a car in the street. Two RUC officers and an off-duty UDR man were among the fatalities.

QUEEN STREET, MAGHERAFELT, 15 MARCH 1974

Corporal Nigel Barnes, BEM, The Royal Hussars

I was one of two dog handlers; I was the Arms/Explosives Search dog handler, and the other being a tracker dog handler, on detachment to the infantry unit based at RUC Magherafelt, Co Londonderry. My recollection of the day was that it was fairly normal with a couple of routine searches in the countryside around the township and then a restful afternoon with a spot of continuation training within the station compound for my dog, a black Labrador called Quin.

An alarm was raised at around 16:00 hours that a lorry bomb had been parked on Queen Street and Moneymore Road but with no warning or time of detonation. I grabbed my equipment, Quin and his equipment and with my armed escort ran down the road; a matter of 200/300 metres. The RV was at the bottom of the road and, in discussion with the ATO (who was also located at the station) I was to ready the dog and approach the vehicle. I was wearing my 'Cromwell' helmet (basically just a normal motorcycle helmet), and my flak jacket and started the approach to the vehicle; God, how lonely is it when all you can hear is your own footfall.

I had got to around 50 metres away from the lorry when I heard a whistle blast from behind me, and I spun around and saw a soldier (rank unknown) signalling for me to come back, post haste. He used the military hand signal of a clenched fist up and down (meaning to double). I shouted for Quin to come to heel, not bothering to put him back on his lead. I got back to the RV and asked what was wrong. They had had a 'coded' message, late, saying that the bomb would be going off at 16:00 hours and, as I looked at my watch: bang! One almighty explosion! I had missed being blown up by seconds! This time, I believe would have been about 16:20 hours; obviously timed to catch out some member(s) of the SF.

Subsequent information found it to be a 600lb bomb in a metal fish transportation tank, similar to those alloy tanks found in most lofts as water header tanks. Newspaper reports said that the explosion claimed the life of one Adam Johnston, father of four young children who was decapitated by a piece of flying shrapnel. A lesser known fact was that a poor pup that was sitting outside a butcher's shop in another street waiting for his daily bone was also killed by shrapnel. I have read since that an RUC Police Sergeant also lost an eye through flying debris. I cannot remember who the soldier was, or the regiment he belonged to, but I guess I owe him my life!

Adam Johnston (28), a father of four, was killed when the IRA detonated a 600lb device in Queen Street. He was standing some 200 yards away from the incident, which demonstrated the incredible killing range of the device and shows their scant concern for peripheral casualties. Mr Johnston, a Protestant, was walking through a previously cleared area and an RUC officer raced after him to save him from the blast. However, as he had almost reached him, the device detonated and he too was injured.

LUCK AND BAD LUCK: LONDONDERRY 1974

Private Pete Whittall Mortar Platoon, 1 Staffords

During another time our section was on foot patrol coming down Beechwood Avenue; it was a Sunday morning and the sky was clear and blue. It was strange because not many people were about and being church day it didn't seem right, then suddenly one of our mobile patrols was ambushed from the shirt factory in Bligh's Lane, across in the Bogside/Creggan area. I don't remember too much about it but do recall that the front Land Rover had slowed down to check the T-junction from Marlborough Road on to Beechwood Avenue to come up towards our foot patrol to check on us. Suddenly there was this distinctive rush of Armalite and Garand gunfire which seemed to come over our heads and hit the lead Land Rover. Corporal Barry Toal (seconded to us from 2 Para), the patrol commander, jumped out of his front passenger seat and took up a defensive position to report the contact and try and spot where the gunfire was coming from. At about the same time, Private Nigel Bourne who was looking forward out of the hatch of the second Land Rover suddenly dropped down and we thought he had been hit. In the meantime our brick of four squaddies legged it down towards the vehicles whilst this gunfire was still taking place.

As I ran towards Barry, I noticed rounds bouncing through the grit box on the pavement by the steps that went down to the 'Bog' and the grit was flying everywhere. Jim quickly radioed base and told them we were hot pursuing into the 'Bog' to follow up. The Bogside was patrolled by the Royal Artillery and we needed base to let them know we were entering their area. As Alan and I ran past the grit box, rounds were bouncing all around us and, as more troops from the RED 1 Response team arrived, the shooting stopped. We went to some houses over by William Street area to check but as it was, the shooting was in fact further up from the shirt factory. This was a lot higher than we were and an ideal place to ambush both mobile and foot patrols. Once the dust had settled we went back to Marlborough Avenue to see how Nigel was and found that the top hatch had been forced into his face because of a sudden gust of wind and had hit him full on the nose; this had knocked him back, giving him a nasty gash and bloody nose. On examination of the lead Land Rover we found several bullet holes in the front and side of the vehicle. One round in particular had continued through the engine block and entered a few centimetres below Barry's seat and in a central position to his groin; a very lucky escape Corporal Toal!

Danny 'Smudger' Smith was seriously wounded during another ambush in the Rosemount area. Our section was out on foot patrol and had gone into a 'safe house' for a cuppa. On the way back we heard gunfire and we were just coming towards the far entrance way to Brook Park. Sergeant Bob Gleeson was patrol commander with me, Jim Swain and Alan Wassall making up the rest of the patrol; as always, I was 'tail end Charlie.' It was 14 August and early evening, but already dark. Danny who was aged 22 at the time and married, had run out of Rosemount Police Station and climbed into a Land Rover with his patrol. Their task was to drive to a road junction and set up an immediate VCP to try and stop a stolen car. As the two-vehicle patrol drove down the Creggan Road, they hit a junction (I think it was Marlborough Road) which required them to slow down and as they did several shots rang out from a range of about 50 yards. A bullet from a Garand high velocity rifle passed through two layers of armoured vehicle protection, through the back of Danny's seat and entered his left lung, shattering it and causing severe trauma. Another bullet was found tangled up in his pullover, luckily not wounding him further. Danny was rushed to hospital and a few days later placed on the critical list.

His wife sat beside him at his bedside throughout the weeks of care and treatment and luckily Danny survived. Danny was no coward, not like those who had shot him and weeks later he was back on patrol on the streets of Derry; a real hero in my book because he had had a significant part of his lung removed. Whilst the gunfire could be heard, I asked Sergeant Gleeson if we should hot pursue through the park and aim to give support to the ambushed mobile patrol. However, he was reluctant and wouldn't let us tab it to their position. I don't know if it would have made much difference to be honest, because from talking to the guys who were involved, as soon as the contact report went in Red1 was dispatched and the RUC were quick on the scene and we were on foot.

I was pissed off because we couldn't pursue and pissed off because Danny was a mate and we had worked together back in Germany in our mechanised mortar platoon role. I was angry because the IRA had injured yet another British soldier who was only doing his job; a job that bloody well protected people from these bastards. I am so pleased that Danny survived. Unfortunately that would not be the case for Lieutenant Michael Simpson who would be mortally wounded in the Shantallow in September and who would lose his fight to live after three brave weeks of trying. Also in that ambush Private Steven Stankavich would suffer serious arm injuries as a result of being hit by gunshot fire in the same incident.

On 3 October 1974 Lieutenant Michael Simpson (21) from Middlesex was shot by an IRA sniper on Racehorse Road in Londonderry. He died of that wound some twenty days later. A Londonderry teenager was tried and found guilty of his murder and though sentenced to life imprisonment was released early. After serving only three years, she was released on medical grounds following pressure from some mainland Labour MPs.

These are just a few incidents which I experienced as a young soldier during my first tour of Ulster in those dark, dangerous days of the worst periods of the Troubles. There were very few days when we were not bricked, or petrol bombed or spat at or told to go home. There were many days where nothing happened and weeks when everything happened. From shootings, to riots, to bombings etc. I did return home but like many other soldiers would return again to experience other evils in different parts of NI.

The Staffords would lose another six men. On 20 January 1981, Private Christopher Shenton was shot and killed by an IRA sniper whilst manning an OP in the Bogside. He was 21 and came from the Stoke-on-Trent area and was shot whilst closing security gates. It later emerged that an IRA informer had warned the RUC of the impending attack but the information was not relayed to the Staffords. Some three years later, when the Regiment was in the Crossmaglen area, Lance Corporal Stephen Anderson (23) was killed by an IRA landmine. The young soldier died instantly; poignantly, the father of a small child was killed on his wedding anniversary.

Two more members of the Regiment, Private Mark Mason (18) from Stoke on Trent and Sergeant Dean Oliver (30) from Peterlee died in 1989 and 1992 respectively. PTE Mason was killed in an accidental discharge; Sergeant Oliver's apparent murder is dealt with in another part of this book.

The last Staffords soldier to be killed in Northern Ireland was Private Wayne Smith (18) tragically killed in a road traffic accident on 1 July 1995.

THE IRA TRY TO KILL ME: AGAIN!

Glen Espie, UDR

Over the years I had worked out that if (East Tyrone) PIRA were to attack me again the only place where I was vulnerable was leaving for work in the morning. This was my only predictable pattern; therefore thinking like a terrorist, how would I ambush myself? I lived in the country to the east of Cookstown up a lane about half mile long. Looking down the lane from my home it merged with a smaller lane to a neighbour's home making a T-junction. I had visual on the lane to the main road from my home. The hedges were cut short to avoid concealment for an ambush team; unfortunately the ground to the right hand side of the lane leaving my home was about one metre below the level of the lane and out of sight from my home. The perfect location to launch an ambush was the two-storey house on the other side of the road about 25 metres up from the end of my lane on the other side of the main road going toward Cookstown.

I believed PIRA would take over this house the night before as a secure location out of sight of patrolling helicopters that carried out dawn patrols in the area of off-duty soldiers. I thought they would put a gun team at the corner of the front garden; it had good cover from view and a firm earth bank, with a two-foot-high hedge on top. This would leave me the target coming into their view about 75 metres from the end of my lane and closing all the time on their position. I walked through numerous ambush scenarios and in all cases I believed the car would become the target and I needed to get away from the car as quickly as possible if I survived the opening burst of gunfire; wounded or not. The drainage ditch at the side of the road across from the house that PIRA would use offered the best possible cover.

On 18 March 1987, I was left for work as usual about 8am and I spotted a car I knew to be driven by a PIRA member parked up a long lane about 50 metres off the main road at an old railway bridge going into Cookstown. This lane had been used previously to launch a mortar bomb attack on the local police station from the concealed lane. On that occasion, I phoned the Battalion ops room and named the PIRA member from the west of Cookstown who at that time I believed to be scouting the area for another mortar attack on the police station.

Some years before the attack on Glen Espie – 26 May 1983 – an INLA gun attack on the RUC station at Cookstown killed Constable Colin Carson, an RUC Reservist. He was 31 and a married father of two children and was killed when an INLA husband-and-wife team opened fire on him as he approached the van they were travelling in.

The following morning was clear with a light drizzle of rain and some light snow was still lying around in the fields and ditches. The mountain Slieve Gallion which dominated the sky line twelve miles north of my home was totally covered. I always thought the mountain looked so powerful and dominant on the skyline; with it covered in snow there was a beauty that only nature could provide.

My children had asked if they could travel to work with me so they could be at school early and spend some time with friends before class commenced, but because they were not quite ready, I told them to get the school bus at the end of the lane as usual at 8.30am. I was in a hurry as a number of problems that had arisen at work the previous afternoon needed to be addressed first thing.

I looked out of the windows around my home as usual and then went out and checked my car for under-vehicle booby trap bombs. I was thinking of how to address the problems at work as I drove along the lane way from my home. I emerged from my lane without stopping and looked right down the main road at the bend; about half a mile from my lane I observed a school bus come into view around the bend. My pistol was holstered and as I drew level with the hedge, a green coloured car emerged from the lane way that was used by the house opposite. When I saw the green bonnet of the Ford Orion car, I thought it was a neighbour who lived further down the lane and drove the same.

This thought was quickly kicked into touch as the car accelerated onto the main road and turned facing my car and screeched to a stop. There were three people in the car; all wearing balaclava masks. My first thought was: 'Not again!' as I took in the scene of the masked terrorists. There is something about a mask that is really frightening. The front and rear passenger doors were thrown open as I stood on the brakes to bring my car to a stop. Two gunmen got out of the car armed with 7.62mm Heckler & Koch G3 assault rifles. My car started to vibrate as the first burst of automatic fire hit the front of the car and windscreen. I could see the gunman using the edge of the car roof as a support to steady his aim and was wearing what looked like a green German Army parka jacket; beneath the car door I could see that his trousers were tucked into the top of his boots.

My car came to a halt about three or four car lengths from the gunmen's car. I thought this is it; three terrorists with assault rifles. I was totally out gunned; my chances of survival looked very slim, but, as always time spent in training is never wasted and I had planned for this ambush. I dived out of the car onto the road as the first burst of automatic fire hit my car and at this moment, my left wrist was shattered by a 7.62 round as I drew my holstered 9mm Beretta SB Compact with my right hand. I ran down the side of the car with rounds cracking past, and I think it was one of these rounds that took out the rear tyre of my car. I ran across the rear of the car, keeping below window level and dived head first into the drainage ditch; Linford Christie couldn't have made it any faster.

When I looked up out of the ditch, my car blocked the view and I could only see the rear boot area of the gunmen's car. I crawled forward along the drainage ditch and the car came fully into view; and I fired my pistol, one handed, as my left wrist was shattered and therefore useless, firing three shots quickly as I hoped this would frighten them off.

The second gunman took cover behind the rear passenger door and after I opened fire took no further part in the attack. The gunman at the front passenger's door moved his body and readjusted his aim onto my position in the ditch; the distance between me and gunmen's car was about 10 to 15 metres at a right angle from my position in the drainage ditch. I tried desperately to hit and kill the gunman who was firing repeated burst of automatic gunfire in my direction. I was low in the ditch and able to use my right hand only. My pistol was resting on the grass bank of the drainage ditch and I could just raise my head enough to sight the pistol through the grass at the gunman. The rounds being fired at me were tearing up the ground around my fire position, lifting sods of grass and throwing dirt in my face with other rounds going over my head, then into and cutting the bushes in the hedge behind me.

During the fire fight I could see the gunman recoil each time he fired, and I was aware of the car engine being constantly revved. It was obvious that the car was in first gear with the driver having his foot on the clutch and gunning the engine ready for a fast getaway. The driver's head was getting lower and lower until he was literally looking out under the steering wheel and I could just see the top of his head. I now know that one of my rounds had hit the driver's door-post and, had it penetrated, he may well have taken a head shot.

One of them was now leaning at a right angle, using the corner of the car roof to support his elbow to steady and support his weapon and firing across the car roof at an angle. During the fire fight the gunman would bend down and yell something into the car, which I was unable to make out over the noise of gunfire and the high revving car engine. I was never going to win the fire fight with a pistol against an assault rifle and, because of the closeness of my positions it would become very obvious if I ran out of rounds. I did have a spare magazine and had practised how to change it one-handed. If I was ambushed again and was lucky to escape the first burst of gunfire, I might be wounded. My first three rounds were fired in quick succession which I hoped would scare off the gunmen, but it quickly became apparent that the gunman using the G3 assault rifle was a professional and had done this before and was not afraid to stand his ground and press home the attack. I was trying to hit and kill him and never in my life before or after have I ever wanted to kill another person so much.

The gunman fired another burst and then slid into the passenger's seat and the car accelerated away; as it passed my position in the ditch, I expected the rear seat gunman to fire at me as he would have a clear field of fire into the bottom of the ditch. I lay on my back with my pistol across my chest and when the car drew level with my position and slowed to provide a clear line of fire for the rear gunman I would fire my last rounds at the gunman's car. The gunman's car did not slow down but accelerated away. It was only then as I turned to follow the car that I saw the school bus had pulled up behind and I ran down the ditch behind the school bus and came out onto the road. The gunman's car had stopped about 200 metres down the road and I dropped onto one knee and fired a shot at the stopped car. I didn't want them coming back again and the relief at having survived a second close quarter assassination attack was overwhelming.

Then my senses started to kick in; why had they stopped? I had not seen the second gunman since when I had first fired. Had they driven off by mistake and left the second gunman in the hedge at the other side of the road? I was wandering around the road fully erect, presenting an excellent target to a gunman if he was still in the ambush area. My adrenalin was pumping and taking in the scene as I turned around and heard shouts, and saw the people who had been held hostage running and shouting. I was unable to make out what they were saying and my eyes were scanning the hedge in case the second gunman was still in the vicinity. Had I disabled the gunmen's car with one of my shots? I saw that the rear tyre of my car was flat, but even so, I jumped in and sped off towards Cookstown Police Station three miles away to raise the alarm and get the Air Reaction Force Airborne hopefully to intercept the gunmen's getaway car.

About a mile down the road out of a side road emerged two Land Rovers of a regular Army patrol that had just arrived in the Province and had literally taken up duty within the last few days. I jumped from the car and ran towards them, shouting I was UDR and had just been ambushed. I asked the officer if I could use their radio to contact the ops room. Just then, a neighbour's car pulled up behind my car and the Army patrol. I asked the patrol commander if he would chase after the gunmen as their car was stopped about a mile up the road. I said I would go into Cookstown with the neighbour and get the RUC to inform all call signs of the ambush and seek medical attention there.

On arrival at the police station I ran past the constable on duty at the gate and into the station and informed them what had happened. In the safety of the police station the adrenalin had worn off, and I now felt the terrible pain in my left arm where I had been shot. I was sitting in a chair and the blood was running down my hand and spilling on the floor. I still had a loaded pistol in my right hand; a policeman took it off me and unloaded it. I only found out later when the patrol officer visited me that when I was pointing and gesturing with my right hand, all he could see was the loaded weapon in my hand with the hammer back and was ducking from side to side to stay away from the weapon.

I found out later the couple in the house that was taken over to launch the assassination attack were devout Christians. The couple prayed and sang hymns and recited a poem to the dedicated young men of East Tyrone PIRA and advised the gunmen of their sins in doing the Devils work, that they would have to answer for their sins one day to Christ our Lord and told them to take away all hatred from their hearts. One of the gunmen said you'll be writing a poem about this and they did. I believe this couple had got to the second gunman and that's why he took no part in the ambush after I fired on their car. I will leave it to the readers to make up their own minds.

Was I scared? You're bloody right I was! However this type of attack is so sudden and violent that training takes over and you find an inner strength to function and the will to survive keeps you in control.

The gunman who did all the firing was in control of the East Tyrone PIRA and the Active Service Unit (ASU) on the day of the ambush and had killed before. The weapon used was traced to the murders of other UDR members from my Battalion. It is clear that the PIRA member that I had observed on my way into work parked up the lane the previous day was not scouting the police station as I thought, but was observing my timing into work for the assassination team who were to carry out the attack on me the next morning.

My son has carried on the family tradition and is currently a serving officer with an infantry regiment having completed tours of both Iran and Afghanistan, about which I am extremely proud. I am telling this story to highlight what it was like to be a part-time soldier in the UDR, on or off duty and for my comrades that weren't as lucky as me and made the supreme sacrifice for Queen and Country, so that Northern Ireland would be a better place for all sections of the community to live in peace.

HOUSE SEARCH

Marty, Royal Green Jackets

We were housed in a base in the Brandywell area of Londonderry that we called 'sandbag city'. You have to remember at this time, in 1972, there were no purpose-built buildings for us to live in. This base consisted more or less entirely of sand bags. It came under constant abuse; shootings and rioters were quite a normal part of everyday life at that sorry time. You were constantly aware of the dangers and were always on the move; you never kept still.

An operation was set up for a house search in the Bogside, and, as a Rifleman, I needed to know very little, just a general outline of what my task was. We had intelligence that gunmen were using a house so a Company operation went into action. My section was responsible for the search and we were given about five minutes to carry it out; three men upstairs, three men down. As we moved into the area the locals were out banging their bin lids and making as much noise as possible, so time was somewhat limited. As we moved from 'sandbag city' towards the house on that damp night, all I had was a baton; no weapon or other kit. My CSM was running beside me and sections took up positions en route. We arrived at our target and stood by as our section commander, a big tall lad ran from the opposite side of the road and crashed through the door. We all then piled in, with two others and me upstairs to carry out a quick search.

We did find weapons, explosives and car plates so the info was good, but what we did miss were the gunmen running out the back door. As the operation was carried out quickly the back of the building had not been secured. They did however catch the last man; he was handed over for me to take back to base. Now the thought of an IRA gunman can make you a little nervous when on ops, but I always remember this particular gunman. By the time I got him back to base he had literally shit himself and stank to high heaven; oh what a brave man, rather a pathetic looking individual!

It was decided to do the same search on the same house some months later; same routine, however, our big lad bounced off the door this time, and I took great delight in smashing in all the windows, our alternative way in.

BLIGH'S LANE FIRE FIGHT

Guardsman Kelvin Brown, Coldstream Guards

It was 5 February 1972 and I was with my company based in Bligh's Lane army base in a disused factory compound between the Republican housing estates of the Creggan and the Bogside. I was 'stagging on' in one of the several sangars and I heard a loud explosion from the direction of Lonemoor Road, followed by a lot of shooting.

Immediately, I heard Lance Corporal Dalgreen over my radio headphones calling that the 'milk run' (the daily ration run) had been attacked by a roadside bomb in an oil drum. As he was unable to get through to the radio room, I was forced to relay this message for him. Apparently the device had exploded midway between the lead PIG and a 4-tonner which had the rations on board. He was ordered to return with the convoy to Fort George which was our main base (a former Royal Navy base) alongside the River Foyle. Later on, after we had been relieved from guard duty, we were tasked to go to the junction of Lonemoor Road and Bligh's Lane to meet our CO who was coming to investigate.

As soon as we had dismounted the PIG and secured the junction, the aggro started immediately and bottles, bricks and paving stones rained down on us. I had a rifle-mounted CS grenade discharger which I had to use several times and we were forced to fire rubber bullets. Shortly afterwards we came under both rifle and automatic fire from several directions. Then, three rounds came in from the direction of Bligh's Lane and struck the corner of the brick wall near us. I started to run in the direction of where the PIGs were, to try and spot the location

Riot gun and a magazine of 7.62 SLR rounds compared to a packet of 20 Rothmans King Size. *(Richard Nettleton)*

of the gunman. As I did so, I saw Guardsman Les Smith take over a six-foot riot shield when a further three shots were fired. I saw Les slide down the wall as he had been hit. Another Guardsman, Bob Power, reversed a PIG back to the corner and I used this as cover to get to Les. He had been shot through his steel helmet and we reached him and quickly got him into the vehicle and raced off and for the first time, I saw a PIG do a 'wheelie' as it took him away.

Our platoon commander came down in another vehicle to pick us up and as we got on, the gunman fired a further three rounds at us, all of which hit the armour and bounced off. Once we were back at the base, we looked at the side of the PIG and found three bullet scars in a one-and-a-half-inch grouping. We then saw Les, sitting in the HQ, head all neatly bandaged with a nice groove across the top of his head where the round had hit him. Had he not been wearing a respirator, no doubt he would have been killed. He had to have been the luckiest man in the Province. So far as I know, he still has that groove. At the time, I looked at his steel helmet and there were two bullet holes, one on either side; one an entry, the other an exit. We also had two other lads who were wounded in that fire fight; we never saw the gunman who fired at us.

The accolade of being the 'luckiest man in the Province' had other claimants. On 5 September that same year, about mid-afternoon, a Scots Guards patrol commanded by a Lieutenant Erskine-Crum was moving along Cable Street, Londonderry. Guardsman Spinks was the rear man of the patrol and as he turned into Drumcliffe Avenue, a single shot rang out. The bullet, a Garrand armour-piercing round hit Guardsman Spinks in the middle of his back and he was thrown about five yards along the pavement. His injuries, however, amounted to only bruising and shock, for the bullet had struck the Federal Riot Gun slung over his back and fragmented on contact with his flak jacket. Within 24 hours he was back out on patrol again – with a new riot gun and new flak jacket.

BOGSIDE GIFTS

RSM Haydn Davies, UDR/Royal Regiment of Wales

I felt the blanked-out stare of the locals. We used to call it the 'thousand metre stare' when they looked right through you, and out into the distance beyond. I did meet some kindness in the Bogside and sometimes at night a bar of chocolate or a home-baked cake was pushed into my hands. One woman used to bake me soda bread on a regular basis. The lads used to say to me: 'Watch it, Sir; crushed glass will kill your kidneys,' but I survived and of course I was always aware of the possible explosives device, so my gifts were from old ladies only.

BLUE ON BLUE: ALMOST

Marty, Royal Green Jackets

Londonderry city was a place that always smelt of CS gas as you arrived. Whilst there on this one tour, we had little in the way of purpose-built buildings but as long as you had a camp bed and a sleeping bag you were fine. We had no pre-training for Northern Ireland; we sort of learned as we went along, so to speak.

I recall an incident on the Foyle Road, in which we had been briefed that a gunman would take on a patrol and we were to take up a position watching the front of the house. This we did and moved in at night. We were out in the open and not wearing headdress, and lay in what could be described as a shell scrape with not a great deal of cover. As the morning arrived another Green Jackets patrol was sent out, and we could see them on the high open ground. Suddenly we heard shots being fired at them, and one of the lads was hit in the shoulder. Then we were spotted by the patrol and they returned fire at us and started to move towards our position firing as they moved. It dawned on us that they had not been briefed that we were there and we very quickly got onto the radio to stop them from attacking us. We obviously lost the gunman but I'm glad to say that the Rifleman survived.

A MISSED FUNERAL

Gunner Nigel Glover, Royal Artillery

It was early August 1979 and I was on weekend guard duty at Horseshoe Barracks, Shoeburyness in Essex. A group of civilians came up to me and asked if this was the place where Gunner Furminger's funeral was to be held. I asked them if it was Dick Furminger from 170 Battery, 45 Regiment, Royal Artillery. They weren't sure which regiment he belonged to, only that he had been killed in Northern Ireland. It then dawned on me that it was Dick who had been killed, as I was aware that my parent regiment, 45 Royal Artillery, were serving in Northern Ireland. However, there was no funeral scheduled to be held there at the barracks.

I was quite shocked by this family group coming up to me that day and asking me this question; it was, after all, someone I knew and this remained with me all of my life. It also produced some questions of my own. I asked them to wait where they were and went into the guardroom and asked the guard commander if he could find out where the funeral was to be held. A short time later he came back with the answer; he confirmed that it was, indeed, Richard Furminger of 170 battery and that the funeral was to be held in Colchester only some 30 miles away. The questions that I asked myself were: why wasn't I informed of his death by my Regiment and why, as I was so close to the lad, couldn't I have attended it? I never received answers to those questions. All that I did know was that it was pretty shocking to find out in this way.

On 2 August 1979, Gunner Richard Furminger (19) an Essex boy, was killed by an IRA landmine near Moy in Co Armagh. Killed alongside Richard was SIG Paul Reece (19), of the Royal Corps of Signals, a native of the Crewe area. Both soldiers had only been in Province for just over a week and were travelling in an Army convoy when a massive culvert bomb planted by PIRA exploded, leaving a 10-foot crater in the road. Their patrol was en route to barracks after investigating the murder of an RUC officer. Shots were fired after the explosion but the Army reported no further casualties.

On 17 July 1975, four soldiers were killed by the 70lb device planted in a beer keg near Fords Cross in South Armagh. The IRA had used milk churns as a 'come on' whilst the real device was in the keg, which was hidden in a hedge. The four soldiers were Major Peter Willis (37) from Chester, of the Green Howards, ATO Edward Garside (34), from Chepstow, RAOC, ATO Calvert Brown (25) from Stockton, and RAOC Sergeant Samuel McCarter (33) from Belfast, Royal Engineers.

This was the side of Army life which the glossy advertising posters depicting a young, healthy man waterskiing off Malta or Cyprus did not show; this was the reality of a war against an implacable, terrorist enemy. As a young soldier, the author also had to collect body parts after an explosion. That will live with me forever.

CULLYHANNA SHOOTING

Lance Corporal Rob Hughes, Royal Green Jackets

It was Friday the thirteenth, just the day to head towards the 'pipe ranges' of Cullyhanna and Crossmaglen. During the brief prior to leaving, we were informed that the latest information was that there was a lot of Intel pointing towards a shoot with a secondary device in the

Nick Smith by a wall with bomb damage.

TAOR. There had been reports of automatic fire being heard in the border areas in the days leading up to this patrol; possibly weapons being zeroed.

We flew by Lynx helicopters to the drop off points south of Newtownhamilton and we carried out our tasks as planned. I can remember glancing over my shoulder and being pleased with the way the brick was performing; perfect spacing and positioning and all looking switched on. It was an eerie dusk around Cullyhanna; as we moved south of the town towards the lakes I could see the smoke coming from the chimneys of this notorious village and scanned the likely firing points for any combat indicators.

I looked at the other bricks and noticed that they were dominating an area of high ground behind my position; so I moved towards a VCP on a road between Crossmaglen and Cullyhanna. As I scanned the area, I was suddenly thrown to the ground (with an 80lb Bergen on) and felt immediate pain in my right leg and saw a blinding flash before my eyes. I say pain; it felt more like somebody had shoved a bloody red-hot poker through my right thigh!

To this day I can remember the noise as automatic fire rained down on us from three separate firing points. I was later to learn it was a GPMG and two AK47s. I reached for my radio hand-piece, which had become dislodged. When I moved, another long burst of automatic fire was aimed at me; I can remember watching the glow of green tracer rounds heading towards me and smashing into the ground around me. I admit to thinking that I was finished because there was no cover around me at all. I just looked up and watched the muzzle flashes of the PIRA gun team shooting at us, but what probably saved me and other casualties was the incredibly aggressive return fire from the blokes who hammered the rounds down back at the terrorist positions.

Cullyhanna, South Armagh, was a dangerous place for British soldiers, being the location of the notorious 'Cullyhanna gun crew'. It was the scene of at least five security forces deaths during the course of the Troubles.

On 10 February 1972, Private David Champ of the Devon & Dorsets was killed by an IRA landmine and in the same year, Captain William Watson of the Argyll and Sutherland Highlanders was killed by an IRA booby trap device there.

On 29 July 1988, having been wounded two days earlier, Sergeant Michael Matthews of the Parachute Regiment died of his wounds following an IRA landmine explosion. The Scots Guards lost Lance Sergeant Graham Stewart on 5 May 1990 in Cullyhanna. He was part of an undercover patrol and was shot and killed by an IRA gunman. On 17 August the following year, Lance Corporal Simon Ware, brother of Royal Green Jacket Darren Ware, was killed by an IRA landmine.

IN 'BANDIT COUNTRY'

Private 'C', Queen's Lancashire Regiment

In July 1977 I did my first patrol in Northern Ireland, Crossmaglen Square, South Armagh; 'bandit country.' I can tell you I was scared as I walked out the gates of the police station for the first time. It was more the fear of the unknown and I was concerned to avoid the embarrassment of being killed on my first patrol; silly now thinking back. My Regiment and I survived that tour and in October 1980 I started my second infantry tour of South Armagh. I was employed as the office manager of the intelligence cell of 'B' Company, 1 Queens Lancashire Regiment based at Bessbrook Mill.

Although mostly office bound, I felt I was going blind due to the short distances I was viewing inside the Mill all the time. So I started going out on more and more patrols, although not the heliborne patrols as space on the helicopters was limited. You see, unlike the other Int lads, who used to take the place of one of the lads in a four-man brick, I attached myself to a brick and let them patrol around me as I chatted to the locals. The lads who I accompanied didn't like me much for not dropping one of them off and taking his place so he could get a break, but I didn't care. My theory was I couldn't fulfil my Intelligence role if I was covering an arc in a brick so it was safer for all of us. In a multiple of three bricks led by an officer or platoon sergeant, we would patrol from the Mill in Bessbrook to Camlough and once there, I would stop someone at random and talk to them. Sometimes I would 'P check' them but most times I would just have a friendly chat. I might ask for ID and take a few notes to collate later back in the Intelligence Cell office, but the main objective was to gain the trust of the locals rather than get any real intelligence information.

As the tour progressed, the OC of the company started to insist that a Saracen was used when patrolling in Camlough because of the extra fire power the .3 inch Browning fitted into the turret on top gave us. I hated riding in it as I thought it was just too good a target and it took over an hour to drive the short distance of just over a mile from the Mill to Camlough. You could hear it coming for miles and every culvert on the way had to be checked for command wires or hidden bombs. The Saracen would have to stop about 100m from any culvert, pipe, tunnel under, or bridge over the road. Then one man on each side of the road would have to climb over the fence into the fields and look into the culverts to check for milk churns. These could be packed with ANFO, an explosive made from finely ground ammonium nitrate-rich fertiliser mixed with diesel oil. This was very time consuming but you're a long time dead if you didn't check the one culvert with a bomb underneath and you could guarantee PIRA would be watching to see which if any were being overlooked on a regular basis.

Sadly the Green Jackets who took over from us in March of 1981 were not so lucky. On 19 May 1981 in a Saracen, C/S 42F, four Green Jackets and a Royal Corps of Transport driver were instantly killed by such a culvert bomb on Chancellor's Road. I was particular saddened when I heard of their deaths because I had been very careful to stress the importance of checking culverts to the lad who took over from me as Int Cell Office Manager. This warning was as a result of an incident which 'B' Company had dealt with on our tour. Years later, my Islander Flight Commander told me that had he had heard that explosion and flown a Scout to the scene of the incident and that he had seen a BBC TV crew filming. It seems they had been tipped off prior to the incident by PIRA.

The incident to which Paul refers took place on 19 May 1981; it was a day of tragedy for the Royal Green Jackets, losing four men, the worst day of the Troubles for this superb infantry regiment. Rifleman Michael Bagshaw (24) from Oxfordshire; Rifleman Andrew Gavin (19) from London; Rifleman John King (20) and Lance Corporal Grenville Winston (27) from Bedfordshire and their RCT Driver, Paul Bulman (19) from near Newcastle-upon-Tyne all lost their lives that day. The five soldiers were killed by an IRA landmine at Camlough Lake in Armagh. Travelling outside of Camlough, a massive device, estimated at over 1,000lbs, was detonated and they were all killed instantly. *Lost Lives* also records that a suspected IRA man who was thought responsible for the attack was later killed in a classic IRA 'own goal' explosion on 29 February 1988.

Soldier, Royal Regiment of Wales, ever alert in the Ardoyne.

On my tour, the company had received information of suspicious activity at a chicken farm close to Chancellor's Road that eventually led down to a VCP on the Newry to Dublin Road. Fearing PIRA wanted us in the area for something nasty such as a come-on for a bomb, a shooting or RPG-7 attack, we kept well clear. Eventually PIRA become bored of us avoiding the area and changed tactics by passing information to the Security Forces that there was an unstable bomb under a culvert close by. This actually was a come on; not for us but for Felix, the call sign of ATO. There was a bomb under the culvert all right, but PIRA had also booby trapped the firing point in an effort to kill Felix, who used up one of his nine lives that day. 'SAS K', the nickname of 'B' Company's Intelligence Sergeant and I analysed this incident for ages; looking at lines of sight for the command wire, and where the nearest phone boxes were situated to give warning of the approach of the Saracen. We came up with a plausible scenario and both of us briefed our Green Jacket replacements who took over from us in March 1981. Maybe a couple of months into their tour the Green Jackets just got careless. I heard later that the lad I had briefed left the Int Cell after the bombing and went to COP, the Close Observation Platoon and was shot dead while on an OP near the border at Glassdrummond; but I don't know this for sure. [It is thought that this may refer to Lance Corporal Gavin Dean who was killed in a fire fight with the IRA near Crossmaglen later that same year.]

The Intelligence Sergeant who took over from 'SAS K' had the nickname of 'Cowley' after the head of CI5 from the TV series *The Professionals*. I met him again some two years later and I asked him how his tour went, which I instantly regretted as I could see the pain in his eyes when he recognised me. He said nothing, so I nodded and found a table to eat my meal and thought how lucky my Regiment had been to once again serve in 'bandit country' and not have any deaths. On the first tour we had one lad blinded in a bomb explosion and sadly that could have been avoided if the Colour Sergeant straight from the depot had not taken a scratch brick past a PIRA bomber's house and had problems tuning in the radio. We had a couple of casualties on my second infantry tour but again fortunately no deaths. One lad was hit in the head from a negligent discharge from an LMG and another lad was shot in the stomach in Crossmaglen. When I passed my air crewman's course I felt lucky to be away from the infantry and not have to do any more tours of Northern Ireland, or so I thought at the time!

'BLOODY POKE'

Nick Bates, Army Dog Handlers Unit

I've recalled this one as 'Bloody Poke', because, as all our Ulster friends will know, a 'poke' is Ulster speak for an ice cream.

I had got the call to make my way down to the Ops room which had an adjoining RUC office at Bessbrook (BBK) which was in the bowels of the infamous Mill. I got a very scant brief from the ops officer who basically told me to grab the dog (Fury) and make my way to the guard room where I would be collected and I would get a more detailed brief once I was on the ground.

As many former soldiers will be aware you only drove into BBK when starting your stint out on location, or finishing it, otherwise chopper was the main means of transport. I quickly got my kit together from the wooden site hut which I used to doss down in, which also doubled up as the barber's shop once a week. Only the best accommodation for the groundhog, which was nice and close to the kennels, guard room, heli pad and LPG, fuel bowser and palletised jerry cans.

Fury and I were conveyed by hard skin transport to Newry town centre, a short distance from the Mill on a day I will never forget, Saturday 26 July 1986. The location was Market Square, Newry. A glorious day with masses of shoppers out enjoying the good weather. This would be the first time we would be working in such a confined area with so many people present. We made our way through the crowds with the help of the accompanying brick and when I got to the perimeter cordon I observed that there was a huge crowd and they were extremely difficult to get through despite having a Rotty on a short leash. All eyes were on the open car doors of an armoured Ford Cortina. Gone were the usual sounds of Saturday shoppers: the pounding of feet; the drone of conversation; the laughter of youngsters and the crying of wee ones strapped in buggies. This was replaced by wide eyed, shocked members of the public; mothers that were shielding and steering their children's eyes away from a truly awful sight

I went firm at the corner of a building with Fury by my side with a cover man immediately behind me who appeared to only look about eighteen. The cover man was my protection as I was only armed with a 9 'milly'. ATO was at the Cortina clearing it, just in case there was anything untoward. As you can imagine Felix's job was not one to be rushed and I was somewhat surprised at what I heard next. Near a place of worship a man of the cloth who was giving off at the ICP commander as he had a wedding to conduct and our presence was holding up the proceedings implying that we should carry out our work expeditiously.

With ATO's work done, I put the dog in his harness which associated him with work and swapped his rope and leather short lead for his 18-foot track line. I was conscious of the following – a hot day, hard surface, masses of people – not the best of conditions for tracking. I put my head over my shoulder gesturing to my young cover man that we were going to move, he nodded and up we stood and moved forward toward the open doors of the car, and in doing so I paid out my track line, ever hopeful of Fury picking up a track.

As I approached the car, I leant back with my hands slightly raised, keeping the line taut just so it didn't get snagged on the bumpers of the car or if Fury would suddenly scoot around the other side of the car and pick up a track. He went immediately to the open rear door of the car and started licking but it wasn't the ice creams the occupants had been consuming, unexpectedly discarded and now melting on the ground. I didn't feel revolted, just straight away saddened, as he was licking the head wounds of a young police officer who was lying down on the bench seat of the car. Looking over the rear door frame of the car and in the front I could see another police officer, sporting a well groomed full ginger beard wearing his heavy black Bristol body armour, motionless and in the sitting position. I moved around the car as Fury was leading me and I can recall checking with my cover man if he was alright; he assured me he was OK but I will never forget the ashen look on his face.

I heard the car police radio crackle and make a short inaudible transmission, and I suddenly looked down, and right before me on the ground was the lifeless body of another police officer who appeared to have tried to make good his escape but to no avail. Poor man; the length of the blood trail told you he didn't die instantly. The dog was snorting the ground, and he led the cover man and me away from the car and in the direction of a butcher's shop on the corner. Showing interest but not entering he carried on with great gusto through the crowds who strangely stepped aside like he was Moses parting the waves. He tracked past the length of a parade of shops right to the end of the street, where all of a sudden he stopped at the curb side where skid marks could be seen. Clearly the perpetrators had made off in a vehicle of some description.

When I later joined the RUC, I worked with a lad who went through the depot with the young officer who was indeed a teenager when he was brutally murdered along with his colleagues. I was informed that for good measure, the IRA had thrown a grenade into the rear of the armoured car but it had not gone off. If it had, God knows what the toll would have been and it just shows you the depths these bastards will stoop to. They had indeed taken cover in the butcher's shop and had dressed in butcher's aprons. They had approached the car and opened up on the unsuspecting police officers who were having an ice cream at the time and had the doors open on a sweltering hot day, leaving themselves very vulnerable.

On 26 July 1986, in the incident which Nick describes, three RUC officers were slaughtered as they sat inside their car in Market Street, Newry. The three were Sergeant Peter Kilpatrick (27) from Carrickfergus, a father of one; Constable Charles Allen (37) from Waringstown, a father of two and Constable Karl Blackbourne from Antrim who was only nineteen years old. The young officer had only been in the RUC for six months when he was shot down by the IRA. 22 years after the event, I interviewed a former police officer who asked me: 'How in God's Holy name, did murdering three officers, relaxing on a sunny day, advance the cause of the bloody IRA?'

SOUTH ARMAGH

Private Martin Webb, Royal Anglians

I toured XMG, South Armagh in the summer of '86 with 2nd battalion Royal Anglian Regiment, as an impressionable nineteen-year-old. It was made clear from the outset that the South Armagh PIRA, with their experience and local knowledge, were the equivalent to our SAS and were not to be underestimated. XMG was seen at the time as probably the most dangerous posting in the British Army and I was amongst a company of 100 men allocated to the task.

My first recollection of the tour was landing at Aldergrove (Belfast) airport. After departing the aircraft, we were corralled into an arrivals hanger, which also doubled as a departure lounge. At the departures area there were soldiers from the Black Watch. I remember thinking how old, hard faced and assured they looked, compared to us fresh faced novices. This had the effect of almost freaking you out – just what had these guys endured to look this way? Some four months later, we went through the same experience, this time with us obviously leaving with a new regiment – the Scots Guards – incoming. Again it struck me, just how young and naïve the Scots Guards looked as opposed to us, being war veterans of a kind. In the early '90s the Hollywood film portraying events in the Vietnam War *Platoon* came out. There is a scene entirely reminiscent of my experience when incoming troops disembark the same plane as returning troops board for their journey home. If you see it, it's a virtual replication of the scene I encountered.

It wasn't a quiet tour by any stretch of the imagination and in May I was involved in a contact that saw the murder of our OC, Major Andrew French and two RUC officers. My multiple was involved in a rural field search, south of XMG and had covered a fair amount of ground in the morning. We set up a cordon and took it in turns to eat our lunch, when suddenly an explosion on a nearby hill only 150 metres away got us swiftly to our feet. I recall seeing someone on the hill in a prone position with a rifle, and we all made ready to engage him if need be. However, it was quickly realised he was one of ours, and he had been concussed by the force of the blast. We rushed to the site and commenced first aid; alas, all three men would not survive. I will never forget seeing the bodies of the dead policemen around the explosion site.

Major Andrew French MBE, from Barnet (35) of the Royal Anglian Regiment, Constable David McBride (27) and Constable William Smyth (25) were all killed by an IRA culvert bomb at Milltown Bridge. The murders, which took place on 22 May 1986 was a second agony for McBride's family as his brother-in-law Malcolm White had been killed by a similar device two years earlier at Omagh.

That night we rounded up several men in the area on suspicion of involvement in the attack, which degenerated into a near riot at one stage. A few days after the explosion, I was given the duty along with two others to search and sweep the area that was the suspected firing point. There we were with a couple of wire coat hangers feeling our way forward looking for booby trap trip wires; thankfully there were none. I remember being scared witless at first, but after a while you relax and adopt the mindset of why worry, if they are going to get you so be it; worrying won't change it. This was pretty much how I felt about the threat for the whole tour, or at least after the first fortnight. I was flown home a week later to attend Major French's funeral in Suffolk, England and I revisited his grave a few years ago.

Within my brick, I had adopted the role as the talker, who basically chatted up people to gain info. I loved it and it was far more interesting than crouching on street corners scanning the surrounds. We were given reference cards that identified certain people who had PIRA links. I'd just about talked to all of these people listed except Gilbert 'Danny' McNamee, who I eventually bumped into in Crossmaglen Square. Unlike everyone else, he flatly refused to get out of his car and show me the contents of his boot. I warned him that he would be arrested on an obstruction charge, particularly as we had high ranking RUC officers on this particular patrol. He told me where to go in no uncertain terms, which was a first as most of the 'players' had been receptive to my requests. I contacted the RUC Officer and a Senior NCO Intelligence guy and told them how we had grounds to nab the man. Unbelievably, they didn't want to know and told me to move him on, which I did, and there was a massive smile on McNamee's face.

My embarrassment, however was short lived, as just four days later, I was on an early morning arrest team that roused the same player from his bed and saw him off in a helicopter to be interviewed at Gough Barracks. I cast a grinning glance in his direction as he was bundled away and I recall it was just days before he was due to get married. Imagine my surprise twelve months later, now as a civilian, when I heard on the lunch time news that McNamee had been convicted of the Hyde Park bombing atrocities in 1982 (subsequently overturned on appeal in 1998). I suspect our lot must have been close to an arrest and didn't want a private soldier like me mucking things up with a relatively minor charge, which, I suspect, judging by his reaction, McNamee knew as well.

We lost a couple of other soldiers later on that tour, one of whom was a mate. They were 'Geordie' Bertram and Carl Davis. Whilst passing through XMG, just days before being blown up by a booby trapped car, Private Geordie Bertram showed me a letter from his girlfriend that was a bit saucy and we had a laugh. A nice guy and a great shame to lose him.

On 9 July 1986, Private Mitchell 'Geordie' Bertram (23) from North Shields and Private Carl Davis (24) from Colchester were both killed by a 700lb car bomb planted by the IRA at Glassdrummond. A car and trailer had been hijacked by terrorists and the driver held hostage under threat of death. Two other soldiers who were examining the car were injured by the remote-controlled detonation. Carl Davis was married with one child and his wife was heavily pregnant with a second.

THE UDR BUTT OF THE JOKE

RSM Haydn Davies, UDR/Royal Regiment of Wales

We had two colour sergeants who ran a post office up the road toward Armagh from Bessbrook. I used to worry about them, so I often took them on extra 'personal protection shooting' on the range at Gough Barracks Armagh. It paid off! They were both in the shop one day when the one brother at the counter looked up and looked straight down the barrel of a Smith & Wesson pistol. He moved sharply and a pistol fight started while the other brother bounced tins of dog food off the assailant's head. The IRA fellow ran for the door slightly wounded. As he passed the tin thrower, he smacked the Colour Sergeant over the bald head with his pistol. It was amusing in my office the next morning when we all viewed his head. It had the whole imprint of the butt of the pistol, a series of serrated criss-cross patterns and the round-head screw mark, complete with the cut in the screw, also the lanyard ring. It was such a good imprint that forensic took photographs of it in order to identify the pistol.

Our man with the wounded head was most upset because the national newspapers described how the IRA man had beaten an 'aged old man' over the head as he left the scene.

RED LIGHT FOR DANGER?

Tom Neary, Royal Artillery

Bessbrook was located in the heart of bandit country in South Armagh, and the SF base was an old factory in the centre of the town, often targeted by the IRA, because it was an easy target with plenty of escape routes. When we arrived for the first time, we were directed into the canteen for some scran before going straight out on a 'footsie'. On entering the canteen there was a table on the right, on which was sat a MK15 mortar. This 5ft gas cylinder was filled with explosives and packed with nails and metal fragments, so as to cause death or at least severe maiming. This mortar had been fired the week before from the carpet factory to the rear of the SF base, by the IRA. The base plate was a white Ford transit van. Thankfully, the place was empty and no one was seriously injured. The hole in the roof was pretty impressive though!

Operations were very heavy and troops were on the ground 24/7. We were working alternate patrol shifts with a troop from 45 Royal Marines; they were good lads, and genned us up as to the situation on the ground. The accommodation was shocking for the temporary troops; we were housed in the attic of the SF base on a wooden floor. The place was devoid of any electricity and the washing facilities were basic to say the least, but I loved it there, because I wasn't stuck in a sangar and was doing my job for real!

Taff 'P', my brick commander, was a good lad to be around; he was always up for a laugh when apt but also kept us younger lads on our toes, which was something I really appreciated when on footsies or mobiles. Our first patrol was interesting because I was the 'White Sifter' man [Electronic Counter Measure]. We were going through a small park when I heard the alarm go off in my headset. I brought it to Taff's attention, and he immediately alerted the Ops room and we carried out a full sweep of the area. There was nothing, and we carried on. About five seconds later it went off again, so I told him of it and he said: 'What the fuck are you on? Do you know what you're listening to?' At this point I realised what was happening and gave him the headset to listen to the noise. The Sifter was being set off by the traffic lights below the park.

We were also tasked with supplying patrols for the Engineers, whilst they set up PVCPs on the main roads into and out of the town. This was interesting because it gave us the opportunity to get some real contact with the natives in the area. The Catholics lived on an estate which overlooked the town, and to get there you had to climb a hill called the High Street. Never was a road so aptly named; this was a 1 in 4 hill and was directly behind the base, which was a bastard if you had been out for five or six hours and were tasked with a quick patrol up there. The place was a hovel and I couldn't understand why they were prepared to live that way. I didn't really care because I had my job to do and they were doing their best to kill me or my muckers if we gave them the opportunity!

DOG GOES MAD IN NEWRY

Colour Sergeant Gordon Vacher

It was just after we lost Winny, Baggy, Kingy and Andy Gavin and the rest in the roadside bomb on their way to Newry. One of our patrols found another roadside bomb and it was decided by Major Pringle to go against the rules and instead of having a controlled explosion, we would put in an OP and try and catch them on the firing point. CSM Jimmy Condon was to lead the OP with Amon Loftus; there were others, but I'm sorry, I can't remember their names.

The trick was to lure the IRA out and we did this by having an armoured RUC sit at the top of the road just to tempt the bad lads in. My job was to land by helicopter on the firing point and take them out. In the brick was Steve Welch, Benny and one other whose name escapes me; we had all the fire power we needed and also a war dog called 'Bear' with its handler.

We got the code word 'Bingo' and had to leg it to the helipad, meeting up with dog and handler, and once aboard, with legs hanging out and feet on the skids, off we went, hedge hopping to the firing point.

I was getting a running commentary from the pilot along with monitoring the company net, and the last thing I remember hearing was the pilot saying: 'One minute to LZ,' and me saying: 'Unmuzzle Bear,' then all hell let loose. The bloody dog attacked and tried to bite everyone in the back, and the pilot lost his nerve, as this brown and tan tornado was ripping up maps and bits of clothing and trying to get at him. The upshot of it was that he put us down miles away from the firing point and once we skidded to a halt, the last thing I saw was Bear chasing a cow and his handler with pistol drawn, chasing Bear.

We got the terrorists on the firing point but that was no thanks to us; we were too busy walking home!

Gordon refers to an incident where several Jackets were killed; this was at Camlough, near Newry on 19 May 1981. Four members of the Regiment's 1st Battalion and their RCT driver were killed in a massive landmine attack by the IRA, whilst on mobile patrol. They were Riflemen: Michael Bagshaw (29), Rifleman Andrew Gavin (19), John King (24), Lance Corporal Grenville Winstone (27) and Driver Paul Bulman (19).

PART FOUR

GOING BACK, LOOKING BACK

People smash cars and lynch two Royal Corps of Signals soldiers during IRA member Kevin Brady's funeral. See page 82. © *Bernard Bisson/Sygma/Corbis*

RETURN TO BELFAST: HOMAGE TO GEORGE MUNCASTER

Graham, Royal Artillery

After a shower and some dinner we walked back into the centre and enjoyed a few more pints of the black stuff at another bar near Customs House and were treated as part of the family. Now full of the proverbial 'Dutch courage' it was time to pay my respects and visit the place a friend lost his life 30 years ago. Walking straight through the back streets, camera in one hand and my loved one on the other, with a heavy heart and close to tears, I whispered to her and quietly pointed out the spot he fell and where he was shot from. We stood in silent tribute in the late afternoon sunshine; a mere 400 or so yards from where we were staying. A totally surreal moment that will never leave me; traffic noise from nearby Cromac Street and Central Station seemed to stop and time stood still. A momentary pause and shiver of the spine, tears rolling down my cheeks then a squeeze of the hand and back to the hotel in silence where she left me with my private thoughts to collect the bags; homage paid and job done.

My impressions? Still a lovely place with lovely people and how hate can overcome humanity still as confusing. But as the tour guide said, hopefully those terrible days have gone, never to return and Belfast can bloom and blossom like never before. Needless to say, I hope it does. A lot of the back to back terraces and slum estates and killing grounds have long gone, and not before time, to be replaced by modern housing. Some of the inter-community initiatives we heard about will take a long time to bear fruit but inevitably will, at least that's what my heart tells me; only time will tell. The guides pulled no punches and some people on the bus were aghast at the tales and were amazed at how close the communities actually lived together; my better half certainly was, especially when she saw the interface areas at first hand and close up. But as someone said, it can only get better now, and someone help us all if the politicians and the people let it go ape again. I don't think I'm particularly naïve but surely it can't happen again can it?

Gunner George Muncaster (19), to whom Graham refers, Royal Artillery, was shot by an IRA gunman near Eliza Street, a hundred metres north of Rhoda Park and died within minutes of being wounded; he was a Liverpool boy. Eyewitnesses noted that two young children were playing nearby and could so easily have been hit.

RETURN TO ULSTER

Ken Wharton

On 22 November 2008, in the company of a comrade, I returned to Northern Ireland after an absence of many years. The years had passed so quickly; two divorces, another six children to add to my little girl at the time and three grandchildren to whom Northern Ireland probably means as much as it did to me back in 1968: absolutely nothing. I took the short flight from Leeds/Bradford airport over England's north-west – Lancashire, the 'dark side' as I call it – and over the Isle of Man and there, on the right were the evergreen fields of Ulster. My eyes filled with tears and I thanked God that I had a seat to myself and that no-one could see them; how could I possibly explain them to someone who hadn't a clue of just how emotional I was feeling? We touched down and after a quick security check I met my mate and off we drove, via

Palace Barracks, towards the old 'killing grounds' of the Falls Road and Divis Street. The odd-shaped blocks we called the 'Zanussi' had gone; Leeson Street looked respectable and even the Royal Victoria Hospital looked more modern than I remembered.

On the Falls – once part of the 'murder mile' – much of the old blackened stone terracing had gone; replaced with newer housing and there seemed to be more businesses than before. We stopped at the site of the former RUC station at Springfield Road – now private housing – where several thousand years ago, Parachute Regiment Sergeant Michael Willetts gave his life, without hesitation to save the lives of civilians after the IRA threw a bomb into a crowded foyer. It was the site of Kingo 'Jimmy' Doglay's death, also from an IRA bomb and where my good friend Paddy Lenaghan was badly injured in the same attack. I paused awhile at Crocus Street, scene of the murders of three Jackets in a 1981 IRA attack. My mate asked me to smile for a photo as I stood on the very corner where the three died; strangely enough, I couldn't.

On we drove and up the Whiterock Road, turning right into the 'Murph – no doubt clocked by the 'dickers' who still feel that they have a role to fulfil – and parked up on Glenalina Crescent. My friend showed me where his King's Regiment colleague Chris Shanley was killed in 1979 and where Stephen Rumble was fatally wounded in the same attack. The houses are cleaner than I remember, the gardens tidier and there was a distinct absence of both the packs of wild dogs which chased our PIGs and the old, rusting Vauxhall Vivas and Ford Anglias propped up on bricks that seemed to adorn every other garden. The Turf Lodge and Andytown still looked the same as before, IRA slogans and tricolours flying everywhere. On Ardmonagh Gardens, on the site of the former 'disco block' where Andy Webster was killed by an IED in 1979, stands the Ardmonagh Family Centre. Not even a minute trace of the life and death of a young Kingo lance corporal. All that now exists is the eternal love of his friends and family. Certainly not the eternal thanks of a grateful nation.

We moved on to the site of the former Andytown RUC station in the 'triangle' at the bottom of Andersonstown Road, sited near the bus depot and over the road from the infamous Milltown Cemetery. The station is now gone and the Belfast City Council has erected large rocks along all three sides of the triangle to stop (vehicle) interlopers. With my back to Milltown, I looked across at the barber's shop from where IRA gunmen shot Blues and Royals Troopers Thornett and Dykes as they ran to close the security gates at the side of the station. The shop is still there; the two lads are not.

We paused at Woodbourn PSNI – once the RUC – and I looked at the armour plating, the barbed wire and the strategically placed rocks to prevent a car bomb getting close. 'This is peace?' I mused to myself, before realising that a black cab – still run by the IRA? – was cruising slowly by me and that I was being clocked by the driver. I crossed Andersonstown Road and entered an estate which, long ago in a past life, I would have never entered alone and was confronted by one of the locals. I use the word 'confronted' but the truth is somewhat more prosaic, because he simply looked at me with a mixture of curiosity and possibly suspicion. Reluctant to let him hear my English accent, I attempted 'What about ye?' in the best Belfast brogue that I could muster and he simply looked at me in a bemused way and hurried past me on a cold Friday afternoon. Some undercover soldier I would have made!

Later, we visited the remains of North Howard Street Mill – a former base of mine – and I stood looking sadly at the old carpets, building rubble and rotting rubbish on the now leveled Mill. An old man – probably, in truth, the same age as myself – walked up to me and asked how I was and it flashed across my mind that he might have been an old adversary. We talked about the seventies and the Troubles and he told me 'Sure enough, it's peaceful enough now.' He pronounced the word now as 'nie' and memories flooded back of my time there in Belfast.

Royal Green Jacket injured by rioters continues on patrol. *(David Barzilay)*

Woodbourne PSNI. *(Ken Wharton)*

It wasn't peaceful when Rifleman David Walker was shot dead on the roof of the Mill in 1971. And it wasn't peaceful on a May day twenty years later when ADU man Terrence O'Neil was killed by an IRA bomb on that same site. But the old man was right; it was quiet on the day I revisited. The peace line still stands – it seems higher now or have I simply shrunk – as a permanent reminder that the sectarian hatred hasn't really gone away; it merely lurks, just under the surface.

The following day, we travelled via Claudy – scene of a savage, inexplicable and unforgivable IRA attack on a sleepy little village which killed six in 1972 – to Londonderry and a trip to the Creggan Estate. I was in a foreign land, with a plethora of tricolours and IRA slogans everywhere, reminding me that 'they' haven't gone away; not completely. We were questioned by a man who came out of a nearby betting shop in the company of two of his mates who stared at me with grave suspicion. They are still wary of strangers in this area where once, hastily and amateurishly scrawled slogans such as 'We stand by the IRA' predominated; the pro-IRA slogans are now done almost professionally. He spoke to my colleague and then moved on, having ascertained that we weren't 'fucking Paratroopers' leaving my heart pounding near fit to burst.

We visited the cemetery just down from the Creggan and there, as if we didn't know, is the evidence of the hatred they feel for the Paras, even 37 years on from the events of 'Bloody Sunday'. The gravestones of some of the dead contain words such as 'Murdered by Paratroopers' or 'Killed by Crown Forces'. This hatred will never go away and as much as the Protestants will never forget the 1690 Battle of the Boyne, nor will the Catholics ever forget that grim day of 30 January 1972. That hatred will outlast the marble and granite headstones with their provocative epitaphs. I felt depressed as we drove away and returned to Belfast and, alone with my thoughts as was every soldier who trod the streets and fields of Northern Ireland, reflected on how things had changed in the physical sense, but how, emotionally, nothing has really changed.

The only difference was that my memories of the early '70s were somehow in black and white; today the nightmare is in technicolour.

RTHERN IRELAND AFTERMATH

Paddy Leneghan, King's Regiment and Australian Army

Ken and I had a verbal disagreement when he maintained that Aussies had never heard of Belfast or Northern Ireland's Troubles and were not really aware of events in other parts of the world. 'So what?' I asked, 'by the same token, the people in the UK, prior to the bombs and killing of their soldiers, were more concerned with the results of their soccer games and how many points they had on Littlewoods Pools.' They were more concerned with other things rather than what was happening a short flight away across the Irish Sea.

I have, even now, not sat down with Josie, my wife of some 40 years and talked about my feelings, my fears or my resentment about what we were doing in the overseas part of Britain; Northern Ireland. My wife has stuck by me through all these years; put up with my mood swings, the black clouds behind my eyes. I have wanted to hurt someone, and that is the one person who has stuck by me. I have had to walk away until that rage, that self-destruct which just simmers below the surface, goes away. Then I feel remorse. Why do I lose the plot; why do I hurt with my words and actions? Why can't I return the love and the feelings that she shows by staying with me?

Our daughter, Marika, born in a British military hospital in Malta, has never forgiven me for what she saw her Mother go through; what I call my 'Irish temper.' Even now, we are only at the 'polite' phase when we do speak or e-mail each other and I do understand her wanting to distance herself and family from the hate and mood swings which she endured as a child. This was her family environment; the drunken Dad who rolled in at all hours, full of hate and self-loathing, the environment for which I have tried to make amends. I do understand her desire just to have contact between her children and Josie.

My son, Kevin, against all expectations and despite his sister's warnings, went off and joined the Australian Army [as did Paddy following the explosion at Springfield Road RUC station and eventual discharge from the British Army]. He pissed me off by becoming Para-qualified, especially after he had heard me say during one of my many binge drinking sessions, that I had not had too many kind experiences with Paras. I had been put on my arse in Aden by one of them and on my first tour I had come across them during the Shankill riots. It was a Saturday afternoon and a riot had started – thanks to the RMPs – and we had just passed Unity Flats when it started. We were there all through the night and most of Sunday and it was just about over, when we were relieved by the Paras. What got my goat were the headlines in the papers the next day: 'Paras Clear Up the Street of Belfast.' Fuck! Fuck!

Kevin has never listened to, or asked me, what happened in Northern Ireland. He has never introduced me to his Army mates as: 'This is my Dad; he got stuffed in Northern Ireland.' I have never been able to get close to him and say: 'Do you know what I went through? Do you know what it was like, what I felt, why I am like I am?' Kevin also went through active service and wears with pride his Infantry Combat Badge he earned in East Timor.

My life is not as ordered as that of the 'average family man', though I have changed either through old age, mellowing, or, God bless her, Josie winning my war of self pity. I only did two tours, one full one and then the last one lasting only 33 days, due to the IRA bomb at Springfield Road police station that killed my mate, Jimmy Doglay. Don't misunderstand me; I loved being a soldier, both in the British and then the Australian Army. I loved the bonding that only comes through communal fear, fear of not showing your emotions; not letting your mates down, even at the expense of the ones who love you. In the Australian Army, I bonded with the

Vietnam vets, because I could relate to the fears, the emptiness felt when preparing for a patrol, even though the terrain was different there and the opposition did not drive Ford Cortinas or shop in Tesco like we did.

As I said, I loved being a soldier; the closeness, being part of a team where you believe that you are invincible, musketeers, all for one and one for all. But guess what? The Army is a way of life; it is not your wife! But why, after all these years do I still cry; why can I remember 1972 more easily than 1992 or 2002?

What a way to live, but I am proud to have been a British soldier; fuck the consequences and I wear with pride the GSM with Northern Ireland bar.

Both Paddy and his wife Josie are friends of mine and although we served in different regiments, I feel the same bond with him as any other British soldier who served Queen and country. Paddy's biggest brush with death, as described elsewhere in this book, took place on 30 May 1972, whilst stationed on Springfield Road, Belfast. Whilst the 'barracks' as it was known to several generations of locals was being redecorated, an IRA sympathiser or member posing as a workman smuggled a 30lb device into the rest area. It exploded without warning, killing Private Marcus 'Jimmy' Doglay, wounding many others, including Paddy who lost a finger and was later discharged from the Army.

PEOPLE WANTED TO FORGET

Colour Sergeant Ken Ambrose, Royal Green Jackets

The author talks about the 'eternal thanks of a grateful nation' or, rather the lack of it. Although that sentiment was true whilst the Troubles were going on it will not be seen as being true now that the more modern conflicts have brought the sacrifices made by our solders to public notice.

It has to be explained that at the time you had to have a relative who was a soldier to appreciate what their time in Ulster was about and know that some came home in body bags and some came home mentally scarred forever more. After the initial shock reports, most civilians did not regard the fact that soldiers were dying within the UK as worthy of more than their passing attention and the sentence read out on the nightly News that 'Last night another soldier ...' was heard without reaction. Or the same sort of emotion that it is treated with now – but the difference between now and then was that we did not have the 'Help For Heroes' campaign or high profile royals such as HRH [serving in Afghanistan] and the national newspapers on our side. But we were in just as much need of them then as modern servicemen are today.

Maybe we were different to modern soldiers and did not whinge enough or as much, in which case maybe it was partly our fault that we were not fully supported by the public or received their gratitude. It was almost as if because it was part of the UK that we were fighting in, people wanted to forget it was going on. Some would say that Ulster was our Vietnam.

IN DUBLIN

Lawrence Jagger, Royal Corps of Transport

I am out of the army; time done and back in civilian life. I tried all sorts of jobs but couldn't 'get it on'. I tried office, factory, etc, but coming from the RCT, being out and about and on the open road was my calling. From being an Army 'trog' I became a civvie 'trog' and am still a 'diesel demon' today.

Belfast and other ops seem to be miles away; just memories and photos. I was driving tourist coaches and everything was fine. Then one day, I was asked to go to Ireland with Americans. I was reluctant to go; it was summer, I have got squaddie tattoos and they can smell ex-soldiers from a mile away. All I could think was: what if? There were bound to be IRA sympathisers and the like all over, but I decided to give it a go. Our arrival in Southern Ireland made my hair stand up and I felt alone and unsure, but met my group for a drink and went to my room.

One evening it was arranged that all tour drivers and managers would eat together on the same table, and that was fine with me. However, the driver next to me, a well built Irishman, was waffling on about he had gone to Belfast and the 'Kesh to see some friends. He was saying some very insulting things about the British Army and what bastards they were. I kept quiet until suddenly my manager who had known me a while said: 'Stop talking about the Troubles; my driver was a soldier.' The Irishman started to say something, but I snapped: 'Shut your fucking mouth!' The paddy stood up and shouted: 'You mean to tell me that I am sharing a table with a British soldier?'

I was angry, but said that I didn't want any trouble, and that I would leave them in peace to enjoy the rest of their meal. I made my exit and went to my room and 'barricaded' myself in by moving the bed and things and sat up all night watching my bus. I was thinking that if they got me, it would be in the morning when I was alone and going for my coach. They're not going to harm my passengers, particularly as they were Americans, but I might get a beating; happily, nothing happened.

I had some free time in Dublin, but I never left the hotel; all I wanted to do was get away, just get away. I was not a glory soldier, just a RCT 'trog' but they don't like us, and they didn't care whether we were a Para or a driver. You wore the Queen's uniform and you were hated for it; to this very day there is still no real peace.

NOT IN VAIN

James Kinchin-White, Royal Green Jackets

I recall my own first trip back was marked with trepidation, not a little anxiety and even less belief that I was doing the right thing. That was despite the fact that I had the ulterior motive of meeting up with my children. But I found that it is easier the more you go, and what has made it easier for me is actually talking to some of those who were on the other side, and given that they knew who/what I had been helped enormously to ensure honest discussion. Also talking to the younger generation – the thirty somethings – who grew up amidst the Troubles and who, by and large, don't want to go there ever again.

On my first trip back I was ferried around by a son-in-law I had known nothing about; guess what? He is a black cab driver from a Republican area; you can't help but smile! He was at pains to ask me what was different about the cars; they all had tax discs he pointed out with a wide grin! Then I went on my own tour, back to the Lower Falls, mostly re-built, no sign of the toothless old witch nor even the street, Little Distillery Street I think. Mulhouse Street was still there back as part of the Royal Victoria, Roden Street is now a dead end; separating the communities still. The RVH is a much more modern building, Springfield Road (aka TAC HQ) is permanently deleted from the pages of our history. I stood at the place where my head managed to stay attached to my shoulders and felt – nothing. I thought I would, but the abnormal normality of it all consigned my own bit of drama to something less than a footnote in a yet to be written autobiography. I drove down Iveagh Parade, Rodney and St James – we always seemed to get shot at there – down Broadway looking up towards the bakery from where one of our lads had been shot.

I bought my ex a bunch of flowers from a shop near the Beehive Bar on the Falls, used my best 'sarf London' accent and didn't even raise an eyebrow – great product, great price and the service was excellent. Went to Milltown to visit a relatives resting place, then went to the 'Murph (the bullring) and looked at a PIRA Remembrance Garden; saw the names of IRA dead listed. It was about ten at night, in summer, and I didn't need to worry about accents as my eldest girl was with me (she grew up in the area); some teenage lads walked past and asked, with sincerity, if we wanted them to go get the key – I smiled again.

I went to the Markets to see if I could locate the place where Bob Bankier was killed, but it seems to have been re-developed. A small plaque in Joy Street to one of the IRA casualties of the day (Joe McCann of M1 Carbine and silhouette picture fame) is all that remained as evidence of the hostilities in that part of town.

Back in the black taxi I was given a midnight tour of the Republican murals; we parked outside a former Republican club watching the comings and goings. My 'driver' asked me how it felt to be sitting outside a Republican club at midnight – I smiled again and told him it was much the same as the last time I did it; actually, it was a bit less comfortable.

The following year in summer they took me into a Republican club on the night of the anniversary of Internment. I didn't say much, but one guy kept looking at me, so I asked him to take a picture of me; that seemed to satisfy his curiosity – and I smiled again. I listened to the local male voice choir and learned a couple of new chorus lines that I had missed the last time; I felt good that I had been there without them knowing who I was; maybe nothing changes, or is it merely an old man's ego. Just like the time I had collected the 'laundry' from a Republican club in South Armagh and my 'van boy' had said, 'Don't go back in there; they think you are a Brit!' Total elation at having been there, done that; overcoming the internal terror I felt while actually inside the place.

My return to Belfast was, in the circumstances, highly emotional. I met my children on their home ground for the first time in almost thirty years. I had returned to the battlefield to face down the terror I had felt during my own extraordinary experiences, and, most importantly, I began to listen to the life my kids had lived throughout the Troubles.

I learned of their fears whilst at school when the teacher would ask 'What does your father do for a living?' – and they couldn't remember what they had said the last time – or whether their sibling was giving a different answer in another room. I mentioned this to a Republican I have become friendly with and he said 'They could simply have given the same answer as 95 per cent of the other Catholic kids; that you were unemployed, or perhaps gained some street cred by saying you were inside.'

I never had much to do with Loyalist elements of the Troubles and therefore have little comment on their standpoint, but I have had the opportunity to talk to former enemies on the Republican side, sharing experiences, musing over the odd light moment and our hopes and fears for the future. I have no doubt that the Republicans consider their struggle to be far from finished, but though the struggle continues, their war is over.

Perhaps the most significant thing for me occurred during one debate about those who were killed. The leader of the group, a well known Republican, said: 'We are not going to make distinctions anymore; we will remember everyone who was lost.' There will always be some dissent, but I have no doubt that the war is over and I have made my peace. My hope is that former comrades can also make theirs and perhaps return to visit a place where they left so much of themselves behind, and they will find out that it was not in vain.

BEAUTY

Private Martin Webb, Royal Anglians

In 2005, I returned to XMG, whilst on a family holiday in Dublin. In a bizarre twist, I ended up in a fast food type outlet, having a cup of tea looking out onto the square, which was almost surreal. Likewise driving around south Armagh for the first time, having previously only ever moved by foot or by air. Perhaps being younger and concentrating on the terrorist threat I had never really taken in the beauty of the area, which is something really to behold. The whole Crossmaglen experience will be etched into my mind forever!

DISCIPLINE

Haydn Davies, RRW and UDR

I always felt and indeed said to the Irish that they were bloody lucky that it was British troops that were deployed against them. They should all be thankful for that. The discipline and restraint of the soldiers, young and old, was amazing to me on so very many occasions. I remember being at Bessbrook Mill when the man who set off the bomb which killed four members of their Company HQ ICP was brought into the Mill and the whole company watched him as he passed by them. There were at least a hundred men; not one said a word to him, they all just stared at him. They were a company of Green Howards and had just lost their company commander, apparently a very popular fellow.

HOMEWORK

Mick 'Benny' Hill, Royal Anglians

A couple of weeks ago one of my grand-daughters came to see me about a project she was doing at school about the Troubles. Her Mum (my daughter) suggested to her that I and her uncle, having spent about six years in the Province between us, might be of help. She didn't know that we had been there; no-one in the family had ever thought to mention it. I looked at the course work she had been given, and it was all about Civil Rights, inequalities, and (mostly) politics. Nothing about us; very little about the enormous death toll, and very little about terrorism, and I couldn't relate to it.

When you are lying in a gutter or trying to hide behind a shield those lofty concepts are not exactly on your mind. She did ask me about the legacy of the peace process, and I'm afraid I wasn't much help. My own legacy is more personal: a failed marriage, the occasional headache that confines me to bed for a couple of days, two fingers that don't work properly, and a slight limp and some medals lying half forgotten in a drawer. I still reckon I'm one of the lucky ones, I'm now over 70; I sleep well every night. I don't get nightmares, and only occasionally do I wake up for no reason soaked in sweat. A lot of our comrades are not so lucky. I'm sure I speak for us all when I say that I hope it was worth it. Only time will tell.

The press take notes as they accompany the patrol on the streets. This woman was from the mainland, the regiment's home town. *(Paul Crispin)*

AFTERWORD

This book has been a labour of love; it has been hard work, often going on long into the night, leaving my partner an 'author's widow'. Over the course of my three books, I have sent or received nearly 18,000 e-mails, dozens of letters, a hundred or more photo exchanges and in excess of 500 telephone calls. In April 2009, I emigrated to Australia and on the long, 24-hour journey and during the awful days of jet lag, I hankered after, yearned for the moment when I could continue *Bloody Belfast*. On completion, I felt immensely proud of what I had achieved, not for myself, but for the thousands of British soldiers who risked their lives for a country and successive governments who lost interest in them.

After I left the Army, I watched and mourned the death and injury of every soldier, policeman, prison officer or innocent civilian, killed as a consequence of the Troubles. I recall during my time at Warwick University following a Union debate on the killing of soldiers, confronting a left wing trendie who proudly announced to me that he 'rejoiced in the deaths of those soldiers'. I will leave the story of what happened to that person to others who were witness to it. I realised on that day, maybe always knew, that the vast majority of the British public simply didn't give a damn. I knew however, that one day, I would do my best to see that the lives – and deaths – of those who served and fell would receive the recognition they so richly deserved.

If you have now read my oral histories of the Troubles from the squaddie's perspective, then hopefully you will know more of the hell that was just 40 minutes flying time away with Easy Jet.

A SOLDIER DIED TODAY

Should you find yourself in danger with enemies at hand,
Would you want a politician with his shifting stand,
Or would you prefer a soldier who has sworn to defend,
His home, his kin and country and would fight until the end.
He was but a common soldier and his ranks are getting thin
But his presence should remind us, we might need his like again.
For when countries are in conflict then we find the soldiers part
Is to clean up all the troubles that the politicians start.

Bill 'Spanner' Jones

Shake and rattle, grunt and grind,
names they called you oft unkind,
never held amongst the great
in use well past your use by date
but when I took you for a drive
you helped me get all back alive,
Going down the Antrim road
those back from leave our precious load
office workers on lunch break
for some the last they'd ever take.
an awful roar rips through the air
the people are no longer there,
lurch and swerve, tossed around
but you kept all four wheels on the ground.
With your armour to protect our heads
we got the lads back to their beds.
tool bins and mud wings bent and battered
hull with blood and gore bespattered
we cleaned you down with broom and hose
a few beers bring the day to close,
and now at times when bad dreams scare me
through that bomb blast you still bear me.
I've driven many a fancier rig,
but owe my life to the humble Humber PIG.

Bill 'Spanner' Jones

THE MILL

The old mill windows rattled,
Dust billowed into the air.
In an instant I knew what that sound meant someone was dying somewhere.
Stand to; get down to the vehicles!
I stumbled, half fell down the stair.
As I tried to get my bearings yet another loud bang rent the air.
Explosion after explosion; a pall hung over the city.
Someone had planted bombs, NO WARNING, NO MERCY NO PITY.
As I knelt down by the station, among fire and screams and smoke,
I saw what had once been a human, now far beyond any hope.
My anger boiled within me, and tears came to my eyes.
If only those bombers could see or hear the dying, pitiful cries.
What I saw that day in Belfast, etched in memory; it haunts me still.
God may forgive those bombers BUT BY GOD I NEVER WILL.

Steve Norman

ROLL OF HONOUR 1969–98

During a long but ultimately rewarding course of research into deaths of soldiers during the troubles, I identified 1,301, thanks to the good offices of the NIVA website, cross-referenced to *Lost Lives* and the Armed Forces memorial. I included those who had died not only as a consequence of terrorist action, but those dying in duty-related traffic and training accidents, accidental shootings and, of course, suicides. I do not feel that I need to justify differing to a huge degree from the MOD's assertion that about 730 were killed because they had their rationale. However, I feel that I must include all the deaths of soldiers who died in, or as a consequence of, the Troubles. After all, had they not been there, the vast majority would not have died so prematurely.

Soldiers who are known to have been members of the TA are included in the roll for their parent regiment with TA indicated.

RTA: Road Traffic Accident
DoW: Died of Wounds

9/12 LANCERS

LT JOHN GARNER-RICHARDS	4/04/75	RTA in Co Armagh in suspicious circumstances
TPR SEAN PRENDERGAST	5/04/77	Cause of death unknown
SGT ROBERT MAUGHAN	8/05/79	Cause of death unknown
SGT PAUL ORAM	21/02/84	Cause of death unknown

13/18 HUSSARS

TPR ROBERT BARRACLOUGH	28/09/75	RTA
TPR PAUL SHEPHERDSON	16/07/78	RTA
TPR PHILIP SMITH	27/07/78	RTA

14/20 KINGS HUSSARS AND 15/19 KINGS ROYAL HUSSARS

SGT JOHN PLATT	03/02/71	Killed in RTA following IRA ambush at Aldergrove
CPL IAN ARMSTRONG	29/08/71	Ambushed at Crossmaglen by IRA
2/LT ROBERT WILLIAMS-WYNN	13/08/72	IRA sniper, West Belfast
TPR JOHN TYSON	28/02/74	RTA
CPL MICHAEL COTTON	20/03/74	Killed in friendly fire, Co Armagh
CPL MICHAEL HERBERT	20/03/74	Killed in same incident
SGT WILLIAM ROBERTSON	08/02/75	Sniper, Mullan, Co Fermanagh
TPR GARY LINES	28/05/79	RTA

15/19 HUSSARS

TPR DAVID JOHNSON	18/10/71	Accidental shooting
TPR JOHN MAJOR	29/11/74	Death by violent or unnatural causes
SGT WILLIAM ROBSON	07/02/75	DoW after being shot by IRA at Mullan, Fermanagh

17/ 21ST LANCERS

TPR JAMES DOYLE	24/11/70	Cause of death unknown; died in Omagh
TPR ROBERT GADIE	17/02/71	RTA at Ballygawley
CPL TERENCE WILLIAMS	05/05/73	Booby Trap bomb Crossmaglen
TPR JOHN GIBBONS	05/05/73	Killed in same incident
TPR KENEALY	14/09/73	Killed in training accident Gosford Castle

16/5TH LANCERS

CPL DAVID POWELL	28/10/71	Bomb attack Kinawley, Co Fermanagh
2/LT ANDREW SOMERVILLE	27/03/73	IRA landmine near Omagh

1ST REGIMENT ROYAL HORSE ARTILLERY

GNR TIMOTHY UTTERIDGE	19/10/84	Shot by IRA, Turf Lodge, Belfast

5 REGIMENT ARMY AIR CORPS

SGT I.C. REID	24/06/72	IRA landmine, Glenshane Pass, Co Antrim
L/CPL D. MOON	24/06/72	Killed in same incident
PTE C. STEVENSON	24/06/72	Killed in same incident
C/SGT A. PLACE	18/05/73	Booby trap bomb, Knock-na-Moe Hotel, Omagh
C.O.FH. BR COX	18/05/73	Killed in same incident
SGT D.B. READ	18/05/73	Killed in same incident
WO D.C. ROWAT	12/04/74	Killed by IRA landmine, location unknown
MAJ J.D. HICKS	18/12/75	Aircraft accident
WO B.A. JACKSON	07/01/76	Aircraft accident
CAPT M.J. KETT	10/04/78	Killed in helicopter accident
CAPT A.J. STIRLING	02/12/78	Killed in helicopter accident
CPL R.D. ADCOCK	02/12/78	Killed in helicopter accident
CPL RAYMOND JACKSON	05/07/80	RTA
CPL BERNARD McKENNA	6/04/82	Died of natural causes on duty
L/CPL SIMON J ROBERTS	28/11/83	RTA
L/CPL TONY ORANGE	20/10/87	RTA
S/SGT JEREMY CROFT	14/08/89	Violent or unnatural causes

5TH ROYAL INNISKILLING DRAGOON GUARDS

SGT FREDERICK WILLIAM DRAKE	03/06/73	DoW, bomb, Knock-na-Moe Hotel, Omagh

ADJUTANT GENERAL'S CORPS

CPL GLEN A. SLAINE	03/11/95	RTA
L/CPL PAUL MELLING	03/09/97	Died whilst on duty

ARGYLL AND SUTHERLAND HIGHLANDERS

L/CPL DUNCAN MCPHEE	10/09/72	IRA landmine, Dungannon
PTE DOUGLAS RICHMOND	10/09/72	Killed in same incident

L/CPL WILLIAM MCINTYRE	11/09/72	DoW from same incident
2/LT STEWART GARDINER	22/10/72	IRA sniper, Drumuckavall, Armagh
PTE D. HARPER	12/11/72	Killed in training accident
CAPT WILLIAM WATSON	20/11/72	IRA booby trap Cullyhanna
C/SGT JAMES STRUTHERS	20/11/72	Killed in same incident
PTE JOHN McGARRY	28/11/72	Friendly fire
PTE DOUGLAS MCKELVIE	20/08/79	RTA
CPL OWEN MCQUADE	11/11/80	Shot outside Altnagelvin hospital, Londonderry
CPL STEWART MARSHALL	20/08/98	RTA
PTE WILLIAM BROWN	20/08/98	RTA
PTE STEVEN CRAW	20/08/98	RTA

ARMY CATERING CORPS

PTE LEONARD THOMPSON	31/12/71	RTA
PTE ROGER KEALEY	18/06/72	Cause of death unknown
SGT PETER GIRVAN	12/02/77	RTA
L/CPL BARRY HYLTON	17/11/77	Cause of death unknown
PTE GEOFFREY DAVIS	18/07/79	Cause of death unknown
PTE TERENCE M. ADAM	06/12/82	INLA bomb attack Droppin' Well pub, (now riverside Bar) Ballykelly
PTE PAUL JOSEPH DELANEY	06/12/82	Killed in same incident
PTE JOHN MAYER	19/03/83	RTA
PTE RICHARD R. BIDDLE	09/04/83	IRA booby trapped car, Omagh

ARMY CADET FORCE

CAPT PAUL RODGERS	19/04/79	IRA sniper, Falls Road, Belfast

ARMY INTELLIGENCE CORPS

CPL PAUL HARMAN	14/12/77	Killed on covert op by IRA Monagh road, Belfast
CPL JOHN ROESER	31/08/78	RTA
CPL MICHAEL BLOOR	31/08/78	Killed in same RTA
CPL MARCUS CHARLES-WILLIAMS	08/11/86	Cause of death unknown
L/CPL BARRY JACKSON	16/02/88	Cause of death unknown

ARMY PHYSICAL TRAINING CORPS

WO2 DAVID BELLAMY	28/10/79	IRA ambush, Springfield Road, Belfast

BLACK WATCH

PTE DAVID STEIN	04/03/71	Accidental death
L/CPL EDWIN CHARNLEY	18/11/71	Sniper, East Belfast
PTE MARK D. CARNIE	19/07/78	IRA bomb, Dungannon
PTE GEORGE IRELAND	21/06/95	Cause of death unknown

BLUES & ROYALS

TPR EDWARD MAGGS	25/02/79	Death by violent or unnatural causes
STAFF CPL JOHN TUCKER	25/02/79	Death by violent or unnatural causes
TPR ANTHONY DYKES	05/04/79	IRA snipers, Andersonstown RUC station
TPR ANTHONY THORNETT	05/04/79	Killed in same incident
LT DENIS DALY	20/07/82	Killed in Hyde Park bomb outrage
SQMC R. BRIGHT	23/07/82	DoW from same incident

TPR SIMON TIPPER	23/07/82	Killed in same incident
L/CPL JEFFERY YOUNG	23/07/82	Killed in same incident

CHESHIRE REGIMENT

PTE ARTHUR SMITH	04/07/74	DoW after being shot, Ballymurphy Estate, Belfast
PTE NEIL WILLIAMS	06/12/82	IRA bomb Droppin' Well pub, Ballykelly
PTE ANTHONY WILLIAMSON	06/12/82	Killed in same incident
L/CPL DAVID WILSON-STITT	06/12/82	Killed in same incident
L/CPL STEVEN BAGSHAW	06/12/82	Killed in same incident
L/CPL CLINTON COLLINS	06/12/82	Killed in same incident
L/CPL PHILIP MCDONOUGH	06/12/82	Killed in same incident
PTE DAVID MURREY	06/12/82	Killed in same incident

COLDSTREAM GUARDS

SGT ANTHONY METCALF	27/08/72	IRA sniper, Creggan Heights, Londonderry
GDSMN ROBERT PEARSON	20/02/73	IRA sniper, Lower Falls, Belfast
GDSMN MICHAEL SHAW	20/02/73	Killed in same incident
GDSMN MICHAEL DOYLE	21/02/73	Sniper, Fort Whiterock, Belfast
GDSMN ANTON BROWN	06/03/74	Sniper, Ballymurphy Estate, Belfast
CAPT ANTHONY POLLEN	14/04/74	Shot on undercover mission, Bogside, Londonderry
GDSMN PAUL SIMMONDS	12/01/76	Cause of death unknown
CPL JOHN SPENSLEY	25/12/81	RTA
CPL RICHARD DREWETT*	15/06/84	Death by violent or unnatural causes
GDSMN STEVEN SHAW	21/01/89	Cause of death unknown
L/CPL SIMON WARE	17/08/91	IRA landmine explosion, Cullyhanna, Armagh

*Att Intelligence Corps

DEVON & DORSET REGIMENT

PTE CHARLES STENTIFORD	21/01/72	IRA landmine, Keady, Co Armagh
PTE DAVID CHAMP	10/02/72	IRA landmine, Cullyhanna, Co Armagh
SGT IAN HARRIS	10/02/72	Killed in same incident
CPL STEVEN WINDSOR	06/11/74	Sniper, Crossmaglen
CPL GERALD JEFFERY	07/04/83	DoW, IRA bomb, Falls Road, Belfast
L/CPL STEPHEN TAVERNER	05/11/83	DoW, IRA bomb, Crossmaglen

DUKE OF EDINBURGH'S ROYAL REGIMENT

CPL JOSEPH LEAHY	8/03/73	DoW, booby trap, Forkhill, Co Armagh
S/SGT BARRINGTON FOSTER	23/03/73	Murdered off-duty by the IRA
CAPT NIGEL SUTTON	14/08/73	Died in vehicle accident, Ballykinler
PTE MICHAEL SWANICK	28/10/74	IRA van bomb attack, Ballykinler
PTE BRIAN ALLEN	6/11/74	Sniper, Crossmaglen
PTE JOHN RANDALL	26/06/93	Sniper, Newtownhamilton, Co Armagh
L/CPL KEVIN PULLIN	17/07/93	Sniper, Crossmaglen

DUKE OF WELLINGTON'S REGIMENT

PTE GEORGE LEE	6/06/72	IRA sniper, Ballymurphy Estate, Belfast
CPL TERRENCE GRAHAM	16/07/72	Landmine attack, Crossmaglen
PTE JAMES LEE	16/07/72	Killed in same incident

PTE BRIAN ORAM	07/04/73	RTA
CPL DAVID TIMSON	07/04/73	Killed in same incident
PTE JOSEPH MCGREGOR	24/05/73	RTA
WO2 PETER LINDSAY	28/08/73	Unknown
2/LT HOWARD FAWLEY	25/01/74	Landmine attack, Ballyronan Co Londonderry
CPL MICHAEL RYAN	17/03/74	IRA sniper, Brandywell, Londonderry
PTE LOUIS CARROLL	07/04/74	Cause of death unknown
CPL ERROL PRYCE	26/01/80	IRA sniper, Ballymurphy Estate, Belfast
PTE JOHN CONNOR	24/02/88	Cause of death unknown
PTE JAMES RIGG	25/11/88	RTA
PTE JASON COST	25/05/95	Cause of death unknown

GLOUCESTERSHIRE REGIMENT

PTE ANTHONY ASPINWALL	17/12/71	DoW after gun battle in Lower Falls area, Belfast
PTE KEITH BRYAN	05/01/72	IRA sniper, Lower Falls area, Belfast
CPL IAN BRAMLEY	02/02/72	IRA sniper, Hastings Street RUC station, Belfast
PTE GEOFFREY BREAKWELL	17/07/73	IRA booby trap, Divis Street Flats, Belfast
PTE CHRISTOPHER BRADY	17/07/73	Killed in same incident
L/CPL ANTHONY BENNETT	04/06/78	Cause of death unknown
PTE D.J. McCHILL	17/08/78	Died during the tour – not as a result of terrorist actions
L/CPL A. P. BENNETT	04/06/80	Killed in vehicle accident, Limavady

GORDON HIGHLANDERS

WO2 ARTHUR MCMILLAN	18/06/72	Booby trapped house in Lurgan, Co Down
SGT IAN MARK MUTCH	18/06/72	Killed in same incident
L/CPL COLIN LESLIE	18/06/72	Killed in same incident
L/CPL A.C. HARPER	08/08/72	RTA
PTE MICHAEL GEORGE MARR	29/03/73	Sniper, Andersonstown, Belfast
CAPT RICHARD LAMB	17/05/77	RTA
L/CPL JACK MARSHALL	28/08/77	Shot in gun battle Ardoyne, Belfast

GREEN HOWARDS

PTE MALCOLM HATTON	09/08/71	Sniper, Brompton Park, Ardoyne
PTE JOHN ROBINSON	14/08/71	Sniper, Ardoyne, Belfast
PTE GEORGE CROZIER	23/08/71	Sniper, Flax Street Mill, Ardoyne
L/CPL PETER HERRINGTON	17/09/71	Sniper, Brompton Park, Ardoyne
PTE PETER SHARP	01/10/71	Shot on Kerrara Street, Ardoyne
PTE RAYMOND HALL	05/03/73	DoW, sniper attack, Belfast
PTE FREDERICK DICKS	05/06/74	IRA sniper, Dungannon
MAJ PETER WILLIS	17/07/75	IRA bomb, Ford's Cross, Armagh
CPL IAN METCALF	15/06/88	IRA booby trapped lorry, Lisburn

GRENADIER GUARDS

CAPT ROBERT NAIRAC GC	14/05/77	Murdered by IRA on undercover mission
GDSMN GRAHAM DUGGAN	21/12/78	Killed in attack on Army patrol, Crossmaglen
GDSMN KEVIN JOHNSON	21/12/78	Killed in same incident
GDSMN GLEN LING	21/12/78	Killed in same incident
GDSMN PAUL WEAVER	23/12/78	Death by violent or unnatural causes
CAPT HERBERT WESTMACOTT	2/05/80	Killed on undercover mission in west Belfast
C/SGT JOHN WIGG	17/01/86	Death by violent or unnatural causes

GDSMN PAUL MACDONALD	05/03/86	RTA on duty at Ballkelly
GDSMN BRIAN HUGHES	11/03/86	Killed in same RTA
L/CPL GARY KITELEY	28/12/86	Death by violent or unnatural causes
GDSMN DANIEL BLINCO	30/12/93	IRA sniper, South Armagh

INTELLIGENCE CORPS

CPL PAUL HARMAN	14/12/77	Killed after his vehicle was hijacked, Turf Lodge, Belfast
SGT JOHN ROESER	31/08/78	RTA
CPL MICHAEL BLOOR	31/08/78	Killed in same incident
CAPT HENRIETTA STEEL-MORTIMER	11/06/98	RTA

IRISH GUARDS

SGT PHILLIP PRICE	21/07/72	Killed by car bomb, 'Bloody Friday', Belfast
GDSMN DAVID ROBERTSON	24/11/73	IRA landmine, Crossmaglen
GDSMN SAMUEL MURPHY	14/11/77	Murdered in front of his mother whilst on leave, Andersonstown, Belfast

KING'S OWN ROYAL BORDER REGIMENT

PTE GEORGE P. RIDING	10/05/72	Died of natural causes
C/SGT WILLIAM BOARDLEY	01/02/73	Shot in Strabane by IRA gunman
CPL JAMES BURNEY	20/12/78	IRA sniper, Newington, Belfast
PTE OWEN PAVEY	11/03/80	Accidental shooting, Crossmaglen
PTE JOHN B. BATEMAN	15/03/80	IRA sniper, Crossmaglen
PTE SEAN G. WALKER	21/03/80	DoW, car bomb, Crossmaglen
L/CPL ANTHONY DACRE	27/03/85	Bomb attack, Divis street flats, Belfast
PTE DAVID HATFIELD	24/02/92	Vehicle accident, Londonderry
PTE MARTIN THOMAS	17/01/95	Vehicle accident, Belfast
PTE DARREN MILRAY	21/02/95	Road accident

KING'S OWN SCOTTISH BORDERERS

S/SGT PETER SINTON	28/07/70	Violent or unnatural causes
L/CPL PETER DEACON SIME	07/04/72	IRA sniper, Ballymurphy Estate, Belfast
L/CPL BARRY GOLD	24/04/72	DoW after gun battle at VCP in Belfast
C/SGT HENRY S. MIDDLEMASS	10/12/72	IRA booby trap, Turf Lodge, Belfast
PTE JOHN GILLIES	06/10/76	Cause of death unknown
S/SGT H. SHINGLESTON, MM	25/11/76	Cause of death unknown
PTE PETER B. SCOTT	10/10/79	RTA
PTE JAMES HOUSTON	13/12/89	Killed at VCP in gun and grenade attack, Fermanagh
L/CPL MICHAEL JOHN PATERSON	13/12/89	Killed in same incident

KINGS REGIMENT

CPL ALAN BUCKLEY	13/05/72	Shot on Turf Lodge, Belfast
PTE EUSTACE HANLEY	23/05/72	IRA sniper, Ballymurphy Estate
PTE MARCEL DOGLAY	30/05/72	IRA bomb, Springfield Road, Belfast
PTE JAMES JONES	18/07/72	IRA sniper, New Barnsley, Belfast
PTE BRIAN THOMAS	24/07/72	IRA sniper, New Barnsley, Belfast
PTE RENNIE LAYFIELD	18/08/72	IRA sniper, Falls Road, Belfast

PTE ROY CHRISTOPHER	30/08/72	DoW after bomb attack, Cupar St, Belfast
SGT DENNIS DOOLEY	15/03/75	RTA outside of Londonderry; died in hospital
PTE DAVID OWEN	14/10/75	Died of natural causes
PTE PETER KAVANAGH	14/11/75	Death by violent or unnatural causes
PTE CHRISTOPHER SHANLEY	11/04/79	Ambushed and shot, Ballymurphy Estate, Belfast
L/CPL STEPHEN RUMBLE	19/04/79	DoW from same incident
L/CPL ANDREW WEBSTER	19/05/79	Bomb attack, Turf Lodge, Belfast
PTE STEPHEN BEACHAM	24/10/90	Killed by IRA 'proxy bomb' Coshquin, near Londonderry
L/CPL STEPHEN BURROWS	24/10/90	Killed in same incident
PTE VINCENT SCOTT	24/10/90	Killed in same incident
PTE DAVID SWEENEY	24/10/90	Killed in same incident
PTE PAUL WORRALL	24/10/90	Killed in same incident

LIFE GUARDS

COH LEONARD DURBER	21/02/73	DoW after riot in Belfast

LIGHT INFANTRY

1st Battalion

PTE RICHARD JONES	18/08/72	Sniper, West Belfast
PTE R. ROWE	28/08/72	Shot accidentally in Ardoyne, Belfast
PTE T. A. STOKER	19/09/72	DoW after accidental shooting in Flex Street Mill, Ardoyne
PTE T. RUDMAN	30/09/72	Shot in Ardoyne, Belfast (brother killed in 1971 in N. Northern Ireland)
PTE STEPHEN HALL	28/10/73	Shot in Crossmaglen
PTE G.M. CURTIS	10/06/83	IRA bomb, Ballymurphy Estate, Belfast
PTE NICHOLAS BLYTHE	12/11/87	Killed in accident
PTE J. J. WILLBY	06/02/88	Violent or unnatural causes
PTE B. BISHOP	20/08/88	Killed in Ballygawley coach bombing
PTE P. L. BULLOCK	20/08/88	Killed in same incident
PTE J. BURFITT	20/08/88	Killed in same incident
PTE R. GREENER	20/08/88	Killed in same incident
PTE A.S. LEWIS	20/08/88	Killed in same incident
PTE M.A. NORWORTHY	20/08/88	Killed in same incident
PTE S.J. WILKINSON	20/08/88	Killed in same incident
PTE J. WINTER	20/08/88	Killed in same incident
PTE GRAHAM SMITH	03/12/88	Violent or unnatural causes
PTE A.J. RICHARDSON	12/03/97	Killed in attempted ambush by IRA after ceasefire

2nd Battalion

PTE J.R. RUDMAN	14/10/71	Shot in Coalisland area
SGT ARTHUR WHITELOCK	24/08/72	IRA sniper, Londonderry
CPL T.P. TAYLOR	13/05/73	Killed in bomb attack, Donegall Road
PTE J. GASKELL	14/05/73	DoW from same incident
PTE R. B. ROBERTS	01/07/73	Sniper, Ballymurphy Estate, Belfast
PTE R. STAFFORD	20/07/79	RTA
PTE PAUL TURNER	28/08/92	IRA sniper, Crossmaglen

3rd Battalion

PTE P.K. EASTAUGH	23/03/71	Shot accidentally in the Ardoyne area of Belfast
CPL I.R. MORRILL	28/08/72	IRA sniper, Belfast (Att from RGJ)
LCPL A. KENNINGTON	28/02/73	IRA sniper, Ardoyne area of Belfast
LCPL C.R. MILLER	18/09/73	Shot in West Belfast
PTE R.D. TURNBULL	29/06/77	Ambushed and shot West Belfast
PTE MICHAEL E HARRISON	29/06/77	Killed in same incident
PTE LEWIS J HARRISON	09/08/77	IRA sniper, New Barnsley, Belfast
CPL D.P. SALTHOUSE	7/12/82	IRA bomb Droppiin' Well pub, Ballykelly

LIGHT INFANTRY (BN UNKNOWN)

L/CPL TERENCE WILSON	01/07/78	RTA
PTE KEVIN MCGOVERN	03/07/78	RTA
PTE GARY HARDY	16/08/78	Cause of death unknown

NORTH IRISH MILITIA

RANGER SAMUEL M. GIBSON	24/10/74	Abducted and murdered off duty (TA)

PARACHUTE REGIMENT

PTE PETER DOCHERTY	21/05/70	Accidental death
PTE VICTOR CHAPMAN	24/06/70	Drowned
SGT M. WILLETTS GC	25/05/71	Killed saving civilians in IRA bomb blast, Springfield Road, Belfast
PTE R. A. BARTON	14/07/71	Shot protecting comrades, Andersonstown, Belfast
SGT GRAHAM	17/10/71	DoW after being shot by IRA gunman in Oldpark area
FATHER GERRY WESTON, MBE	22/02/72	Killed in IRA bomb outrage, Aldershot
PTE A. KELLY	18/03/72	Killed in accident, Holywood, Co Down
PTE C. STEPHENSON	24/06/72	IRA landmine, Glenshane Pass, Londonderry
PTE FRANK T. BELL	20/09/72	DoW after being shot on Ballymurphy Estate, Belfast
CPL S.N. HARRISON	07/04/73	IRA landmine, Tullyogallaghan
L/CPL T.D. BROWN	07/04/73	Killed in same incident
L/CPL D.A. FORMAN	16/04/73	Accidentally shot, Flax Street Mill, Ardoyne
WO2 W.R. VINES	05/05/73	IRA landmine, Crossmaglen
A/SGT J. WALLACE	24/05/73	IRA booby trap, Crossmaglen
PTE R. BEDFORD	16/03/74	Shot in IRA ambush, Crossmaglen
PTE P. JAMES	16/03/74	Killed in same incident
PTE WILLIAM SNOWDON	28/06/76	IRA bomb, Crossmaglen
PTE J. BORUCKI	08/08/76	IRA booby trap, Crossmaglen
L/CPL D.A. JONES	17/03/78	Shot in gun battle, Glenshane Pass, Londonderry
PTE J. FISHER	12/07/78	IRA booby trap, Crossmaglen
CPL R.D. ADCOCK	02/12/78	Killed in helicopter accident
MAJ. P. J. FURSMAN	27/08/79	Killed in IRA double bomb blast, Warrenpoint. One of 16 Paras and two other soldiers killed
WO2 W. BEARD	27/08/79	Killed in same incident
SGT I. A. ROGERS	27/08/79	Killed in same incident
CPL N. J. ANDREWS	27/08/79	Killed in same incident
CPL J.C. GILES	27/08/79	Killed in same incident

CPL L. JONES	27/08/79	Killed in same incident
L/CPL C.G. IRELAND	27/08/79	Killed in same incident
PTE G.I. BARNES	27/08/79	Killed in same incident
PTE D.F. BLAIR	27/08/79	Killed in same incident
PTE R. DUNN	27/08/79	Killed in same incident
PTE R.N. ENGLAND	27/08/79	Killed in same incident
PTE R.D.U. JONES	27/08/79	Killed in same incident
PTE T.R. VANCE	27/08/79	Killed in same incident
PTE J.A. VAUGHAN-JONES	27/08/79	Killed in same incident
PTE A.G. WOOD	27/08/79	Killed in same incident
PTE M. WOODS	27/08/79	Killed in same incident
PTE P.S. GRUNDY	16/12/79	IRA booby trap, Forkhill
LT S.G. BATES	01/01/80	Shot accidentally, OP at Forkhill
PTE G.M.R. HARDY	01/01/80	Killed in same incident
A/SGT B.M. BROWN	09/08/80	IRA booby trap, Forkhill
L/CPL PETER HAMPSON	25/12/81	Violent or unnatural causes
L/CPL MICHAEL C. MAY	26/07/82	RTA
SGT A.I. SLATER MM	02/12/84	Killed in anti-IRA operation, Fermanagh
SGT MICHAEL MATTHEWS	29/07/88	DoW, IRA landmine, Cullyhanna
PTE ROBERT SPIKINS	25/03/89	RTA, Belfast
L/CPL STEPHEN WILSON	18/11/89	IRA landmine, Mayobridge (3 soldiers killed)
PTE DONALD MACAULAY	18/11/89	Killed in same incident
PTE MATTHEW MARSHALL	18/11/89	Killed in same incident
PTE ANTHONY HARRISON	19/06/91	Murdered by IRA in fiancés' home, East Belfast
L/CPL RICHARD COULSON	27/06/92	Drowned crossing a river
L/CPL PETER H. SULLIVAN	27/06/92	Drowned trying to rescue his friend
PTE MICHAEL B. LEE	20/08/92	Violent or unnatural causes
PTE P.F.J. GROSS	13/05/93	Accidental death at Holywood
PTE CHRISTIAN D. KING	04/12/94	Violent or unnatural causes
PTE MARC RAMSEY	21/08/97	Accidental death

PRINCE OF WALES OWN REGIMENT OF YORKSHIRE

PTE JAMES LEADBEATER	11/02/73	Cause of death unknown
S/SGT ARTHUR PLACE	18/05/73	Booby trap bomb, Knock-na-Moe Hotel, Omagh
PTE DAVID WRAY	10/10/75	DoW after being shot Creggan area, Londonderry
L/CPL GRAHAM BIRDSALL	23/08/86	Cause of death unknown
PTE WILLIAM CARNE	20/07/96	Cause of death unknown

PRINCESS OF WALES ROYAL REGIMENT

MAJ JOHN BARR	26/11/92	Helicopter crash, Bessbrook Mill
L/CPL PAUL PARKIN	08/10/95	Cause of death unknown

QUEEN ALEXANDRA'S ROYAL ARMY NURSING CORPS

CAPT LYNDA SMITH	22/04/81	Cause of death unknown

QUEENS LANCASHIRE REGIMENT

SGT JAMES SINGLETON	23/06/70	Died on duty
PTE STEPHEN KEATING	03/03/72	IRA sniper, Manor Street, West Belfast
PTE MICHAEL MURTAGH	06/02/73	Killed in rocket attack Lower Falls area, Belfast
PTE EDWIN WESTON	14/02/73	IRA sniper, Divis Street area, Belfast

PTE GARY BARLOW	04/03/73	Gun battle, Lower Falls area, Belfast
PTE JOHN GREEN	08/03/73	Shot whilst guarding school in Lower Falls area, Belfast
L/CPL WILLIAM RIDDELL	06/01/76	RTA
PTE IAN O'CONNER	03/03/87	Grenade attack, Divis Street flats, Belfast
PTE JOSEPH LEACH	04/06/87	IRA sniper, Andersonstown, Belfast

QUEENS OWN HIGHLANDERS

PTE JAMES HESKETH	10/12/73	Shot dead on Lower Falls, Belfast
PTE ALAN JOHN MCMILLAN	08/07/79	Remote-controlled bomb in Crossmaglen
L/CPL D. LANG	24/08/79	Killed in helicopter crash with another soldier
L/CPL D.A. WARES	24/08/79	Killed in same accident
LT/COL DAVID BLAIR	27/08/79	Killed in IRA double bomb blast, Warrenpoint (one of 18 soldiers killed in same incident)
L/CPL VICTOR MACLEOD	27/08/79	Killed in same incident
CPL RICHARD TURNER	27/02/90	Accidentally shot

QUEENS REGIMENT

PTE DAVID PITCHFORD	27/06/70	RTA
PTE PAUL CARTER	15/09/71	DoW after being shot at Royal Victoria Hospital, Belfast
PTE ROBERT BENNER	29/11/71	Abducted and murdered by IRA off duty at Crossmaglen
PTE RICHARD SINCLAIR	31/10/72	IRA sniper, New Lodge, Belfast
PTE STANLEY EVANS	14/11/72	IRA sniper, Unity Flats complex, West Belfast
PTE PETER WOOLMORE	19/03/79	Mortar bomb attack, Newtownhamilton, Co Armagh
PTE ALAN STOCK	15/10/83	Remote-controlled bomb, Creggan, Londonderry
PTE NEIL CLARKE	24/04/84	IRA sniper, Bishop Street, Londonderry
PTE STEPHEN RANDALL	23/05/84	Cause of death unknown
WO1 JEFFERY BUDGEN	31/10/84	Cause of death unknown
CPL ALEXANDER BANNISTER	08/08/88	IRA sniper, New Barnsley, Belfast
SGT CHARLES CHAPMAN	16/07/90	IRA booby trap, Army recruiting office, Wembley, London

QUEEN'S ROYAL IRISH HUSSARS

TPR HUGH MCCABE	15/08/69	Killed by friendly fire, Divis Street, Belfast

ROYAL AIR FORCE

FLT SGT JOHN WILLOUGHBY	07/12/69	Died of natural causes
LAC ROBERT CALDERBANK	10/07/71	RTA
SAC STEPHEN HENSELER	12/03/80	RTA
JNR TECH DAVID GILFILLAN	13/10/81	RTA
SGT DAVID RIGBY	25/10/85	Killed in helicopter crash at Forkhill
CPL ISLANIA MAHESHKUMAR	26/10/89	Shot by IRA in Wildenrath, West Germany and killed alongside baby daughter, Nivruti (6 months old)
SQN LDR MICHAEL HAVERSON	26/10/92	Helicopter crash, Bessbrook Mill base, Armagh
FLT LT SIMON S.M.J. ROBERTS	26/10/92	Killed in same accident
FLT SGT JAN PEWTRESS	26/10/92	Killed in same accident

RAF REGIMENT

AIRMAN JOHN BAXTER	01/05/88	IRA booby trap, at Nieuw-Bergan, Holland
AIRMAN JOHN MILLER	01/05/88	Killed in same incident
AIRMAN IAN SHINNER	01/05/88	IRA sniper, Roermond, Holland
CPL IAN LEARMOUTH	30/08/89	Unlawfully killed at VCP

ROYAL ANGLIAN REGIMENT

MAJ PETER TAUNTON	26/10/70	Violent or unnatural causes
PTE BRIAN SHERIDAN	20/11/70	RTA
PTE ROGER WILKINS	11/10/71	DoW after being shot on Letterkenny Road, Londonderry
L/CPL IAN CURTIS	09/11/71	IRA sniper, Foyle Road, Londonderry
2/LT NICHOLAS HULL	16/04/72	IRA sniper, Divis Street flats, Belfast
PTE JOHN BALLARD	11/05/72	IRA sniper, Sultan St. Lower Falls, Belfast
L/CPL MARTIN ROONEY	12/07/72	IRA sniper, Clonnard St., Lower Falls, Belfast
CPL KENNETH MOGG	13/07/72	IRA sniper, Dunville Park, Belfast
L/CPL JOHN BODDY	17/08/72	IRA sniper, Grosvenor Road area of Belfast
CPL JOHN BARRY	25/09/72	DoW after gun battle, Lower Falls, Belfast
PTE IAN BURT	29/09/72	IRA sniper, Albert Street, Lower Falls, Belfast
PTE ROBERT MASON	24/10/72	IRA sniper, Naples Street, Grosvenor Road area, Belfast
PTE ANTHONY GOODFELLOW	27/04/73	Shot manning VCP Creggan Estate, Londonderry
PTE N. MARWICK	12/09/73	Cause of death unknown
L/CPL ROY GRANT	02/11/73	Death by violent or unnatural causes
PTE PARRY HOLLIS	13/11/74	Died of natural causes
PTE STEPHEN FOSTER	13/11/78	Accidental death
PTE PAUL WRIGHT	08/10/79	Killed on covert operation, Falls Road area
PTE KEVIN BREWER	29/08/81	RTA
PTE ANTHONY ANDERSON	24/05/82	Killed by vehicle in confusion after petrol bomb attack, Butcher Street, Londonderry
PTE MARTIN PATTEN	22/09/85	Murdered off duty Limavady Road, Waterside, Londonderry
MAJ ANDREW FRENCH	22/05/86	Killed by remote-controlled bomb, Crossmaglen
PTE MITCHELL BERTRAM	09/07/86	Remote-controlled bomb Glassdrumman, Crossmaglen
PTE CARL DAVIES	9/07/86	Killed in same incident
PTE DAVID J. KNIGHT	26/07/86	RTA
PTE NICHOLAS PEACOCK	31/01/89	Remote-controlled bomb Falls Road area, Belfast

ROYAL ARMY DENTAL CORPS

SGT RICHARD MULDOON	23/03/73	Murdered by the IRA whilst off duty

ROYAL ARMY EDUCATION CORPS

MAJ RHODRI HOWELL	19/07/79	Cause of death unknown

ROYAL ARMY MEDICAL CORPS

PTE 'TAFFY' PORTER	21/04/72	Violent or unnatural causes
CAPT HARRY MURPHY	15/03/73	Violent or unnatural causes

CAPT JANIS CANT	8/11/84	Cause of death unknown
PTE BRIAN ARMSTRONG (TA)	25/08/85	RTA
WO2 PHILLIP CROSS	02/11/91	IRA bomb planted at Musgrave Park Hospital (killed with one other soldier)
CPL JOHN NEILL	13/04/92	Cause of death unknown

ROYAL ARMY PAY CORPS

PTE MICHAEL PRIME	16/02/72	Shot in ambush at Moira roundabout near Lisburn
WO2 GEORGE JOHNSON	16/03/76	Cause of death unknown
L/CPL ANDREW SNELL	19/03/80	Cause of death unknown
L/CPL HENRY M. MCGIVERN		RTA

ROYAL ARMY ORDINANCE CORPS

CAPT D.A. STEWARDSON	09/09/71	Defusing IRA bomb Castlerobin, Antrim
WO2 C.J.L. DAVIES	24/11/71	Killed by IRA bomb in Lurgan
PTE T.F. McCANN	14/02/72	Abducted and murdered by the IRA, Newtownbutler
SSGT C.R. CRACKNELL	15/03/72	IRA booby trap, Grosvenor Road, Belfast
SSGT A.S. BUTCHER	15/03/72	Killed in same incident
MAJ B.C. CALLADENE	29/03/72	IRA car bomb outside Belfast City Hall
CAPT J.H. YOUNG	15/07/72	Defusing IRA bomb, Silverbridge near Forkhill
WO2 W.J. CLARK	03/08/72	Defusing IRA bomb at Strabane
SGT R.E. HILLS	05/12/72	Attempting to make live shell safe, Kitchen Hill
CAPT B.S. GRITTEN	21/06/73	Killed inspecting explosives, Lecky Road, Londonderry
SSGT R.F. BECKETT	30/08/73	Killed pulling bomb out of a post office, Tullyhommon
CAPT RONALD WILKINSON	23/09/73	Defusing IRA bomb, Edgbaston, Birmingham
2/LT L. HAMILTON DOBBIE	03/10/73	IRA bomb, Bligh's Lane post, Londonderry
SSGT A.N. BRAMMAH	18/02/74	Examining IRA roadside bomb, Crossmaglen
CPL GEOFFREY HALL	20/09/74	Cause of death unknown
SSGT V.I. ROSE	7/11/74	IRA landmine, Stewartstown, Tyrone
WO2 J.A. MADDOCKS	02/12/74	Examining milk churn bomb, Gortmullen
WO2 E. GARSIDE	17/07/75	Killed with three other soldiers, IRA bomb near Forkhill
CPL C.W. BROWN	17/07/75	Killed in same incident
CPL DOUGLAS WHITFIELD	13/03/76	RTA
SGT MICHAEL G. PEACOCK	13/03/76	Killed in same incident
SGT M.E. WALSH	09/01/77	Killed dismantling IRA bomb, Newtownbutler
L/CPL MICHAEL DEARNEY	31/05/77	RTA
SIG P.J. REECE	02/08/79	IRA landmine near Armagh
GNR R.A.J. FURMINGER	02/08/79	Killed in same incident
WO2 M. O'NEIL	31/05/81	Examining IRA bomb near Newry
L/CPL ROBERT PRINGLE	24/08/81	Cause of death unknown
PTE IAN ARCHIBALD	15/02/83	RTA
L/CPL DEREK W. GREEN	15/06/88	One of six soldiers killed by IRA booby trap, Lisburn
WO2 JOHN HOWARD	08/08/88	IRA booby trap, Falls Road, Belfast
L/CPL ANDREW DOWELL	17/08/92	Cause of death unknown

ROYAL ARMY VETERINARY CORPS

CPL BRIAN CRIDDLE, BEM	22/07/73	DoW after being injured whilst defusing IRA bomb
CPL TERENCE O'NEIL	25/05/91	Hand grenade, North Howard Sreet, Belfast

ROYAL ARTILLERY

GNR ROBERT CURTIS	06/02/71	Shot by IRA gunmen, New Lodge area, Belfast
L/BDR JOHN LAURIE	15/02/71	DoW after same incident
BDR PAUL CHALLENOR	10/08/71	IRA sniper, Bligh's Lane post, Londonderry
GNR CLIFFORD LORING	31/08/71	DoW after being shot at VCP, Belfast
SGT MARTIN CARROLL	14/09/71	IRA sniper, Creggan, Londonderry
GNR ANGUS STEVENS	27/10/71	IRA bomb attack, Rosemount RUC station, Belfast
L/BDR DAVID TILBURY	27/10/71	Killed in same incident
GNR IAN DOCHERTY	31/10/71	DoW after being shot in Stockmans Lane, Belfast
GNR RICHARD HAM	29/12/71	Shot dead in the Brandywell area of Londonderry
L/BDR ERIC BLACKBURN	10/04/72	Killed in bomb attack, Rosemount Avenue
L/BDR BRIAN THOMASSON	10/04/72	Killed in same incident
GNR VICTOR HUSBAND	02/06/72	IRA landmine, Rosslea, Co Fermanagh
GNR BRIAN ROBERTSON	02/06/72	Killed in same incident
SGT CHARLES COLEMAN	07/06/72	IRA sniper, Andersonstown, Belfast
GNR WILLIAM RAISTRICK	11/06/72	IRA sniper, Brooke Park, Londonderry
BDR TERRENCE JONES	11/07/72	Shot in the back by IRA, Londonderry
GNR LEROY GORDON	07/08/72	IRA landmine, Lisnaskea, Co Fermanagh
L/BDR DAVID WYNNE	07/08/72	Killed in same incident
MAJ DAVID STORRY	14/08/72	Booby trap, Casement Park base, Andersonstown
GNR ROBERT CUTTING	03/09/72	Accidentally shot, New Lodge area of Belfast
S/SGT JOHN GARDNER CRAIG	15/09/72	RTA
GNR PAUL JACKSON	28/11/72	Hit by bomb shrapnel, Strand Road, Londonderry
SGT IVOR W. SWAIN	23/03/73	RTA
GNR IDWAL EVANS	11/04/73	IRA sniper, Bogside area of Londonderry
GNR KERRY VENN	28/04/73	IRA sniper, Shantallow Estate, Londonderry
SGT THOMAS CRUMP	03/05/73	DoW after being shot in Londonderry
GNR JOSEPH BROOKES	25/11/73	Shot in IRA ambush in Bogside area of Londonderry
BDR HEINZ PISAREK	25/11/73	Killed in same incident
SGT JOHN HAUGHEY	21/01/74	Remote-controlled bomb, Creggan Estate, Londonderry
GNR LEONARD GODDEN	04/02/74	Killed by IRA bomb on M62 in Yorkshire
BDR TERRENCE GRIFFIN	04/02/74	Killed in same incident
GNR DAVID FARRINGTON	13/03/74	Shot by IRA gunmen at Chapel Lane Belfast city centre
LT/COL JOHN STEVENSON	08/04/74	Murdered by IRA gunmen at his home in Northumberland
GNR KIM MACCUNN	22/06/74	IRA sniper, New Lodge, Belfast
SGT BERNARD FEARNS	30/07/74	IRA sniper, New Lodge area of Belfast
GNR KEITH BATES	04/11/74	RTA Central Belfast
GNR RICHARD DUNNE	08/11/74	IRA bomb in Woolwich, London pub bombings

GNR GEOFFREY B. JONES	09/06/75	RTA
GNR CYRIL MACDONALD	18/12/75	IRA bomb attack at Guildhall Square, Londonderry
GNR MARK ASHFORD	17/01/76	Shot at checkpoint, Great James Street, Londonderry
GNR JAMES REYNOLDS	13/03/76	RTA
GNR WILLIAM MILLER (TA)	3/07/76	IRA sniper at checkpoint Butcher Street, Londonderry
SGT DAVID EVANS	21/07/76	Cause of death unknown
GNR ANTHONY ABBOT	24/10/76	Ambushed and killed by IRA, Ardoyne, Belfast
GNR STEPHEN NICHOLSON	05/11/76	Cause of death unknown
GNR MAURICE MURPHY	22/11/76	DoW from same incident
GNR EDWARD MULLER	11/01/77	IRA sniper at VCP in Old Park area of Belfast
GNR GEORGE MUNCASTER	23/01/77	IRA sniper, Markets area, Belfast
GNR PAUL SHEPPARD	01/03/78	Shot in gun battle Clifton Park Avenue, Belfast
GNR ROGER EDWARDS	02/07/78	Cause of death unknown
GNR RICHARD FURMINGER	02/08/79	Killed in IRA landmine attack with RAOC comrade Cathedral Road, Armagh
GNR ALAN AYRTON	16/12/79	Killed in landmine explosion, Dungannon
GNR WILLIAM BECK	16/12/79	Killed in same incident
GNR SIMON EVANS	16/12/79	Killed in same incident
GNR KEITH RICHARDS	16/12/79	Killed in same incident
GNR PETER A. CLARK	09/08/80	RTA
SGT SAMUEL MCCLEAN	30/05/81	Cause of death unknown
L/BDR KEVIN WALLER	20/09/82	Remote-controlled INLA bomb Divis Street flats, Belfast
BDR PAUL CREE	05/02/88	Cause of death unknown
GNR LYNDON MORGAN	26/04/88	IRA booby trap Carrickmore
GNR MILES AMOS	08/03/89	IRA landmine, Buncrana Road, Londonderry
L/BDR STEPHEN CUMMINS	08/03/89	Killed in same incident
L/BDR DAVID SHEPPARD	18/03/89	Cause of death unknown
MAJ MICHAEL DILLION-LEE	02/06/90	Murdered outside his quarters in Dortmund, Germany
GNR DARREN OLDFIELD	01/06/92	Death by violent or unnatural causes
CAPT NIGEL FRENCH	12/03/92	Cause of death unknown
L/BDR PAUL GARRETT	02/12/93	IRA sniper, Keady, Co Armagh
2 LT JAMES C. FOX	21/01/95	Violent or unnatural causes
L/BDR STEPHEN RESTORICK	12/02/97	IRA sniper at VCP at Bessbrook Mill Army base
GNR JON COOPER	22/02/97	Violent or unnatural causes

ROYAL CORPS SIGNALS

L/CPL MICHAEL SPURWAY	13/09/69	Accidentally shot, Gosford Castle
SIG PAUL GENGE	07/11/71	Shot by IRA whilst off-duty in Lurgan
SGT DAVID MCELVIE	13/03/73	Unknown
CPL JOHN AIKMAN	06/11/73	Shot by IRA gunmen Newtownhamilton
SIG MICHAEL E. WAUGH	04/02/74	Killed by IRA bomb, M62, Yorkshire
SIG LESLIE DAVID WALSH	04/02/74	Killed in same incident
SIG PAUL ANTHONY REID	04/02/74	Killed in same incident
SGT DEREK BASSFORD	24/10/75	Cause of death unknown
SIG DAVID ROBERTS	13/03/76	RTA
CPL ARTHUR FORD	07/01/76	Aircraft accident

L/CPL RICHARD DAVIES	25/02/79	RTA
SIG PAUL J REECE	02/08/79	IRA landmine, Armagh
L/CPL ROBIN LISTER	18/02/80	Cause of death unknown
L/CPL PAUL HOLT	03/11/80	Cause of death unknown
SIG BRIAN RICHARD CROSS	04/07/81	Killed in road traffic accident, Lisburn
CPL MICHAEL WARD	01/04/82	Shot with REME soldier by IRA in Bogside, Londonderry
SGT LESLIE MCKENZIE	24/05/83	RTA
SIG KENNETH ROYAL	28/03/85	RTA
CPL DEREK T WOOD	19/03/88	Beaten by mob, shot by IRA, Penny Lane, Belfast
CPL DAVID HOWES	19/03/88	Killed in same incident
L/CPL GRAHAM P LAMBIE	15/06/88	Killed by IRA bomb, Lisburn (one of six sol diers killed)
SGT MICHAEL JAMES WINKLER	15/06/88	Killed in same incident
SIG MARK CLAVEY	15/06/88	Killed in same incident
CPL WILLIAM J. PATERSON	15/06/88	Killed in same incident
S/SGT KEVIN A FROGGETT	16/09/89	Shot by IRA repairing radio mast Coalisland RUC station
SIG WILLIAM DRYDEN	07/08/91	Cause of death unknown
SGT MICHAEL NEWMAN	14/04/92	Shot by INLA at Army Recruiting office, Derby, England
SIG JONATHAN EDMONDS	27/05/92	Cause of death unknown
CPL PAUL SMITH	22/09/94	RTA
SGT JOHN LIVINGSTONE	21/04/98	Cause of death unknown

ROYAL CORPS TRANSPORT

MAJ PHILIP COWLEY	13/01/70	Died on duty
CPL CHRISTOPHER YOUNG (TA)	29/07/71	RTA
DVR STEPHEN BEEDIE	26/03/72	RTA
DVR LAURENCE JUBB	26/04/72	Killed in vehicle crash after mob attack, Armagh
L/CPL MICHAEL BRUCE	31/05/72	IRA sniper, Andersonstown, Belfast
S/SGT JOSEPH FLEMING (TA)	09/07/72	Shot dead by IRA in Grosvenor Road area of Belfast
DVR PETER HEPPENSTALL	14/07/72	IRA sniper, Ardoyne area of Belfast
DVR STEPHEN COOPER	21/07/72	IRA car bomb on 'Bloody Friday', Belfast bus depot
DVR RONALD KITCHEN	10/11/72	IRA sniper at VCP in Old Park Road, Belfast
DVR MICHAEL GAY	17/03/73	IRA landmine, Dungannon
SGT THOMAS PENROSE	24/03/73	Murdered off-duty with two others, Antrim Road, Belfast
CPL ANDREW GILMOUR	29/08/73	RTA
L/CPL EDMOND CROSBIE	23/11/73	RTA
DVR NORMAN MCKENZIE	11/04/74	IRA landmine, Lisnaskea, Co Fermanagh
DVR HAROLD J. KING	19/04/75	RTA
DVR WILLIAM KNIGHT	17/05/76	RTA
DVR VICTOR DORMER	01/10/76	Cause of death unknown
SGT WILLIAM EDGAR	15/04/77	Abducted and murdered by IRA whilst on leave in Londonderry
LT NIGEL BREWER	31/05/79	Cause of death unknown
DVR JOHN DORRITY	30/09/79	Cause of death unknown
DVR STEVEN ATKINS	29/11/80	RTA

DVR IAN MACDONALD	08/03/81	Cause of death unknown
DVR PAUL BULMAN	19/05/81	Killed in IRA landmine attack along with 4 RGJs at Camlough, South Armagh
DVR PAUL JOHNS	25/10/81	Cause of death unknown
CAPT JOHN MEADOWS	08/08/84	Cause of death unknown
L/CPL NORMAN DUNCAN	22/02/89	Shot by IRA waterside area of Londonderry
THOMAS GIBSON (TA)	20/10/89	Murdered by IRA as he waited for lift in Kilrea
DVR C. PANTRY	02/11/91	Killed by IRA bomb at Musgrave Park hospital, Belfast
PTE MAURICE CARSON (TA)	13/06/81	RTA

ROYAL DRAGOON GUARDS

TPR GEOFFREY KNIPE	07/08/72	Armoured vehicle crashed after mob attack, Armagh

ROYAL ELECTRICAL & MECHANICAL ENGINEERS

CFN CHRISTOPHER EDGAR	13/09/69	Violent or unnatural causes
CFN ANDREW PATON	26/05/71	
SGT S.C. REID	24/06/72	IRA milk churn bombs at Glenshane Pass, Londonderry
L/CPL D. MOON	24/06/72	Killed in same incident
CFN BRIAN HOPE	14/08/72	IRA booby trap Casement Park, Andersonstown, Belfast
L/CPL COLIN HARKER	20/12/72	IRA sniper, Lecky Road, Londonderry
CPL DAVID BROWN	14/03/73	Unknown
SGT M E SELDON	30/06/74	Violent or unnatural causes
L/CPL ALISTER STEWART	09/10/74	RTA
L/CPL DEREK NORWOOD	05/03/75	Cause of death unknown
CFN COLIN MCINNES	18/12/75	IRA bomb attack on Army base in Londonderry
CPL ROBERT MOORE	15/09/79	RTA
CPL PETER BAILEY	05/04/80	RTA
CFN ALAN COOMBE	16/02/81	RTA
L/CPL PHILIP HARDING	30/03/82	Cause of death unknown
SGT MICHAEL BURBRIDGE	01/04/82	IRA sniper, Rosemount barracks, Londonderry
SGT RICHARD GREGORY	22/10/82	Died of natural causes on duty
CFN WILLIAM PARR	06/07/90	Cause of death unknown
WO1 (ASM) JAMES BRADWELL	11/10/96	DoW after car bomb attack by IRA on Army base Lisburn

ROYAL ENGINEERS

SPR JOHN CONNACHAN	27/06/71	Cause of death unknown
SPR DEREK AMOS	28/12/71	RTA
SPR RONALD HURST	17/05/72	IRA sniper whilst working on base in Crossmaglen
S/SGT MALCOLM BANKS	28/06/72	Shot by IRA Short Strand area of Belfast
SPR EDWARD STUART	02/10/72	Shot whilst working undercover Dunmurry, Belfast
WO2 IAN DONALD	24/05/73	IRA bomb, Cullaville, Co Armagh
MAJ RICHARD JARMAN	20/07/73	IRA booby trap Middletown, Co Armagh
SPR MALCOLM ORTON	17/09/73	Cause of death unknown

S/SGT JAMES LUND	19/01/74	Cause of death unknown
SPR JOHN WALTON	02/07/74	IRA booby trap Newtownhamilton
L/CPL IAN NICHOLL	15/05/74	RTA
SGT DAVID EVANS	21/07/74	IRA booby trap, Army base, Waterside, Londonderry
WO1 JOHN NEWTON	24/06/75	
SGT ROBERT MCCARTER	17/07/75	IRA bomb, Forkhill
GNR ANTHONY JEAL	11/07/75	Cause of death unknown
SPR GARETH GRIFFITHS	06/11/76	Cause of death unknown
SPR HOWARD EDWARDS	11/12/76	IRA sniper, Bogside area of Londonderry
SPR DAVIS THOMPSON	13/01/77	Cause of death unknown
SPR MICHAEL LARKIN	10/02/77	Cause of death unknown
CPL JOHN HAYNES	28/07/77	Cause of death unknown
SPR STEPHEN WORTH	01/08/77	Cause of death unknown
SPR JAMES VANCE	14/11/77	RTA
CPL JAMES ANDREWS	04/09/78	Cause of death unknown
SPR FRASER JONES	03/02/80	RTA
COL MARK COE	16/02/80	Murdered by IRA gunmen at Army home in Bielefeld Germany
SGT KENNETH ROBSON	18/02/80	Aircraft accident
WO2 EMANUEL MARIOTTI	22/08/81	Cause of death unknown
SPR CHRISTOPHER BEATTIE	06/04/82	Cause of death unknown
CPL THOMAS PALMER	08/02/83	RTA
L/CPL DAVID HURST	06/10/86	RTA
L/CPL MICHAEL ROBBINS	01/08/88	Killed by IRA bomb at Mill Hill Army camp, London
L/CPL PAUL CASSIDY	15/03/88	RTA
S/SGT DAVID HULL	22/08/89	RTA
S/SGT JAMES H. HARDY	12/06/90	RTA
SGT MICHAEL CASHMORE	01/07/90	Cause of death unknown
SPR DEAN PITTS	03/08/91	Cause of death unknown
L/CPL C.M. MONTEITH	05/08/91	RTA
CPL M.D. IONNOU	15/04/95	RTA
S/SGT S.J. THOMPSON	30/06/95	Died of natural causes whilst on duty
SPR JOHN ROBINSON	21/04/96	Cause of death unknown

ROYAL GREEN JACKETS

L/CPL MICHAEL PEARCE	24/09/69	Violent or unnatural causes
RFN MICHAEL BOSWELL	25/10/69	RTA caused by rioters
RFN JOHN KEENEY	25/10/69	Died in same incident
CPL ROBERT BANKIER	22/05/71	IRA sniper, Markets area of Belfast
RFN DAVID WALKER	12/07/71	IRA sniper, Northumberland Street, Lower Falls, Belfast
RFN JOSEPH HILL	16/10/71	Shot by gunman during riots in Bogside, Londonderry
MAJ ROBIN ALERS-HANKEY	30/01/72	DoW after being shot in Bogside area of Londonderry
RFN JOHN TAYLOR	20/03/72	IRA sniper, William Street, Londonderry
RFN JAMES MEREDITH	26/06/72	Shot in Abercorn Road, Londonderry
L/CPL DAVID CARD	04/08/72	Killed by IRA gunman in Andersonstown, Belfast

CPL IAN MORRILL	28/08/72	IRA sniper, Beechmount Avenue, Belfast
RFN DAVID GRIFFITHS	30/08/72	IRA sniper, Clonnard Street, Lower Falls, Belfast
L/CPL IAN GEORGE	10/09/72	Thought to have been shot by an IRA sniper, Belfast
RFN RAYMOND JOESBURY	08/12/72	DoW after being shot whilst in Whiterock area of Belfast
RFN NICOLAS ALLEN	26/11/73	Death by violent or unnatural causes
RFN MICHAEL GIBSON	14/12/74	Shot along with RUC constable at Forkhill on joint patrol
CPL WILLIAM SMITH	31/08/77	IRA sniper, Girdwood Park Army base, Belfast
LT/COL IAN CORDEN-LLOYD	17/02/78	Helicopter crash near Bessbrook
RFN NICHOLAS SMITH	04/03/78	IRA booby trap Crossmaglen
MAJ THOMAS FOWLEY	24/04/78	Died of natural causes whilst on duty
RFN CHRISTOPHER WATSON	19/07/80	Shot and killed off-duty in Rosemount, Londonderry
RFN MICHAEL BAGSHAW	19/05/81	IRA landmine at Camlough
RFN ANDREW GAVIN	19/05/81	Killed in same incident
RFN JOHN KING	19/05/81	Killed in same incident
L/CPL GRENVILLE WINSTONE	19/05/81	Killed in same incident
L/CPL GAVIN DEAN	16/07/81	IRA sniper, near Crossmaglen
RFN DANIEL HOLLAND	25/03/82	Killed with two others in gun attack on Springfield Road, Belfast
RFN NICHOLAS MALAKOS	25/03/82	Killed in same incident
RFN ANTHONY RAPLEY	25/03/82	Killed in same incident
WO2 GRAHAM BARKER	20/07/82	Killed in IRA bomb outrage, Regents Park, London
BDSM JOHN HERITAGE	20/07/82	Killed in same incident
BDSM ROBERT LIVINGSTONE	20/07/82	Killed in same incident
CPL JOHN MCKNIGHT	20/07/82	Killed in same incident
BDSM GEORGE MEASURE	20/07/82	Killed in same incident
BDSM KEITH POWELL	20/07/82	Killed in same incident
BDSM LAURENCE SMITH	20/07/82	Killed in same incident
RFN DAVID GRAINGER	10/04/83	Thought to have been shot by IRA in Belleek
RFN DAVID MULLEY	18/03/86	IRA bomb, Castlewellan, Co Down
L/CPL THOMAS HEWITT	19/07/87	IRA sniper, Belleek, Co Fermanagh
CPL EDWARD JEDRUCH	31/07/87	Killed in helicopter accident in South Armagh
SGT THOMAS ROSS	18/09/91	RTA
L/CPL WAYNE HARRIS	08/11/91	RTA. Hit a bridge in Armagh
RFN CHRISTOPHER WILLIAMS	08/11/91	Killed in same incident
CPL MATTHEW MADDOCKS	14/11/91	Helicopter crash, Gortin Glen, Omagh
CPL LARRY WALL	12/12/91	Death by violent or unnatural causes
RFN JAMIE SMITH	10/08/92	RTA
RFN RICHARD DAVEY	29/10/92	Death by violent or unnatural causes
RFN DAVID FENLEY	17/02/93	Death by violent or unnatural causes
WO2 KEITH THEOBOLD	02/10/95	Death by violent or unnatural causes

ROYAL HAMPSHIRE REGIMENT

PTE JOHN KING	13/03/73	IRA booby trap, Crossmaglen
PTE ALAN WATKINS	03/08/73	INLA sniper, Dungiven, Co Londonderry
CPL JOHN LEAHY	03/08/73	DoW following IRA bomb, Mullaghbawn, Forkhill

DRUMMER FRANK FALLOWS	10/11/76	Accidental shooting, Magaheralin, Co Armagh
SGT MICHAEL P. UNSWORTH	02/01/77	Drowned after helicopter accident, River Bann
PTE COLIN CLIFFORD	30/04/82	IRA landmine, Belleek, Co Fermanagh
PTE ANDREW COCKWILL	17/05/89	Cause of death unknown

ROYAL HIGHLAND FUSILIERS

FSLR JOHN B. MCCAIG	10/03/71	Abducted and murdered by the IRA at Ligoniel, Belfast
FSLR JOSEPH MCCAIG	10/03/71	Murdered in the same incident
FSLR DOUGALD P. MCCAUGHE	10/03/71	Murdered in the same incident
L/CPL DAVID HIND	02/01/77	Shot by IRA, Crossmaglen
CPL ROBERT M THOMPSON	20/07/80	IRA car bomb, Moy Bridge, Aughnacloy

ROYAL HUSSARS

S/SGT CHARLES SIMPSON	7/11/74	IRA booby trap, Stewartstown, Co Tyrone
LT ROBERT GLAZEBROOK	14/11/76	RTA

ROYAL HORSE GUARDS

L/COH KEITH CHILLINGWORTH	14/06/72	RTA

ROYAL IRISH RANGERS

SGT THOMAS MCGAHON	19/01/71	RTA
CPL JAMES SINGLETON	19/01/71	Killed in same incident
RANGER WILLIAM J. BEST	21/05/72	Abducted and murdered when on home leave
RANGER THOMAS MCGANN	26/05/72	RTA
MAJ DONALD FARRELL	23/03/74	Cause of death unknown
L/CPL MICHAEL NORRIS	27/07/74	Cause of death unknown
RANGER H THOMPSON	06/12/77	RTA
RANGER ROBERT QUAIL	05/07/79	Cause of death unknown
RANGER SEAN REILLY	04/09/81	Cause of death unknown
RANGER DAVID LANHAM	10/01/83	RTA
SGT TREVOR ELLIOTT (TA)	13/04/83	Cause of death unknown
RANGER LAWRENCE PITMAN	05/07/84	Cause of death unknown
RANGER WALTER LLEWELLYN	22/05/86	Cause of death unknown
SGT JOHN PEDEN	07/10/86	Cause of death unknown
RANGER CYRIL J. SMITH QGM	24/10/90	Killed saving colleagues during bomb attack at Newry

ROYAL IRISH REGIMENT

L/CPL MICHAEL W.A. PATTERSON	06/09/92	RTA (Home Service Force)
SGT ROBERT IRVINE	20/10/92	Shot by IRA in his sister's home, Rasharkin
PTE BRIAN MARTIN	20/10/92	RTA (Home Service Force)
L/CPL IAN WARNOCK	19/11/92	Shot by IRA as he met his wife in Portadown
PTE STEPHEN WALLER	30/12/92	Shot by IRA when on home leave, Belfast
L/CPL MERVYN JOHNSTON	15/02/93	Shot by IRA at his in-laws' house West Belfast
PTE WILLIAM HARKNESS	27/03/93	RTA
PTE ROBERT GARDNER	28/03/93	RTA
CPL ROBERT NEWELL	05/03/93	Cause of death unknown
PTE CHRIS WREN	31/05/93	Killed by IRA bomb under his car in Moneymore
CPL ROBERT ARMSTRONG	21/11/93	RTA

PTE SEAN MAIR	17/04/94	RTA
PTE WILLIAM SALTERS	30/04/94	Cause of death unknown
PTE WILLIAM TOSH	30/04/94	Cause of death unknown
PTE ADRIAN ROGERS	15/05/94	Cause of death unknown
PTE REGGIE MCCOLLUM	21/05/94	Abducted and murdered by the IRA whilst off-duty
PTE SIMON LECKY	31/07/94	RTA
CPL TRELFORD T. WITHERS	08/08/94	Shot in his shop, Downpatrick Street, Crossgar
CPL RONALD JACKSON	10/10/95	RTA
PTE WILLIAM MCCREA	10/10/95	RTA
PTE PAUL KILPATRICK	13/12/95	Cause of death unknown
CPL ROBERT ANDERSON	19/05/96	Cause of death unknown
PTE ALAN MCCORMICK	01/06/96	RTA
L/CPL STEVE RANKIN	23/09/96	Death by violent or unnatural causes
PTE JAMIE CATER	25/10/96	Cause of death unknown
PTE WILLIAM WOODS	03/09/97	Violent or unnatural causes
WO2 ROBERT BELL	09/01/98	Died on duty
PTE MATTHEW FRANCE	01/05/98	Violent or unnatural causes
PTE RONALD MCCONVILLE	30/06/98	Died on duty
CPL JACKY IRELAND	13/07/98	RTA
PTE JOHN MURRAY	28/08/98	RTA
L/CPL STUART ANDREWS	16/09/98	Died on duty
CPL GERALD BLAIR	21/10/98	Died on duty

ROYAL IRISH REGIMENT (V)

WO2 HUGH MCGINN	28/12/80	Killed by INLA in his own home in Armagh
SGT TREVOR A. ELLIOT	13/04/83	Killed by IRA at his shop in Keady
CPL TREVOR MAY	09/04/84	IRA bomb under his car in Newry outside his work

ROYAL LOGISTIC CORPS

CPL TERENCE HEFFY	07/12/93	Cause of death unknown
PTE MATTHEW EDWARDS	29/12/93	Cause of death unknown
L/CPL DAVID WILSON	14/05/94	Killed by bomb attack at VCP at Keady, Co Armagh
L/CPL MARK TREHERNE	29/07/94	Cause of death unknown
PTE PAUL SHEPHERD	25/12/95	Cause of death unknown
L/CPL RICHARD FORD	30/10/98	Died whilst on duty

ROYAL MARINES

BAND CPL DEAN PAVEY	22/09/89	Killed in IRA bomb outrage, Marine Barracks, Deal
BAND CPL TREVOR DAVIS	22/09/89	Killed in same incident
BAND CPL DAVE McMILLAN	22/09/89	Killed in same incident
MUSICIAN RICHARD FICE	22/09/89	Killed in same incident
MUSICIAN BOB SIMMONDS	22/09/89	Killed in same incident
MUSICIAN MICK BALL	22/09/89	Killed in same incident
MUSICIAN RICHARD JONES	22/09/89	Killed in same incident
MUSICIAN TIM REEVES	22/09/89	Killed in same incident
MUSICIAN MARK PETCH	22/09/89	Killed in same incident
MUSICIAN ANDY CLEATHEROE	22/09/89	Killed in same incident
MUSICIAN CHRIS NOLAN	18/10/89	DoW from same incident

ROYAL MARINE COMMANDOS

40 Cdo

MNE LEONARD ALLEN	26/07/72	Shot by IRA, Unity Flats, Belfast
MNE ANTHONY DAVID	17/10/72	DoW after being shot by IRA on Falls Road
MNE JOHN SHAW	26/07/73	RTA in controversial circumstances*
MNE ANDREW GIBBONS	28/05/83	Died Camlough Lake, Co Armagh

* Marine John Shaw's death is recorded by the Royal Marines as 'killed in action'

42 Cdo

MNE IVOR SWAIN	23/03/73	RTA North Belfast
MNE GRAHAM COX	29/04/73	IRA sniper, New Lodge, Belfast
MNE JOHN MACKLIN	28/03/74	DoW after being shot in the Antrim Road, Belfast
CPL ROBERT MILLER	17/08/78	IRA bomb attack, Forkhill
MNE GARY WHEDDON	12/11/78	DoW after bomb attack, Crossmaglen
MNE ADAM GILBERT	15/06/89	Shot in friendly fire incident, New Lodge Road

45 Cdo

MNE ROBERT CUTTING	28/08/72	Killed in friendly fire incident, Turf Lodge
CPL DENNIS LEACH	13/08/74	IRA bomb, Crossmaglen
MNE MICHAEL SOUTHERN	13/08/74	Killed in same incident
MNE NEIL BEWLEY	21/08/77	IRA sniper, Turf Lodge, Belfast
SGT WILLIAM CORBETT	23/08/81	Accidentally shot, Musgrave Park Hospital, Belfast

ROYAL MILITARY POLICE

L/CPL WILLIAM G. JOLLIFFE	01/03/71	Killed in crash in Londonderry after petrol bombing
CPL ALAN HOLMAN	11/02/73	Cause of death unknown
CPL RODERICK LANE	20/05/73	RTA
SGT SHERIDAN YOUNG	18/05/73	Killed in IRA atrocity at Knock Na Moe Hotel
CPL RICHARD ROBERTS	30/05/73	RTA
CPL STUART MILNE	20/02/74	RTA
L/CPL PAUL MUNDY	20/02/74	Killed in same incident
CPL THOMAS F. LEA	21/01/75	DoW eight months after IRA bomb attack, Belfast
CPL JOHN BOOTH	29/01/75	Cause of death unknown
CPL MICHAEL HARDS	17/04/76	Cause of death unknown
CPL WILLIAM SNAITH	25/01/79	Cause of death unknown
CPL GEORGE MIDDLEMAS	08/11/77	RTA
SGT DAVID ROSS	27/03/84	Killed in Londonderry after explosion
L/CPL DUNCAN CHAPPELL	19/09/91	Cause of death unknown
CPL MICHAEL HEIGHTON	09/10/91	Cause of death unknown

ROYAL NAVY

L/SMN GAVIN STEWART	01/10/73	RTA
L/WREN ANNIE BYRNE	29/08/75	RTA
CK1 THOMAS GILLEN	29/03/82	RTA
NA (AH) DAVID SHIPLEY	11/01/87	RTA
AB MARK CARTWRIGHT	11/01/87	Killed in same incident
LT A.R. SHIELDS	22/08/88	IRA bomb in Belfast; was Naval recruiter

STWD ROBERT STEWART	03/10/87	RTA
MEM ALAN BALMER	29/7/88	RTA

ROYAL PIONEER CORPS

PTE IRWIN BOWEN	02/08/72	RTA
SGT JAMES ROBINSON	08/02/73	Died of natural causes whilst on duty
PTE PHILIP DRAKE	26/08/74	IRA sniper, Craigavon, Co Armagh
PTE GRAHAM HAYES	02/05/75	Cause of death unknown
PTE DAVID P. BONSALL	29/03/75	RTA
PTE L. ROTHWELL	25/10/76	Cause of Death unknown
L/CPL GRAHAM LEE	22/08/80	RTA
PTE SOHAN VIRDEE	05/08/81	Murdered by the IRA whilst off duty
PTE S. HUMBLE	26/08/81	Killed in shooting accident
CPL DEREK HAYES	21/06/88	IRA booby trap, Crossmaglen

ROYAL REGIMENT FUSILIERS

1st Battalion

FSLR ANTHONY SIMMONS	15/11/74	Shot by IRA at Strabane
CPL B. BARKER	25/01/81	Shot at VCP in Belfast
CPL T.H. AGAR	18/05/84	Killed by IRA bomb under car at Enniskillen
L/CPL R.V. HUGGINS	18/05/84	Killed in same incident
L/CPL P.W. GALLIMORE	18/10/84	Died of heart attack after bomb attack, Enniskillen

2nd Battalion

MAJ J.J.E. SNOW	08/12/71	DoW after being shot by IRA in New Lodge area
FSLR K. CANHAM	14/07/72	IRA sniper, Lenadoon
FSLR ALAN P. TINGEY	23/08/72	IRA sniper, West Belfast
CPL D. NAPIER	09/03/73	RTA
FSLR GEORGE FOXALL	16/06/80	Violent or unnatural causes
FSLR ANDREW GRUNDY	01/05/92	IRA bomb at VCP at Killeen
L/CPL MICHAEL J. BESWICK	09/02/93	DoW after IRA bomb in Armagh

3rd Battalion

CPL JOHN L. DAVIS	15/09/72	Shot by IRA in Bogside, Londonderry
FSLR C.J. MARCHANT	09/04/73	Shot in ambush at Lurgan
CPL DAVID LLEWELLYN	28/09/75	RTA
CPL E. GLEESON	09/10/75	IRA landmine, Lurgancullenboy
SGT S.J. FRANCIS	21/11/75	IRA booby trap, Forkhill
FSLR M.J. SAMPSON	22/11/75	Killed in major gun battle with IRA at Drumuckaval
FSLR J.D. DUNCAN	22/11/75	Killed in same incident
FSLR P.L. McDONALD	22/11/75	Killed in same incident
CPL DONALD TRAYNOR	30/03/76	IRA booby trap, Ballygallan
L/CPL WAYNE MAKIN	03/01/83	Violent or unnatural causes
L/CPL JAMES J. MCSHANE	04/02/74	Killed in IRA bomb outrage, M62, Yorkshire
FSLR JACK HYNES	04/02/74	Killed in same coach bombing
CPL CLIFFORD HAUGHTON	04/02/74	Killed in same coach bombing
FSLR STEPHEN WHALLEY	04/02/74	Killed in same coach bombing

BATTALION UNKNOWN

FSLR TERRY THOMAS	25/01/72	Cause of death unknown
CPL DEREK NAPIER	09/03/73	RTA
FSLR THOMAS FOXALL	19/06/80	Cause of death unknown

ROYAL REGIMENT OF WALES

PTE ALAN ROY ROGERS	13/03/71	RTA
L/CPL JOHN HILLMAN	18/06/72	IRA sniper, Flex Street Mill, Ardoyne, Belfast
L/CPL ALAN GILES	12/06/72	Shot in gun battle with IRA, Ardoyne, Belfast
PTE BRIAN SODEN	19/06/72	IRA sniper, Ardoyne, Belfast
PTE DAVID MEEK	13/07/72	IRA sniper, Hooker Street, Ardoyne, Belfast
PTE JOHN WILLIAMS	14/07/72	Killed in gun battle with IRA, Hooker St., Ardoyne
PTE GARY CHANNING	21/11/86	Accidental death at VCP in Omagh
PTE GEOFFREY JONES	05/01/87	Death by violent or unnatural causes
WO1 (RSM) MIKE HEAKIN	12/08/88	Murdered at traffic lights by IRA, Ostende, Belgium
PTE WILLIAM DAVIS	01/06/90	Murdered in Litchfield railway station by IRA

ROYAL SCOTS

PTE RODERICK D W C. BANNON	31/03/76	IRA landmine explosion, Co Armagh
PTE DAVID FERGUSON	31/03/76	Killed in same incident
PTE JOHN PEARSON	31/03/76	Killed in same incident
C/SGT NORMAN REDPATH	02/02/81	Died of heart attack whilst on duty
PTE PATRICK J. MCKENNA	15/03/81	Accidentally shot
PTE ALAN BRUCE	17/09/82	RTA
L/CPL LAWRENCE DICKSON	17/03/93	IRA sniper, Forkhill

ROYAL SCOTS DRAGOON GUARDS

TPR IAN CAIE	24/08/72	IRA landmine attack, Crossmaglen

ROYAL TANK REGIMENT

L/CPL JOHN WARNOCK	04/09/71	IRA landmine attack, Derrybeg Park, Newry
TPR JAMES NOWOSAD	03/03/78	Shot by gunmen in 'Rag Day' killing, Belfast city centre
TPR JULIAN MILLS	18/09/77	Cause of death unknown
L/CPL NICHOLAS BUSHWELL	02/10/80	RTA
CPL STEVEN SMITH	02/07/89	IRA bomb under his car, Hanover, Germany

ROYAL WELSH FUSILIERS

CPL GERALD BRISTOW	16/04/72	IRA sniper, Bishops Street, Londonderry
FSLR KERRY MCCARTHY	21/06/72	IRA sniper, Victoria RUC station, Londonderry
CPL DAVID SMITH	21/06/73	IRA booby trap, Strabane
CPL ALAN COUGHLAN	28/10/74	Van bomb attack at Ballykinler Army camp
FSLR ANDREW CROCKER	24/11/76	Killed by IRA at Post Office robbery, Turf Lodge
LT STEVEN KIRBY	14/02/79	IRA sniper, Abercorn Road, Londonderry
CPL DAVID WRIGHT	16/12/93	RTA whilst on duty

SCOTS DRAGOON GUARDS

TPR ANTHONY SUTTON	06/12/77	RTA
TPR DONALD DAVIES	17/11/74	Cause of death unknown

SCOTS GUARDS

GDSMN JOHN EDMUNDS	16/03/70	Drowned
GDSMN BRIAN HALL	04/10/71	IRA sniper, Creggan heights base, Londonderry
GDSMN GEORGE HAMILTON	17/10/71	Ambushed and killed by IRA, Cupar Street, Lower Falls
GDSMN NORMAN BOOTH	30/10/71	Killed in same incident
GDSMN STEPHEN MCGUIRE	04/11/71	IRA sniper, Henry Taggart base, West Belfast
GDSMN PAUL NICHOLS	27/11/71	IRA sniper, St James Crescent, Falls Road, Belfast
GDSMN JOHN VAN-BECK	18/09/72	DoW after being shot by IRA, Lecky Road, Londonderry
GDSMN GEORGE LOCKHART	26/09/72	DoW after being shot by IRA, Bogside, Londonderry
L/SGT THOMAS MCKAY	28/10/72	IRA sniper, Bishop Street, Londonderry
GDSMN ALAN DAUGHTERY	31/12/73	IRA sniper, Beechmount Avenue, Falls Road, Belfast
GDSMN WILLIAM FORSYTH	05/10/74	Killed in IRA bomb outrage, Guildford (with four others)
GDSMN JOHN HUNTER	05/10/74	Killed in same outrage
COL/SGT DAVID NADEN	07/06/78	RTA
L/CPL ALAN SWIFT	11/08/78	Killed on covert ops, Letterkenny Road, Londonderry
COL/SGT EDWIN MURRISON	09/04/80	RTA
L/SGT IAIN HANNA	20/10/80	Cause of death unknown
MAJ DONALD NICOL OF ARDMONACH	21/10/86	Died of natural causes whilst on duty
L/SGT GRAHAM STEWART	05/05/90	Killed on covert ops, Cullyhanna, Co Armagh
GDSMN PAUL BROWN	02/08/90	RTA
GDSMN ALEX IRELAND	11/09/90	Death by violent or unnatural causes
GDSMN DAMIAN SHACKLETON	03/08/92	IRA sniper, New Lodge, Belfast
GDSMN ANDREW WASON	03/09/92	Death by violent or unnatural causes

STAFFORDSHIRE REGIMENT

S/SGT JOHN MORRELL	24/10/72	DoW after IRA booby trap, Drumargh, Armagh
2/LT MICHAEL SIMPSON	23/10/74	DoW after being shot by IRA sniper, Londonderry
PTE CHRISTOPHER SHENTON	20/01/81	IRA sniper whilst in OP Bogside, Londonderry
L/CPL STEPHEN ANDERSON	29/05/84	IRA landmine, Crossmaglen
PTE MARK MASON	15/08/89	Death by violent or unnatural causes
SGT DEAN OLIVER	09/05/92	Death by violent or unnatural causes
PTE WAYNE G. SMITH	01/07/95	RTA

THE HIGHLANDERS

HIGHLANDER SCOTT HARRINGTON	09/07/95	Accidentally shot

THE ROYAL GLOUCESTERSHIRE, BERKSHIRE AND WILTSHIRE REGIMENT

CPL GARY LLEWELLYN FENTON	22/06/98	Run down and killed by lorry at VCP, Crossmaglen. Posthumous Mention in Dispatches

ULSTER DEFENCE REGIMENT

2nd Battalion

SGT HARRY D. DICKSON	27/02/72	Murdered by the IRA at his home
PTE SIDNEY W. WATT	20/07/73	Ambushed by the IRA at a friend's house
PTE KENNETH HILL	28/08/73	Shot in Armagh City whilst attending an incident
CPL JAMES A. FRAZER	30/08/75	Killed by IRA at a friend's farm
L/CPL JOE REID	31/08/75	Murdered at home by IRA
L/CPL D. JOHN BELL	06/11/75	Killed by IRA as he returned from work
C/SGT JOE NESBITT	10/11/75	Shot by the IRA on his way to work
PTE JOSEPH A. McCULLOUGH	25/02/76	Shot by IRA
CPL ROBERT McCONNELLl	05/04/76	Murdered at his home in Tullyvallen, Newtownhamilton
L/CPL JEAN LEGGETT	06/04/76	Ambushed and shot by IRA on patrol in Armagh
LT JOE WILSON	26/10/76	Killed at work by the IRA
PTE MARGARET A. HEARST	08/10/77	Murdered at home by IRA near Middletown
CAPT CHARLIE HENNING	06/10/78	Shot by IRA whilst at work
L/CPL THOMAS ARMSTRONG	13/04/79	Ambushed and killed by IRA on his way home
PTE JAMES PORTER	24/06/79	Murdered at home by IRA
PTE JAMES H. HEWITT	10/10/80	Killed by bomb under his car
L/CPL FREDDIE A. WILLIAMSON	07/10/82	Killed with a woman prison officer in INLA-caused crash
SGT THOMAS G. COCHRANE	22/10/82	Abducted and murdered by IRA
CPL CHARLIE H. SPENCE	10/11/82	Shot by IRA as he left work in Armagh
CPL AUSTIN SMITH	19/12/82	Shot by IRA after parking his car near home
MAJ CHARLIE ARMSTRONG	14/11/83	Killed by IRA bomb in Armagh City
PTE STEPHEN MCKINNEY	25/09/88	Murdered by IRA as he arrived home after quitting UDR
L/CPL DAVY HALLIGAN	17/11/89	Shot by IRA as he drove home
PTE PAUL D. SUTCLIFFE	01/03/91	DoW after IRA mortar attack in Armagh
PTE ROGER J. LOVE	01/03/91	DoW from same incident
PTE PAUL R. BLAKELY	31/05/91	Killed in IRA bomb at the Glenane base
PTE SIDNEY HAMILTON	31/05/91	Killed in same incident
L/CPL ROBERT W. CROZIER	31/05/91	Killed in same incident

3rd Battalion

L/CPL JOE JARDINE	08/03/72	Shot by IRA whilst working
CPL JIM D. ELLIOTT	19/04/72	Abducted and murdered by IRA; body then booby trapped by his killers
C/SGT JOHN RUDDY	10/10/72	Shot by IRA on his way to work
PTE THOMAS MCCREADY	17/11/74	Shot by the IRA in Newry
CPL CECIL GRILLS	12/01/78	Shot by IRA as he drove home from work
PTE JIM COCHRANE	06/01/80	Killed by IRA bomb at Castlewellen
PTE RICHARD SMITH	06/01/80	Killed in same incident
PTE RICKY WILSON	06/01/80	Killed in same incident
PTE COLIN H. QUINN	10/12/80	Shot by INLA as he left work
MAJ W.E. IVAN TOOMBS	16/01/81	Shot by IRA in Warrenpoint where he worked
L/CPL RICHARD W.J. MCKEE	24/04/81	Shot by IRA at Kilcoo whilst on duty
CAPT GORDON HANNA	29/11/85	Killed when IRA bomb exploded under his car at home

CPL D. BRIAN BROWN	28/05/86	Killed by IRA bomb when searching after a warning
PTE ROBERT W HILL	01/07/86	Killed when IRA bomb exploded under his car at home
CPL ALAN. T. JOHNSTON	15/02/88	Shot by the IRA as he arrived for work
PTE W. JOHN MORELAND	16/12/88	Shot in his coal lorry at Downpatrick
PTE MICHAEL D. ADAMS	09/04/90	Killed by IRA landmine at Downpatrick
L/CPL J. (BRAD) BRADLEY	09/04/90	Killed in same incident
PTE JOHN BIRCH	09/04/90	Killed in same incident
PTE STEVEN SMART	09/04/90	Killed in same incident

4th Battalion

PTE FRANK VEITCH	03/09/71	Shot by IRA at Kinawley RUC station
PTE JOHNNY FLETCHER	01/03/72	Abducted and murdered by IRA in front of his wife
L/CPL W. HARRY CREIGHTON	07/08/72	Murdered by IRA at his house near Monaghan
PTE JIMMY E. EAMES	25/08/72	IRA booby trapped car at Enniskillen
L/CPL ALFIE JOHNSTON	25/08/72	Killed in same incident
PTE TOMMY R. BULLOCK	21/09/72	Murdered along with his wife at their home
PTE J. ROBIN BELL	22/10/72	Shot by IRA whilst with his father
PTE MATT LILLY	07/09/73	Shot by the IRA on his milk round
PTE ALAN R. FERGUSON	25/06/78	Killed in IRA landmine and gun attack
CPL HERBIE. G. KERNAGHAN	15/10/79	Shot by the IRA as he delivered to a school; witnessed by dozens of children
CPL AUBREY ABERCROMBIE	05/02/80	Murdered by the IRA on his farm
PTE W. RITCHIE LATIMER	07/06/80	Shot by the IRA at his hardware store
PTE NORMAN H. DONALDSON	25/11/80	Shot by IRA as he collected charity money at RUC Station whilst off-duty
L/CPL RONNIE GRAHAM	05/06/81	Shot by IRA as he delivered coal; one of three brothers murdered by IRA
PTE CECIL GRAHAM	11/11/81	DoW after being shot by IRA at his wife's house
CPL ALBERT BEACOM	17/11/81	Murdered by IRA at his home
PTE JIMMY GRAHAM. BEM	01/02/85	Shot in front of school children by IRA
PTE JOHN F. EARLY	03/02/86	IRA landmine
CPL JIMMY OLDHAM	03/04/86	Shot by IRA gunmen as he arrived where he worked
CPL WILLIE BURLEIGH	06/04/88	Killed by IRA bomb under his car

5th Battalion

CAPT MARCUS MCCAUSLAND	04/03/71	Abducted and murdered by the IRA
PTE THOMAS CALLAGHAN	16/02/72	Abducted and murdered in the Creggan, Londonderry
PTE SAMUEL PORTER	22/11/72	Shot and killed by the IRA as he walked home
PTE GEORGE E. HAMILTON	20/12/72	Shot by the IRA as he worked on repairs at a reservoir
CAPT JAMES HOOD	04/01/73	Murdered by the IRA at home
SGT DAVID C.DEACON	03/03/73	Abducted and murdered by the IRA
CPL JOHN CONLEY	23/07/74	IRA car bomb in Bridge Street, Garvagh
PTE ROBERT STOTT	25/11/75	Shot by the IRA on the way home from work
PTE JOHN ARRELL	22/01/76	Shot on board his firm's mini bus

PTE JACK MCCUTCHEON	01/04/76	Shot at work by the IRA
S/SGT BOBBY H.LENNOX	02/04/76	Postman, lured to an isolated farm and shot
CAPT W. RONNIE BOND	07/11/76	Shot outside his home in Londonderry as he got home
L/CPL JIMMY SPEERS	09/11/76	Shot by the IRA at his garage in Desertmartin
L/CPL WINSTON C. MCCAUGHEY	11/11/76	Shot by the IRA as he stood outside his house in Kilrea
MAJ J. PETER HILL	23/02/77	Shot by IRA as he got home from work, Londonderry
PTE DAVID MCQUILLAN	15/03/77	Shot by IRA as he waited for a lift to work, Bellaghy
L/CPL GERALD C. CLOETE	06/04/77	Shot by the IRA as he drove to work in Londonderry
LT WALTER KERR	02/11/77	DoW after IRA bomb under his car
CPL WILLIAM J. GORDON	8/02/78	Killed along with daughter (10) after IRA bomb exploded under their car
L/CPL SAMUEL D. MONTGOMERY	10/02/81	Shot by the IRA as he left work
PTE T. ALAN RITCHIE	25/05/81	Killed in IRA ambush at Gulladuff near Bellaghy
PTE ALLEN CLARKE	12/09/81	Shot by IRA as he walked through Maghera
L/CPL BERNIE V. MCKEOWN	17/12/83	Murdered by the IRA in front of his 13-year-old son in their car
SGT BOBBY F. BOYD	18/11/85	Murdered by the IRA at his front door
SGT TOMMY A. JAMISON	08/03/90	Ambushed and killed by the IRA at work
PTE MICKEY BOXALL	06/11/91	Killed in IRA mortar attack at Bellaghy

6th Battalion

PTE WINSTON DONNELL	09/08/71	1st UDR man killed by the IRA; manning VCP at Clady, Tyrone
SGT KENNETH SMYTH	10/12/71	Shot whilst off duty by the IRA
PTE TED MEGAHEY	09/06/72	DoW after IRA shooting
PTE WILLIAM J. BOGLE	05/12/72	Murdered in his car as he sat with his children
PTE ROBERT N. JAMESON	17/01/74	Shot by IRA as he got off a bus at Trillick
PTE EVA MARTIN	03/05/74	Killed by IRA in rocket and gun attack at Clogher
CPL W. DEREK KIDD	18/11/76	Shot and killed at work
CPL WILLIAM J. MCKEE	14/04/78	Shot and killed by gunmen as he drove a school bus
PTE JOHN GRAHAM	25/04/79	Shot by the IRA as he collected milk from farms
PTE JOHN A. HANNIGAN	19/06/79	Shot by IRA as he came out of a shop in Omagh
PTE JAMES A. ROBINSON	19/10/79	Shot and killed on his his milk round
PTE WILLIE J. CLARKE	03/08/80	Shot in the Republic visiting relatives
L/CPL JOHNNY MCKEEGAN	19/11/81	Lured to a house in Strabane and shot by IRA
LT J. LESLIE HAMILTON	27/04/82	Shot whilst delivering to a Londonderry supermarket
PTE H.A. (LEXI) CUMMINGS	15/06/82	Shot by IRA as he prepared to drive home from work
PTE RONNIE ALEXANDER	13/07/83	IRA landmine at Drumquin
PTE OSSIE NEELY	13/07/82	Killed in same incident

PTE JOHN ROXBOROUGH	13/07/82	Killed in same incident
CPL THOMAS HARRON	13/07/82	Killed in same incident
CPL RONNIE D. FINDLAY	23/08/83	Shot by IRA as he left work
PTE GREG ELLIOTT	02/01/84	Shot as he got into his van at Castlederg
L/CPL THOMAS A. LOUGHLIN	02/03/84	Killed by IRA bomb planted underneath his works van
C/SGT IVAN E. HILLEN	12/05/84	Shot and killed at his farm in Augher by IRA
CPL HEATHER C. J. KERRIGAN	14/07/84	IRA landmine, Castlederg
PTE NORMAN J. MCKINLEY	14/07/84	Killed in same incident
PTE W.VICTOR FOSTER	15/01/86	IRA bomb planted under his car at Castlederg
PTE THOMAS J. IRWIN	26/03/86	Shot and killed by IRA at his work in Omagh
PTE WILLIAM C. POLLOCK	08/04/86	Killed by IRA booby trap at home in Castlederg
CAPT IVAN R.K. ANDERSON	21/05/87	Shot by IRA as he drove home from his school
L/CPL MICHAEL DARCY	04/06/88	Murdered at home by IRA in Castlederg
PTE OLVEN L. KILPATRICK	09/01/90	Shot by IRA at his shoe shop in Castlederg

7th Battalion

PTE JOHN B. HOUSTON	29/11/75	Shot at work by the IRA
PTE PETER MCCELLAND	28/08/79	Killed at VCP
PTE SEAN RUSSELL	27/03/81	Murdered at home by IRA, Belfast; daughter injured
PTE JOHN D. SMITH	27/03/81	Shot by IRA as he walked to work in Belfast

8th Battalion

PTE W. DENNIS WILSON	07/12/71	Murdered at home in Curlough
L/CPL HENRY GILLESPIE	20/05/72	Shot by IRA patrolling near Dungannon
PTE FRED D. GREEVES	15/12/72	Shot by IRA as heft work in Armagh
CPL FRANK CADDOO	10/05/73	Shot by IRA at his farm in Rehagey
CAPT CORMAC MCCABE	19/01/74	Abducted and murdered by IRA in Irish Republic
CPL ROY T. MOFFETT	03/03/74	IRA landmine on Cookstown to Omagh road
WO2 DAVID SINNAMON	11/04/74	IRA bomb in house in Dungannon
PTE EDMUND R.L. STEWART	29/04/76	Lured to relatives house and shot by IRA
L/CPL STANLEY D. ADAMS	28/10/76	Lured to remote farmhouse as mailman and shot by IRA
PTE JOHN REID	09/03/77	Ambushed and shot by IRA as he fed his cattle
CPL DAVY GRAHAM	25/03/77	DoW after being shot at work by IRA, Gortonis
CAPT W. ERIC SHIELDS	29/04/77	Shot by IRA outside his home in Dungannon
2ND/LT ROBIN SMYRL	13/09/77	Shot by IRA as he drove to work at Plumbridge
PTE BOB J. BLOOMER	24/09/77	DoW after being shot at home by IRA in Eglish
SGT JOCK B EAGLESHAM (MID)	07/02/77	A postman, shot by IRA on his rounds
PTE G. SAMMY GIBSON	29/04/79	Shot by IRA as he cycled to work in Tyrone
CPL FRED H. IRWIN	30/10/79	Shot by IRA driving to work in Dungannon
PTE W. JACK DONNELLY	16/04/81	Shot by INLA at his local pub in Moy
L/CPL CECIL W. MCNEILL	25/02/83	Shot by IRA at his work in Tullyvannon
PTE ANDY F. STINSON	04/06/83	Killed by INLA booby trap on his digger at work
PTE CYRUS CAMPBELL	24/10/83	Shot by IRA at Carnteel as he drove to farm
PTE N. JIMMY JOHNSTON	08/05/84	Shot by IRA disguised as ambulance men at his hospital
PTE ROBERT BENNETT	07/09/84	Shot by IRA at his work in Pomeroy

PTE TREVOR W. HARKNESS	28/02/85	Killed by IRA bomb at Pomeroy on foot patrol
PTE MARTIN A.J. BLANEY	06/10/86	Shot by IRA as he drove home in Eglish
MAJ GEORGE SHAW	26/01/87	Murdered by IRA at his home in Dungannon
PTE WILLIE T. GRAHAM	25/04/87	Shot by IRA at his farm in Pomeroy
CAPT TIM D. ARMSTRONG	16/01/88	Murdered by unknown gunmen (Falklands veteran)
PTE JOHN STEWART	16/01/88	DoW after being shot by IRA at his home in Coalisland
PTE NED GIBSON	26/04/88	Shot by IRA as he worked on dustbins in Ardboe
PTE RAYMOND A. MCNICOL	03/08/88	Shot by IRA as he drove to work in Desertcreat
PTE JOHN HARDY	14/03/89	Shot by IRA as he drove his lorry to Granville
WO2 ALBERT D. COOPER	02/11/90	IRA bomb planted in car left at his garage in Cookstown

9th Battalion

SGT MAYNARD CRAWFORD	13/01/72	Shot as he waited in a car at Newtownabbey
CPL ROY STANTON	09/06/72	Shot by IRA as he drove home
PTE HENRY J. RUSSELL	13/07/72	Abducted, tortured and shot by the IRA, Carrickfergus
CPL DAVID W. BINGHAM	16/01/73	Abducted and killed by the IRA
PTE THOMAS J. FORSYTHE	16/10/73	Killed in a shooting accident
PTE STEVEN CARLETON	08/01/82	Shot by the IRA at petrol station in Belfast
PTE LINDENCOLIN HOUSTON	20/01/84	Murdered by the IRA at his home in Dunmurry

10th Battalion

PTE SEAN RUSSELL	08/12/71	Murdered by IRA at his home, New Barnsley, Belfast
PTE SAMUEL TRAINOR	20/03/72	IRA bomb, Belfast city centre
PTE ROBERT MCCOMB	23/07/72	Abducted and murdered by IRA in Belfast
PTE TERENCE MAGUIRE	14/10/72	Abducted and murdered in Belfast
PTE WILLIAM L. KENNY	16/03/73	Abducted and murdered on way to UDR barracks
CPL JOHN GEDDIS	10/05/77	Killed by UVF in explosion in Crumlin Road, Belfast
L/CPL GERALD W.D. TUCKER	08/06/77	Shot by IRA as he left work at Royal Victoria Hospital
CPL JAMES MCFALL	27/7/77	Murdered by IRA at his home in Belfast
CPL HUGH A. ROGERS	08/09/77	Shot by IRA as he left for work in Dunmurry
SGT ROBERT L. BATCHELOR	27/11/78	Shot by IRA as he left work in Belfast
PTE ALEXANDER GORE	06/06/79	Shot by IRA at UDR base, Malone Road, Belfast
PTE MARK A. STOCKMAN	29/09/81	Shot by INLA at work in Belfast
SGT RICKY CONNELLY	21/10/81	Murdered at his home by IRA, Belfast
PTE BILLY ACHESON	04/09/82	Death by violent or unnatural causes
PTE ALEX YOUNG	01/10/84	Death by violent or unnatural causes
PTE FRED GALLAGHER	03/10/84	Death by violent or unnatural causes
LT DUNCAN CARSON	06/04/85	Death by violent or unnatural causes

11th Battalion

L/CPL VICTOR SMYTH	06/09/72	IRA bomb underneath his car, in Portadown
2/LT R. IRWIN LONG	08/11/72	Shot by IRA in Lurgan driving to collect his daughter

SGT ALFIE DOYLE	03/06/75	He and two friends shot dead by IRA as they returned from a meeting in Irish Republic
PTE GEORGE LUTTON	15/11/76	Shot by IRA on duty in Edward Street, Lurgan
PTE ROBERT J. MCNALLY	13/03/79	Killed by INLA bomb under his car, Portadown
PTE S. DAVID MONTGOMERY	08/03/84	Shot by IRA at his works, Moira on the Airport Road
PTE DAVID CHAMBERS	04/06/84	Shot by IRA as he arrived for work, Dollingstown
PTE WILLIE R. MEGRATH	23/07/87	Killed by IRA as he drove home to Lisburn
PTE COLIN J. MCCULLOUGH	23/09/90	Shot by IRA as he sat in his car with fiancé, Lurgan

4–6th Battalion

L/CPL KENNY A. NEWELL	27/11/91	Abducted and murdered by IRA at Crossmaglen

7–10th Battalion

SGT DENIS TAGGART	04/08/86	Shot dead outside his home by IRA in Belfast
PTE JOE MCILLWAINE	12/06/87	Shot by IRA at his work in Dunmurry
PTE G. JOHN TRACEY	26/06/87	Shot by IRA at his work in Belfast
PTE STEVEN W MEGRATH	17/09/87	Shot by IRA at his relatives' house
PTE JAMES CUMMINGS	24/02/88	Killed by IRA bomb in Belfast city centre
PTE FREDERICK STARRETT	24/02/88	Killed in same incident
L/CPL ROY W. BUTLER	02/08/88	Shot dead by IRA in front of his family in West Belfast shopping centre
PTE BRIAN M. LAWRENCE	17/06/91	Shot by IRA as he arrived for work, Belfast

UDR (Battalion Unknown)

PTE THOMAS WILTON	22/10/70	Died on duty
PTE JOHN PROCTOR	24/10/70	RTA
S/SGT GEORGE GILKESON	11/10/71	RTA
CPL THOMAS ADDIS	04/12/71	Unknown
PTE EDWARD BROWN	13/12/71	Unknown
L/CPL PHILIP THOMPSON	31/12/71	RTA
PTE THOMAS MOFFETT	26/02/72	Unknown
PTE GEORGE CURRAN	12/03/72	Unknown
PTE DONALD KANE	04/04/72	Unknown
CPL BRIAN HERON	18/05/72	Unknown
CPL SIDNEY HUSSEY	20/05/72	Unknown
SGT WILLIAM REID	28/05/72	Unknown
PTE WILLIAM WILKINSON	12/07/72	Unknown
MAJ ERIC BEAUMONT	25/07/72	Unknown
CPL ALBERT JOHNSTON	01/08/72	Unknown
PTE ANDREW SIMPSON	18/09/72	RTA
PTE THOMAS OLPHERT	06/10/72	Unknown
PTE EDMUND SIMPSON	10/10/72	Unknown
PTE ROBERT MCKEOWN	13/10/72	RTA
SGT WILLIAM CALDERWOOD	15/10/72	Unknown
MAJ JOHN MUNNIS	16/10/72	RTA
PTE THOMAS BOYD	28/12/72	Unknown
PTE JOHNSTONE BRADLEY	23/01/73	Unknown
CPL PATRICK DAVIDSON	17/03/73	Unknown
PTE ALEXANDER MCCONAGHY	10/04/73	Unknown

PTE SAMUEL BEATTIE	14/04/73	Unknown
L/CPL HUGH WATTON	24/05/73	Unknown
PTE COLIN MCKEOWN	17/10/73	RTA
PTE WILLIAM MAGILL	19/10/73	Unknown
L/CPL THOMAS BEATTY	04/11/73	Unknown
CPL WILLIAM MARTIN	20/11/73	RTA
PTE DAVID SPENCE	20/11/73	RTA
PTE EDWARD GIBSON	30/05/74	Unknown
PTE NOEL SEELEY	26/06/74	Unknown
PTE ROBERT RAINEY	27/07/74	RTA
PTE SAMUEL WORKMAN	25/08/74	RTA
PTE WILLIAM BELL	21/10/74	Unknown
PTE ROBERT ALLEN	25/10/74	Unknown
PTE JOHN S. MARTIN	18/11/74	RTA
PTE JOHN TAYLOR	30/11/74	RTA
PTE DAVID ARMSTRONG	28/01/75	Unknown
S/SGT IVAN NIXON	31/03/75	RTA
SGT WILLIAM MILLAR	19/09/75	RTA
PTE DAVID MOSGROVE	21/11/75	RTA
L/CPL JOHN NIBLOCK	20/12/75	RTA
PTE WILLIAM OVENS	27/03/76	RTA
L/CPL ROBERT MCCREEDY	24/04/76	RTA
PTE ISAAC STEWART	06/05/76	RTA
LT JOHN HIGGINS	08/08/76	RTA
W/PTE ANN GAYNOR	09/08/76	RTA
CAPT ERIC SCOTT	28/08/76	RTA
CPL WILLIAM DUNN	27/11/76	RTA
SGT FREDERICK PULFORD	18/02/77	RTA
PTE ROBERT PURDY	29/05/77	RTA
PTE RAYMOND MCFARLAND	31/08/77	RTA
PTE ALAN MCFARLAND	31/08/77	RTA
PTE WILSON PENNEY	21/09/77	RTA
CPL ALISTAIR COOKE	19/09/78	RTA
PTE TREVOR HERRON	04/12/78	RTA
PTE WILLIAM MORTON	29/04/79	RTA
L/CPL IVAN MCCORKELL	08/06/79	RTA
PTE ALAN MCCELLAND	04/09/79	RTA
PTE ALEXANDER ROWE	12/12/79	RTA
PTE GEORGE BROWN	27/12/79	RTA
W/PTE MARY COCHRANE	28/02/80	RTA
PTE WILLIAM KEITH DONNELL	16/04/81	RTA
LT DAVID PATTERSON	24/04/81	RTA
PTE SAMUEL WHITESIDE	20/08/81	RTA
L/CPL BRENDEN MCKEOWN	26/03/82	RTA
PTE BRIAN WALMSLEY	01/05/82	RTA
PTE LEONARD GREER	16/04/83	RTA
PTE BRIAN KIRKPATRICK	01/10/83	RTA
PTE ROBERT ALEXANDER IRWIN	21/12/83	RTA
PTE FRAZER BROWN	22/01/84	RTA
PTE SAMUEL JOSEPH BRADFORD	21/12/84	RTA
PTE ALBERT BROWN	21/04/85	RTA

PTE MERVYN SALMON	28/01/86	RTA
PTE BRIAN NICHOLL	28/03/86	RTA
PTE ROY ALLEN	26/06/86	RTA
PTE ANDREW MONTGOMERY	30/06/86	RTA
W/CPL CIARA OUSBY	20/07/86	RTA
LT PAUL MAXWELL	04/08/86	RTA
PTE JOHN MCKERAGHAN	14/03/87	RTA
CPL JAMES ANDERSON	25/04/87	RTA
PTE THOMAS AICKEN	11/08/87	RTA
PTE CARL PEARCE	11/08/87	RTA
PTE WILLIAM REILLY	08/11/87	RTA
PTE FRANCIS GIBSON	26/04/88	RTA
PTE THOMAS JONSTON	08/05/89	RTA
PTE MATTHEW CHRISTIE	11/09/89	RTA
PTE ALEXANDER PHOENIX	16/03/90	RTA
PTE BRIAN CORDNER	04/11/90	RTA
PTE DAVID WILLIAMSON	15/11/90	RTA
PTE ALAN C. MCCONNELL	09/09/91	RTA
SGT GEORGE ROLLINS	27/09/91	RTA
PTE STEPHEN SCANLON	11/05/92	RTA
L/CPL THOMAS MCDONNELL	08/06/97	Violent or unnatural causes

THE FOLLOWING UDR SOLDIERS WERE KILLED IN ACCIDENTS, PLACES UNKNOWN

WO2 BERNARD ADAMSON	31/05/72	
PTE GEORGE ELLIOTT	26/06/72	
PTE WILLIAM HAMILTON	04/08/72	
PTE KENNETH TWADDELL	05/08/72	
PTE THOMAS I. MCCLELLAND	26/04/87	
L/CPL DAVID GASS	16/06/88	
PTE KEVIN HUTCHINGS	12/07/89	
W/PTE ELIZABETH SLOAN	13/04/92	in Ballymena area

EX ULSTER DEFENCE REGIMENT SOLDIERS KILLED IN NORTHERN IRELAND

MR D.J. MCCORMICK	10/12/71	Shot by IRA on way to work
MR ISAAC SCOTT	10/07/73	Shot by IRA in Belleek, Co Armagh
MR IVAN VENNARD	03/10/73	Shot dead by IRA on his postal round, Lurgan
MR GEORGE SAUNDERSON	10/04/74	Shot by IRA at his school in Co Fermanagh
MR BRIAN SHAW	20/07/74	Abducted and killed, Grosvenor Road, Belfast
MR WILLIAM HUTCHINSON	24/08/74	Shot by IRA at work
MR GEORGE MCCALL	02/08/75	Shot by IRA in Moy, Co Tyrone
MR KENNETH WORTON	05/01/76	One of 10 men murdered in Kingsmill Massacre
MR NICOLAS WHITE	13/03/76	Shot at youth club, Ardoyne, Belfast
MR SIDNEY MCAVOY	12/06/76	Shot at his shop in Dunmurry
MR JOHN FREEBURN	28/06/76	Shot in Lurgan
MR NORMAN CAMPBELL	15/12/76	Joined RUC and shot in Portadown
MR ROBERT HARRISON	05/02/77	RUCR shot by IRA Gilford, Co Down
MR JOHN LEE	27/02/77	Shot by IRA in club in Ardoyne, Belfast
MR JAMES GREEN	05/05/77	Shot by IRA whilst working as taxi driver, Belfast
MR GILBERT JOHNSTON	19/08/78	Shot by IRA at his shop in Keady, Co Armagh

MR MICHAEL RILEY	07/06/78	Shot at his home by IRA in Shankill Road, Belfast
MR ROBERT LOCHART	17/04/79	RUCR killed by IRA bomb at Camlough
MR JACK MCCLENAGHAN	19/05/79	Shot by the IRA whilst delivering bread in Fermanagh
MR DAVID STANLEY WRAY	20/05/79	Shot by IRA on his way to church in Claremont
MR DAVID ALAN DUNNE	02/06/79	RUCR shot by INLA in Armagh
MR GEORGE HAWTHORNE	05/10/79	Shot by IRA in Newry
MR JAMES FOWLER	16/12/79	Shot by IRA as he drove his fish van in Omagh
MR CLIFFORD LUNDY	02/01/80	Shot at work by IRA near Bessbrook, Co Armagh
MR HENRY LIVINGSTONE	06/03/80	Shot by IRA at his farm at Tynan, Co Armagh
MR VICTOR MORROW	17/04/80	Shot by IRA at Newtownbutler, Co Fermanagh
MR JOHN EAGLESON	01/10/82	RUCR shot by IRA on way to work
MR WILLIAM ELLIOT	28/06/80	Shot by IRA at cattle market in Ballybay, Co Monaghan
MR JOHN ROBINSON	23/04/81	Shot by IRA driving works van in Armagh
MR PTE JOHN PROCTOR	14/09/81	Shot by IRA at hospital after visiting his wife and newborn baby at Magherafelt
MR HECTOR HALL	05/10/81	Shot by IRA outside Altnagelvin hospital
MR CHARLES NEVILLE	10/11/81	Shot by IRA at work in Co Armagh
MR JAMES MCCLINTOCK	18/11/81	Shot by IRA on his way home from work, Londonderry
MR NORMAN HANNA	11/03/82	Shot by IRA at his works in Newry
MR THOMAS CUNNINGHAM	12/05/82	Shot by IRA whilst working in Strabane
MR WILFRED MCILVEEN	27/08/82	IRA bomb underneath his car in Armagh
MR CHARLES CROTHERS	05/10/82	Shot by IRA at Altnagelvin
MR ROBERT IRWIN	16/11/82	RUCR shot by INLA at Markethill
MR SNOWDEN CORKEY	16/11/82	RUCR killed in same incident
MR JAMES GIBSON	02/12/82	Shot by IRA driving school bus at Coalisland
MR JOHN TRUCKLE	20/09/83	IRA bomb underneath his car in Portadown
MR RONALD FUNSTON	13/03/84	Shot by IRA on his farm at Pettigoe, Co Fermanagh
MR HUGH GALLAGHER	03/06/84	Taxi driver; he was lured by IRA to Omagh and shot
MR MELVIN SIMPSON	08/10/84	Shot by IRA at work in Dungannon
MR DOUGLAS MCELHINNEY	25/02/85	Shot by INLA at friend's house in Londonderry
MR GEOFFREY CAMPBELL	25/02/85	RUCR. One of nine killed IRA mortar attack, Newry
MR HERBET MCCONVILLE	15/05/86	Shot dead by IRA whilst delivering in Newry
MR HARRY HENRY	21/04/87	Murdered by IRA at his home in Magherafelt
MR CHARLES WATSON	22/05/87	Murdered by the IRA at his home, Clough, Co Down
MR NATHANIEL CUSH	15/06/87	IRA bomb underneath his car in Belfast
MR WINSTON G. FINLAY	30/08/87	Shot by IRA at his home in Ballyronan
MR JOHN GRIFFITHS	04/05/89	IRA bomb underneath his car
MR ROBERT J. GLOVER	15/11/89	IRA bomb underneath his car near Dungannon
Mr DAVID STERRITT	24/07/90	RUCR killed with four others by IRA landmine, Armagh
MR DAVID POLLOCK	20/10/90	IRA sniper, Strabane
MR NORMAN KENDALL	10/11/90	Murdered with three others by IRA, Castor Bay, Lurgan

MR HUBERT GILMORE	01/12/90	Shot by IRA Kilrea, Co Londonderry
MR ERIC BOYD	05/08/91	Shot by IRA as he left work Cappagh, Co Tyrone
MR RONALD FINLAY	15/08/91	Shot at work by the IRA, Co Tyrone
MR DAVID MARTIN	25/04/93	IRA bomb underneath his car, Kildress, Co Tyrone
MR JOHN LYNESS	24/06/93	Shot by IRA at his home in Lurgan
MR JOHN ALEXANDER BURNS	30/10/93	Shot by UFF at Eglington
MR ALAN SMYTH	25/04/94	Shot by IRA in Garvagh
MR ERIC SMYTH	28/04/94	Shot by IRA at his home in Co Armagh
MR DAVID CALDWELL	01/08/02	Working on Army camp in Londonderry; killed by 'Real' IRA booby trap

(David Caldwell's name, although outside the date parameter, is included, because it is believed that he was targeted by the 'Real' IRA because of his former UDR involvement)

WELSH GUARDS

SGT PHILIP PRICE	21/07/72	IRA car bomb on 'Bloody Friday' Belfast bus depot
GDSMN PAUL FRYER	13/11/79	IRA bomb, Fords Cross, South Armagh
L/CPL MARK HOWELLS	12/07/92	RTA
GDSMN DAVID ROBERTS	24/11/73	Killed by IRA bomb, South Armagh

WORCESTER & SHERWOOD FORESTERS

PTE MARTIN ROBINSON	16/04/72	Killed in gun battle at Brandywell base, Londonderry
PTE MARTIN JESSOP	20/09/82	Killed in rocket attack, Springfield Road RUC station
CPL LEON BUSH	27/09/82	IRA booby trap, West Circular Road, Belfast
CPL STEPHEN MCGONIGLE	04/05/89	IRA landmine, Crossmaglen
L/CPL STEPHEN KENT	02/02/90	RTA
CPL GARY KIRBY	02/02/90	Killed in same accident

WOMEN'S ROYAL ARMY CORPS

W/PTE ANN HAMILTON	05/10/74	Killed with four others in IRA bomb outrage, Guildford
W/PTE CAROLINE SLATER	05/10/74	Killed in same outrage
L/CPL ROBERTA THAIN	25/03/75	Accidentally shot dead in Shipquay Street, Londonderry
W/SGT ALISON STRYKER	04/06/76	RTA
W/PTE KATHRYN WATERLAND	16/08/79	RTA
W/CPL ELAINE MARRISON	14/02/83	RTA
W/PTE MARIA HORNSBY	11/12/84	RTA
W/PTE KAREN R. COWAN	10/11/85	RTA

CIVILIAN SEARCHERS

NORMA SPENCE	03/03/78	Shot by IRA in Belfast city centre by IRA
BRIAN RUSSELL	28/09/78	Shot by IRA Waterloo Place, Londonderry

SECURITY SERVICES (DATE AND CAUSE OF DEATH WITHHELD BY MOD)

CHARLES APCAR

ARMY WOMEN AND CHILDREN KILLED AS A RESULT OF TERRORISM

MRS LINDA HAUGHTON	04/02/74	M62 Coach Bomb outrage
MASTER LEE HAUGHTON	04/02/74	Killed in same outrage
MASTER ROBERT HAUGHTON	04/02/74	Killed in same outrage
MISS LESLEY GORDON	08/02/78	Murdered with her father, by IRA, Maghera
MISS NIVRUTI MAHESKKUMAR	26/10/89	Murdered with her father, Wildenrath, Germany

ARMY CIVILIAN PERSONNEL KILLED IN ALDERSHOT IRA BOMB OUTRAGE 22/02/72

THELMA BOSLEY
JOAN LUNN
MARGARET GRANT
JILL MANSFIELD
JOHN HASLAR
CHERIE MUNTON

ARMY CIVILIAN WORKERS MURDERED IN TERRORIST INCIDENTS

NOOR BAZ KHAN	26/06/73	Murdered by the IRA in Londonderry
MOHAMMED ABDUL KHALID	22/04/74	Murdered by the IRA at Crossmaglen
PATSIE GILLESPIE	24/10/91	Killed by IRA at Coshquin by 'Proxy' Bomb

FORMER ARMY PERSONNEL KILLED AS A DIRECT CONSEQUENCE OF THE TROUBLES

BRIAN SHAW	21/07/74	(ex-RGJ) Murdered by IRA in Lower Falls area

Other soldiers, military families and civilian workers were killed or died during their time in Northern Ireland and the author invites anyone with further knowledge of these people with regiments, dates, or causes of death, to contact him at ken_wharton@hotmail.co.uk. I apologise for any erroneous information, for missing names or for misspelled names.

I gratefully and wholeheartedly acknowledge the incredible services of Emma Beaumont without whom, the compiling of this comprehensive Roll of Honour could never have happened. Great assistance by individual regimental associations was also given and I would like to mention Norman Brown of the Royal Pioneer Corps, Kevin Gorman of the Scots Guards, Kevin Stevens, Royal Green Jackets, Pete Whittall, Staffords, Richard Nettleton, Grenadier Guards and Robert Osborne, QLR. I gratefully acknowledge the Armed Forces Memorial Roll of Honour and the Northern Ireland Veterans' Association; cross-referencing between these two excellent websites was fundamental to this list.

SELECT BIBLIOGRAPHY

Gamble, Ronnie, *'Echo' Company: The History of E Company 5th Battalion of the Ulster Defence Regiment*, Regimental Association of the Ulster Defence Regiment, Coleraine Branch, Coleraine (2007)

Hamill, Desmond, *Pig in the Middle; The Army in Northern Ireland, 1969–95* (Methuen Books)

Harnden, Tim, *Bandit Country* (Hodder & Stoughton)

McGartland, Martin, *Dead Man Running* (Hastings House Publishers)

McKittrick, Kelters, Feeney, Thornton and McVea, *Lost Lives* (Mainstream Publishing)

Urban, Mark, *Big Boy's Rules* (Faber & Faber)

Ware, Darren, *A Rendezvous With the Enemy; My Brother's Life and Death; With the Coldstream Guards in Northern Ireland* (Helion Books)

Wharton, Ken, *A Long Long War; Voices of the British Army in Northern Ireland, 1969–98* (Helion Books)

Wharton, Ken, *Bullets, Bombs and Cups of Tea; Further Voices of the British Army in Northern Ireland* (Helion Books)

Controlled explosion at an abandoned factory. *(Paul Crispin)*

The Wheelbarrow. Used to detonate bombs by remotely approaching the suspect device. *(Paul Crispin)*

The RUC knew all too well that the innocence of the kids would soon die out as the sectarianism of west Belfast got its evil hold on them as they grew. *(Paul Crispin)*

INDEX

NB: The IRA are not indexed as there are references to them on virtually every page. Similarly, the RUC are not indexed, as there are so many references, virtually every other page.